DATA STRUCTURES AND ALGORITHMS

SERIES ON SOFTWARE ENGINEERING AND KNOWLEDGE ENGINEERING

Series Editor-in-Chief
S K CHANG (*University of Pittsburgh, USA*)

Vol. 1 Knowledge-Based Software Development for Real-Time Distributed Systems
Jeffrey J.-P. Tsai and Thomas J. Weigert (Univ. Illinois at Chicago)

Vol. 2 Advances in Software Engineering and Knowledge Engineering
edited by Vincenzo Ambriola (Univ. Pisa) *and Genoveffa Tortora* (Univ. Salerno)

Vol. 3 The Impact of CASE Technology on Software Processes
edited by Daniel E. Cooke (Univ. Texas)

Vol. 4 Software Engineering and Knowledge Engineering: Trends for the Next Decade
edited by W. D. Hurley (Univ. Pittsburgh)

Vol. 5 Intelligent Image Database Systems
edited by S. K. Chang (Univ. Pittsburgh), *E. Jungert* (Swedish Defence Res. Establishment) *and G. Tortora* (Univ. Salerno)

Vol. 6 Object-Oriented Software: Design and Maintenance
edited by Luiz F. Capretz and Miriam A. M. Capretz (Univ. Aizu, Japan)

Vol. 7 Software Visualisation
edited by P. Eades (Univ. Newcastle) *and K. Zhang* (Macquarie Univ.)

Vol. 8 Image Databases and Multi-Media Search
edited by Arnold W. M. Smeulders (Univ. Amsterdam) *and Ramesh Jain* (Univ. California)

Vol. 9 Advances in Distributed Multimedia Systems
edited by S. K. Chang, T. F. Znati (Univ. Pittsburgh) *and S. T. Vuong* (Univ. British Columbia)

Vol. 10 Hybrid Parallel Execution Model for Logic-Based Specification Languages
Jeffrey J.-P. Tsai and Bing Li (Univ. Illinois at Chicago)

Vol. 11 Graph Drawing and Applications for Software and Knowledge Engineers
Kozo Sugiyama (Japan Adv. Inst. Science and Technology)

Vol. 12 Lecture Notes on Empirical Software Engineering
edited by N. Juristo & A. M. Moreno (Universidad Politécrica de Madrid, Spain)

Forthcoming titles:

Acquisition of Software Engineering Knowledge
edited by Robert G. Reynolds (Wayne State Univ.)

Monitoring, Debugging, and Analysis of Distributed Real-Time Systems
Jeffrey J.-P. Tsai, Steve J. H. Yong, R. Smith and Y. D. Bi (Univ. Illinois at Chicago)

Series on Software Engineering and Knowledge Engineering

Vol. 13

DATA STRUCTURES AND ALGORITHMS

Series Editor

S K Chang

Editor

Shi-Kuo Chang

University of Pittsburgh, USA

World Scientific

New Jersey • London • Singapore • Hong Kong

Published by

World Scientific Publishing Co. Pte. Ltd.
5 Toh Tuck Link, Singapore 596224
USA office: Suite 202, 1060 Main Street, River Edge, NJ 07661
UK office: 57 Shelton Street, Covent Garden, London WC2H 9HE

British Library Cataloguing-in-Publication Data
A catalogue record for this book is available from the British Library.

DATA STRUCTURES AND ALGORITHMS

ISBN 981-238-348-4

Printed in Singapore by World Scientific Printers (S) Pte Ltd

Preface

The Macro University is a worldwide consortium of virtual universities. The consortium was established in the Spring of 1999 and now has more than fifteen international members. With a worldwide consortium, there will be a wide variety of curricula and educational programs for people with different linguistic skills, different cultures, and different perceptual preferences. Therefore the Marco University should support the multilevel, multilingual and multimodal usage of the shared content codeveloped by many teachers. (a) **Multilevel Usage**: The same course materials can be organized in different ways to be used in a regular semester course, a short course, an introductory exposition, an advanced seminar, etc. (b) **Multilingual Usage**: The same course materials can be transformed into different languages. (c) **Multimodel Usage**: The same course materials can be used by people with different perceptual preferences. These considerations have led to the Growing Book Project.

A *Growing Book* is an electronic book codeveloped by a group of teachers who are geographically dispersed throughout the world and collaborate in teaching and research. Since the course materials are constantly evolving, the Growing Book must be constantly updated and expanded. The Growing Book is used by each teacher both in the local classroom as well as in the worldwide distance learning environment. Therefore the Growing Book must be accessible by multilingual students. The chapters of the Growing Book are owned by different authors who may utilize and/or provide different tools for distance learning, self-learning and assessment.

The participants of the Macro University worked together to develop a prototype Growing Book, which has the following characteristics: course materials accessible with a browser; common look-and-feel and common buttons; common assessment tool with adjustable granularity; individual tools downloadable as plug-ins; examples in C and later Unicode; adaptive learning with embedded audio/video clips; collaboration in content and tools evaluation, and availability in hard copy and CD. The prototype Growing Book is intended as an online textbook for an undergraduate course on *Data Structures and Algorithms.* The initial version of the Growing Book is available for instructional usage by members of the Macro University. Inquiries to join the Macro University can be sent to `chang@cs.pitt.edu`.

Data Structures and Algorithms is the first textbook in hard copy produced by the Macro University Consortium. It is intended for undergraduate students in computer science and information sciences. The thirteen chapters written by an international group of experienced teachers cover the fundamental concepts of algorithms and most of the important data structures as well as the concept of interface design. The book is illustrated by many examples and visual diagrams. Whenever appropriate, program codes are included to facilitate learning. This textbook is entirely self-contained and can be used by itself. It can also be used together with the online version of the Growing Book to enhance the student's learning experience.

Shi-Kuo Chang
University of Pittsburgh and Knowledge Systems Institute
January 8, 2003

Contents

Chapter 1

Introduction to the Fundamentals of Algorithms

PAOLO MARESCA
University Federico II of Naples, Italy
paomares@unina.it

1.1. Introduction

In this introductory chapter we examine some ancient algorithms with the intent of introducing the concept of algorithm in a more natural way. From those examples, the reader will be able to derive important characteristics inherited in the area of computer science. The concept of execution time of an algorithm will be introduced.

1.2. Ancient Algorithms

Computer science is deeply rooted in history. It is not just an academic discipline initiated forty years ago. With this intention, we make a brief reflection upon one of the concepts that is at the base of computer science: the concept of "algorithm".

What is an algorithm? The word "algorithm" seems to have been derived from the Arabic "Al Kuvaritm", even though we know that the Egyptians and the Babylonians had already used algorithms.

A recent archaeological expedition has brought to light, in an area of Mesopotamia (currently Iraq) near ancient Babylon (currently Baghdad), some tablets covered with cuneiform signs.[1]

[1] A form of writing used since 3000 B.C.

These finds have been of great scientific and mathematical interest since, although they were written about the time of the Hammurabi dynasty (1800–1600 B.C.), they showed that the Babylonians had a knowledge of algebra. In fact beyond the knowledge of the operations of addition, subtraction, multiplication and division, they were able to solve many types of algebraic equations as well. But they did not have an algebraic notation that was quite as transparent as ours. Actually, they didn't have any powerful algebraic notation: they didn't know the use of formulas!

Each concise formula was seen as a list of elementary actions whose execution had the same effect as the application of the concise formula.

In other words applying the concise formula is equivalent to applying the corresponding sequence of elementary actions to resolve the problem.

This sequence of elementary actions is called an "algorithm". Each elementary action is an "instruction".

In effect, we can affirm that Babylonians worked with a kind of "machine language" for the representation of formulas, instead of a symbolic language.

One can appreciate better the level of the mathematical conquests of these people if we examine some examples.

Before starting, remember that the ancient Babylonians used a base-60 number system. Our present system of counting the hours, minutes and seconds are vestiges of their system. But it is less widely known that Babylonians actually worked with base 60 numbers, using a rather peculiar notation that did not include any exponent part. They had 60 different digits. In order to represent the base 60 numbers we will use decimal numbers 0 to 59, with a comma separating the digits in a number. For example, the number $5,30_{\text{base }60}$ (note that in the following we write for simplicity $5,30_{60}$) is a two digit number: the digit 5 and the digit 30. The comma explains the correct separation of the digits. To give an idea of the way Babylonians worked with numbers, consider the following example. Given two digits, for example 2 and 20, respectively, the number $2,20_{60}$ can represent

$$\mathbf{2^*60^1 + 20^*60^0 = 140_{10}}\ \textbf{or}$$

$$\mathbf{2^*60^0 + 20^*60^{-1} = 2 + 20/60 = \left(2\tfrac{1}{3}\right)_{10} = 140_{10}{}^*60^{-1}}\ \textbf{or}$$

$$\ldots\ldots$$

In other words it represents the more general number $\mathbf{140^*60^n}$ for $-\infty \leq n \leq \infty$. As we can see, this shows the way Babylonians were representing ***floating-point numbers***.

At first sight this manner of representing numbers may look very awkward, but in fact it has significant advantages when multiplications and

Table 1.1. Table of reciprocals.

$x_{\text{base } 10}$	$(1/x)_{\text{base } 60}$	$x_{\text{base } 10}$	$(1/x)_{\text{base } 60}$	$x_{\text{base } 10}$	$(1/x)_{\text{base } 60}$
2	30	16	3, 45	45	1, 20
3	20	18	3, 20	48	1, 15
4	15	20	3	50	1, 12
5	12	24	2, 30	54	1, 6, 40
6	10	25	2, 24	1	1
8	7, 30	27	2, 13, 20	$64_{10} = 1, 4_{60}$	56, 15
9	6, 40	30	2	$72_{10} = 1, 12_{60}$	50
10	6	32	1, 52, 30	$75_{10} = 1, 15_{60}$	48
12	5	36	1, 40	$80_{10} = 1, 20_{60}$	45
15	4	40	1, 30	$81_{10} = 1, 21_{60}$	42, 26, 40

divisions are involved. We use the same principle when we do calculation by slide rule, performing the multiplications and divisions without regard to the decimal point location and then supplying the appropriate power of 10 later. A Babylonian mathematician, when computing with numbers that were meaningful and familiar to him, could easily keep the appropriate power of 60 in mind since it is not difficult to estimate the range of a value within a factor of 60. Only few cases of additions performed incorrectly because the radix points were improperly aligned [2, p. 28] have been found in the literature, but such examples are surprisingly rare.

As an indication of the utility of this floating-point notation, consider the following table of reciprocals (see Table 1.1).

The table is a useful tool for the Babylonian floating-point notation. The reciprocal of a number x is $1/x$ and $1/x_{\text{base } 60} = 1/(x^*60^{-1})_{\text{base } 10}$. For example the reciprocal of $2_{10} = 2_{60}$ is computed in the following way $(1/2)_{60} = 1/(2^*60^{-1}) = 60/2 = 30$. In the same way $(1/12)_{60} = 1/(12^*60^{-1}) = 60/12 = 5$. The numbers that are not divisible by 60 without a remainder generate pairs or triples of coefficients. For example $(1/8)_{60} = 1/(8^*60^{-1}) = 60/8 = 7$ with remainder 4, now $(4/8)_{60} = (1/2)_{60} = 30$ as we have seen above. So the number $(1/8)_{60}$ generates the pair of coefficients 7 and 30, which creates the number $7, 30_{60}$.

Dozens of tablets containing this information have been found and some of them go back as far as the "Ur III dynasty", about 2250 B.C. There are also many multiplication tables which list the multiples of the numbers; for example, dividing by $81 = 1, 21$ is equivalent to multiplying by $44, 26, 40$ and tables of $44, 26, 40^*k$ for $1 \leq k \leq 20$ and $k = 30, 40, 50$ were commonplace. Over two hundred examples of multiplication tables have been catalogued.

In the next sections we will describe some "old" algorithms and we derive the corresponding algorithm in our number system.

1.3. Algorithm 1: Sum of the Powers of 2 with an Exponent from 1 to 10 (1800–1600 B.C.)

Original
What is the sum of the powers of 2 from 1 to 10?

p1) Compute the last term of the sum which is $8,32$
p2) Subtract 1 from $8,32$ and obtain $8,31$
p3) Add $8,31$ to $8,32$ and obtain the answer $17,3$
p4) End

Correspondent in base 10
What is the sum of the powers of 2 from 1 to 10?

p1) Compute the last term of the sum which is 1024
p2) Subtract 1 from 1024 and obtain 1023
p3) Add 1024 to 1023 and obtain the answer 2047
p4) End

1.4. Algorithm 2: Sum of the Squares of Numbers from 1 to 10 (1800–1600 B.C.)

Original
The square of $1 \times 1 = 1$ and of $10 \times 10 = 1,40$. Consider the square of the numbers from 1 to 10. What is their sum?

p1) Multiply 1 by 20, namely by one-third, giving 20
p2) Multiply 10 by 40, namely by two-thirds, giving $6,40$
p3) $6,40$ plus 20 is 7
p4) Multiply 7 by 55 (which is the sum of 1 through 10), obtaining $6,25$
p5) $6,25$ is the desired sum
p6) End

Correspondent in base 10
Consider the square of the numbers from 1 to 10. What is their sum?

p1) multiply 1 per 1/3, obtaining 1/3
p2) multiply 10 per 2/3, obtaining 20/3
p3) 1/3 plus 20/3 is 7
p4) multiply 7 by 55 (which is the sum of 1 through 10) obtaining 385

p5) 385 is the desired sum
p6) End

These two algorithms, so complex to understand, contain the correct formulas, respectively, for the

$$\sum_{k=1}^{n} 2^k = 2^n + (2^n - 1) \qquad \textbf{sum of a geometric series}$$

$$\sum_{k=1}^{n} k^2 = \left(\frac{1}{3} + \left(\frac{2}{3}\right) * n\right) * \sum_{1}^{n} k \qquad \textbf{sum of a quadratic series}$$

These formulas, as written above, have not been found in Old-Babylonian texts, but we can see from their algorithms that they knew how to solve them.

The algorithms described above were accompanied by an example in the original tablets, but in some rare cases, an example showing a different style, like the following one displayed at the British Museum, has been found. The explanation of such a difference in style is probably due to the fact that this algorithm comes from a later period of Babylonian history (**1800–1600 B.C.**), called the Seleucid period. We think that in this period, there has been an evolution in the use of the algorithms and therefore no detailed explanations were required.

The algorithm described below was a typical problem of the time and belongs to this late period. It computes the measurement of a rectangular land. In particular, the total sum of the length, the width and the diagonal of a rectangle ($l+w+d$), as well as the area of the land (A), are provided and the algorithm computes the value of each of the three measures individually. Actually there are three distinct versions of the problem in the same text: two of them include an example, the third does not. We present all the three distinct versions in the original notation. Wherever the notation is misleading, because formulas were not used, an explanation is given.

1.5. Algorithm 3: (1800–1600 B.C.)

Original

first version

The sum of length, width, and diagonal of a rectangle is 1, 1 and 7 is the area.
Compute the measures of the length, of the width, and of the diagonal, respectively.
The relative measures are unknown but we know their sum.

p1) $1,10$ times, $1\ 10$ is $1,21,40$. (read $1,10_{60} \times 1,10_{60} = 1,21,40_{60}$)
p2) 7 times 2 is 14
p3) Subtract 14 from $1,21,40$, which is equal to $1,7,40$
p4) Now multiply $1,7,40$ times 30, which is equal to $33,50$
p5) Which number should $1,10$ multiply in order to obtain $33,50$?
p6) $1,10$ times 29 is $33,50$
p7) 29 is the diagonal

——— second version ———

The sum of length, width, and diagonal of a rectangle is 12 and 12 is the area.
Compute the measures of the length, of the width, and of the diagonal, respectively.
The relative measures are unknown.

p1) 12 times 12 is $2,24$
p2) 12 times 2 is 24
p3) Subtract 24 from $2,24$ and obtain 2
p4) 2 times 30 is 1
p5) Which number should 12 be multiplied by to obtain 1?
p6) 12 times 5 is 1
p7) 5 is the diagonal

——— third version ———

p1) The sum of length, width, and diagonal of a rectangle is 1 and 5 is the area
p2) Multiply the length, the width, and the diagonal-times the length, the width, and the diagonal
p3) Multiply the area by 2
p4) Subtract the products and multiply what is left by one-half
p5) Which number should the sum of length, of the width, and of the diagonal be multiplied by to obtain this product?
p6) The diagonal is the factor

So let l be the length, w be the width, $A = lw$ be the area of a rectangle, and $d = (l^2 + w^2)^{1/2}$ (note: there is great evidence from other texts that the old-Babylonian mathematicians knew the so-called Pythagorean theorem, over 1000 years before the time of Pythagoras!) be the length of its diagonal, the solution of the previous problem is based on the rather remarkable formula:

$$\boldsymbol{d = \frac{1}{2}((l + w + d)^2 - 2A)/(l + w + d)}$$

The first two versions of the previous example, compute the problem for the case in which the triple $(l, w, d) = (20, 21, 29)$ and (3, 4, 5) respectively, but without calculating the length l and the width w, respectively. We know from other texts that the Babylonians knew the solution to the equations $x + y = a$ and $x^2 + y^2 = b$. The description of the calculation in these two versions is unusually terse and does not name the quantities it is dealing with. On the other hand, the third section gives the same procedure entirely *without* numbers. The reason for this may be the fact that the stated parameters 1 and 5 cannot possibly correspond to the length + width + diagonal and the area, respectively, of any rectangle, no matter what power of 60 is attached! From this perspective, a teacher of computer science will recognize that the above text looks very similar to the attempt to solve an impossible problem.

What we have learned

Different concepts emerge from an careful analysis of the algorithms described in the previous paragraph. The first is the concept of data. The second is the concept of a job's environment: the environment that characterizes the algorithm. The third is tied up with the characteristics that each algorithm must possess. We will examine all these concepts one by one in the following sections.

1.6. Data: Definition and Characteristics

From the analysis of any of the Babylonian algorithms given in the precedent paragraph we can conceive the concept of "data". The Babylonians used numerical data almost exclusively. But what is data? Information, or data, is an object with which the algorithm works. For example, from the p2 step of the power of 2 algorithm, (p2) the last term you add is 1024 it is easy to understand that 1024 is data. But let us give a more rigorous definition. An information item (or data) has three components [5]:

$$\mathbf{I} = \{\mathbf{Type}, \mathbf{Attribute}, \mathbf{Value}\}$$

A well defined information item will have all three components, as a matter of fact the value represents an object selected from a set named "type" while the attribute represents the semantics of the same information item. An information item that possesses only a value and a type is a constant. As an example of a constant recall the value 1024 from step p2 of the power of 2 algorithm.

In the Babylonian algorithms many constants are found. Some were named, much like typed constants in the programming languages of a few millennium later.

Actually there are many things in common but also many differences, for instance, the types used in computer languages are not only numerical therefore the value of a data item is not always a number. For instance, in the type "day of the week" the value (day) is obtained by selecting a day in a set having the following values:

$$\{\textbf{Monday}, \textbf{Tuesday}, \textbf{Thursday}, \textbf{Wednesday}, \textbf{Friday}, \textbf{Saturday}, \textbf{Sunday}\}$$

Besides, the observation that the value should not be confused with the particular representation is also reasonable. If we consider the seleucid algorithm we can have two versions: the translated one and the original one. The translated version is easier to use since the values of the data are represented in base 10 while the original version uses a base 60 and floating-point representation. The algorithms are the same and they operate on the same data. The difference is that they are represented in different numeration bases because a Babylonian operated in base 60 while an inhabitant of this millennium has more familiarity with base 10!

Finally, the state of an information item consists of the pair (Attribute, Value). This means that we can modify an information item by modifying the attribute and/or the value. We will speak in this case of the concept of elaboration of information and we will mean the modification of the state of any information that is a part of the algorithm. Frequently elaborations exist that also modify the value in the intermediate elaborations. In the seleucid algorithms step p2 is an example. It is less usual to modify an attribute in order to construct an elaboration: in the Babylonian algorithms it doesn't ever happen!

1.7. Algorithm Environment

In the preceding sections the descriptions of the algorithm also implied the environment in which the algorithm must be performed. The environment is that of the performer that in all the cases of tablets so far found in Babylonia was a human being. In this short section we will take a first look at the concept of environment. This will also serve as the starting point for some reflections on the Babylonian algorithms.

The concept of environment derives from the specific application of computer science. We continually use the phrase "job environment" without any difficulty. The desktop environment, for instance, is perhaps the most well known for persons who spend a lot of time studying or working on it. In this environment the objects used are evident (pen, paper, eraser, ruler, etc.) and the simple actions that we can do with them (writing, erasing, moving, etc.) are evident as well. But by themselves the actions applied to the objects are not enough to realize complex actions, for instance: draw a triangle on a sheet of paper.

It is necessary for "algorithms" to encapsulate the actions you need to apply to the objects in order to realize one specific hand-made object (the triangle in this case).

For example how many elementary actions would be necessary in order to decompose the problem: draw a triangle!

It can be realized from endless sequences of different actions (algorithms). One of these could be:

— take a sheet of paper,
— take a pencil,
— take the ruler,
— trace the first side,
— rotate the ruler of 30° with respect to the first side,
— trace the second side,
— [etc].

The concept of environment therefore is a very powerful tool abstraction. It could be represented in this way:

OBJECTS
ACTIONS (1)
ALGORITHMS

The **OBJECTS** represent the static part of the environment and represent the entities on which it makes sense to carry out the actions.

The defined **ACTIONS** on the objects are of a very elementary type (see the preceding example) and, therefore, almost always are not sufficient by themselves to resolve the problem. These actions must be organized in **ALGORITHMS** in order to resolve a specific problem, as shown in the preceding example.

An object can be seen at different levels of abstraction; for instance the object "car" is an abstraction of a very complex object. In fact, depending on the context in which it appears can be a complex object (for the builder it represents the assembly of an enormous number of parts) or simple (for the car dealer it could be the code from a catalogue). Still the car can become much more complex if other job environments are considered, for instance: body worker, mechanic, etc.

In general therefore an object is characterized by the environment of which it is a part. We can define a level of abstraction for it (comparable to the degree of complexity): the more elevated is the level of abstraction the less complex is the object in accord with the principles of Top–Down design.

The actions are also tightly tied to the environment (that is to the objects) in which they are defined and they characterize the behavior of it. A level of abstraction is also definable for them. In fact, an action that may seem elementary in a certain environment may not be in another one.

In the environment of mathematical knowledge everyone will know the meaning of the product of two whole numbers. But this action is not so elementary in the environment of mathematical knowledge of a six-year-old child!

Finally, algorithms offer the possibility to create new products in the environment. They are strongly influenced by the technology used in the environment. We may compare, for example, the process of auto making at the beginning of the XX century with that of the present day.

Some objects (assembly lines, etc.) and actions (those relative to the assembly lines) even disappear in the comparison, while others that are used to produce the same product (car) appear (robot, actions on these, etc.).

Assuming that any environment can be characterized by the triple (1) it is evident that the same can be done for environments for information processing.

It is not surprising that the concept of environment is central to computer science. It is enough to formulate the following definition to understand why:

"Computer science is a set of theories, techniques, and methodologies, used for the definition, design, implementation and use of environments for automatic processing of information."

It is often true that we make use of "environments in environments" in order to realize a kind of "Chinese box". In this case we speak about Integrated Environments for information processing. Many software tools currently in commercial use are of this type.

1.8. Algorithm: Definition and Characteristics

1.8.1. *Definition*

An algorithm is a sequence of actions whose task is to resolve a problem. An algorithm is composed of a sequence of actions, each organized in steps.

Each step modifies the states of the set of information items. Each action corresponds to a step that the performer completes. A sequence of actions does not always evoke the same execution sequence. This problem is the prologue to the introduction of the instructions that control the execution. A sequence of actions is organized sequentially and causes a plurality of dynamic sequences. This conclusion was also well known in the Babylonian algorithms. And despite the fact that the performer was a man they already used conditional and iterative instructions.

1.8.2. *Characteristics*

The concept of algorithm, as one can guess, is one of the most important elements of computer science. It is useful to frame a problem and to transform it into a solution that is correct and efficient. This is the first property of an algorithm that forms a part of it. Correctness is the property reflecting the extent to which the algorithm is able to reach a solution without errors. Think for example of the sequence of actions necessary for the collection of a sum of money through ATM machines. The sequence of actions is, necessarily, prearranged and therefore any alteration of the sequence can cause an error jeopardizing its result (missing issue of banknotes, ejection of the card, etc.). The efficiency of an algorithm is the property that regards the rapidity by which a solution is reached. It is clear that, for instance, the assembly instructions of an appliance are often not even read by the installer. Why is that? Evidently the repetition of this activity, by the expert has conferred to him such a speed that he is able to efficiently repeat the assembly much more quickly than someone doing it for the first time. On the other hand, the beginner may try their solution of the problem without reaching the solution immediately (some steps may need to be redone). The computer scientist should therefore seek or design algorithms that are both correct and efficient.

An algorithm should have numerous other properties that we will now list. Generality is the property that confers to the algorithm a fundamental value: it must be designed to solve a class of problems. The algorithm must be finite in terms of the sequence of actions to do and defined by these individual actions. Besides, it must be effective, that means that each single action can be recognizable through its effect, in a word it should be reproducible. Finally the algorithm must be comprehensible by the one who performs it.

What we have said allows us to return to the concept of algorithm only to point out that it is not only known but also widely used in daily life. Make a phone call, make a coffee, get dressed, etc. are examples of algorithms and each of us carry them out in different ways. The algorithm

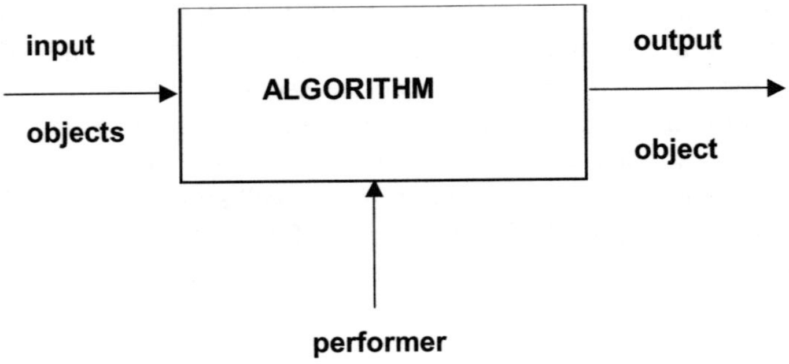

Fig. 1.1. The relationship between algorithm, input, output and performer.

therefore depends on the performer that can be, for example, a human or a computer. It must describe in all details, the actions and the entities necessary for the resolution of a problem.

More generally in an algorithm there are static entities called objects. These could be of three types:

— input,
— output,
— algorithm,

1.8.3. *Algorithm and Program*

What difference is there between an algorithm and a program? The first thing to underline is that an algorithm is meant in general to be performed by a human while the computer performs a program. Also, a program is a sequence of instructions, each of which causes an action. But does a sequence of instructions cause a sequence of actions? The answer is not only negative but we can point out that each sequence of actions causes dynamic sequences which are not only unknown beforehand but are in fact infinite (the algorithm for a phone call is an example, assembly of an appliance another).

In a program the static sequence (lexicographical sequence) describes multiple dynamic sequences (possible different executions). In short, associated with the instructions that cause the actions we need phrases or linguistic mechanisms that, according to whether a certain event is verified or not, drives the performer to carry out one sequence of actions rather than another. These instructions are called control instructions.

This is not an observation that has recent origin since the Babylonians already knew control structures although they did not write them as we do write in programming languages. Besides, they did not know the use of the "0"; the known mathematics of that time was essentially functional for measurement so of what interest could have been a geometrical figure whose perimeter is a number equal to zero?

They did not know the use of such a test as "go to step 4 if $x < 0$" but they had already realized that there exist possible executions for which they constructed different algorithms for different cases. Instead of having such tests, there would effectively be separate algorithms for the different cases. For example see [3, pp. 312–314] for a case in which one algorithm is step-by-step the same as another, but simplified since one of the parameters is zero.

What kinds of control instructions are necessary in order to describe the algorithms? The definition of the dynamic sequences happens through linguistic mechanisms that implement three fundamental operations:

(a) **sequence**: the instructions are performed in "sequence" that is in the order in which they were written.
(b) **selection**: the instructions to be executed are selected according to whether a logical event is verified or not.
(c) **iteration**: a block of instructions must be repeated; the execution and the repetition of the block are stopped when a logical event is verified or not.

There are not many instances of iteration either. The basic operations underlying the multiplication of high precision base 60 numbers obviously involve iteration, and these operations were clearly understood by the Babylonian mathematicians; but the rules were apparently never written down. No example showing intermediate steps in multiplication have been found.

In [3, pp. 353–365; 4, Tables 32, 56, 57; 5, p. 59; 6, pp. 118–120] an example dealing with compound interest, taken from the Berlin Museum collection, is one of the few examples of a "DO I = 1 TO N" construct in the Babylonian tablets that has been excavated so far.

References

1. D. Knuth, "Ancient Babylonian algorithms," *Comm. ACM* **15**(7), 671–677, July 1972.
2. O. Neugebauer, *The Exact Science in Antiquity*, Brown U. Press, Providence, R.I., 2nd edition), 240 pp. plus 14 photographic plates, 1957.

3. O. Neugebauer, "Mathematishe keilschrift-texte," In *Quellen und Studien zur Geschichte der Mathematik, Astronomie und Physik*, Vol. A3, Pt.1, 516 pp., 1935.
4. A. V. Aho and J. D. Ullman, "Fondamenti di Informatica," Zanichelli, 1998.
5. B. Fadini and C. Savy, "Elementi di Informatica," Liguori, 1998.
6. F. Thuream-Dangin, *Textes Mathematiques Babylonians*, E. J. Brill, Leiden, The Netherlands, 243 pp., 1938

Exercises

Beginner's Exercises

1. The type of an information is:
   (a) The set in which you make a choice
   (b) The length of an information item (data)
   (c) The attribute of an information item (data)
2. An algorithm is:
   (a) A sequence of elementary actions that resolves a problem
   (b) The given instructions, without any order, to a performer in order to resolve a problem
   (c) An ordered and finished sequence of actions that resolves a problem automatically
3. An information item (data) is composed of:
   (a) His value
   (b) His three components: {Type, Attribute, Value}
   (c) His two components: Attribute, Value
4. A constant item is:
   (a) A real number
   (b) The pair: {Type, Value}
   (c) The pair: {Attribute, Value}
5. The types used in computer languages:
   (a) Are always numerical
   (b) Are not only numerical
   (c) Depend on the user
6. The state of an information is:
   (a) The pair: {Type, Value}
   (b) The pair: {Attribute, Value}
   (c) The triple: {Type, Attribute, Value}

7. The elaboration of an information mean:
   (a) The ordered pairs {Attribute, Value}
   (b) The modification of the state of any information that is a part of the algorithm
   (c) The modification of the state of all information that is a part of the algorithm
8. The environment is composed of:
   (a) {Type, Attribute, Value}
   (b) Objects, Actions and Programs
   (c) Objects, Actions and Algorithms
9. An algorithm is:
   (a) An algorithm of any type
   (b) A sequence of actions whose task is to resolve a problem
   (c) A sequence of programs whose task is to resolve a problem
10. A sequence of actions:
    (a) Always evoke the same execution sequence
    (b) Does not always evoke the same execution sequence
    (c) Sometimes evoke the same execution sequence
11. What is the property of generality for an algorithm?
    (a) The characteristic for which the algorithm must be designed to solve a problem
    (b) The characteristic for which the algorithm must be designed to solve a part of problem
    (c) The characteristic for which the algorithm must be designed to solve a class of a problems
12. What does correctness mean?
    (a) Is the property reflecting the extent to which the algorithm is able to reach a solution without errors
    (b) Is the property reflecting the extent to which the algorithm is composed of finite actions
    (c) Is the property reflecting the extent to which the algorithm is able to solve a problem with rapidity
13. What kind of control instructions are necessary in order to describe the algorithms ?
    (a) Sequence, selection, iteration
    (b) Selection, iteration, repetition
    (c) Iteration, induction, recursion

Advanced Exercise

14. Compute the algorithm execution time of the following fragment of code

```
for (int i = 1; i <= n - 1; i++)
        for (int j = i + 1; j <= n; j++)
                for (k = i; k <= n; k++)
                        A(j, k) = A(j, k) - A(i, k)*A(j, i)/A(i, i);
```

Chapter 2

The Running Time of an Algorithm

PAOLO MARESCA
University Federico II of Naples, Italy
paomares@unina.it

In this chapter we will show a method to compute the running time (or execution time) of an algorithm or a program. The running time of an algorithm helps the programmer to choose the algorithm with the best performance that solves a determined problem. We measure the execution time of an algorithm or of a program (a program is the translation of an algorithm into a determined language) and then we show how to build more efficient programs, wherever possible.

2.1. General Considerations about the Execution Time

What are the characteristics that a good algorithm should have? The answer to this question requires answering another question: What it is the goal of an algorithm (or of a program)? This second question is more important than the first because, if you do not have a clear idea of the objective to reach, writing an algorithm could be a complex activity. The first principle to keep in mind is the KISS principle: Keep It Simple, Stupid! Simplicity or comprehensibility makes an algorithm easy to read and it lowers the probability and the quantity of errors that will naturally emerge. Clarity in a program is obtained by writing in a simple way and by adding detailed documentation. A clear and well-documented program is simple to read and is easy to explain a long time after its creation, and the possible modifications (maintenance) can be made in a fastest way either by its author or by other programmers. The efficiency of an algorithm becomes fundamental when an algorithm must be repeated in certain conditions (e.g. within a certain time). Attaining a high efficiency requires a cost in the use of the resources that the algorithm needs to reach such efficiency. For instance, how much memory is required by the variables? How much data must be transferred from or to memory? How much data must be transferred from or to another computer (this generates traffic on the net)?

It is worthwhile to observe that the characteristics of an algorithm are often in contrast: some are objective some are subjective. We try to explain these concepts. For example, suppose we have a program that controls the chemical reaction of a melting furnace and we estimate that it must execute in 10 ms. Then the efficiency of that program is an objective matter because the time must be rigorously respected if you want the result of the chemical process to be safeguarded. On the other hand, comprehensibility is a subjective attribute. For example, how much and how well documented should a program be? That depends on the performer of the program: is the performer a capable person able to understand the documentation methodologies or should the documentation be for novices? Efficiency and comprehensibility are two features that can conflict. Suppose we have to sort a vector and we consider two possible algorithms for the solution of the problem: one uses the method of merging, the other the method of selection. The first method is surely more complex than the second, no matter how much documentation we use, and it is also longer than the second, however more efficient it is for big quantity of data. In order to compute the running time of the chosen algorithm, we could execute the program on all the input data. This approach can be unrealistic because with a huge amount of data the program could take an infinite time. We need a better way to compute the efficiency of a program; we need a measure of the execution time that synthesizes its performance with respect to the number of input data. For example, the expression $\boldsymbol{log\ n}$ can be used to describe the running time of an algorithm whose execution time takes logarithmic time with respect to the size of the input $\boldsymbol{n}$.

If we agree that the execution time of a program is an objective measure of a program then we should provide an objective way to compute and compare the execution times of algorithms. There are two possible ways:

(1) Benchmark
(2) Analysis

But we are interested in algorithm analysis. When we analyze an algorithm we look at the input data and at their dimension. The dimension of the data depends on the specific problem solved by the program. For instance, a good measure of the dimension of a sorting algorithm is the number of elements to order. We are also interested in determining where the program spends most of his time. A rule of thumb (the 90/10 rule) tells us that 90% of the execution is spent in 10% of the code. One way to measure the efficiency of a program is to perform a profile of the program (through a tool called *profiler*) in order to identify the critical points and improve them. For instance, if we could halve the execution time of that 10% of the code, which is 90% of the total execution time, the total execution time would be reduced by 45%!

2.2. Execution Time

To represent the *execution time* of a program on a datum of dimension $\boldsymbol{n}$, we use the function $\boldsymbol{T(n)}$. If $\boldsymbol{T(n)} = \mathbf{c^*n}$, where c is a constant, then the program has an execution time proportional to the dimension of the datum n. In this case, we say that the program has a ***linear execution time***.

We can think of the execution time as the sum of the times spent for each instruction of a program. In this hypothesis it is easy to verify that the execution of a program does not depend only on the dimension of the datum but also on the specific input. In general, we define $T(n)$ to be the execution time in the worst case; in other words the execution time of the program on a generic input of dimension n.

Another common measure of the performance of a program is the *average execution time*, $\boldsymbol{T_{\mathbf{med}}(n)}$, of a program on an input of dimension n. Although this is a more realistic measure of the performance of a program, it is more difficult to measure with respect to the worst-case execution time. In fact the average execution time requires that all the data of dimension n has the same probability to be executed.

2.2.1. *The Execution Time of a Program as Function of the Dimension of the Data*

As an example, let us calculate the execution time of the C++ code fragment (only the most internal loop) of a Bubble Sort algorithm.

The purpose of the fragment is to "exchange" the element **a[i]** with **a[i+1]** if **a[i]** is greater than **a[i+1]**. If we assume that a unit of time is spent on each instruction to be executed, then one unit is used by the assignment statement in lines (3)–(5). In the **for** statement, one unit is used for the increment of i and one unit to compare i with *arraySize-1*, each time the loop is repeated (line 1). In the body of the loop, the statement of lines (3)–(5) is executed only if the test in line (2) is successful. Therefore, in the worst case, four units of time are required to execute lines (2)–(5), for

Example

```
1) for ( i = 0; i< arraySize – 1; i++)
2) if (a[i] > a[i+1] {
3) temp = a[i];
4) a[i] = a[i+1];
5) a[i+1] = temp; }
```

line 2) to 5) **4 time unit**
line 1) to 5) ⇒ **8 time unit *(arraySize) + 2 time unit**

Fig. 2.1. A fragment of *BubbleSort* code.

a total of four units for each loop. Since each loop is repeated *arraySize* times, the total execution time for the loop is equal to $8(\mathit{arraySize})$. To obtain the total execution time, we still need to add two more units of time for the statement in line (1) at the end of the iteration loop, i.e. when the test $i > \mathit{arraySize}$ successful. Therefore, the total execution time of this code fragment is $8(\mathit{arraySize})$.

The dimension of the data used by this fragment is *arraySize* and is related to the length of the input vector $\mathrm{A}[0..n]$. So, we have that

$$\boldsymbol{T(j) = 8(\mathrm{arraySize}) + 2 = 8(\mathrm{arraySize}); \mathrm{with}\ j = \mathrm{index}}$$

is the execution time of the fragment of code shown in Fig. 2.1.

2.3. Comparisons Between Different Execution Times

One aspect for the measure of a quantity is the identification of a "weight" of the component entity. This is obtained by first defining a measure and then a methodology to compute the measure. In our specific case we have defined a temporal measure in a conventional manner and we are going to describe a methodology for measuring the performance of a program. However, one of the problems to consider is the comparison between the execution time of programs of different complexity, when executed on the same computer. In the field of linear measures, space, etc. comparisons are simple. In fact, given the measure of two rooms, 40 m^2 and 45 m^2, the comparison is immediate, i.e. the second is larger than the first. Unfortunately this does not happen all the time the two programs are compared.

What we have learned

The execution time of a program determines the maximum dimension of the problem that can be solved by a program. By increasing the speed of the computers, the dimension of the problem solvable with a program whose execution time grows slowly, increases more than the dimension of the problems solvable with a program whose execution time grows quickly.

2.4. Big-O Notation: The Approximation of the Execution Time

2.4.1. *Introduction*

Once we have written the program in a language and we have defined the input data, the execution time of the program still depends on two factors: the computer on which it will be executed and the compiler that will execute it. The first factor is clear: there are computers that execute instructions faster than others. Consider, for example, a supercomputer and a personal computer. The second factor concerns the compiler and its way of implementing a single instruction. It is well known that the implementation depends on the choices performed by the compiler but also on the operating system running on the computer.

These considerations allow us to conclude that given a program and its data, we are not able to say, for example, that: "the following program will perform its job in 8.34 seconds."

However, the problem of the measure of the real execution time of a program remains complex to determine even if we know the type of computer, the compiler, the program and the test cases used to execute the program. This is the reason why it is necessary to choose a measure that is independent of the implementation details of the compiler (independent of the average number of machine instructions generated) and of the computer. This notation is called "Big-O". If we recall the code fragment of the BubbleSort program of Fig. 2.1, we say that the execution time of that fragment is $O(m)$ and we read it "Big-O of m", instead of saying that the program requires an execution time equal to $4m - 1$ on a vector of length m. In other words, we are saying that the execution time of that fragment of code is "a constant multiplied by m". This definition not only allows to ignore the implementation details related to the computer and the compiler but also to formulate a simple hypothesis for the calculation of the execution time.

2.4.2. *Big-O Notation*

The formal definition of the execution time of a program follows.

Let $T(n)$ be the execution time of a program and n the dimension of the input data, we assume that

$$\begin{array}{ll} \textbf{a) } \boldsymbol{n} & \textbf{is a non-negative integer} \\ \textbf{b) } \boldsymbol{T(n)} & \textbf{is non-negative } \forall\, \boldsymbol{n} \end{array}$$

Let $f(n)$ be a function defined over non-negative integer values of n, then

$$\boldsymbol{T(n)} \textbf{ is } \boldsymbol{O(f(n))} \Leftrightarrow \exists \mathbf{n_0},\ \mathbf{c} > \mathbf{0} : \forall \mathbf{n} \geq \mathbf{n_0}\ \boldsymbol{T(n)} \leq \boldsymbol{cf(n)} \quad (1)$$

In other words $T(n)$ is $O(f(n))$ if $T(n)$ is at most a constant multiplied by $f(n)$, with the exception for some values of n.

We can apply the Big-O definition to prove that $T(n)$ is $O(f(n))$ for particular functions T and f. To do this, given two fixed variables n_o and c, we need to demonstrate that

$$\boldsymbol{T(n) \leq cf(n)}$$

If we assume that n is a non-negative integer and is greater than or equal to n_o, this proof requires just a little algebraic manipulation. Let us look at some examples.

2.4.3. *Some Examples*

(1) Let us consider a program with execution time equal to $T(n) = (n + 1)^3$, we say that "$T(n)$ is $O(n^3)$" or that "$T(n)$ is cubic". To show that this is true from (1) we need to choose an n_o and a constant c so that $\boldsymbol{T(n) \leq cf(n)}$. For $n_o = 1$ and $c = 8$ we need to prove that $(n + 1)^3 <= 8n^3$ with $n >= 1$. In fact, $(n + 1)^3 <= n^3 + 3n^2 + 3n + 1$ and for $n >= 1$ we have that $n^3 >= n^2$, $n^2 >= n$ and $n^2 >= 1$. Therefore

$$\boldsymbol{n^3 + 3n^2 + 3n + 1 <= n^3 + 3n^3 + 3n^3 + n^3 = 8n^3}$$

(2) The function $(n + 1)^3$ can also be considered "Big-O of a n^2 fraction", for instance, $O(n^3/1000)$. In fact, let $n_o = 1$ and $c = 8000$, if $n >= 1$ we have:

$$\boldsymbol{(n + 1)^3 <= 8000\ (n^3/100) = 8n^3}$$

From the above examples we derive the properties for the manipulation of $T(n)$ listed below.

Property 1. ***The constant factors are not meaningful.***
This is derived from the definition (1). In fact in Examples 1 and 2, $\forall$ positive constant x and $\forall T(n)$, $\boldsymbol{T(n) <= c(xT(n))}$, independently from the fact that x is a big number or a very small fraction, provided that $x > 0$.

Property 2. ***The terms of inferior degree are insignificant.***
If $T(n)$ is a polynomial of degree k with the positive coefficient a_k, it is possible to neglect all the terms of the polynomial except the first.

$$\boldsymbol{a_k n^k + a_{k-1} n^{k-1} + \cdots + a_2 n^2 + a_1 n + a_0}$$

Moreover, the constant $\boldsymbol{a_k}$ can be replaced by 1, according to Property 1. Then, we say that **"$\boldsymbol{T(n)}$ is $\boldsymbol{O(n^k)}$"**

An example of the application of Property 2 follows. Let $T(n)$ be

$$T(n) = 2n^5 + 3n^4 - 10n^3 + 2n + 1$$

According to Property 2 "$T(n)$ *is* $O(n^5)$". To prove it, we apply the definition (1). Let $n_0 = 1$ and c be the sum of the positive coefficients, that is $c = 7$. Then for $n >= 1$ we can write:

$$2n^5 + 3n^4 - 10n^3 + 2n + 1 <= 2n^5 + 3n^5 + n^5 + n^5 <= 7n^5$$

since $a_j n^j <= a_j n^k$ for $j <= k$. The negative coefficients can be replaced by 0 since $a_j n^j <= 0$. Therefore we conclude that "$T(n)$ *is* $O(n^5)$".

The principle of elimination of the terms of inferior degree can be applied to any sum of expressions. It derives from the fact that

$$\lim_{n \to \infty} h(n)/g(n) = 0 \Rightarrow \textbf{ } h(n) \textbf{ grows more slowly than } g(n) \textbf{, therefore } h(n) \textbf{ cannot be neglected}$$

which means that

$$\text{"}O(h(n) + g(n)) \textit{ is } O(g(n))\text{"}$$

$T(n) = 2^n + n^2$ $\lim_{n \to 0} n^2/2^n = 0$ n^2 is insignificant with respect to 2^n since n^4 grows more slowly than 2^n. Therefore $T(n) = O(2^n)$.

To show formally that $2^n + n^2$ is $O(2^n)$, let $n_o = 10$ and $c = 2$. For $n \geq 10$ we have $2^n + n^2 \leq 2 * 2^n$. In fact, for $n = 10$

$$2^{10} = 1024 \quad 10^2 = 100$$

that is, when $n > 10$, n^2 becomes smaller and smaller than 2^n, therefore $n^2 \leq 2^n$, for $n >= 10$. This means that **"$\boldsymbol{2^n + n_2}$ is $\boldsymbol{O(2^n)}$"**.

2.5. Simplification of the Expressions in Big-O Notation

The simplification of the expressions in Big-O notation is important because it represents an assessment of the execution time. According to the 90/10 rule, the greatest time spent by a program is in 10% of the code of the program, therefore we expect a significant simplification of the expression. In this paragraph we examine the laws that govern the simplification of the expression in Big-O notation.

2.5.1. *Transitive Law for Big-O Notation*

The transitive laws say that if "$f(n)$ *is* $O(g(n))$ *and* $g(n)$ *is* $O(h(n))$ then $f(n)$ is $O(h(n))$". For example, we know that $T(n) = 10n^5 + 5n^4 + 2n^3 - 2n + 2$ $T(n)$ is $O(n^5)$. If n^5 is $O(0.1n^5)$, for the transitive law, then $T(n)$ is $O(0.1n^5)$.

2.5.2. *The Choice of the Precision*

The laws so far introduced allow us to compute the execution time in a more precise manner. In other words if a fragment of program has an execution time $T(n) = O(n^2)$, we could think that we could be more precise and say, for example, that $T(n) = O(0.03n^2)$. However, since the constant factors are insignificant in the Big-O notation, the problem is not relevant, i.e. there is not difference between $O(0.03n^2)$ and $(0.01n^2)$. This simplifies the calculation of the execution time. In addition, if we associate a semantic name to each execution time, we can group them in a simple list. The most common execution times are listed in Table 2.1.

Table 2.1. Most common execution times.

Big-O	Informal name
O(1)	constant
O(logn)	logarithmic
O(n)	linear
O(nlogn)	nlogn
$O(n^2)$	quadratic
$O(n^3)$	cubic
$O(2^n)$	exponential

We can also say that $f(n)$ is a tight Big-O limit of $T(n)$ in the following cases:

1. If $T(n)$ is $O(f(n))$
2. If $T(n)$ is $O(g(n))$ then it is also true that $f(n)$ is $O(g(n))$.

In an informal way, this means that we cannot find a function $g(n)$ that grows with the same speed of $T(n)$ but more slowly than $f(n)$.

If $T(n) = n^3 + 2n$ and $f(n) = n^3$ then $f(n)$ is a tight limit of $T(n)$ and is also simple (n^3 is simple but n^3 and $n^3 + n$ are not).

2.5.3. *Rule of the Sum*

Suppose that $T_1(n)$ is $O(f_1(n))$ and that $T_2(n)$ is $O(f_2(n))$ and suppose that f_2 grows less quickly than f_1 (that is that $f_2(n)$ is $O(f_1(n))$). We conclude that $T_1(n) + T_2(n) = O(f_1(n))$.

Example

The following fragment program transforms the matrix A into a matrix in which the diagonal elements have i value

(1) cin $>> n;$
(2) for $(i = 1; i <= n; i{+}{+})$
(3) for $(j = 1; j <= n; i{+}{+})$
(4) $A[i, j] = 0;$
(5) for $(i = 1; i <= n; i{+}{+})$
(6) $A[i, i] = i;$

Let us compute the execution times of each line. Line (1) reads the value of n from the keyboard and requires an execution time equal to $T_1(n) = O(1)$. The same execution time is required by line (6) which is contained in the ***for*** loop of line (5). The ***for*** loop of line (5) is executed n times. Therefore the whole loop requires $T_{5-6}(n) = O(n)$. The loop of line (2) is also executed n times as well as the ***for*** loop of line (3). Since for each loop of line (2) we execute the whole loop of line (3), the whole loop of line (2) requires an execution time equal to $T_{2-3-4}(n) = O(n^2)$. In conclusion, we have $1 + O(n^2) + O(n) = T_1(n) + T_{2-3-4}(n) + T_{5-6}(n)$. What is the upper limit of this sum? According to the rule of the sum it is surely $O(n^2)$. By applying the rule of the sum, since $1 <= O(n^2)$ and $O(n) <= O(n^2)$, we obtain that $T_1(n) + T_{2-3-4}(n) + T_{5-6}(n) = O(n^2)$, which is the execution time of the whole program.

In the previous fragment we have applied the property by which the terms of inferior degree are insignificant for the calculation of the execution time of the program. In reality, there is something more: the rule of the sum affirms that given a sequence of instructions, every instruction that is weighted equal to $O(1)$, can be "absorbed" in $O(1)$. This means that the sum of two constants is still a constant. It is not admissible, however, to confuse the "constant number" sum of terms $O(1)$ with "the sum of number of terms that varies with respect to the dimension of the data". This is the case of a ***for*** loop, for instance. In this case we deal with the sum of n terms, each one, eventually, constant, where n is a variable that depends on the dimension of the data and is used in the loop. In this case the execution time is $O(n)$.

2.5.4. *Incommensurable Functions*

Given two functions $f(n)$ and $g(n)$, it is not always possible to compare their Big-Os since there exist pairs of incommensurable functions, which are neither one, the "Big-O" of the other.

2.6. Analysis of the Execution Time of a Program

In this paragraph, we introduce the analysis of the execution time of a program. We begin by analyzing the execution time of simple instructions, then we deal with the control instructions and finally we show a methodology for the computation of the execution time of a program.

2.6.1. *The Execution Time of Simple Instructions*

Simple instructions, such as *cin*, *cout*, *goto*, etc., have a constant execution time equal to $O(1)$. This is due to the fact that these instructions are implemented by using a finite and definite number of operations, which can be

(1) arithmetic operations $(-, +, *, /)$
(2) an access function to a structured type (i.e. the parenthesis [ ] to access a vector, pointer, etc.)

The same consideration is valid for instructions such as *cin* (*cout*) that copy a number of data from the input file to the output file.

We will assume that in all these cases, except when there is a call to a function, the execution time is $O(1)$. For example, in the fragment of Fig. 2.2, the lines 4–6 have a "weight" equal to $O(1)$.

It is also interesting to observe that often, in a program, we can locate blocks of instructions of the same weight to which, using the rule of the sum, we assign the same weight. This is the case of lines 4–6.

```
(1) for (i = 0; i < arraySize; i++)
(2) for (i = 0; i < arraySize - 1; i++)
(3) if (a[i] > a[i + 1] {
(4) temp = a[i];
(5) a[i] = a[i + 1];
(6) a[i + 1] = temp; }
```

Fig. 2.2. Bubble sort: fragment.

2.6.2. *The Execution Time of the "for" Loop*

The analysis of the execution time of a loop is quite simple. In fact if a loop repeats its body n times we have found the exact upper limit. We will always satisfy this hypothesis because we use control structures of the type 1-in/1-out (i.e. it is not possible to have more than one entry and exit from the loop). In order to find the upper limit of the loop we must evaluate the execution time of each iteration of the loop. The analysis of the execution time of each iteration of the loop requires the division of the loop into several parts (see Fig. 2.3, it helps if the student represents the loop by using a flow chart). Let us assign the "weights" as shown in Fig. 2.3.

a) cin, cout, goto → $O(1)$

b) Loop for → Composed of:

```
for (i = 1; i < n; i++)
        A[i, j] = 0;
```

1) The loop's initialization time requires $O(1)$
2) The time to increment the variable "i" of the loop is $O(1)$
3) The time for the first comparison between the index of the loop and the upper limit (n) is $O(1)$
4) The time for the comparison (i.e. $i \geq n$) is $O(1)$
5) The time for each loop repetition is $O(n)$ (if repeated n times)

Then

$$\boldsymbol{O(for)} = O(1) + O(1) + O(1) + O(1) + O(n) \to O(n)$$

Following the same analysis methodology, we see that the execution time of the next three lines of instructions is $O(n^2)$

for $(i = 1;\ i < n; i++)$
for $(j = 1;\ j < n;\ j++)$
$A[i, j] = 0;$

Fig. 2.3. Evaluation of the execution time of a "for" loop.

In addition, let us consider again the example of Fig. 2.2. It is easy to show that the execution time of the internal loop (lines 2–6) is $O(\text{arraySize})$ because the number of iterations depends on *arraySize*. For the same reasons and using the example of Fig. 2.3, the external loop has the execution time equal to $O(\text{arraySize}^2)$.

2.6.3. *The Execution Time of the "if" Structure*

Figure 2.4 shows the steps for the computation of the execution time of an if structure. The evaluation of the execution time of the condition is constant and is equal to $O(1)$, always in the hypothesis that the condition is not a call to function. Let $f(n)$ and $g(n)$ be the upper limits of the execution time of the "then" and "else" branches. If $f(n)$ is $O(g(n))$ [$g(n)$ is $O(f(n)$] we say that $O(g(n))$ [$O(f(n))$] is an upper limit for the execution time of the *if* structure. This is the case of the *if* instruction in Fig. 2.4. Problems arise when f and g are not the Big-O of the other. In that case the upper limit of the time execution is the max execution time between the two.

(c) If (condition) {} else {}

- Condition $\to O(1)$
- "else" branch $\to$ the upper limit of the execution time is $g(n)$.
- "then" branch $\to$ the upper limit of the execution time is $O(g(n))$ because $f(n)$ is $O(g(n))$

If $f(n)$ and $g(n)$ are not Big-O of each other then $O(\text{if}) = O(\max(f(n), g(n)))$

Example

if $A[1][1] = 0$

for $(i = 1;\ i < n;\ i{+}{+})$

for $(j = 1;\ j < n;\ i{+}{+})$

$A[i][j] = 10;$

else

for $(i = 1;\ i < n;\ i{+}{+})$

$A[i][j] = 1;$

$O(\max(n^2, n)) = O(n^2)$

Fig. 2.4. The execution time for the "if" structure.

2.6.4. *The Execution Time of a Sequence of Instructions*

Blocks of instructions composed of the Input/Output instructions, the assignment and test instructions, require an execution time equal to $O(1)$. We apply the rule of the sum, which allows us to neglect all the execution times of the sequence (block) except one. In general, the execution time of a sequence is calculated by adding the upper limits of the executions times of the single instructions, of which it is composed. For instance, in the program of Fig. 2.2, the internal cycle has an execution time equal to

$$[O(arraySize) + O(1) + O(1) + O(1)] = O(arraySize)$$

2.6.5. *The Execution Time of Iterative Structures* (*While and Do-While*)

The execution time of a *while* or *do-while* structure is similar to that of a *for* loop. In this case, however, we deal with iterative structures for which the upper limit of the loop is not known *a priori*. The search for the upper limit of the number of iterations of that structure is the focus of the computation of the execution time of the structure itself. What we say for the *while* structure can be said, in an analogous way, for the *do-while* structure and is left to the reader as an exercise. In the meanwhile, we recall that for a *while* structure (resp. a *do-while* structure) the test condition must become false (resp. false) after a certain number of iterations. In order to determine the upper limit of each loop iteration, we examine its body, compute the execution time and we add to this time the execution time for the verification of the test condition, i.e. ($O(1)$). The upper limit of the execution time of the whole *while* loop is obtained by multiplying the upper limit of the number of iterations for the upper limit of the execution time of each iteration. To be more precise, we should add to it the execution time of the first verification of the test condition, but since this time is $O(1)$ it is usually skipped. In the example of Fig. 2.5 it is easy to verify that the execution time of lines (1) and (3) is $O(1)$. The *while* loop (lines (2) and (3)) is performed at most n times if the vector contains the x element. Since the body of the loop is $O(1)$, the execution time of the whole loop, by the rule of the sum, is $O(n)$.

```
(1)        i := 1;
(2)        while number <> A[i] do
(3)        i := i + 1;
```

$$\mathbf{T}(\boldsymbol{while}) = O(1) + O(1) + O(1) + O(n) \rightarrow O(n)$$

Fig. 2.5. The execution time of the “while” structure .

2.7. Recursion Rules for Execution Time Evaluation: The Nesting Tree Approach

In this section we define a recursive rule for the calculation of the execution time of algorithms. The algorithms are supposed to be written in C++ language but the method is easily extendable to algorithms written in any other language.

If we observe the construction rules for the computation of the execution time for the simple and structured instructions of the C++ language, we notice that behind these there is the inductive rule for the construction of complex algorithms starting from the simple phrases of the language (instruction of evaluation of expression, instruction of assignment, input, output and unconditional jump) that correspond to simple algorithms. Formally we have:

2.7.1. *Construction Rules of the Instructions*

***Base*:**

An assignment, an input or an output instruction, an unconditional jump are elementary instructions.

***Induction*:**

The following rules allow us to build instructions from elementary instructions.

1. **block** If $S1$; $S2$; ...; Sn is a sequence of instructions then

$$\{S1; S2; \ldots; Sn\} \text{ is an instruction}$$

2. **while instruction.** If $S1$; $S2$; ... Sn is a sequence of instructions and R is a logical relation

$$\textbf{\textit{while}}\ R\{S1; S2; \ldots; Sn\} \text{ is an instruction}$$

3. **do-while instruction.** If $S1$; $S2$; ...; Sn is a sequence of instructions and R is a logical relation

$$\textbf{\textit{do}}\ \{S1; S2; \ldots; Sn\}\ \textbf{\textit{while}}\ R \text{ is an instruction}$$

4. **for instruction.** If $S1$; $S2$; ...; Sn is a sequence of instructions and expression_i is an expression with an integer or an enumerated value then

$$\textbf{\textit{for}}\ (\text{expression}_1; \text{expression}_2; \text{expression}_3)\ \{S1; S2; \ldots; Sn\}$$
$$\text{is an instruction}$$

5. **conditional instruction if.** If $S1$; $S2$; ...; Sn is a sequence of instructions and R is a logical relation then

$$\textbf{\textit{if}}\ R\{S1; S2; \ldots; Sn\} \text{ is an instruction}$$

6. **conditional instruction if else.** If $S1$; $S2$; ...; Sn is a sequence of instructions and R is a logical relation then

$$\textbf{\textit{if}}\ R\{S1; S2; \ldots; Sn\} \text{ else } \{S1; S2; \ldots; Sn\} \text{ is an instruction}$$

The previous recursive rules gives us a way to construct a program in a bottom–up way starting from simpler instructions and going up to more complex.

Analogously, the Big-O upper limit of the execution time of a program can be defined in an inductive manner using the recursive definition scheme of the program structure. In the hypothesis that the program contains neither procedure nor functions calls, we have:

2.7.2. *Rule for the Construction of Upper Limit of the Execution Time of a Program*

Base:

The upper limit of a simple instruction (an assignment, an input or output instruction, or an unconditional jump) is $O(1)$.

Induction: The upper limit of the structured instructions is defined as follows:

1. **while structure:**
   Let $O(f(n))$ be the upper limit of the body and
   let $g(n)$ be the upper limit of the number of iterations of the loop (at least 1 time for each n),
   then $O(f(n), g(n))$ is the upper limit of the execution tim of the while structure.
2. **do-while structure:**
   Let $O(f(n))$ be the upper limit of the body and
   let $g(n)$ be the upper limit of the number of iterations of the loop (at least 1 time for each n) (remember that in the do-while structure $g(n)$ is always at least equal to 1!)
   then $O(f(n), g(n))$ is the upper limit of the execution time of the do-while structure.
3. **for structure**
   Let $O(f(n))$ be the upper limit of the body and
   let $g(n)$ be the upper limit of the number of iterations of the loop (at least 1 time for each n),
   then $O(f(n), g(n))$ is the upper limit of the execution time of the for structure.
4. **conditional structure**
   Let $O(f1(n))$ be the upper limit of the body "then" and
   let $O(f2(n))$ be the upper limit of the body "else" (if there is),
   then $O(\max(f_1(n), f_2(n)))$ is the upper limit of the execution time of the conditional structure.
5. **block**
   Let $O(f_1(n))$, $O(f_2(n))$, ..., $O(f_k(n))$ be the upper limit of the instructions composing the block
   then $O(f_1(n)) + f_2(n)) + \cdots + (f_k(n))$ is the upper limit of the execution time of the block.

These rules are applied to derive and to analyze the "nesting tree" that represents the program in a bottom–up manner (from simplest instruction to most complex one).

2.7.3. *Example for a Simple Program: The Execution Time of the Bubble Sort Program*

In this paragraph we analyze the bubble sort algorithm that, for convenience, we rewrite below.

```
void BubbleSort (float A[ ], const int arraySize);
int i,temp;
{
1      for (i = 0; i < arraySize; i++)
          {
2         // external loop
3         for (i = 0; i < arraySize −1; i++)
4            if A[i] > A[i + 1]
5      //       (* exchange *)
6         temp := A[i];
7         A[i] := A[i + 1];
8         A[I + 1] := temp;
       }
}
```

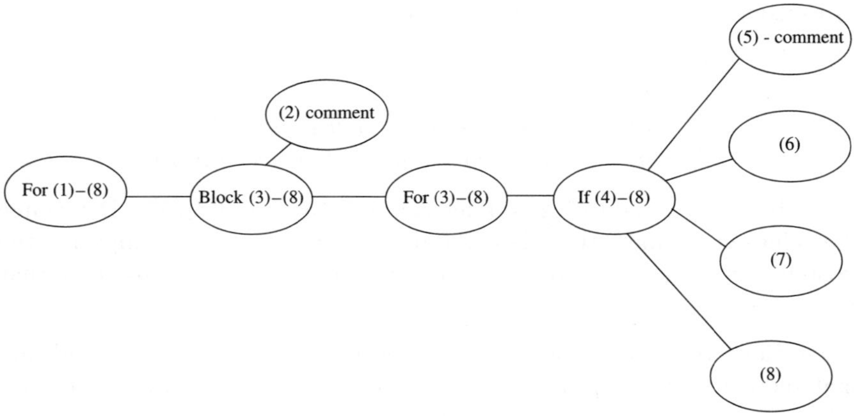

Fig. 2.6. The sort algorithm.

The analysis of the execution time is obtained by visiting the nesting tree of the program in a bottom–up way and by associating to each node the Big-O contribution:

(4)–(8)	$O(\text{arraySize} - 1)$
(5)	—
(6)	$O(1)$
(7)	$O(1)$
(8)	$O(1)$

On the contrary, the external loop is executed arraySize times while the internal block has an execution time equal to O(arraySize -1). Then the complexity is (arraySize -1)* O(arraySize) = O(arraySize^2 – arraySize) that is O(arraySize^2), which is an upper limit for the execution time of the whole program of bubble sort. Therefore bubble sort has a quadratic complexity.

This is an exact limit, in fact we can prove that if the elements are initially ordered in a reverse order, the bubble sort algorithm performs $n^*(n-1)/2$ comparisons.

We will not show the execution time of an algorithm of merging, but we simply say that an algorithm of merging (such as QuickSort) has an upper and lower limit equal to $(n^* \log 2(n))$. This shows that an algorithm of merging is faster than a selection algorithm (except for some values of n) due to the fact that $O(n^* \log 2(n))$ actually hides a bigger constant than that hidden by $O(n^2)$.

Examples

1) Consider the following four functions:

$$f_1 = n^2\,;$$
$$f_2 = n^3\,;$$
$$f_3 = n^2 \ if\ n\ is\ odd,\ and\ n^3\ if\ n\ is\ not\ odd$$
$$f_4 = n^2 \ if\ n\ is\ prime,\ and\ n^3\ if\ n\ is\ composed$$

for each i and j equal to $1, 2, 3, 4$ determine if $f_j(n)$ is $O(f_j(n))$. Determine the values of n_0 and c that show the relationship Big-O, or, supposing the existence of values n_0 and c draw a contradiction in order to show that $f_j(n)$ is not $O(f_j(n))$.

Suggestion: remember that all the prime numbers except 2 are odd and that there are endless prime numbers and endless composed numbers (not prime)

2) Consider the function ***SquareofTwo*** that take an argument $n <> 0$ and compute the number of times that 2 is divided into n. How many times did 2 divide n? What is the execution time of **SquareofTwo**

```
int SquareofTwo (int n)
{
        int i = 0;
        while not (n % 2 <> 0)
        {
                n = n/2;
                i++;
        }
}
```

3) Compute the execution time of the following fragment of code

```
cin >> n;
for (int i = 1; i <= n; i++)
    for (int j = 1; j <= n; j++)
            A(i, j) = 0;
for (i = 1; i <= n; i++)
    A(i, j) = 1;
```

4) Build the nesting tree of the following algorithm and compute the execution time

```
int main ()
{
        int sum = 0;
        for (int i = 1; i <= n; i++)
            sum = sum + A(i);
        middle = sum/n;
        int nearer = 1;
        i = 2;
        while not (i <= n)
    {
            if (A[i]-middle)* (A[i]-middle)
                              <
            (A[nearer]-middle)* (A[nearer]-middle)
            nearer = i;
            i++;
    }
return 0;
}
```

5) Compute the execution time of the following fragment of code

```
for (int i = 1; i <= n - 1; i++)
    for (int j = i + 1; j <= n; j++)
      for (int k = i; k <= n; k++)
                A(j, k) = A(j, k) - A(i, k)* A(j, i)/A(i, i);
```

6) Compute the execution time of the following fragment of code

```
void SelectionSort (float A[ ], const int n);
int i, j, little,temp;
{
1       for (i = 0; i < n- 1; i++)
```

```
        {
                              /*"little" is the index of the first
                              occurrence of the smallest element*/
        little = i;
        for (j = i + 1; j <= n; j++)
            if A[j] < A[little]
                little := j;
                              (* at this point "little" is the index of the
                              smallest elements in A[i ... n] and we
                              change A[little] with A[i]*)
        temp := A[little];
        A[little] := A[i];
        A[i] := temp;
      }
}
```

Exercises

Beginner's Exercises

1. How many ways do you know to compute and compare the execution time of an algorithm?
   (a) Benchmark and analysis
   (b) Analysis and execution
   (c) Compilation and execution
2. A set of test cases representing an algorithm is:
   (a) A particular execution of a program
   (b) The results of a program
   (c) A sample of data that the algorithm uses
3. We say that a program has a linear execution time:
   (a) If the program has an execution time that does not depend on the dimension of the datum n
   (b) If the program has an execution time proportional to the dimension of the datum n
   (c) If the program has an average execution time proportional to the dimension of the datum n
4. The notation "Big-O":
   (a) Is a measure dependent of the implementation details of the compiler

(b) Is a measure independent of the implementation details of the compiler and of computer
(c) Is a measure independent of the implementation details of the compiler

5. The formal definition of the execution time $T(n)$ of a program with the dimension of input data equal to n is:

(a) $T(n)$ **is** $O(f(n)) \Leftrightarrow \exists n_0, \quad c > 0 : \forall n \geq n_0 \quad T(n) < cf(n)$
(b) $T(n)$ **is** $O(f(n)) \Leftrightarrow \exists n_0, \quad c > 0 : \forall n \geq n_0 \quad T(n) \leq cf(n)$
(c) $T(n)$ **is** $O(f(n)) \Leftrightarrow \exists n_0, \quad c > 0 : \forall n \geq n_0 \quad T(n) = cf(n)$

6. The properties for the manipulation of $T(n)$ are:

(a) The constant factors are sometimes meaningful and if $T(n)$ is a polynomial of degree k the terms of inferior degree are insignificant
(b) The constant factors are not meaningful and if $T(n)$ is a polynomial of degree k the terms of inferior degree are insignificant
(c) If $T(n)$ is a polynomial of degree k the terms of inferior degree are insignificant

7. The transitive law for Big-O notation says that:

(a) If "$f(n)$ is $O(g(n))$ and $g(n)$ is $O(f(n))$ then $f(n)$ is $O(h(n))$"
(b) If "$f(n)$ is $O(g(n))$ and $g(n)$ is $O(h(n))$ then $f(n)$ is $O(h(n))$"
(c) If "$f(n)$ is $O(g(n))$ and $f(n)$ is $O(h(n))$ then $f(n)$ is $O(h(n))$"

8. The execution time of simple instructions is:

(a) Equal to $O(\frac{1}{2})$
(b) Equal to $O(n)$
(c) Equal to $O(1)$

9. The execution time of the "for" loop is:

(a) Equal to $O(n - i)$
(b) Equal to $O(n)$
(c) Equal to $O(n^2)$

10. The execution time of the "if" structure is:

(a) The min execution time between the two branches
(b) Let $f(n)$ and $g(n)$ be the upper limits of the execution time of the "then" and "else" branches. If $f(n)$ is $O(g(n))$ [$g(n)$ is $O(f(n)$] we say that $O(g(n))$ [$O(f(n))$] is an upper limit for the execution time *of the if structure*
(c) The max execution time between the two branches

11. The execution time of a sequence of instructions is:

(a) The lower limits of the executions times of the single instructions, which compose it

(b) Always equal to $O(1)$
(c) The upper limits of the executions times of the single instructions, which compose it

12. The execution time of iterative structures (while and do-while) is:
    (a) Equal to $O(n)$
    (b) Equal to $O(n^2)$
    (c) Equal to $O(n - i)$
13. What is the recursive rule for the calculation of the execution time of algorithms?
    (a) It is a way to construct the Big-O upper limit in an inductive manner using the recursive definition scheme of the program structure
    (b) It is a way to construct the Big O upper limit in an inductive manner using the iterative definition scheme of the program structure
    (c) It is a way to construct the Big O upper limit in an deductive manner using the iterative definition scheme of the program structure

Advanced Exercises

14. Consider the following four functions:
    $f_1 = n^2$;
    $f_2 = n^3$;
    $f_3 = n^2$ if n is odd e n^3 if n is not odd
    $f_4 = n^2$ if n is prime, e n^3 if n is composed
    for each i and j equal to $1, 2, 3, 4$ determine if $f_j(n)$ è $O(f_j(n))$. Determine the values of n_0 and c that show the relationship Big-O, or, supposing the existence of values n_0 and c draw a contradiction, show that $f_j(n)$ is not $O(f_j(n))$.
    Suggestion: remember that all the first numbers except 2 are odd and that there are endless numbers first and endless composed numbers (not first)
15. Consider the function SquareofTwo that take an argument $n <> 0$ and compute the number of times that 2 is divided to n. How many times did 2 divide n? What is the execution time of SquareofTwo

```
int SquareofTwo (int n)
{
        int i = 0;
        while not (n % 2 <> 0)
```

```
        {
                n = n/2;
                i++;
        }
}
```

16. Compute the algorithm execution time of the following fragment of code

```
cin >> n;
for (int i = 1; i <= n; i++)
        for (int j =; j <= n; j++)
                A(i, j) = 0;
for (i = 1; i <= n; i++)
        A(i, j) = 1.
```

17. Build the nesting tree of the following algorithm and compute the algorithm execution time

```
int main ()
{
        int sum = 0;
        for (int i = 1; i <= n; i++)
                sum = sum + A(i);
        middle = sum/n;
        int nearer = 1;
        i = 2;
        while not (i <= n)
        {
                if (A[i]-middle)* (A[i]-middle)
                                <
                (A[nearer]-middle)* (A[nearer]-middle)
                nearer = i;
                i++;
        }
return 0;
}
```

Chapter 3

The Execution Time of an Algorithm: Advanced Considerations

PAOLO MARESCA
University Federico II of Naples, Italy
paomares@unina.it

3.1. The Execution Time Analysis of a Program: The Case of Nonrecursive Functions

In this section we discuss the analysis of the execution time of a program which contain function calls. We distinguish two cases: the programs in which the function call is recursive and the programs in which the function call is iterative. Let us start with the analysis of the iterative function calls and postpone the analysis of recursive function calls to the next section.

In the case of iterative function calls we consider each function one at a time and evaluate their execution time independently from the others (this is possible since they constitute units with autonomous compilation). The order of the evaluation of the functions is derived from the call stack, starting from the function call that does not call any other function (which will be at the top of the stack), and then proceeding up in the call stack until we reach the evaluation of the main program. Let us observe that if the function F calls the function $F1$, we must relate the measure of the dimension of the arguments of F to that of $F1$.

There is not one generally valid rule to compute the execution time in this case, but it is possible with some examples, to fix some good rules for the evaluation of the execution time.

Imagine that we have determined that a good upper limit for the execution time of the function F is $O(f(n))$ where n is the measure of the dimension of the arguments of F. Then for all the functions that call the function F we can use $O(f(n))$ to indicate the execution time of the instruction that calls F. This instruction can be part of a block or of an if, or of a while or do-while instruction.

It also happens that a call to a function or several calls to the same or different functions can appear inside assignment instructions or conditional instructions. We assume that for an assignment or an output instruction that contains one or more calls to a function the execution time of the instruction is the sum of the upper limits of each call.

If the call to one or more functions appears in the test condition of an if instruction, in the initialization or in the limit of a for and the call to the function has an upper limit of $O(f(n))$, the execution time is computed as follows.

1. If the call to the function appears in the test condition of a while or do-while loop, add $f(n)$ to the upper limit of the execution time of each iteration. This time is then multiplied by the upper limit of the number of iterations, as usual. In the case of a while loop, add $f(n)$ to the cost of first verification of the condition, in case the loop is executed zero times.
2. If the call to the function appears in the initialization or in the final limit of a for loop, add $f(n)$ to the total cost of the loop.
3. If the call to the function appears in the test condition of a conditional instruction, add $f(n)$ to the cost of the instruction.

3.2. Examples for Nonrecursive Function Calls

```
int fun1(int x, n);
{
        (1) for (i = 0; i <= n; i++)
        (2) x = x + fun2(i, n);
}

int fun2(int a, n); {
        (3) for (i = 0; i <= n; i++)
        (4) x = x + i;
        (5) fun2 = x; }

main ()
{
        (6) cin >> n;
        (7) Sum = 0;
        (8) fun1(Sum, n);
        (9) cout << fun2
            (Sum, n);
}
```

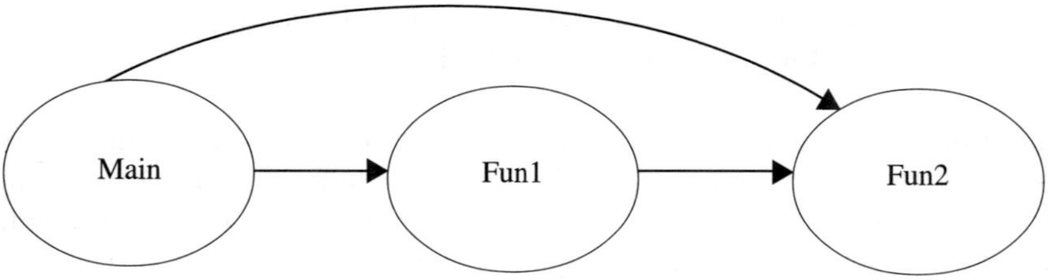

Fig. 3.1. Program without recursive function call.

It is possible see from the call graph that there are neither recursive functions nor loop. We can compute the execution time of the function main starting from the function that does not call any other functions (Fun2, in our case) going up until we reach the function main. The loop of lines (3) and (4) sums the integers from 1 to n and assigns it to x. This summation is equal to $n(n + 1))/2$. It follows that Fun2$(x, n) = x + n(n + 1)/2$. The function Fun1 adds to x the function $\sum_{i=1}^{n}$ Fun2 (i, n), which is $\sum_{i=1}^{n}(i+n(n+1)/2)$. It is easy to show that the quantity that the function Fun1 sums to x is $((n^3 + 3n^2 + 2n)/2)$. Finally we analyze the function main, which reads n in the line (6), assigns the value 0 to a in line (7) and invokes, in line (8), the procedure Fun1. After the execution of this function the value of a is $a + ((n^3 + 3n^2 + 2n)/2)$. Line (8) prints Fun2$(a, n)$ that sums to a the value $(n(n + 1))/2)$. Finally, the result $((n^3 + 3n^2 + 2n)/2)$ is printed.

Let us evaluate the upper limit of the execution times of each single function starting from the most nested function (Fun2 $\rightarrow$ Fun1 $\rightarrow$ main). To make things simpler, we assume that n is the dimension of the datum for all three functions even though it would be more precise to consider different input dimension for the different functions. The function Fun2 requires a time complexity equal to $O(1)$ to execute the line (4), a time complexity equal to $O(n)$ to execute the lines (3) and (4) (the for loop) and finally a time complexity equal to $O(1)$ to execute the line (5). The total execution time for the function Fun2 is $O(n)$. The function Fun1 requires a time equal to $O(1)$ to execute the line (2). We add to this the time to execute the call to Fun2 that is $O(n)$. Line (2) is nested in a for loop (line (1)) that is performed n times. Therefore the execution time of the function Fun1 is equal to $O(n^2)$. The execution time of the function main is then $O(1) + O(1) + O(n^2) + O(n)$ that, for the sum rule, is $O(n^2)$. In this example, the most time-consuming function is Fun1.

3.3. The Execution Time Analysis of a Program: The Case of Recursive Function Units

The computation of the execution time of a recursive function is more complex than that of an iterative one. Let F be the function, $T_F(n)$ represents the execution time of F with respect to the dimension n of its arguments. We need to define a recurrence equation for $T_F(n)$ in terms of the function $T_G(k)$ correspondent to the G functions of the program and to their dimension k. If F has a simple recursion then one or more than one function G will coincide with F. Since $T_F(n)$ is defined by induction on n, the dimension of the arguments, the value of n during recursion is modified so that the next function is called with progressively smaller arguments. This guarantees that the base of the recursion is met.

After having determined a reasonable dimension (physical limits considered) we have two cases:

1. The dimension of the argument is so small that F does not trigger any recursive call. That corresponds to the base of the inductive definition of $T_F(n)$.
2. The dimension of the argument is big enough to trigger recursive calls. We will assume however that the recursive calls made from F either to itself or to any other function G have parameters of smaller dimension. That corresponds to the inductive step of the definition of $T_F(n)$.

The recurrence equation that defines $T_F(n)$ is derived from the examination of the code of the F procedure in the following way:

(a) For each call to the function G or use of the function G inside an expression (it is worth to observe that G could coincide with F) we use $T_G(k)$ as the execution time of the call to G, where k is the dimension of the arguments of the call.

(b) The execution time of the body of the function F is determined with the same technique used so far leaving the terms in the $T_G(k)$ as unknown functions (i.e. n). These terms cannot be simplified (i.e. with the rule of the sum). The function F is analyzed two times. The first in the hypothesis that the dimension of F is sufficiently small to trigger any recursive call; the second that n is not sufficiently small. In this way we obtain two expressions that will compose the recurrence equation of F: the first of the recurrence equation of $T_F(n)$ describes the inductive base while the second describes the inductive step.

(c) The expressions of the execution time of G are replaced by the Big-O terms, such as $O(f(n))$ multiplied by a specific constant c (for example $cf(n)$).

(d) If a is an input dimension, we set $T_F(a)$ equal to the expression that results from the step (c) in the hypothesis that there are no recursive calls.

The execution time of the whole procedure is computed by solving this recurrence equation. In the next paragraph we show the techniques to solve a recurrence equation.

3.3.1. *Examples of Nonrecursive Calls*

A good example for the application of the recurrence equation is the computation of the factorial function of n. It requires a simple recursion. The function calls itself, therefore we use $T(n)$ to indicate the execution time on an input parameter of dimension n.

```
int factorial(int n);
{
    (1)  if (n <= 1)/* base */
    (2)              factorial = 1
    (3)  else/* induction*/
    (4)              factorial = n* factorial(n − 1);
}
```

Fig. 3.2. Factorial of n.

Let us analyze the base and the inductive step of the recursion. From Fig. 3.2 it can be seen that if $n <= 1$, the condition expressed in line (1) is true. Therefore the call of the function *factorial* with parameter $n \leq 1$ executes only lines (1) and (2), which have an execution time equal to $O(1)$. So for $n \leq 1$, the total execution time of the base case is equal to $O(1)$.

For $n > 1$, the condition of line (1) is false. Therefore the function executes the lines (1) and (4). Line (1) requires an execution time equal to $O(1)$ while line (4) requires an execution time equal to $O(1)$ for the multiplication and assignment statement, and $T(n-1)$ for the recursive call to factorial.

In conclusion for $n > 1$ the total execution time of *factorial* is $O(1) + T(n-1)$. At this point it is possible to define the recurrence equation $T(n)$ of the recursive function.

Base $T(1) = O(1)$ for $n \leq 1$

Induction $T(n) = O(1) + T(n-1)$ for $n > 1$

We replace $O(1)$ with the constants a and b respectively to the base and to the inductive step as allowed from rule (c) and we obtain

Base $T(1) = a$ for $n \leq 1$

Induction $T(n) = b + T(n-1)$ for $n > 1$

Let us solve the recurrence equation for simple cases:

$$\begin{aligned} T(1) &= a \\ T(2) &= b + T(1) = a + b \\ T(3) &= b + T(2) = b + (a + b) = a + 2b \\ T(4) &= b + T(3) = b + (a + 2b) = a + 3b \end{aligned}$$

Therefore

$$T(n) = a + (n-1)b \text{ for } n >= 1$$

The most common method to solve the recurrence equation is to calculate the value of some simple cases. From those cases we hypothesize the general solution and then we prove that the hypothesis is correct using the induction technique.

In some cases, it is possible to compute the solution by applying the substitution method.

Suppose we have the recurrence equation

$$T(n) = b + T(n-1), \quad \text{for } n > 1$$

Observe that

1. $T(n) \quad = b + T(n-1)$
2. $T(n-1) \quad = b + T(n-2)$
3. $T(n-2) \quad = b + T(n-3)$

....

$n-1.$ $\quad T(2) \quad = b + T(1)$

If we replace the second equation in the first we have $T(n) = b + (b + T(n-2)) = 2b + T(n-2)$. Again we can replace $T(n-2)$ with the equation of line 3 and we obtain $T(n) = 2b + (b + T(n-3)) = 3b + T(n-3)$. After $i-1$ steps the recurrence relation looks like: $T(n) = ib + T(n-i)$. We continue to replace until the recurrence equation is expressed in terms of $T(1)$. The final equation is the following[1]:

$$\boldsymbol{T(n) = (n-1)b + T(1)}\,. \tag{1}$$

[1] To be formal, we should prove by induction on i what occurs when we replace $T(n-i)$ repeatedly in the formula.

We observe that the formula (1) is a polynomial of degree n. Therefore, if $T(1)$ does not require an execution time greater than linear, the recurrence equation, for the rule of the sum, says that the execution time is $T(n) = O(n)$. This is what happens in the computation of the factorial of n. In fact the function factorial is called n times and each of the calls requires an execution time equal to $O(1)$ including $T(1)$.

3.4. Other Methods for the Solution of the Recurrence Equations

When the substitution method shown in the previous paragraph cannot be applied, there is another technique, which tries to guess the solution $f(n)$ of the equation and then use the same recurrence equation to prove that $T(n) \leq f(n)$. With this technique we do not get an exact value of $T(n)$ but we are satisfied to obtain an exact upper limit of the execution time. This approach allows us to hypothesize a parametric form of the function and to specify the parameters later. For instance, given a and b, a solution $f(n) = an^b$ could be guessed. The exact value for a and b will have to be obtained when we try to show that $T(n) \leq f(n)$ for all n.

It certainly seems strange that accurate solutions for $T(n)$ can be guessed just looking at a few small n. It is not so strange if we think that the theory of differential equations resembles to that of recurrence equations and is based on the knowledge of the solution of certain common forms of equations. Differential equations of different types are solved by attempts. In an equal matter we proceed for the recurrence equations.

Good examples for the construction and the solution of the recurrence equations can be found in the sorting algorithms, such as the Merge Sort.

Exercises

Advanced Exercises

1. Supposing that **prime**(n) is a function that requires an execution time equal to $O(\sqrt{n})$ consider a function whose body is the following.

```
if prime(n)
        A
else
        B
```

Give a simple and precise superior limit for the execution time of this function supposing that

(a) ***A*** requires a time equal to $O(n)$ and ***B*** requires an execution time equal to $O(1)$;
(b) Both ***A*** and ***B*** require an execution time equal to $O(1)$.

2. Replace the line (1) of the function ***Fun1*** (see Example 3.2)

$$\textbf{for}\ (i = 0;\ i <= \textbf{Fun2}(n, n);\ i++)$$

and determine the algorithm execution time.

3. Assign the following function

```
int sum = 0;
for (int i = 1; i <= f(n); i++)
        sum = sum + i;
```

where $\mathbf{f}(n)$ is a call to function **f**. Give a simple and precise superior limit for the execution time of this function supposing that:

(a) The execution time of **f(n)** is $O(n)$ and the value of **f(n)** is $n!$
(b) The execution time of **f(n)** is $O(n)$ and the value of **f(n)** is n
(c) The execution time of **f(n)** is $O(n^2)$ and the value of **f(n)** is n
(d) The execution time of **f(n)** is $O(1)$ and the value of **f(n)** is 0

4. Show that the time of execution of the $\mathbf{MCD}(i, j)$ function is equal to $O(\log i)$.
Suggestion: Show that after two calls we invoke **MCD** (m, n) with $m <= i/2$

```
int MCD (int m, int n)
{
  int mcd = 0;                              // mcd computed
  int remainder = 0;                        // remainder
  remainder = m % n;
                                            // inductive assertion
  if (remainder == 0)
                 mcd = n;                   // base step
     else
                 mcd = MCD(n, remainder);   // inductive step
  return mcd;
}
```

5. Try to show the time of execution of the **fibonacci** (n)

```
long fibonacci(long n);
{
    if (n == 0 || n == 1)/* base */
            return n;
        else /* induction*/
            return fibonacci (n - 1) + fibonacci (n - 2);
}
```

Chapter 4

Abstract Data Types

TIMOTHY ARNDT
Cleveland State University, USA
arndt@cis.csuohio.edu

4.1. Introduction to Abstract Data Types

When programming large systems, one of the most important objectives of programmers is to understand how the various components of the system work. This is a difficult task since in these large systems programming is done by teams of programmers rather than by a single individual. So if we want to use, for example, a data structure designed by someone else, we first have to understand how the data structure works. Fortunately, with a little extra work we can design the data structure in such a way that it is easy to understand. In particular, we can use the principle of *data abstraction* to enhance understandability. *Abstraction* allows us to consider the high-level characteristics of something without getting bogged down in the details. *Process abstraction*, for example, is supported in most modern programming languages through the various types of subprograms (functions, procedures, etc.). This process abstraction allows one to ignore the details of portions of a large program. Besides the ability to ignore these details, it is also useful to be able to assign portions of a large program to different teams of programmers and to allow these programmers to work independently. In order to support this type of division of labor, it is necessary to be able to compile only the portion of the program that one particular team is working on. In other words, it is necessary to support *separate compilation*. In C, files can be separately compiled. Languages such as Ada and FORTRAN 90 support separately compilable modules.

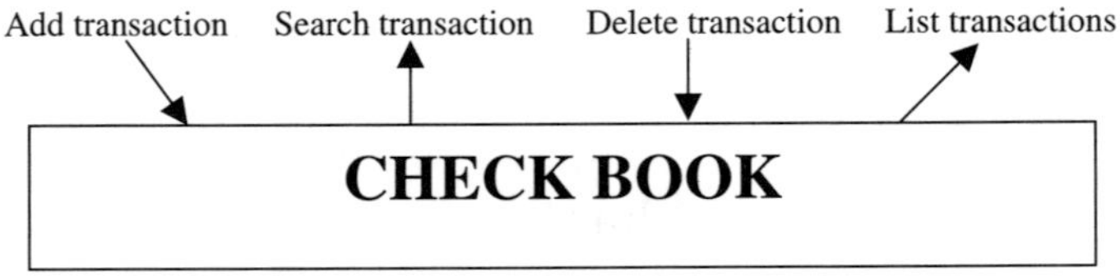

Fig. 4.1. A checkbook ADT.

Data abstraction allows us to design and use a *data structure* without considering how it is implemented. This is an extremely effective approach for controlling complexity. In particular, an *abstract data type* (ADT) is defined in terms of the operations that can be performed on instances of the type rather than by how those operations are actually implemented. In other words, an ADT defines the interface of the objects. The operations are performed on some data that is also a part of an object of a given type.

As an example of an abstract data type, consider a *check book* ADT. The data type is defined by the operations we can perform on it, e.g. add a transaction; search for a transaction; delete a transaction; list transactions, etc. We say nothing about the *implementation* of the check book. This allows us to ignore the (unimportant) details to concentrate on the (important) overall behavior and support modular design since we can change the implementation without affecting how other modules which use this ADT will work.

ADTs are not a part of a particular programming language (even though it is possible to consider built-in data types like integers or characters as ADTs); rather they are implemented by a programmer to solve a particular problem or some class of problems. On the other hand, some programming languages offer features that can be used to easily implement ADTs. In object-oriented languages like Java and C++, ADTs can be easily implemented as *classes*. In this approach, both the operations and data of the ADT are encapsulated in a class. In modular languages like C, ADTs can be implemented as libraries of datatypes and functions that manipulate those data types. In this second approach, the operations and data are defined separately, but they are grouped together in a library so that they seem to be part of a single entity to other programmers. In this chapter we will give examples in several programming languages to give an idea of how different languages support ADTs.

As an example, the header file for a library implementing a simple set ADT including the usual set operations of union, intersection and difference is given below. The implementations of the functions would be provided in a separate source code file that would be compiled into an object file or a static or dynamic library. The header file would be visible to users of the ADT, but the implementation would be hidden since the code would be compiled.

```
/* File set_adt.h */

#define MAX_SET_SIZE            100
#define SET_ELEMENT_TYPE        float
typedef struct SET {
        SET_ELEMENT_TYPE elements[MAX_SET_SIZE];
        int current_elements;
        int current_position;
} set_type;

/* Prototypes
**      initialize_set must be called before any of the other
**      operations. Each of the operations has a return value
**      an error code — 0 means the operation failed, 1 means
**      it succeeded. The operation set_get_next element can
**      be used along with get_set_size to retrieve all of
**      the elements of the set. After n elements of an set of
**      size n have been retieved, the 1st element is retrieved
**      again.
*/

int set_add (*set_type set, SET_ELEMENT_TYPE element_to_add);
int set_remove (*set_type set, SET_ELEMENT_TYPE
                element_to_remove);
int get_set_size (*set_type set);
int set_union (*set_type set1, *set_type set2, *set_type result_set);
int set_intersect (*set_type set1, *set_type set2,
      *set_type result_set);
int set_difference (*set_type set1, *set_type set2,
      *set_type result_set);
int set_get_next_element (*set_type set1, SET_ELEMENT_TYPE
                          retrieved);
int initialize_set (*set_type set);
```

Other programs can now use this library by including the header file and then linking the library. The following program fragment illustrates this use.

```
/* File client.c */

#include "set_adt.h"
```

```
. . .
set_type my_set;
. . .
/* Initialize and use a set */
result = initialize_set(&my_set);
result = set_add(&my_set, 7.0);
printf("The size of my_set is %d\", get_set_size(&my_set);
. . .
```

Now we can see the utility of using ADTs when working on a large project. Rather than having to understand the detailed implementation of the set operations, the user only has to study the interface — the abstraction is at a much higher level so much time can be saved. There are other advantages to using ADTs as well. When the ADT can be used in a variety of different programs (as in our set example), we achieve the highly desired goal of *software reuse*. It is more cost effective for organizations to use existing, well-tested components in large projects than it is to write the component from scratch. One of the reasons that reuse is not more widespread is the difficulty in understanding legacy code written by another programmer. ADTs avoid this problem by hiding the implementation. This emphasizes yet another advantage of ADTS — *information hiding*. The reason that information hiding is generally desirable is because it makes code more modular. This allows the implementation of the component to be changed without affecting some other component. Since the implementation is hidden, we cannot base our code on that implementation (which could cause our code to break if the implementation is changed). On the other hand, it is critical that the interface not change. The interface is considered a kind of contract between the implementers and the users of the ADT.

Figure 4.2 shows another view of an abstract data type. It presents an interface to the world that consists of a number of operations that can be performed on the data structure encapsulated by the ADT. The data structure itself is not visible to the outside world. When the ADT makes

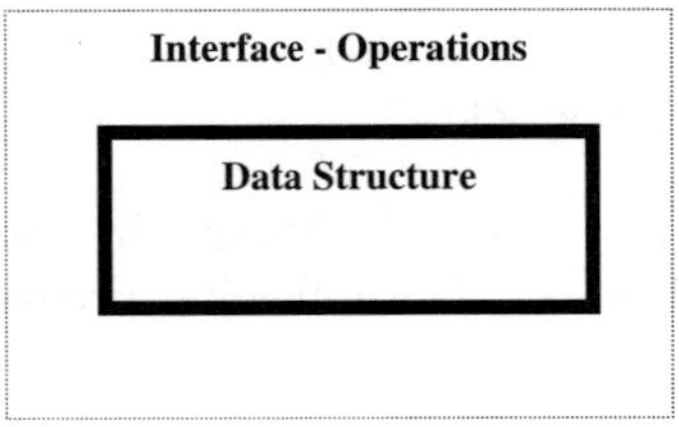

Fig. 4.2. An abstract data type.

its interface visible, it is said to *export* the interface. The hiding of the data structure inside the ADT is referred to as *encapsulation* and it is the means by which we accomplish the desired information hiding.

4.2. Abstract Data Types and Object-Oriented Languages

Earlier we stated that object-oriented languages like C++ and Java make implementing ADTs easy by providing the *class* construct. The reader may be wondering what exactly the relation between ADTs and object-orientation as a programming language paradigm is and what differences, if any, exist between the two concepts. In this section we will explore these questions.

One type of operator often provided as part of an ADT is called a *constructor*. It creates a new *instance* of the ADT. In object-oriented languages, the ADT is modeled by a class, while the instance is called an *object*. A constructor operation is provided for each class of objects and a destructor operator that destroys the object is provided for each class as well. Objects, in this programming paradigm, are dynamically created and destroyed. As we saw in the sets example from the previous section, this is not necessarily the case when using ADTs in a non object-oriented language. Notice that there is no constructor function provided as part of the ADT, instead the instance of the ADT is declared as being of the ADT type, and an initialization operation is provided.

Objects are sometimes said to communicate by exchanging *messages* in the object-oriented paradigm. In practice, this usually boils down to having a message cause one of the operations of the object to be executed. The operations in turn are usually referred to as *methods*. The data structures of the objects are called *properties*.

One large addition to the ADT idea in object-oriented languages is *inheritance*. Inheritance allows us to define one class of objects as a *subclass* of another, previously existing class. The subclass is then said to inherit from the *superclass*. What this means is that the newly defined class has all of the same methods (operations) and properties (data structures) as the superclass. New operations and properties can be added to the subclass and existing methods can be replaced (overridden) as well. Subclassing allows existing classes to be *specialized*, thus supporting software reuse. A simple example is the use of a preexisting shape class to define new rectangle and triangle classes. We would subclass the shape class to produce new rectangle and triangle classes, adding new methods such as get_area and get_perimeter, while reusing methods such as get_color, set_color, get_line_width, and set_line_width. Some object-oriented languages (e.g. C++) allow a class to inherit from more than one superclass while others (e.g. Java) do not. This capability is called *multiple inheritance*. Inheritance is such a fundamental property of object-oriented languages such that languages as the early versions of Ada which support ADTs but not inheritance are sometimes referred to as object-based rather than object-oriented.

One further feature supported by some object-oriented languages like Smalltalk is *run-time binding* or *polymorphism*. This allows the determination of the class of an object in a program to be put off until the program runs, allowing for a very flexible programming style. Other object-oriented languages like C++ require the class of an object (or the most general class an object can belong to) to be specified when the program is written. This is known as compile-time binding.

The C++ header file corresponding to the previous set ADT is shown below.

```
//***************************************************************************
//
// File set_adt.h
//
//***************************************************************************

#define MAX_SET_SIZE            100
#define SET_ELEMENT_TYPE        float

class Set
{
public:
        bool is_full ( ) const;
                // Postcondition:
                //     Return value is true if list is full
                //     false otherwise
        bool is_empty ( ) const;
                // Postcondition:
                //     Return value is true if list is empty
                //     false otherwise;
        int set_add (SET_ELEMENT_TYPE element_to_add);
                // Precondition:
                //     NOT is_full ( ) and element_to_add has a value
                // Postcondition:
                //     element_to_add is in Set and get_set_size ( ) ==
                //     get_set_size ( ) entry + 1
```

```
    int set_remove (SET_ELEMENT_TYPE element_to_remove);
        // Precondition:
        //     NOT is_empty ()
        // Postcondition:
        //     If element_to_remove is in set entry
        //         element_to_remove is no longer in set
        //     and get_set_size () == get_set_size () entry - 1
    int get_set_size () const;
    int set_union (Set& set2, Set& result_set) const;
    int set_intersect (Set& set2, Set& result_set) const;
    int set_difference (Set& set2, Set& result_set) const;
    int set_get_next_element (SET_ELEMENT_TYPE retrieved);

    Set (); // Constructor
    ~Set (); // Destructor

private:
    SET_ELEMENT_TYPE elements[MAX_SET_SIZE];
    int current_elements;
    int current_position;
};
```

We can make several interesting observations about the C++ code. Notice first of all that the class construct incorporates both the data structures that implement a set as well as the functions (methods) that manipulate these data structures. By declaring the data structures as *private*, we specifically prevent the manipulation of these data structures by any means other than the public methods of the class. These methods are made available to other objects by declaring them in the public section. Among the public methods are a *contructor* method which creates a new instance of the class (allocating the necessary memory) and a destructor method that destroys an instance (de-allocating the object's memory).

Another interesting point regards the use of *preconditions* and *postconditions* in the documentation of the methods. These represent a kind of contract between the implementers and the users of the methods. If the condition specified in the precondition holds when the method is invoked, then the postcondition is guaranteed to hold when the method completes. This type of standard documentation makes it easier to understand the methods.

Finally, the const keyword specifies that the method so tagged does not modify the data values of the object when it is executed. The use of this tag can make understanding the code easier for programmers who did not write the code.

The relationship between ADTs and object-oriented languages is summarized in the following figure.

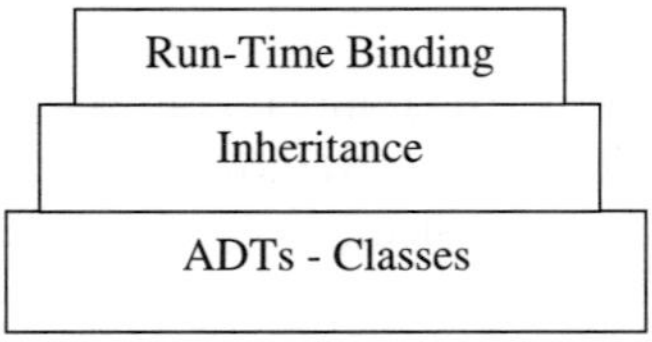

Fig. 4.3. Object-oriented languages and ADTs.

4.3. Packages

We have seen in the previous section that classes provide a natural way to implement ADTs. Another programming language structure that is widely used for this purpose is the *package*. A package actually has two important features. First of all it can be used for partitioning a program or for the construction of reusable units. Part of this partitioning might also include the ability to partition the *namespace* of a program.

In very large programs with many libraries of classes, functions, procedures, variables, constants, etc., it is quite possible that one of these entities that we define in our program can have the same name as an entity defined in a library (or somewhere else in the program). This can be a very difficult problem to understand since we have to keep in mind the definitions for all of the entities defined in all of the libraries that our program uses. In languages that use packages to partition the namespace, we must explicitly import the package to make the classes, functions, etc. of the package usable. All the other entities in packages that we do not explicitly import are invisible. In other words, the classes, constants, etc. are hidden from us so we can give one of our entities the same name and no confusion will result — ours is the only visible entity with that name, so any reference to that name refers to the entity we have defined. We will explore this use of packages later using Java as our example language.

The second use of packages is as an encapsulation mechanism. Some languages (e.g. Ada) use the package as the basic encapsulation mechanism. In object-oriented languages like Java which support packages the package is a more general encapsulation mechanism than classes and may include classes in the package.

Ada packages are the basic unit for both encapsulation and reuse. Packages have two parts (stored in two different files) — the *package specification* and the *package body*. The package specification contains the interface of the package while the package body contains the implementation of the functions and procedures contained in the package. Generally, only the package specification is available (visible) to users of the package. The package may contain functions, procedures (the difference between procedures and functions is that functions return a value while procedures do not. In C all subprograms are functions, but the return value can be ignored — it need not be used in an expression), data structures, constants, etc. Packages have two parts — public and private. The entities declared in the public part of the package are available to all users of the package while only the functions and procedures of the package may use the entities in the private part of the package. The first part of the package is the public part while the keyword private starts the private part. In order to achieve our information-hiding goal, we usually declare only the ADTs operations in the public part of the package while the implementation of the ADT (its data structure) is declared in the private part.

It may seem counterintuitive to make the implementation visible to users of the package by including it in the private part of the package specification. If our goal is information-hiding why not leave it out of the package specification altogether? The reason is so that the package body need not be available at compilation time. In order to compile the program that uses the package the compiler needs information about the implementation of the ADT. This information is available in the private part of the package specification. Modula-2 handles this problem by requiring that all ADTs whose representation is hidden in a module (package) be pointers. This hides the implementation of the ADT from its users, but it raises new problems of security.

An Ada package is used inside of a program by importing it via the *with* keyword at the beginning of the file containing the program. This makes the package visible in the program. In order to use the operations (functions and procedures) as well as the data structures (variables, constants, etc.) of the package, the operations and data structures are prefixed with the package name followed by a '.' operator. If we want to avoid giving the package name in (for example) the names of the procedures in the package we can do this with the use keyword. This assumes that we do not have conflicting entity names in our program.

It is important to notice that, in general, an Ada package represents a single object (e.g. a single set). To avoid this limitation (i.e. to define multiple sets for use in a program) we can use the *new* operator inside of a program. We simply create a duplicate of the original package creating in the process (e.g.) another set. The use of the new operator is necessary when we have a parameterized package (as we do in the example given below).

Consider an Ada package for a set containing integers. In Ada, the integer type is called natural. We can parameterize the package so that the user can provide the maximum number of elements that can be contained in the set.

The Ada package specification for the set of naturals package is given below.

— Set package specification

— Element type: Natural numbers

— Constraints: 0 <= get_set_size <= max_set_size

package natural_set_package is

type set(max_set_size : positive) is limited private;

set_full :exception;
set_empty :exception;

function is_full (the_set : stack) return boolean;
— Return value is true if list is full, false otherwise

function is_empty (the_set : stack) return boolean;
— Return value is true if list is empty, false otherwise

procedure set_add (the_set : in out stack; element : natural);
— element is added to the set
— exceptions: set_full is raised if number of elements in the
— set = max_set_size.

procedure set_remove (the_set : in out stack; element : natural);
— If element is a member of the set, it is removed.
— exceptions: set_empty is raised if number of elements in the
— set = 0.

function get_set_size (the_set : set) return natural;
— The size of the set is returned.

function set_union (first, second : set) return set;
— Returns the union of the first and second sets.

function set_intersect (first, second : set) return set;
— Returns the intersection of the first and second sets.

function set_difference (first, second : set) return set;
— Returns the difference of the first and second sets.

function set_get_next_element (the_set : set) returns natural;
— Returns the next set element.

```
private
    type array_of_elements is array(positive range < >) of natural;
    type set(max_set_size : positive) is record
        current_elements  :natural := 0;
        current_position  :natural := 1;
        elements          :array_of_elements (1..max_set_size);
    end record;
end natural_set_package;
```

The package body corresponding to the set of naturals package specification is given below (in part).

```
package_body natural_set_package is
    function is_full (the_set : set) return boolean is
    begin
        if the_set.current_elements = max_set_size then
            return true;
        else
            return false;
    end is_full;
    function is_empty (the_set : set) return boolean is
    begin
        if the_set.current_elements = 0 then
            return true;
        else
            return false;
    end is_empty;
    procedure set_add (the_set : in out stack; element : natural) is
    begin
        the_set.elements(current_elements + 1) := element;
        the_set.current_elements := the_set.current_elements + 1;
    exception
        when contraint_error => raise set_full;
    end set_add;
    . . .
    end natural_set_package;
```

This package could then be used as follows.

```
with natural_set_package;
procedure main_program is
```

```
package my_natural_set_package is new natural_set_package(100);
. . .
my_natural_set_package.set_add(my_natural_set_package.set, 100);
```

Another example of the use of packages is provided by Java. As in Ada, Java packages provide a way to group together logically related subprograms (classes in the case of Java). Unlike in Java, packages usually consist of multiple files, rather than a single file. This reflects the Java paradigm of one (public) class per file.

A class is defined to be part of a file by including a line of the following type at the beginning of a file, before the class defined in the file.

```
package com.widgets.smallwidgets;
public class Firstsmallwidget extends Object {
. . .
```

This defines the class firstsmallwidget to be part of the package com.widgets.smallwidgets. Similar declarations would appear in every other file containing a class for this package.

The name of the package reflects an attempt to supply a unique name for every package. The name starts with the Internet domain name of the furnisher of the package (in this case widgets.com) in reverse order. We can add further modifiers to the name started in this manner (i.e. com.widgets.products2001.* and com.widgets.products2002.*). Starting with Java 2, the classes pertaining to a package are stored in a particular directory depending on the name of the package. This directory is always relative to the classes directory. In a Windows system, this directory might be c:\jdk1.2.1\jre\classes while on a UNIX machine it might be \usr\local\jdk1.2.1\jre\classes where \usr\local is the directory where the JDK (Java Developer's Kit) has been installed.

After the classes contained in a package are compiled they are installed in the directory implied by the package name. In our case (assuming a standard Windows installation) the directory is c:\jdk1.2.1\jre\classes\com\widgets. Note that com is a directory as well. After compilation of the class which is part of the package, then name of the package becomes part of the name of the class. In our case com.widgets.smallwidgets. In order to use this class, we can use this complete name, or more easily, we can use the *import* command to avoid using the complete name as shown below.

```
import com.widgets.smallwidgets;
public class Example {
. . .
```

```
Firstsmallwidget f1;
f1 = new Firstsmallwidget ( );
. . .
```

Java also provides a way to allow access to the methods and data members of one class to be given to other classes which are part of the same package while not allowing access to other classes. For example, we typically restrict access to the data members of classes, allowing them only to be accessed using public methods — this is the basic philosophy of ADTs.

```
package com.widgets.smallwidgets;

public class Firstsmallwidget extends Object {
    private double widgetweight;
. . .
    public double getWeight ( ) { return widgetweight; }
. . .
```

The *private* keyword prevents other classes from directly accessing the widgetweight. Instead they must use the getWeight method, which is declared *public.* On the other hand, we may have auxiliary classes as part of the package which should be able to access the widgetweight directly. We can have that result by declaring widgetweight to be *protected.*

```
package com.widgets.smallwidgets;

public class Firstsmallwidget extends Object {
    protected double widgetweight;
. . .
```

In order to have the same type of access in C++, it is necessary to explicitly list all of the classes which are to have access to a private member as friend classes of the class in question.

4.4. Generic Abstract Data Types

When we are working with ADTs like sets, queues and stacks, two distinct ADTs may vary only in the type of element that is to be stored in the data structure. We may have sets of integers, characters or strings, for example. Using the language constructs we have seen so far, we would need to specify separate interfaces and have separate implementations (i.e. a completely separate ADT) for each type of element we want to be able to store in a structure. A little bit of thought will surely show that these separate ADTs are in fact very much alike. Following this reasoning a little further, it would be nice for the programming language we are using to allow us to give this common structure once, rather than repeatedly, and have the parts specific for a particular element type filled in when needed. This idea of giving the common part of an ADT and *instantiating* it (specializing it) for a particular data type is the idea behind *generic abstract data types.*

Generic abstract data types are supported in some, but not all, modern programming languages. Ada supports generic ADTs through the *generic package* construct while C++ provides *templates* for the same purpose. We will focus on Ada generic packages in this section.

In order to allow ADTs which work on various data types, Ada supports the generic package construct. These packages are instantiated by users of the package. The instantiation specializes the package, specifying the data type of the elements and also, perhaps, some other parameters. In order to make a package generic, it is necessary to make sure that there are no operations that are specific for one particular data type in the procedures and functions in the package. This is usually not a problem since the types of operations we are interested in are issues like assignment and comparison that are valid for most data types. The instantiation is accomplished using the *new package* operator.

The Ada package specification for a generic set ADT is given below.

```
— Generic set package specification
— Constraints: 0 <= get_set_size <= max_set_size
generic
        type element_type is private;
package set_package is
        type set(max_set_size  : positive) is limited private;

        set_full            :exception;
        set_empty           :exception;

        function is_full (the_set : stack) return boolean;
        — Return value is true if list is full, false otherwise

        function is_empty (the_set : stack) return boolean;
        — Return value is true if list is empty, false otherwise

        procedure set_add (the_set : in out stack; element :
element_type);
        — element is added to the set
```

```
    — exceptions: set_full is raised if number of elements in the
    — set = max_set_size.

    procedure set_remove (the_set : in out stack; element :
element_type);
    — If element is a member of the set, it is removed.
    — exceptions: set_empty is raised if number of elements in the
    — set = 0.

    function get_set_size (the_set : set) return natural;
    — The size of the set is returned.

    function set_union (first, second : set) return set;
    — Returns the union of the first and second sets.

    function set_intersect (first, second : set) return set;
    — Returns the intersection of the first and second sets.

    function set_difference (first, second : set) return set;
    — Returns the difference of the first and second sets.

    function set_get_next_element (the_set : set) returns
element_type;
    — Returns the next set element.
private

    type array_of_elements is array(positive range <>) of
element_type;

    type set(max_set_size : positive) is record
        current_elements  :natural := 0;
        current_position  :natural := 0;
        elements          :array_of_elements(1..max_set_size);
    end record;

end natural_set_package;
```

The set type has been defined to be of type *limited private*. This is the more restrictive alternative that Ada provides. If the set type had been declared private we would not be able to manipulate its internal representation except through the given functions and procedures of the type, but we would be able to assign it (using the assignment operator) and to compare it to other sets using the equality operator. By declaring the type to be limited private, these possibilities are not allowed. If we want, we can provide our own assignment and equality operators for the set functions. So we can see that Ada provides a very powerful information hiding capability that is useful in the implementation of ADTS.

By making the size of the set a parameter, we give the user the ability to define the maximum size of the set when it is declared. In this way Ada provides flexibility for the different needs of different users.

4.5. Software Design with Abstract Data Types

The design of a software system is traditionally divided into a number of successive *phases*. The phases are nonoverlapping and each phase results in the production of one or more documents. Two of the earliest stages are the analysis phase and the design phase. The analysis phase is a detailed study of the problem to be solved. This is a crucial phase in the production of large-scale software systems since even if we correctly implement a solution, if the problem we are solving is not the one that the users are interested in, we have not correctly solved the problem. Correcting such mistakes, which often show up only when testing with real users begins, is very expensive since the whole system may need to be reprogrammed. The design phase begins with a precisely detailed description of the problem to be solved (the document which is the output of the analysis phase) and gives a (possibly programming language independent) solution to the problem. Only when the document describing this solution is produced, does actual coding in a programming language begin. These two phases may consume a large part of the resources expended in developing a software system. Experience certainly suggests that they should.

Even when implementing a software system using a programming language like C that does not provide much support for the implementation of ADTs the use of ADTs in the analysis and design phases of software development can be quite useful since it provides a principled approach to the software development process.

Software design with ADTs generally begins with the description of a real-world problem that needs to be understood. In the case of problems that require large systems to solve, the real-world situation is often full of complicating details that make understanding the problem difficult at best. Abstraction is a key tool in overcoming this difficulty. The idea is to separate the pertinent details from those which are superfluous, abstracting away the unnecessary details by creating a model of the problem as shown in Fig. 4.4.

Consider, for example, a simple system to keep track of grades for students on exams at a university. We might start the design of a solution to this problem by identifying the objects that are part of this problem — students, exams, instructors, etc. The next step in the design

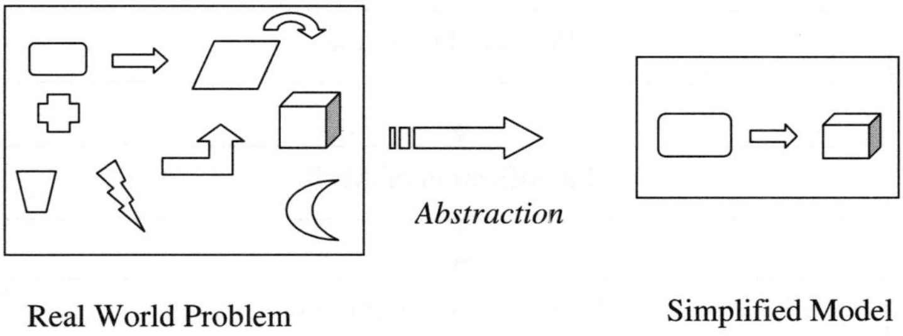

Fig. 4.4. Abstraction in system design.

might be to identify the attributes of these objects. For example, for *student* ADTs we might have attributes such as:

- Name
- Age
- Address
- Identification number
- Major
- Eye color
- etc.

Clearly, some of these attributes (age, address, eye color) are not relevant to the problem being solved and can be ignored in our model of the *student* ADT. In more realistic problems, not just attributes of objects but entire objects may be safely ignored.

The next step in the design process is to establish the operations that the various data types should support. So, for example, the *exam* ADT will have operations such as add_grade, change_grade, add_exam, etc. The interactions between the various ADTs which comprise the system may also be established at this point as part of the documentation of the system. All of the activities outlined until this point have been independent of the language to be used in the implementation of the system. In the final step, the ADTs will have to be implemented, and the ease with which this can be accomplished will depend on the language to be used. If one has a library of previously developed ADTs available and an object-oriented language is to be used for the implementation, then part of the development process will likely include the identification of a hierarchical organization of the ADTs (objects) in order to reuse as much as possible of the programming work already done. The complete development process outlined above is illustrated in Fig. 4.5.

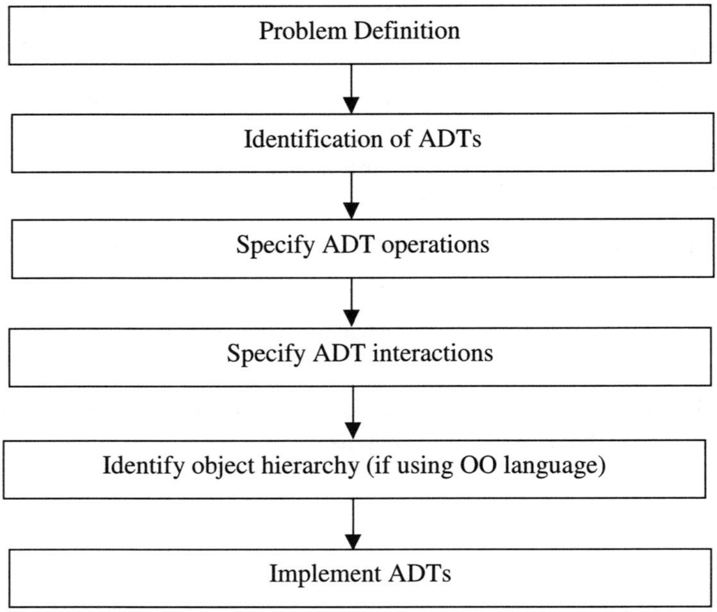

Fig. 4.5. System design with ADTs.

4.6. Conclusions

Data abstraction is one of the most important ideas to emerge in the area of software development in the last 30 years. Data abstraction was conceived as an idea to control the explosion in program complexity that led many software projects to be completed late and to contain many errors, and other projects to fail completely. Abstraction is an effective tool to control complexity since it allows software designers to concentrate on pertinent portions of a software project while ignoring irrelevant details. Data abstraction is one of the two fundamental types of abstraction widely used in software design, along with the older process abstraction, represented by the use of subprograms. Data abstraction and the associated concept of ADTs did not become widely used, however, until programming languages that support ADTs became widely available. Among these languages, SIMULA 67 was a very early example (as was Smalltalk), but it was not widely used in many application areas. Ada and Modula-2 were among the first widely used languages that could easily support ADTs. They appeared in the early 1980s and were followed by such important and popular object-oriented languages as C++ and Java.

Table 4.1. ADT supporting features of some popular languages.

	Separate Compilation	Classes	Packages	Generics
C	Yes	No	No	No
C++	Yes	Yes	No	Yes
Java	Yes	Yes	Yes	No
Ada	Yes	No	Yes	Yes

The primary characteristics of ADTs are the collocation of a data structure and the operations that manipulate that data structure and information hiding by allowing access to the ADT only through the operations provided. SIMULA 67, Smalltalk, C++, Java and other object-oriented languages support ADTs directly through their class structure. Other languages, like Ada and Modula-2 provide a general encapsulation feature (packages or modules) that can be used to indirectly simulate ADTs. Language structures supporting ADTs for some of the languages we have examined in this chapter are summarized below in Table 4.1.

The use of ADTs for software design was popularized by authors such as Grady Booch, who developed the Booch methodology primarily for systems to be implemented in Ada. The Booch methodology was later incorporated in the Uniform Modeling Language which has been standardized by the Object Management Group and forms the basis for many popular Computer-Aided Software Engineering (CASE) tools for the production of large-scale software systems.

Exercises

Beginner's Exercises

1. Consider a telephone as an Abstract Data Type. List the operations for the telephone ADT.
2. Consider an automobile as an Abstract Data Type. List the operations for the telephone ADT.

Intermediate Exercises

3. Research a particular programming language and discuss its strengths and weaknesses as a language for constructing ADTs.
4. Use ADTs to design a climate control system for a university campus. Give the ADTs and their operations and show their interactions.

Advanced Exercises

5. Use ADTs to design a system for automatic payment at toll road booths. Give the ADTs and their operations and show their interactions.
6. Give the header file describing the ADTs, written in C, for either problem 4 or problem 5.

Chapter 5

Stacks, Recursion and Backtracking

FREDERICK THULIN
Knowledge Systems Institute, USA
fthulin@ksi.edu

5.1. Stacks

5.1.1. *The LIFO Nature of Stacks*

A stack is a data structure analogous to those encountered in everyday life. For example, consider a stack of books on a desk. One may easily put a new book on top of the stack, and one may easily remove the top book. Adding books to, or removing them from, the middle of the stack may be perilous. In the stack data structure accessing items in the middle is prohibited. Items may be added to or removed from only the top of the stack.

Saving an item on a stack is referred to as pushing the item, and retrieving an item is called popping the item. Popping an item removes the item from the stack. Pushes and pops are done at the top of the stack, which may be thought of as a distinguished end of the stack. This means that if two items are pushed and then one popped, the second one pushed will be popped. This order of data access is called last in, first out or LIFO access.

5.1.2. *Reversing with a Stack*

Suppose a sequence of items is presented and it is desired to reverse the sequence. Various methods could be used and the beginner programmer will usually suggest a solution using an array. A conceptually very simple solution, however, is based on using a stack. The LIFO property of stack access guarantees the reversal.

Suppose the sequence ABCDEF is to be reversed. With a stack, one simply scans the sequence, pushing each item on the stack as it is encountered, until the end of the sequence is reached. Then the stack is popped repeatedly, with each popped item sent to output, until the stack is empty. The following illustrates this algorithm.

input ==> ABCDEF

push A:

A <== top of stack

input ==> BCDEF

push B:

B <== top of stack
A

input ==> CDEF

push C:

C <== top of stack
B
A

input ==> DEF

push D:

D <== top of stack
C
B
A

input ==> EF

push E:

E <== top of stack
D
C
B
A

input ==> F

push F:

F <== top of stack

E
D
C
B
A

The end of the input has been reached, and so popping the stack begins.

pop F to output:

E <== top of stack
D
C
B
A

pop E to output:

D <== top of stack
C
B
A

pop D to output:

C <== top of stack
B
A

pop C to output:

B <== top of stack
A

pop B to output:

A <== top of stack

pop A to output:

stack empty; stop.

5.1.3. *Stack Operations*

Besides the push and pop operations on a stack, it is desirable to have at least two more: an *initialize* operation, which prepares the stack for use and sets it to an empty state, and an *empty* operation, which is simply a test to see whether the stack is empty. The empty operation is useful to guard against an attempt to pop an empty stack, which is an error. Ideally stacks should be unlimited in capacity so that another item can always be pushed no matter how many are already on the stack. However, stacks as implemented on an actual computer will always have some finite maximum capacity. Sometimes these stacks are referred to as stacks with a roof. When the roof is reached, items can no longer be pushed on the stack. In view of this fact, it is sometimes desirable to supply a *full* operation for a stack.

Other stack operations may be conceived, such as peek (examine the top item of the stack without popping it), traverse (go through all the items on the stack, performing some action for each item) and count (find the number of items on the stack). Here, however, attention will be restricted to only the five mentioned in the preceding paragraph.

Stack Operations

push:	**add an item to the top of the stack**
pop:	**remove an item from the top of the stack**
empty:	**test whether the stack is empty**
full:	**test whether the stack is full**
initialize:	**set up the stack in an empty condition**

In C programs the above operations are often implemented as functions to provide a degree of data hiding. A program which uses stacks would access the stacks only through these functions, and not be concerned with the inner workings of the stack. It is also convenient to access a stack through a pointer. The pointer can be considered a handle whereby the program can make use of the stack. These techniques can provide implementation independent code, so that a program using stacks would not need to be changed if the stack functions themselves were changed. This will be illustrated in the following two sections.

5.1.4. *Contiguous Implementation*

A contiguous implementation means that each stack item is adjacent in memory to the next stack item, and so arrays are the natural structures for contiguous implementations. For a contiguous stack implementation the stack items are kept in an array and the top position in an integer field of a structure which also contains the array. The stack will be accessed through a handle which is a pointer to this structure. For flexibility, the type itemtype will be used in the code for stack items. Then the actual type used in a program can simply be specified with a typedef. The constant N is the maximum size of the stack and may be redefined to a suitable value for different applications.

Reversing an Input Line with a Contiguous Stack

```
#include <stdio.h>
#include <stdlib.h>

#define N 80

typedef char itemtype;

typedef struct{
        int top;
        itemtype items[N];} stackstruct;

typedef stackstruct * stack;

stack initialize(stack s){
        s = (stack)malloc(sizeof(stackstruct));
        s->top = -1;
        return s;}

void push(stack s, itemtype x){
        s->items[++s->top] = x;}

itemtype pop(stack s){
        return s->items[s->top--];}

int empty(stack s){
        return s->top == -1;}

int full(stack s){
        return s->top == N - 1;}

void main(){
        stack s;
        char c;
        s = initialize(s);
        while((c = getchar( )) != '\n' && !full(s))
                push(s, c);
        while(!empty(s))
                putchar(pop(s));
        getchar( );}
```

Input

palindromes

Output

semordnilap

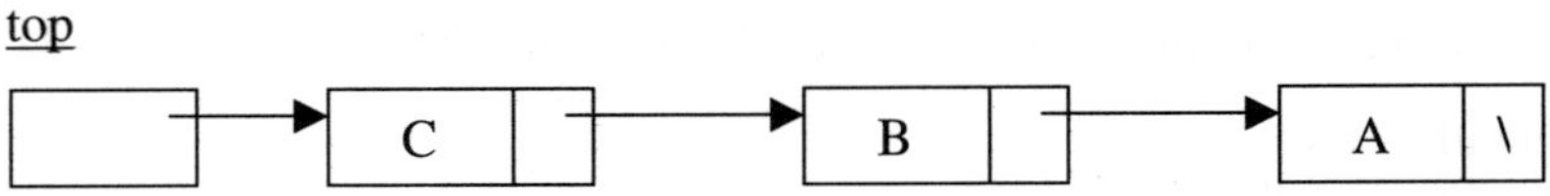

Fig. 5.1. A linked structure.

5.1.5. *Linked Implementation*

A stack can also be implemented as a linked structure, as illustrated in Fig. 5.1. In such an implementation the stack consists of a sequence of *nodes*. Each node is a record (structure in C) containing a data item and a pointer to the next node if one exists. This pointer is called a link (to the next node). The first node is considered to be the top of the stack, and a pointer called top will be directed to it. The last node is the bottom of the stack and its pointer field is set to NULL. An empty stack will have top == NULL. A linked stack with elements C, B, A in order (C on top) may be represented as below, where \ denotes a NULL pointer.

Recall that it is desirable for a program to access a stack through a handle. To achieve this, we simply enclose the top field in a structure, and then a pointer to this structure is the desired handle. It may seem strange to have a structure with only one field, but this ensures that a program can use a linked stack in exactly the same way it would use a contiguous stack.

The memory for each node is dynamically allocated on the heap using malloc. So when an item is pushed, a node for it is created, and when an item is popped, its node is freed (using free).

The following program illustrates appropriate types and functions for a linked stack. The main function below is identical to the main function above using a contiguous stack. Note that the behavior of this program is the same as the one for a contiguous stack, at least for input lines of 80 characters or less. This is because the same function names are used for the linked stack operations and they provide the same functionality for the linked stack as the previous ones do for the contiguous stack. The only difference is that the capacity of a linked stack is generally greater than a contiguous stack since a linked stack will not become full until dynamic memory is exhausted.

Reversing an Input Line with a Linked Stack

```
#include <stdio.h>
#include <stdlib.h>

typedef char itemtype;
```

```
typedef struct node{
        itemtype item;
        struct node * next;} Node;

typedef struct {Node * top;} stackstruct;

typedef stackstruct * stack;

void push(stack s, itemtype x){
        Node * p = (Node*)malloc(sizeof(Node));
        p->item = x;
        p->next = s->top;
        s->top = p;}

itemtype pop(stack s){
        Node * p = s->top;
        itemtype x = p->item;
        s->top = p->next;
        free(p);
        return x;}

int empty(stack s){
        return s->top==NULL;}

int full(stack s){
        Node * p = (Node*)malloc(sizeof(Node));
        if(p == NULL) return 1;
        else{    free(p);
                 return 0;}}

stack initialize(stack s){
        s = (stack)malloc(sizeof(stackstruct));
        s->top = NULL;
        return s;}

void main(){
        stack s;
        char c;
        s = initialize(s);
        while((c = getchar( )) != '\n' && !full(s))
                push(s, c);
        while(!empty(s))
                putchar(pop(s));
        getchar( );}
```

5.2. Recursion

5.2.1. *Introduction*

Recursion in computer science is generally identified with the use of recursive procedures; that is, procedures which call themselves. The call (or calls) of the procedure to itself is an explicit form of self-reference. These self-calls are referred to as recursive calls. Recursion also includes indirect recursion, in which a procedure may call another, which may then call still another, and so on, until one calls the first. An algorithm which uses recursion is called a recursive algorithm.

Recursion is a form of repetition, one of the three basic control structures: sequence, selection and repetition. Repetition is usually first studied as iteration or looping. Iteration is typically more easily understood than recursion at first. Iteration occurs frequently in everyday life where recursion is rare. As an example of iteration, most of us are familiar with seasoning food to taste. We add a little of the seasoning, taste, add more if necessary and taste again, repeating until the food is appropriately seasoned. Many other examples of iteration in daily life may easily come to mind, but examples of recursion do not. The main feature of recursion, self-reference, does not often play a part in ordinary life. However, programming with recursive procedures may yield simple and elegant code that is easy to verify, primarily because of the self-reference involved.

Recursive procedures suffer a performance penalty compared to equivalent iterative code because of the overhead of repeated procedure calls. The reasons for this overhead will be discussed in a later section, but note for now that the overhead includes both space and time. That means that a recursive procedure generally uses more memory and takes more time than an equivalent iterative one. If the clarity of a recursive solution is sufficiently great and the performance penalty small, the recursive solution may be preferred to an equivalent iterative one. It is interesting to note that in the early days of programming any performance penalty was frequently thought to be unacceptable and so recursion was not much used. In fact, many early programming languages did not support recursion, but nowadays almost all do.

Recursion does not need to be used in programming because any recursive procedure or set of procedures may be translated into an equivalent iterative version using only loops for repetition and no recursive calls (direct or indirect). A recursive algorithm thus has a corresponding equivalent non-recursive or iterative version. One may speak of the recursive and iterative versions of an algorithm. Just as recursive algorithms can be translated into iterative ones, iterative algorithms may be translated into recursive ones. That is, any code containing loops may have the loops eliminated and replaced by appropriate recursive calls. The term "removing recursion" is often used to describe the process of translating from a recursive version to an iterative version. In the general case, removing recursion requires the explicit use in the code of a stack data structure. The general case, however, will not be considered here. Most programming systems provide a special stack, invisible to the programmer, called the run-time stack.

5.2.2. *Procedure Calls and the Run-Time Stack*

When a procedure is called, a pointer to the position in the code following the call must be saved so that when the procedure returns, it can return to the proper place. The run-time stack is used for this purpose. The run-time stack is also used for passing parameters and for local variable storage for the called procedure.

In the following diagrams the run-time stack will be pictured as growing downward toward the bottom of the page. This means that the top of the stack actually appears at the bottom in the diagrams. This reflects the orientation used in most computers, where the stack starts at a particular address in memory and grows toward lower addresses in memory.

When a procedure is called, a number of items are pushed on the stack. Together these items constitute what is known as a *stack frame* for the procedure. The calling procedure (the caller) pushes the parameters and the return address. The called procedure (the callee) reserves space on the stack for its local variables. The building of the stack frame is then a cooperative venture between the caller and the callee. When a procedure returns, the stack frame is torn down via reversing (roughly) the steps used to build it. A stack frame is called an activation record by some authors.

As an example, suppose a procedure has parameters P0 and P1 and local variables L0, L1 and L2. Its stack frame can be diagrammed as shown in Fig. 5.2 (this is a simplification of the actual frame but suffices for the main ideas of stack frames):

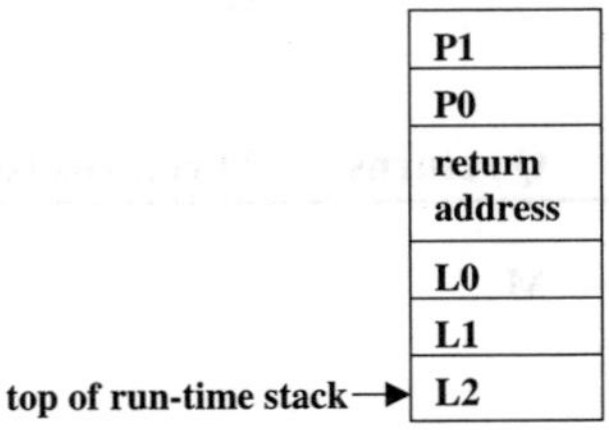

Fig. 5.2. A stack frame.

As a further example, consider a program with a main procedure (M) and procedures N, O, P, Q and R. These letters will stand for either the procedures or their stack frames in the following discussion. Suppose that in a particular run of the program M calls N which then returns, M calls O which calls P which then returns and then O returns, M calls Q which calls R which calls itself and then calls itself again, and then all return. R is recursive, and the important thing to note is that it has a different stack frame for each time it is called. The different stack frames for R mean that there are multiple copies of its parameters and local variables, which may have different values. The following diagrams show the frames on the run-time stack at different points in the execution of the program.

Run-Time Stack Sequence

As illustrated in Fig. 5.3, M calls N which then returns, M calls O which calls P which then returns and then O returns, M calls Q which calls R which calls itself and then calls itself again, and then all return.

A tree diagram called the procedure call tree is a succinct representation of the growth and shrinkage of the stack as the program executes. The tree is conventionally drawn growing downward as illustrated in Fig. 5.4.

M starts	**M calls N**	**N returns**	**M calls O**	**O calls P**	**P returns**
M	**M**	**M**	**M**	**M**	**M**
	N		**O**	**O**	**O**
				P	

O returns	**M calls Q**	**Q calls R**	**R calls R**	**R calls R**	**R returns**
M	**M**	**M**	**M**	**M**	**M**
	Q	**Q**	**Q**	**Q**	**Q**
		R	**R**	**R**	**R**
			R	**R**	**R**
				R	

R returns	**R returns**	**Q returns**	**M returns (stack empty)**
M	**M**	**M**	
Q	**Q**		
R			

Fig. 5.3. Run-time stack sequence.

Procedure Call Tree

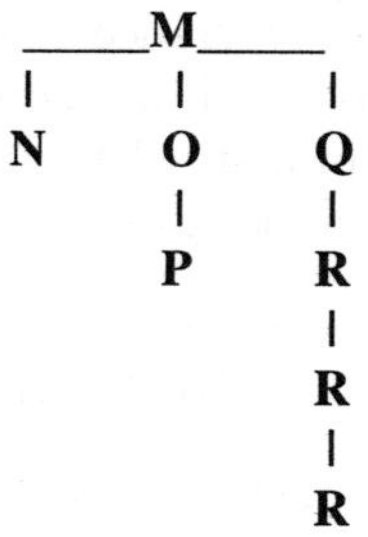

Fig. 5.4. The procedure call tree.

In order to promote the reader's understanding of recursion, a number of code examples in C using recursive functions (recall that all procedures in C are called functions) will be presented and discussed in the following sections. In some cases iterative versions will be presented also for comparison and contrast. The earlier examples will be simple and mostly impractical since the true power and usefulness of recursion is evident only in more advanced applications which will be presented in later chapters.

5.2.3. *Sum of the First n Positive Integers*

As a first example, consider the problem of determining the sum of the first n positive integers (= the sum of the first $n+1$ non-negative integers, including 0). There is a simple formula for this sum: $n(n+1)/2$, but let us ignore that for a while so as to clarify certain concepts needed to understand recursive algorithms. Of course this means that the only practical use of this example is in teaching and studying recursion. Denoting the sum by S_n, and noting that

(1) $S_n = n + (n-1) + (n-2) + \cdots + 2 + 1 + 0,$

it is easy to see that S_n satisfies a *recurrence relation*:

(2) $S_n = n + S_{n-1}$, for $n > 1$.

A recurrence relation may form part of a *recursive definition* in which something is defined in terms of itself. A proper recursive definition contains two parts: one or more base cases in which the item being defined is defined *not* in terms of itself, and one or more recursive cases where the item is defined in terms of smaller or more basic versions of itself. Recursive definitions frequently may be easily translated into recursive implementations in code.

Recursive definitions are often called inductive definitions, especially in the mathematical literature.

It is evident that in the recurrence relation (2), S_n, a sum of $n+1$ numbers (including 0), is expressed in terms of S_{n-1}, a sum of n numbers. So S_n is expressed in terms of a smaller version of itself and (2) may then be included in a recursive definition of S_n:

$S_n = 0$, if $n = 0$ (base case);
$S_n = n + S_{n-1}$, for $n > 1$ (recursive case).

Now this definition may be directly translated into a C function, where the type unsigned int is used since only non-negative arguments are of interest:

```
unsigned int S(unsigned int n){
        if(n == 0) return 0;    /*base case*/
        return n + S(n - 1);}  /*recursive case*/
```

Consider invoking this function with $n = 2$. The call $S(2)$ results in evaluating the expression $n + S(n-1)$ for the return, and $n - 1 = 1$ so the call $S(1)$ is made. This call then results similarly in the call $S(0)$. $n = 0$ is the base case, so 0 is returned. Then $S(1)$ returns $1 + 0$ $(= 1)$, and then $S(2)$ returns $2+1$ $(= 3)$. This sequence of calls and returns may be conveniently represented in the following manner:

```
S(2)  (return 3)
      S(1)  (return 1)
            S(0)  (return 0)
```

The return values may be omitted from some such diagrams later in the chapter.

The parameters in the stack frames of S may be represented in a manner similar to that of the whole stack frames done earlier, as illustrated in Fig. 5.5:

For reference below, (1) and (2) are here repeated:

(1) $S_n = n + (n-1) + (n-2) + \cdots + 2 + 1 + 0$,
(2) $S_n = n + S_{n-1}$, for $n > 1$.

call of S(2)	S(2) calls S(1)	S(1) calls S(0)	return 0	return 1	return 3
2	2	2	2	2	
	1	1	1		
		0			

Fig. 5.5. Parameters in the stack frames.

Now consider an iterative version of the function S. Just as the recursive version follows from the recurrence relation (2), the iterative version follows from the definition (1). The variable s is used to accumulate the sum that becomes the return value of the function.

```
unsigned int S(unsigned int n){
        unsigned int s = 0, i;
        for(i = n; i > 0; i--)
                s+ = i;
        return s;}
```

Note that the recursive version of S contains an if statement, and the iterative version contains a for loop. In the recursive version, repetition is handled by recursion and the if statement serves to stop the recursion at the right point. In the iterative version, repetition is handled by the for loop and is stopped at the right point by the test of the $i > 0$ condition. Some students just beginning to study recursion will incorrectly use a loop in a recursive function. Sometimes a loop is required, but more frequently not.

Other issues worthy to note are that the iterative version uses two local variables while the recursive version uses none, and the recursive version has two fewer lines of code. Sometimes the recursive version of an algorithm also requires more parameters than the iterative version, though this is not the case in this example.

The comparisons above generalize to a fairly large proportion of algorithms in practical use. A summary of these observations follows.

Recursion versus Iteration

recursive versions frequently have:

- **more parameters**
- **fewer local variables**
- **if statement(s)**
- **no loops**
- **less code**
- **more overhead**

iterative versions frequently have:

- **fewer parameters**
- **more local variables**
- **loops (always)**
- **more code**
- **less overhead**

Beginners sometimes forget to include the base case in a recursive function, which leads to a condition known as infinite recursion. In this case the function simply calls itself again and again until the system runs out of the memory required for the recursive calls. This is to be avoided for the same reasons that infinite loops are to be avoided.

5.2.4. *Factorials*

An example similar to the sum of the first n positive integers is the product of the first n positive integers. Unlike the case with the sum, there is no simple formula for this quantity, and so functions that compute it after the manner of the sum example may be of some practical use. There is a standard term for this product: n factorial. There is also a standard notation: $n!$ The factorial function in mathematics is defined by $f(n) = n!$ A so-called "empty product," a product of 0 numbers, is by convention equal to 1. So considering the product of the first 0 positive integers to be 0!, it is seen that $0! = 1$. Iterative and recursive definitions of $n!$ are then evident:

iterative:

$n! = n(n-1)(n-2)\ldots 2^*1$

recursive:

$n! = 1$, if $n = 0$ (base case);
$n! = n(n-1)!$, for $n > 1$ (recursive case).

These definitions lead to the following two versions of the function factorial.

Recursive Factorial

```
unsigned int factorial(unsigned int n){
        if (n == 0) return 1;  /*base case*/
        return n * factorial(n - 1);}  /*recursive case*/
```

Iterative Factorial

```
unsigned int factorial(unsigned int n){
        unsigned int p = 1, i;
        for (i = n; i > 0; i--)
                p *= i;
        return p;}
```

Just as s was used in the iterative function S to accumulate the sum, p is used in the iterative factorial function to accumulate the product. It is usually recommended to use the iterative instead of the recursive factorial function in practical applications, but in fact the performance penalty is quite small so that either version could be used unless it is required to compute a great many factorials quickly. Also note that a practical factorial function would probably use type double rather than unsigned int. Computing factorials with type unsigned int will produce overflow for factorials greater than 8! in 16 bits and greater than 12! in 32 bits.

5.2.5. *Collatz* $3x + 1$ *Problem*

An interesting example comes from the Collatz $3x+1$ problem, which relates to generating a sequence of numbers by either dividing the previous number by 2 (if it is even) or multiplying it by 3 and adding 1 (if it is odd). In the late 1930's the mathematician Lothar Collatz, for whom the problem is named, investigated sequences of integers satisfying the following:

$x_n = 3x_{n-1} + 1$ if x_{n-1} is odd;
$x_n = x_{n-1}/2$ if x_{n-1} is even.

These are recurrence relations and so may be incorporated into a recursive definition. Note that if the number 1 ever occurs in such a sequence, then the sequence proceeds:

$1, 4, 2, 1, 4, 2, 1, \ldots$

and so stopping such a sequence when 1 occurs is a common convention. These sequences are called Collatz sequences. If the sequence starts with an integer x, it is called the Collatz sequence of x. Collatz hypothesized that the Collatz sequence of any positive integer x eventually contained 1 and so, with the stopping convention, was finite. Many mathematicians have tried to prove this, but none has yet done so. The mathematician Stanislaw Ulam did some work with Collatz sequences and the length of a number's Collatz sequence is named after him: the Ulam length of x is the length of the Collatz sequence of x. Recursive definitions of the Collatz sequence and Ulam length of x and corresponding recursive functions are easy to create, and so are the iterative versions. Here Collatz sequences are only considered for positive integers. Those for negative integers are also of interest (and for $x = 0$ of very little interest). For further information on this topic one may consult Martin Gardner's book *Wheels, Life and Other Mathematical Amusements*.

One difficulty with any recursive functions to compute Collatz sequences or Ulam lengths is the lack of a mathematical proof that the sequence is always finite (terminates in 1). This means that the recursion may be infinite, a situation to be avoided, as previously mentioned. The sequences have, however, been tested for very many values of x and have always terminated in such tests. So we have empirical evidence that the recursion will terminate but not actual knowledge that it will. The problem occurs because the recurrence

$x_n = 3x_{n-1} + 1$ if x_{n-1} is odd

apparently does not define x_n in terms of smaller or more basic entities. Nonetheless let us consider the recursive definitions and functions and also the iterative versions, whose loops may possibly be infinite for some values of x just as the recursion may be infinite for those values.

Recursive Definition for the Collatz Sequence of a Positive Integer x

$x_n = x$ if $n = 0$,
x_n undefined if $x_{n-1} = 1$ (sequence stops),
$x_n = 3x_{n-1} + 1$ if $n > 0$ and $x_{n-1} > 1$ is odd;
$x_n = x_{n-1}/2$ if $n > 0$ and $x_{n-1} > 1$ is even.

Collatz Sequence Display (Recursive)

```
void collatz(unsigned int x){
        printf("%u\n", x);      /*%u is proper format for unsigned int*/
        if(x <= 1) return;      /*base case*/
        if(x%2 != 0) collatz(3*x + 1);
        else collatz(x/2);}
```

Collatz Sequence Display (Iterative)

```
void collatz(unsigned int x){
        printf("%u\n", x);
        while(x > 1){
                if(x%2 != 0) x = 3*x + 1;
                else x = x/2;
                printf("%u\n", x);}}
```

Recursive Definition for Ulam Length of Positive Integer x

Ulam length$(x) = 1$ if $x = 1$,
Ulam length$(x) = 1 +$ Ulam length$(3x + 1)$ if $x > 1$ and odd,
Ulam length$(x) = 1 +$ Ulam length$(x/2)$ if $x > 1$ and even.

Recursive Ulam Length Function

```
unsigned int ulam_length(unsigned int x){
        if(x <= 1) return 1;    /*base case*/
```

```
        if(x%2 != 0) return 1 + ulam_length(3*x + 1);
        else return 1 + ulam_length(x/2);}
```

Iterative Ulam Length Function

```
unsigned int ulam_length(unsigned int x){
        unsigned int ul = 1;
        while(x > 1){
                if(x%2 != 0) x = 3*x + 1;
                else x = x/2;
                ul++;}
        return ul;}
```

5.2.6. *Greatest Common Divisor*

Another example is one of the first known algorithms to be described in an unambiguously algorithmic manner. This algorithm was known to the ancient Greeks and is given in essentially a recursive form in Euclid, and is often called Euclid's algorithm. It is the algorithm for finding the greatest common divisor of two given positive integers. This number is the largest integer that evenly divides the two given integers and is abbreviated GCD. It is sometimes called the greatest common factor. The algorithm may be understood by studying the code below.

Recursive Greatest Common Divisor Function

```
unsigned int gcd(unsigned int x, unsigned int y){
        if(x == 0) return y;
        return gcd(y%x, x);}
```

It is instructive to consider a trace of gcd function calls for a variety of arguments. A modified gcd with a printf to display a trace of the arguments is given in a complete program below.

GCD with Argument Trace

```
#include <stdio.h>

unsigned int gcd(unsigned int x, unsigned int y){
        printf("%u, %u\n", x, y);
        if(x == 0) return y;
        return gcd(y%x, x);}

void main(){
        printf("%u\n", gcd(91, 156));
        getchar();}
```

Output:

91, 156
65, 91
26, 65
13, 26
0, 13
13

Using the indentation technique previously described to indicate function calls, the sequence of recursive calls may be illustrated in Fig. 5.6.

```
gcd(91, 156)
       gcd(65, 91)
              gcd(26, 65)
                     gcd(13, 26)
                            gcd(0, 13)     (return 13)
```

Fig. 5.6. Call sequence for gcd(91, 156).

5.2.7. *Towers of Hanoi*

The Towers of Hanoi problem is based upon a children's game popular in Europe in the 1800's. The game consisted of several wooden disks of different sizes and three wooden pegs mounted upright on a wooden base. The disks had holes in the middle to allow them to fit on the pegs. To play the game, the disks were first stacked on one peg, largest first and so on in order of size to the smallest. The object was to move all the disks to one of the other pegs, one disk at a time, subject to the rule that no disk could rest on a disk smaller than itself. A manufactured legend was supplied with the game saying that in a temple in Hanoi (or Benares, or some other location) there were similar disks but 40 (or 64) of them, made of gold and stacked on diamond needles. In this temple monks were transferring the disks one at a time, following the rule. When they completed the task, the world would come to an end.

It is not immediately clear that a solution exists for the towers of Hanoi problem. Thinking recursively, however, provides a demonstration that there is a solution. The idea is that transferring the disks from one peg to another involves the use of the third peg to help the transfer. This third peg is called the auxiliary peg. If the pegs are numbered 0, 1, 2, then the problem may be phrased: transfer the disks from peg 0 to peg 2 using peg 1 as the auxiliary. The problem may be generalized, where i, j and k are distinct integers in the range 0 to 2: transfer the disks from peg i to peg k using peg j as auxiliary.

Now the power of recursive thinking becomes apparent if the original problem is reduced to the following: to transfer n disks from peg 0 to peg 2 with peg 1 as auxiliary, first transfer $n-1$ disks from peg 0 to peg 1 using peg 2 as auxiliary. Then move one disk from peg 0 to peg 2. After this, transfer the $n-1$ disks from peg 1 to peg 2 using peg 0 as auxiliary.

There is the remaining question of how the $n-1$ disks are to be transferred. But using recursion, only the base case needs to be addressed. The base case may be chosen as $n = 0$, so now only the explicit method of transferring 0 pegs need to be considered. It is clear that to transfer 0 pegs, one does nothing. This results in the following recursive algorithm for towers of Hanoi, which shows that a solution indeed exists. The word "by" indicates the auxiliary peg:

Pseudocode for Towers of Hanoi

to move n disks from i to k by j:
    if $n = 0$ do nothing; otherwise:
    move $n-1$ disks from i to j by k,
    move 1 disk from i to k;
    move $n-1$ disks from j to k by i.

Using the above pseudocode, a simple proof by mathematical induction shows that the minimum number of moves to transfer n disks is $2^n - 1$.

Proof that at Least $2^n - 1$ Moves are Needed for n Disks

For $n = 0$, $2^0 - 1 = 1 - 1 = 0$ and 0 moves are required.

For $n > 0$, the inductive assumption is that $2^{n-1} - 1$ moves are needed for the transfer of the first $n-1$ disks and $2^{n-1}-1$ moves required for the second $n-1$ disks. One move is required for the lowest disk. Then the moving of all n disks requires (at least) $2^{n-1} - 1 + 1 + 2^{n-1} - 1 = 2{*}2^{n-1} - 1 = 2^n - 1$ moves, QED.

Towers of Hanoi is an Exponential Algorithm (impractical for large n)

The preceding proof shows that the towers of Hanoi algorithm is of order 2^n or, using the Big-O notation to be fully explained in a later chapter, $O(2^n)$. Such algorithms are called exponential. This implies that the algorithm takes twice as long to execute on n disks as on $n-1$ disks. So if it takes 1 second to run on 20 disks, it will take about 2 seconds on 21, about 4 seconds on 22 and so on. 40 disks would require about 2.14 days. 64 disks would require about 557,845 years.

For certain practical problems sometimes the most obvious solution turns out to be an exponential one like towers of Hanoi. In practice, these solutions are to be avoided wherever possible. Sometimes algorithms can be found which give approximate solutions in much less time. These algorithms are to be preferred over exact solutions when the approximation is acceptable.

Below is a complete program for towers of Hanoi, with its output following. The output is a set of instructions for moving four disks from peg 0 to peg 2 by peg 1. The function towers follows the pseudocode given above. The move_disk function may be modified to show a graphic display of disks moving from peg to peg.

Towers of Hanoi Program

```
#include <stdio.h>

void move_disk(int peg1, int peg2){
        printf("Move a disk from peg %d to peg %d.\n", peg1, peg2);}

void towers(int n, int i, int j, int k){
        if(n == 0) return;
        towers(n − 1, i, k, j);
        move_disk(i, k);
        towers(n − 1, j, i, k);}

void main( ){
        towers(4, 0, 1, 2);
        getchar( );}
```

Output

Move a disk from peg 0 to peg 1.
Move a disk from peg 0 to peg 2.
Move a disk from peg 1 to peg 2.
Move a disk from peg 0 to peg 1.
Move a disk from peg 2 to peg 0.
Move a disk from peg 2 to peg 1.
Move a disk from peg 0 to peg 1.
Move a disk from peg 0 to peg 2.
Move a disk from peg 1 to peg 2.
Move a disk from peg 1 to peg 0.
Move a disk from peg 2 to peg 0.
Move a disk from peg 1 to peg 2.
Move a disk from peg 0 to peg 1.
Move a disk from peg 0 to peg 2.
Move a disk from peg 1 to peg 2.

5.2.8. *Reversing a Line of Input*

Recursion may be used to reverse a line of input without using an explicit stack or an array. The idea is to get a character of the input line, save it, display the rest of the line in reverse (recursively), and then display the saved character. The base case occurs at the end of the line when the newline character is encountered. Here is an implementation as the function line_rev included in a complete program.

```
#include <stdio.h>

void line_rev( ){
        char c = getchar( );
        if(c == '\n') return;
        line_rev( );
        putchar(c);}
void main( ){
        line_rev( );
        getchar( );}
```

Input:
abracadabra
Output:
arbadacarba

Displaying an Input Line in Order

The code for line_rev above when given a slight modification displays the line forward instead of backward. If the character *c* is displayed before rather than after the recursive call, the line is displayed forward. Calling the new function line_for, the following code results:

```
#include <stdio.h>

void line_for( ){
        char c = getchar( );
        if(c == '\n') return;
        putchar(c);
        line_for( );}

void main( ){
        line_for( );
        getchar( );}
```

Input:
abracadabra
Output:
abracadabra

5.3. Backtracking

5.3.1. *Introduction*

Backtracking is the exploration of a sequence of potential partial solutions to a problem until a solution is found or a dead end is reached, followed by a regression to an earlier point in the sequence and exploring a new sequence starting from there, and so on. This process may be used to find one or all solutions to a problem, or to verify that no solution exists. Recursion is often used to implement backtracking since the resulting code may be clearer and simpler than in iterative (looping) implementations.

In the exploration of a sequence of potential partial solutions the regression to an earlier point in the sequence and exploring a new sequence starting from there causes a branching in the search for a solution. The sequences thus branch off from one another and form a tree structure. Backtracking is essentially a *depth-first search* (DFS) of this tree, a concept to be explored more fully in Chapter 11. This tree structure is much like a tree of procedure calls as discussed previously. In fact, the tree is of exactly the same form as the tree of recursive function calls when the backtracking is implemented with a recursive function.

Two examples will help to clarify the concepts used in backtracking. The first example is the eight queens problem and some variants of it. The second example is the problem of escaping from a maze.

5.3.2. *The Eight Queens Problem*

The game of chess is played on an 8 by 8 board with 64 squares. There are a number of pieces used in the game. The most powerful one is called a queen. The eight queens problem refers to a configuration which cannot occur in an actual game, but which is based on properties of the queen. The problem is: place 8 queens on the board in such a way that no queen is attacking any other.

The queen attacks any other piece in its row, column, or either of its two diagonals. In Fig. 5.7 shown below, the queen (Q) is attacking all squares marked X. Squares not under attack are marked by –.

			X				X
X			X			X	
	X		X		X		
		X	X	X			
X	X	X	Q	X	X	X	X
		X	X	X			
	X		X		X		
X			X			X	

Fig. 5.7. The eight queens problem.

The power of the queen is such that there is some difficulty in placing all eight queens. It may not even be clear that such a placement is possible, but in fact it is possible, as will be seen later. First consider an easier version of the problem: the four queens problem, in which four queens are to be placed on a 4 by 4 board, none attacking any other. This problem will illustrate some of the basic principles of backtracking.

The Four Queens Problem

Since it is evident that only one queen can occupy each row, the solution may proceed by attempting to place one queen in each row. As a first try the queen is put in the first position in the row that is not under attack. The following Fig. 5.8 indicates this attempt.

The above is a dead end since now no queen may be placed in the third row. But now we backtrack to the second row and place the queen in the next unattacked position and continue,as shown in Fig. 5.9.

But now there is no place to put a queen in the fourth row and a dead end is reached again. Backtracking to the third row, we find no other position for the queen, and so we backtrack to the second row. Here again there

Q			
		Q	

Fig. 5.8. Placing one queen in a row.

Q			
			Q
	Q		

Fig. 5.9. Backtracking and placement.

	Q		
			Q
Q			
		Q	

Fig. 5.10.

		Q	
Q			
			Q
	Q		

Fig. 5.11.

is no remaining position since the queen is already at the end of the row. So backtracking to the first row, we place the queen in the next allowable position and continue. This results in the following Fig. 5.10.

So eventually backtracking yields a solution in the four queens case. Further backtracking can be used to give all solutions. Backtracking to the first row again and placing the queen in the third position yields the solution shown in Fig. 5.11.

This solution is a mirror image of the first and in fact is the only other solution, as can be determined by further backtracking.

So backtracking yields the two solutions of the four queens problem. Consider now the n queens problem in which n queens are to be placed on an n-by-n board, none attacking any other. The goal will be to implement the recursive backtracking algorithm described for the four queens problem but generalized to n queens. The implementation may then be used to find solutions for eight queens or any other number for which machine resources are adequate.

A dynamic array of n^2 characters will be used to represent the board and will be initialized to all '-'. This array, named board, will be treated as an n-by-n array, but in the code we will actually use a one-dimensional array, which is easier to allocate dynamically. Thus we will not be able to write board$[i][j]$ (since board is one-dimensional) and board will be treated as the pointer it actually is and in place of board$[i][j]$ will appear *(board+i*n+j).

A queen is placed by overwriting a board position with 'Q'. Before placing the queen, the code must check whether the upper left diagonal, the column above, and the upper right diagonal are free of other queens and only place the queen if so. Only positions above need to be checked since the queens are placed starting in row 0 and proceeding down to row $n-1$ (success) or a row less than $n-1$ (failure). A queen that was placed needs to be removed before backtracking.

The above ideas are used in the following complete program for the n queens problem.

Program for the n Queens Problem

```
#include <stdio.h>
#include <stdlib.h>

int solution;

void printboard(char * board, int n){
        int i, j;
        puts("\nPress Enter for next solution.\n");
        getchar( );
        printf("\nSolution # %d:\n\n", ++solution);
        for(i = 0; i < n; i++){
                putchar('\t');
                for(j = 0; j < n; j++)
                        printf("%c", *(board +i*n + j));
                putchar('\n');}}

int aboveOK(char * board, int i, int j, int n){
        for(i--; i >= 0; i--)
                if(*(board + i*n + j) == 'Q')
                        return 0;
                return 1;}

int upleftOK(char * board, int i, int j, int n){
        for(i--, j--; i >= 0 && j >= 0; i--, j--)
                if(*(board + i*n + j) == 'Q')
                        return 0;
                return 1;}
```

```
int uprightOK(char * board, int i, int j, int n){
        for(i--, j++; i >= 0 && j < n; i--, j++)
                if(*(board + i*n + j) == 'Q')
                        return 0;
                return 1;}

void putqueen(char * board, int row, int n){
        int j;
        if(row == n){
                printboard(board, n);
                return;}
        for(j = 0; j < n; j++){
                if(upleftOK(board, row, j, n)
                        && aboveOK(board, row, j, n)
                        && uprightOK(board, row, j, n)){
                        *(board + row*n + j) = 'Q';
                        putqueen(board, row+1, n);
                        *(board + row*n + j) = '-';}}}

void initboard(char * board, int n){
        int i;
        for(i = 0; i < n*n; i++)
                *(board + i) = '-';}

void main(){
        char * board;
        int n, c;
        do{
                solution = 0;
                puts("\nEnter size of board:");
                scanf("%d", &n);
                getchar();
                board = (char *)malloc(n*n*sizeof(char));
                initboard(board, n);
                putqueen(board, 0, n);
                free(board);
                printf("\n%d solutions total for %d queens problem.",
                        solution, n);
                puts("\n\nContinue? (y/n):");
                while((c = getchar()) == '\n');
        }while(c == 'y' || c == 'Y');}
```

Partial Output

```
Enter size of board:
4

Press Enter for next solution.

Solution # 1:

    - Q - -
    - - - Q
    Q - - -
    - - Q -

Press Enter for next solution.

Solution # 2:

    - - Q -
    Q - - -
    - - - Q
    - Q - -

two solutions total for 4 queens problem.
Continue? (y/n):
y
Enter size of board:
8

Press Enter for next solution.

Solution # 1:

    Q - - - - - - -
    - - - - Q - - -
    - - - - - - - Q
    - - - - - Q - -
    - - Q - - - - -
    - - - - - - Q -
    - Q - - - - - -
    - - - Q - - - -
```

Press Enter for next solution.

......

Solution # 92:

```
- - - - - - - Q
- - - Q - - - -
Q - - - - - - -
- - Q - - - - -
- - - - - Q - -
- Q - - - - - -
- - - - - - Q -
- - - - Q - - -
```

92 solutions total for 8 queens problem.

Continue? (y/n):
n

5.3.3. *Escape from a Maze*

Another classic backtracking problem is that of escaping from a maze. The main idea is to proceed into the maze until a dead end is reached and then backtrack to an earlier position and continue from there, backtracking again if a dead end is reached, and so on. If an escape route exists, it will eventually be found by this method. In order for the backtracking to be done, the route so far taken must be remembered. This is most easily accomplished by marking the path.

For definiteness let us assume the maze is represented by an n-by-n character array with the following conventions. A path is to be constructed as a sequence of moves from a designated starting position to an exit position (assumed to be on one edge or corner of the array). The only moves allowed are up 1 position, down 1, left 1 and right 1 (to an open position). No diagonal moves are allowed. Open positions will be represented by blanks and blocked positions (hedges) by X's. An E marks the exit position. The path will be marked by asterisks.

Figure 5.12 is an example of a maze represented in the above fashion.

Assuming a starting position of (0, 0), a successful path would be represented as shown in Fig. 5.13.

The path above is a direct path to the maze exit, but a path constructed by backtracking would generally include some branches into dead ends. The implementation of a recursive backtracking solution is left as an exercise.

```
  X X X         X
          X X   X
X X X X   X   X X
X         X     E
  X   X X X   X X
          X     X
X X X X   X X   X
X         X     X
X   X X       X X
```

Fig. 5.12.

```
* X X X         X
* * * * * X X   X
X X X X * X   X X
X   * * * X * * E
  X * X X X * X X
    * * * X * * X
X X X X * X X * X
X       * X * * X
X   X X * * * X X
```

Fig. 5.13.

Exercises

Beginner's Exercises

1. What operation adds an item to the top of a stack?
2. What operation removes an item from the top of a stack?
3. Which stack operation is prohibited on an empty stack?
4. What does LIFO mean?
5. What is a recursive function?
6. Recursion is a form of which of the three basic control structures?
7. For a recursive function to terminate, it must contain at least one _____ case.
8. If a recursive function is called by another function, then calls itself and then calls itself again, how many stack frames for the function are now on the run-time stack?

9. Would a recursive function for a particular task tend to have more or fewer parameters than an equivalent iterative function?
10. How many moves does the towers of Hanoi algorithm make for (a) 10, (b) 20, (c) 30 disks?

Intermediate Exercises

11. In the following sequence, a letter means push that letter on the stack and $*$ means pop a character from the stack. Indicate the sequence of characters resulting from the pops. LAST***IN***FIRST***OUT***STACK***
12. Write a recursive function to compute the nth Fibonacci number F_n. Follow the recurrence relation: $F_0 = 0$, $F_1 = 1$, $F_n = F_{n-1} + F_{n-2}$ for $n > 1$. This will yield a highly inefficient function that should not be used for practical computation.
13. Write an iterative function to compute the nth Fibonacci number.
14. Write a recursive function to compute the binomial coefficient $C(n, k)$ (n and k non-negative) defined by the recurrence relation: $C(n, 0) = 1$, $C(n, n) = 1$, $C(n, k) = C(n-1, k) + C(n-1, k-1)$ for $n > k > 0$. This, as in (12) above, will yield a highly inefficient function that should not be used for practical computation.
15. Write an iterative function to compute the binomial coefficient $C(n, k)$.
16. Write a recursive function to compute Ackermann's function, defined by: $A(0, n) = n + 1$, $A(m, 0) = A(m - 1, 1)$ for $m > 0$, $A(m, n) = A(m - 1, A(m, n - 1))$ for m, $n > 0$. This is a function whose values can be extremely large for small arguments. It can be used to test how well a particular compiler on a given computer implements recursion. Technically it is a recursive function that is not primitive recursive. The definition of primitive recursive is beyond the scope of this work, but Ackermann's function may informally be thought of as an extremely recursive function.

Advanced Exercises

17. Write a program which allows a user to push an integer on a stack, pop an integer and display it, or quit. The user should be able to repeat these choices until quitting. Do not allow the user to pop an empty stack.
18. Repeat problem 17 but with strings in place of integers.
19. Modify any of the recursive functions to display the recursive call sequence with proper indentation, such as the following for gcd.

```
gcd(91, 156)
        gcd(65, 91)
                gcd(26, 65)
                        gcd(13, 26)
                                gcd(0, 13)
```

20. Write a recursive function queencount(int n) which returns the number of solutions for the n queens problem.
21. Modify the towers of Hanoi program to allow user input of the number of disks and to repeat until the user chooses to quit.
22. Modify the solution of problem 21 to allow suppression of printing and timing of the execution of the towers function as called from main. Determine the number of disks that can be processed in one second on your computer. Investigate timings for higher numbers of disks.
23. Write a program which uses either of the ulam_length functions to find and display the number with the maximum Ulam length from 1 up to a user-supplied input.
24. Write a program which times the execution of finding the number with the maximum Ulam length from 1 up to a user-supplied input using each ulam_length function. The program should display the times for the recursive version and the times for the iterative version.
25. Implement a recursive solution to the maze escape problem. The maze should be read from a text file that has the starting coordinates and size of the maze on the first line and the character representation of the maze in subsequent lines. The maze array should be displayed when a path is found or when it is determined that no path exists.
26. Modify the solution of problem 25 to display all successful paths.

Chapter 6

Queues

ANGELA GUERCIO
Hiram College, USA
guercioa@hiram.edu

6.1. Introduction

A user can build a wide variety of data types, and if we consider them, we can distinguish between data types that have a *low level of abstraction* and that have a *higher level of abstraction*. The *low level of abstraction* data types are predefined in most of the programming languages, such as the arrays, the records, and the pointers. These data types are used to build almost all the other data types that have a *higher level of abstraction*.

In this chapter we study one of the abstract data types at a higher level of abstraction: the **queue**.

The queues are built thanks to the use of some predefined abstract data types such as arrays and pointers, and are one of the abstract data types that have a linear structure. The simplest example of linear structure is a ***list***, a very common and important kind of structure. It is a very natural structure and many examples of lists can be found in the daily life as well as in computing. The phonebook directory is a list of people having a telephone number. When we need a specific phone number we search the list for the data. Other examples of lists are the teams participating in a championship, the airplanes ready to take off, the pharmaceutical products in commerce, the characters in a text line of a file, the courses to take for a university degree, the steps to follow for a recipe, the jobs to be executed, the doctors of an hospital.

6.2. The Concept of Queue

The concept of line explains very clearly the concept of a queue. Have you ever been in line in a bank or in a super market? That line is a queue. When you enter the line you put yourself at the end of the line, "*the tail*," and the person who is at the front of the line, "*the head*," is the next who will be served as soon as the cashier is available. The person will exit the queue and will be served. The next person who will enter the line will put himself behind you and so on. In the meanwhile the queue is served and the next person at the head of the line will exit the queue and will be served. While the queue is served, you will move towards the head of the line since each person that is served will be removed from the head of the queue. You will be, then, in the middle of the line waiting patiently for all the persons in front of you to be served and will exit the line one by one in the order they entered the queue. Finally you will reach the head of the line and you will exit the queue and be served. The behavior of this line is said a ***first-in-first-out (FIFO)*** behavior, that is the person that is removed from the line is the one that entered earliest the line. This behavior is very useful, in any case the order of arrival has to be maintained. Example of queues can be seen in the everyday life, but are common in computing applications as well. For example, processes or threads may be scheduled to run on the CPU in FIFO order. These processes may be stored by the operating system using a queue data structure. I/O requests are queued for service on a disk in a multi-user time-shared server. The I/O requests have to be served in a FIFO order. Messages are queued in a buffer in a client–server communication while waiting for the server to be available to receive the message.

Summarizing, let us consider a finite set of data of type T, a ***queue*** is an abstract data type which exhibits a first-in-first-out behavior (Fig. 6.1).

The FIFO behavior contrasts the ***last-in-first-out (LIFO)*** behavior, which is typical of the stack abstract data type. In the LIFO behavior the last element inserted in the list is the first to be removed. Even though such example of list seems a little awkward in daily life, it has

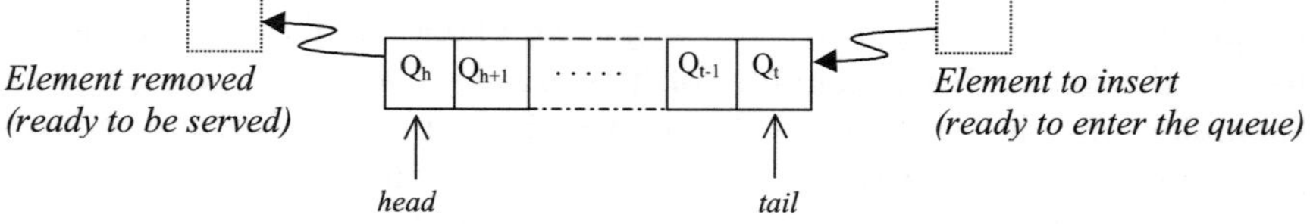

Fig. 6.1. The queue data type.

a great importance in computing. In fact, procedure calls are handled by using stacks to keep track of the sequence of calls and of returning points. Many stack-based architectures have been built and have machine level instructions that operate hardware stacks. The discussion about the notion of stack data type and its implementation is covered in a different chapter.

6.3. An Array-Based Implementation of a Queue

One way to implement the FIFO behavior is by using the array abstract data type to indicate the list of elements of the queue. Suppose a secretary works in a medical office for a doctor who sees each day, no more than 15 patients. The secretary has a magnetic table with fifteen slots in which she writes the names of the patients in order of arrival. The magnetic table can be abstractly implemented by using an array and the queue of the patients can be simulated on it.

```
/* definition of the abstract data type of the queue */
char list_of_patients[15];
```

In the morning, when the office opens, there are no patients. No patients have been inserted in the table nor removed yet from it. These specifications are described by the following instructions.

```
/* initialization of the queue pointers              */
/* the pointer to the head of the queue is empty */
int in = 0;
/* the pointer to the tail of the queue is empty   */
int out = 0;
```

As soon as the first patient arrives, the secretary asks for the name of the patient and diligently writes the name in the queue.

```
/* code for insertion of an element in a queue */
printf("Good morning. May I have your name please? The doctor will
be available as soon as possible."\n);
scanf("%s\n", Name);
list_of_patients[in] = Name;
/* one cell of the table has been occupied then the next
   available cell is pointed by in+1 */
in = in + 1;
```

The second patient arrives and the same procedure is executed. Finally, the doctor arrives and serves the first patient. The patient is removed from the queue and served

```
patient = list_of_patients[out];
out = out + 1
/* serve(patient) */
. . .
```

Let us consider now all the possible limit situations that can occur.

Suppose all the 15 patients showed up and another patient enters and asks if he can see the doctor. The nurse turns him down because she has no more space available in her table.

How is this situation expressed in code? What has happened is the value of in has reached the upper limit of the space available in the queue. This is tested by the following conditional statement:

```
if (in == 15)
{
        printf("the queue is full\n");
        return;
}
```

Suppose now that the doctor has served his patients rather quickly, and the waiting room is empty, while waiting for the next patient to come.

How is this situation coded? Testing for the empty queue means testing the values of the pointers in and out. When (out >= in) then the queue must be empty because we are trying to remove more items than already inserted. The following conditional statement checks for the emptiness of the queue

```
if (out >= in)
{
        printf("Empty queue\n");
        return;
}
```

The complete algorithm of the agenda of the secretary is shown in the following.

```
void secretary (void) {
      /* definition of the abstract data type of the queue */
      char list_of_patients[15];

      /* initialization of the queue pointers              */
      /* the pointer to the head of the queue is empty     */
      int in = 0;
      /* the pointer to the tail of the queue is empty     */
      int out = 0;
```

```
    for (;;) { /* Loop until day is done */
        /* Check for empty queue */
        if (out >= in)
        {
            printf("Empty queue\n");
        }
        /* code for insertion of an element in a queue */
        printf("Good morning. May I have your name please?",
        "The doctor will be available as soon as possible."\n);
        scanf("%s\n", Name);
        /* See if day is done */
        if (!stcmp(Name, "End of day!") /* Time to quit! */
            return;
        /* Otherwise, process patient */
        list_of_patients[in] = Name;
        /* one cell of the table has been occupied then the
        next available cell is pointed by in+1 */
        in = in + 1;
        /* Check for full queue */
        if (in == 15)
        {
            printf("the queue is full\n");
            break;
        }
        patient = list_of_patients[out];
        out = out + 1;
        /* Service the patients */
        serve(list_of_patients);
    }
}
```

The use of the array-based implementation of a queue is generally referred as the *static implementation* of the queue. This definition is due to the fact that the allocation of the elements of the queue in memory is sequential and the memory is allotted immediately after the declaration of the array. The removal or the insertion of elements in the queue does not cause memory reallocation of the queue, and neither enlarges or reduces the numbers of words allocated. The two indices of the array, in and out, play the role of the pointers of the structure and the code above implemented for the insertion and the removal of the elements of the queue, simulates the FIFO behavior of the queue.

6.4. Pointers

A variable, record (a struct in C), or an array used in a program has an associated *address* in memory. This address (expressed in bytes) is the location where the value (or values for records and arrays) are stored when the program runs. The actual location will vary from one program execution to another (that is, the variable may be stored in a different location in the RAM memory of your computer), however most modern operating systems avoid this problem through the use of *virtual memory systems.* Using this method the (fixed) virtual location is translated at the run time of the program to the (varying) physical location. The details are hidden from the programmer by the operating system and the hardware. The (virtual) location for variables, records and arrays is fixed by the compiler.

Notice that records and arrays will occupy more than one memory location. This is true, even for many simple variables — an integer variable typically uses four bytes of memory. The address of the data structure is the first byte occupied by the data structure. By knowing the type of the data structure we can find out exactly which addresses (bytes of memory) are occupied by the data structure. This is because each data type has a fixed size (e.g. four bytes four integers and 40 bytes for arrays of length 10 of integers).

We can refer to a variable or data structure in one of two ways, either using a symbolic name or using its (numerical) address. The second of these methods refers to the use of *pointers.* Consider what happens when we have an assignment statement like the following.

```
int a, c;
. . .
a = c;
```

The compiler converts the symbolic names a and c to their addresses — suppose they are 101 and 135. At run time the (integer) values stored in the four bytes beginning at memory location 135 are copied to the four bytes beginning at memory location 101. A somewhat more complex process is used for access to array elements as in the following example.

```
int a, c[9];
. . .
a = c[2];
```

Once again the compiler converts the symbolic names a and c to their addresses — suppose again that they are 101 and 135. At run time the location of element c[2] is found by multiplying the number of the element by the size of the element and adding it to the beginning location of the array (remember that in C arrays begin with element 0). In this case the address we want is $2^*4 + 135 = 143$.

The calculation for the field of a struct is a little bit more complicated. The location is calculated by adding up all sizes of the fields that precede the one we are looking for and adding this amount to the address of the struct.

Usually it is more convenient for programmers to use the symbolic names of variables (which, good programming style dictates, should have meaningful names). The use of pointers, however, can lead to data structures that are more complex than arrays and records, and these in turn can lead to more efficient implementations of data structures such as queues.

Consider three integer variables x, y and z. Suppose that x is stored at location 1000, y at 1004, and z at 1008 as shown in Fig. 6.2.

In C, we declare a pointer to an integer as follows.

```
int *myPtr;
```

The * operator in front of the variable name myPtr tells the compiler that myPtr is a pointer to an object of type int. Pointers to other types are declared similarly. What this means is that the value of myPtr will be a memory location (not the value of the integer stored at that location).

We need to define one more operator in order to work with pointers. That is the & operator. This operator is used with a variable and returns the address in memory of that variable. So we can have an assignment like the following.

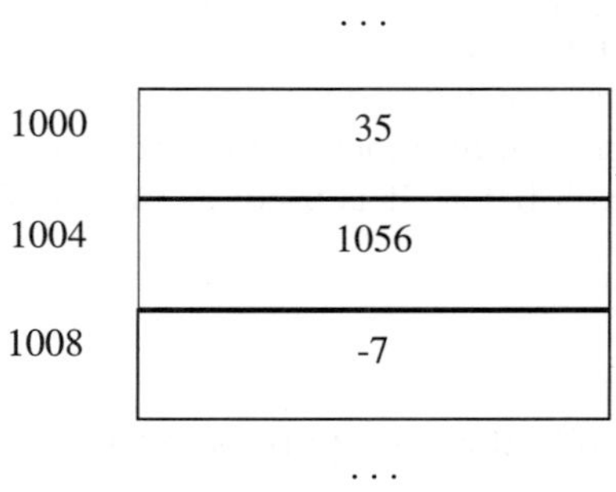

Fig. 6.2. Variables in memory.

```
int *myPtr;
int x, y, z;
. . .
myPtr = &x;
. . .
```

Applying the & operator to x gives the address of x (1000) in this case and assigns it to myPtr. This operation is on x is called ***dereferencing***. We can get to the value stored at that location by using the * operator as follows.

```
y = *myPtr;
```

The result of the above assignment is to give y the value 35. If we leave out the * operator the assignment will give y the address of x (1000) which will not generate an error, but is probably not the result that we wanted.

The * and & operators may only be used with variables or data structures, not with literals (e.g. 5, 'a', "string"). The * operator is used only with variables declared as pointers. Attempting to use it with a variable that has not been declared as a pointer will almost certainly cause the program to crash. This operator is used in expressions and should not appear on the left-hand side of an assignment statement. The & operator is typically used with variables which have *not* been declared as pointers. The most common use of this operator is to assign a value to a pointer variable (as above).

It is important to understand that the assignment statement given above with the & operator on the right-hand side of the assignment does not result in two values of 35 being stored in two different locations in memory, instead it results in two different references to the same value (35 in this case) in memory. As a consequence if we assign (for example) 40 to *myPtr, the value of x will be changed to 40 as well since both *myPtr and x refer to the same location in memory.

A pointer that does not have any value is said to be null. It is usually considered good programming practice to initialize pointers to null and to check if a pointer is null before it is used, as in the following code.

```
. . .
int *myPtr, x;
. . .
*myPtr = NULL; /* Initialize myPtr to be NULL */
. . .
if (myPtr != NULL) { /* Check if NULL before using */
. . .
```

Pointers need to be used with caution since if an incorrect memory address is referenced (e.g. using a NULL pointer results in accessing memory location 0) the program will probably crash. Even worse, languages like C will allow you to accidentally overwrite other memory locations using pointers. This is easy to do in C due to the loose type checking. Such errors can result in difficult to track errors since the effect may only be seen much later. Suppose, for example, we have a pointer to a character. The character data type requires only one byte. Now if we assign an integer value to this pointer (something which C allows), the following three bytes get overwritten. The result of this will only be seen when we attempt to use whatever was stored in those three bytes sometime later. For these and for other reasons, some languages (e.g. Java) do not allow the use of pointers.

6.5. Linked Lists

Often when we are designing a program we need to process lists of data items: patients; students; homework grades; etc. Sometimes we will know in advance exactly how many items will be in the list (e.g. we are processing the 100 best-selling albums). Other times we do not know in advance, or, even if we do know in advance, the program may be run many times with different numbers of items in the list each time. When we know exactly how many items are in the list then it can be used.

The **linked list** data structure is useful whenever we do not know *a priori* how many items will be in the list (otherwise we could use an array). The linked list data structure also simplifies inserting an element into the middle of an ordered list or deleting an element from a list. The former implemented as an array forces us to move (shift to the right) about half of the elements of the array — a costly operation, especially if the array is very large.

Likewise, deleting an element from the middle of an array implementation of an ordered list causes us to move (shift to the left) about half the elements of the array. An alternative for deletion is to change the value of the array element to some nonlegal value to signal that the element is invalid (or empty). This results in "holes" in the list that can be inefficient.

The elements of a linked list are records with fields for the elements being stored in the list plus one extra element that points to the next element in the list. In C, the element is a **struct** with one field that points to a **struct** of the same type (the next element in the list). An example of a linked list structure is shown in Fig. 6.3.

Imagine that we want to have a list of coordinates (x and y positions). We can declare a struct type for the elements of the list as follows.

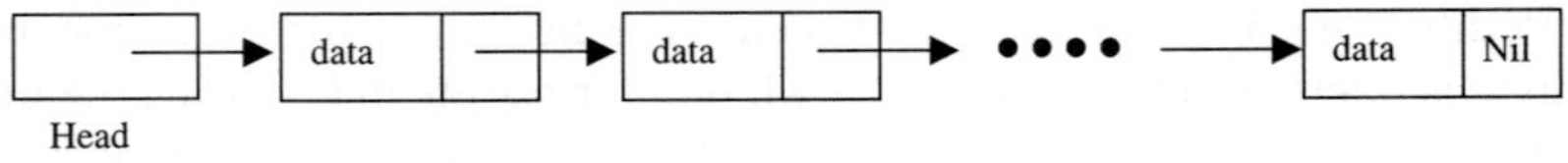

Fig. 6.3. The general structure of a circular queue.

```
typedef struct COORD_LIST_ELEMENT { /* An element of the linked
list */
      int x, y; /* The x and y coordinates */
      struct COORD_LIST_ELEMENT next; /* Next element in the list
*/
} COORD_LIST_ELEMENT;
```

Minimally, we need to keep track of the front of the list. Given the previous definition, we can declare an element to point to the first element in the list. Since the list is previously empty, we initialize the pointer to NULL.

```
COORD_LIST_ELEMENT* head_of_list = NULL; /* Create an empty
list */
```

Consider functions to add and delete elements from the list. Assuming that we are not interested in maintaining an ordered list, the easiest way to insert an element in the list is to add it at the front of the list.

```
int add_element_to_list(COORD_LIST_ELEMENT* head_of_list,
                        COORD_LIST_ELEMENT* to_be_added) {

      to_be_added->next = head_of_list->next;
      /* The new element points to the former head of the list */

      head_of_list->next = to_be_added;
      /* The new element is now the head of the list */

      return(1); /* Success */
}
```

Deleting an element from the list is a little bit more difficult since we must search for the element starting from the beginning of the list and find it before we can delete it. The following function searches for the element containing a given coordinate in the list.

```
int find_element (COORD_LIST_ELEMENT to_be_found,
                  COORD_LIST_ELEMENT* position,
                  COORD_LIST_ELEMENT* head_of_list) {
```

```
    COORD_LIST_ELEMENT* temp;

    temp = head_of_list;
    if (temp == NULL) return(0); /* Empty list */

    for ( ; temp->next != NULL; temp = temp->next) {
        if (temp->next.x == to_be_found.x &&
            temp->next.y == to_be_found.y)
            break;
    }

    if (temp->next != NULL) { /* Element found */
        position = temp; /* position->next is the found element
*/
        return(1); /* Success */
    } else return(0); /* Failure — not found */
}
```

We can now use this function to delete an element from a linked list as shown in the following code.

```
int delete_element_from_list (COORD_LIST_ELEMENT
                              to_be_deleted,
                              COORD_LIST_ELEMENT*
                              head_of_list) {

    COORD_LIST_ELEMENT* temp, temp2;

    if (find_element(to_be_deleted, temp, head_of_list) == 0)
        return(0); /* No deletion — element not in list */
    else {
        temp2 = temp; /* Remember element to be deleted */
        temp->next = temp->next->next; /* Delete the element */
        free(temp2->next); /* Release deleted element memory */
        return(1); /* Element deleted */
    }
}
```

In the following section we will show how to use pointers to implement queue operations using pointers.

6.6. Pointers and Their Use in a Queue

Either ordered or not ordered, this simple structure finds many applications in the user life. The elements of a list have something in common and each element of the list can be reached as if they were attached in a long chain. Once again, note the advantages of using linked lists to implement the queue data structure:

- We do not have to know beforehand how big the queue will be. We just allocate another element on the fly when we need to add to the queue.
- Insertion of an element in a queue (the enqueue operation) can be done in a single step. If we keep the elements in order in an array, we have to shift the *whole* array *each* time we enqueue an element!
- Dequeue (removal from a queue is not as bad with an array. We can just decrease a counter, which indicates end of queue.

Of course, we can also implement a queue ADT without having access to the linked list ADT. In the following paragraphs we give the code for the Enqueue and Dequeue operations. Note that in this implementation we insert at the end of the list and delete from the front of the list. This is just an implementation detail!

```
lR * Enqueue (lR *lR1, int Value) { /* The Enqueue operation */
/* lR1 is a pointer to the Queue */
      lR *lR2 = lR1;
      /* start at the beginning ... */
      /* look for the end */
      if (lR1 != NULL) {
       while (lR1->nextRec != NULL)
              lR1 = lR1->nextRec;
       lR1->nextRec =
                        (lR *)malloc(sizeof(LR));
       /* Now fill in the new element */
       lR1 = lR1->nextRec;
       lR1->nextRec = NULL;
       lR1->myValue = Value;
       return lR2;
      }
      else {
       /* The queue was empty ! */
       lR1 = (lR *)malloc(sizeof(lR));
       lR1->nextRec = NULL;
       lR1->myValue = Value;
       return lR1;
      }
}
```

```
lR * Dequeue (lR *lR1) { /* The Dequeue operation */
    lR * lR2;
    /* Skip the element */
    lR2 = lR1->nextRec;
    /* We need to free it so we don't */
    /* leak memory! */
    free(lR1);
    return(lR2);
}
```

6.7. Variations of Queues

Queues have very interesting and useful applications in real life. They have been used, for example, in operating system applications such as scheduling, where in a multiprogramming system the order of the processes that are ready to run, has to be determined by the system. They are used in helping the communication between processes when several messages are sent from one process to another. They are used in a multiuser system to coordinate the list of user processes that use the I/O facilities, such as the printer. And a very large set of daily life problems can be solved with the use of a queue, look for example at the situation described in the previous paragraphs.

While some problems can be easily solved with the use of regular queues, (the previously described queues) there are some problems, which can benefit from the use of simple variations of the queue. In this paragraph, we present the most interesting and common variations of the queues.

Imagine being in a delivery office where two employees work. The first one takes the orders and retrieves the ordered object from the warehouse while the second employee prepares the delivery of the order by packing the object and mailing it. The two employees work in two different parts of the office separated by a grid of slots that are filled by the first employee with the retrieved object and are emptied by the second employee by removing and delivering the object. The orders as well as the deliveries are served in their arrival order. Only a constant and limited number of slots are available. Every morning the first employee starts his work by filling the first slot, then the second slot, the third and so on. The delivery man, as well, starts every morning by removing the object put by the first employee from the first slot and then from the second slot and so on. The employees guarantee that each order is served according to their arrival. When they close the office at night, all the slots are empty.

In this example, the use of queue is essential to satisfy the specification relative to the order in which the requests must be served, but there is an interesting problem to observe. We have a fixed number of slots. What does the first employee do when he has filled the last slot available? Since the number of slots is physically limited, this situation is realistic. There are two options, either he will stop for the day (not a good solution from the business point of view!) or he can go back and start filling the first slot again if it is empty. In other words the first employee can go back "in circle" and start filling the empty slots that are available, still in order. This circular behavior does not alter the correct sequence of the orders to be served since we suppose that the delivery employee has been working and must have emptied some of the slots in order, starting from the first. Of course, if the delivery employee has not worked at all, the first employee will not find any empty slot since the queue is full. Then he can rest for a while until the other employee starts working and delivers some orders, making room in the slots for the other incoming orders. The deliveryman, on the other side, can rest if no orders are available, that is when all the slots are empty (empty queue).

This example requires a variation of the queue that is called ***circular queue***.

The essential condition for the existence of a circular queue is a finite constant number of elements available. In general purpose queues, implemented as a linked list, the number of elements can be considered unlimited, since there is always the possibility to allocate one more element in memory and then enlarge the queue. We will show that it is possible to implement a circular queue both with an array structure as well as with a linked list structure.

Let us consider a circular queue implemented by using an array of length n, which contains at most n elements of type T.

In the circular queue (Fig. 6.4), the data enters the queue from the tail of the queue and in removed from the head of the queue. The two indices, *head* and *tail* are used to keep track of the retrieval point and the insertion point of the queue, respectively. When a data is removed from the head,

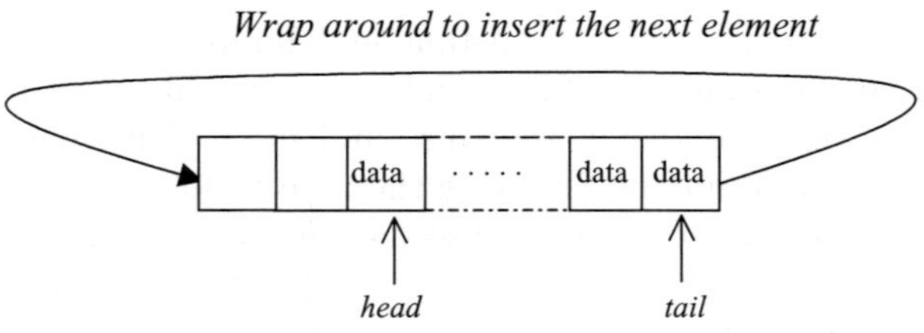

Fig. 6.4. A circular queue implemented with an array.

the *head* increases. When the *head* reaches n then *head* is set to 0 (wrap around). This is obtained by using the instruction:

$$\text{head} = (\text{head} + 1)\ \%\ \text{n}\,;$$

where % in the module operation. Analogously, when a new data is inserted, the *tail* is increased. When the *tail* reaches the value n, then we wrap around and *tail* gets the value 0 thanks to the instruction:

$$\text{tail} = (\text{tail} + 1)\ \%\ \text{n}\,;$$

A counter variable counter, which keeps track of the number of elements in the queue, is added to the program. Variable counter is set to zero at the beginning when the queue is empty, and it is increased when an element is inserted into the queue, decreased if an element is dequeued. If the queue is full, then counter = n; if the queue is empty, then counter = 0.

The variable counter is vital to know how many elements are in the queue. In fact, if head == tail == 0 is the instantiation of the variables, the queue is full when tail == head, and the queue is empty when head == tail. Without the counter variable there is no possibility to understand if the condition occurred because the queue is full or because the queue is empty. Serious consequences could be produced by this situation. A solution that does not use an extra variable is possible and is left as an exercise.

If the queue is implemented with a linked list, only a fixed number of elements have to be available. The general structure of the circular list looks like the one depicted in Fig. 6.5.

The useful feature of a circular list is that you can start traversing the entire queue beginning at any node instead of beginning necessarily from the front.

Suppose that I now want to look for an element in a circular queue and my queue is implemented as a linked list. Starting from my current position, I go forward testing all the elements for equality. I wrap around and check all the other elements that are in the queue. I stop either when I have visited the whole queue, a situation that occurs when I return to the starting point, or when I find the element.

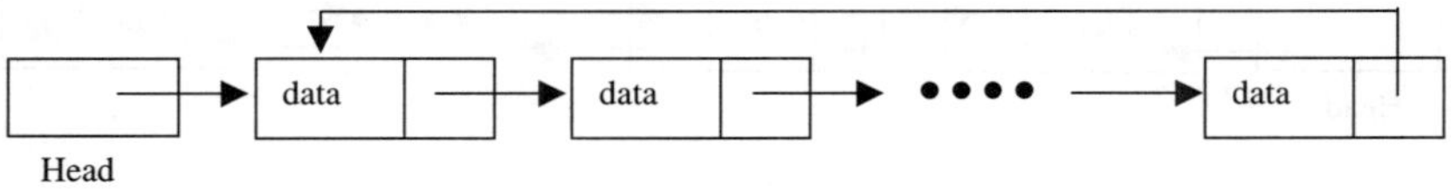

Fig. 6.5. The general structure of a circular queue.

If the queue is full and the element is in the queue and it is my unlucky day, the element I am looking for could be the last element I visit which is, in this case, the element immediately to the left of the element in the position I was at as soon as I started my search. In other words I went all the way through the queue before finding my element! Is there any way I could have done this search any better? Since the pointers of the queue go only in one direction, there is no way I could have done this differently. I had to follow the pointers all the way until I reached the element! But what if I had the opportunity to go in the opposite direction and inspect the queue backward? That would be a great opportunity because I could have discovered my element in just one step! This problem suggests another variation of a queue: a doubly linked list queue.

A doubly linked queue is a list with two pointers: *next*, which points forward to the next element in the queue and *previous*, which points backward to the previous element in the queue. In this case, there are two **Nil** pointers to indicate the end of the queue.

The doubly linked queue can be declared as a struct type as follows.

```
typedef struct DOUBLY_LIST_ELEMENT { /* An element of the doubly linked list */
        int element; /* The data element */
        struct DOUBLY_LIST_ELEMENT next; /* Next element in the doubly linked list */
        struct DOUBLY_LIST_ELEMENT previous; /* Previous element in the doubly linked list */
        } DOUBLY_LIST_ELEMENT;
```

The general structure of a doubly linked queue is shown in Fig. 6.6.

The step from a doubly linked queue to a doubly circular linked queue is trivial at this point. The doubly circular linked queue combines all the properties of a doubly linked queue with the one of a circular queue. Figure 6.7 shows the general structure of a doubly circular linked queue.

Another example of queue variation is the priority queue. A **priority queue** is another special queue in which besides the value and pointer, each element has a non-negative *priority* (0 is the lowest priority).

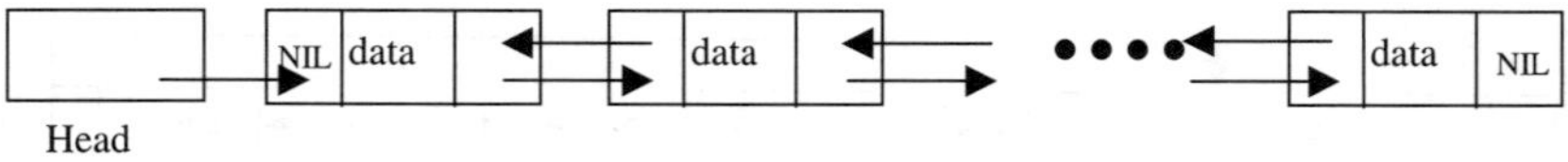

Fig. 6.6. The general structure of a doubly linked queue.

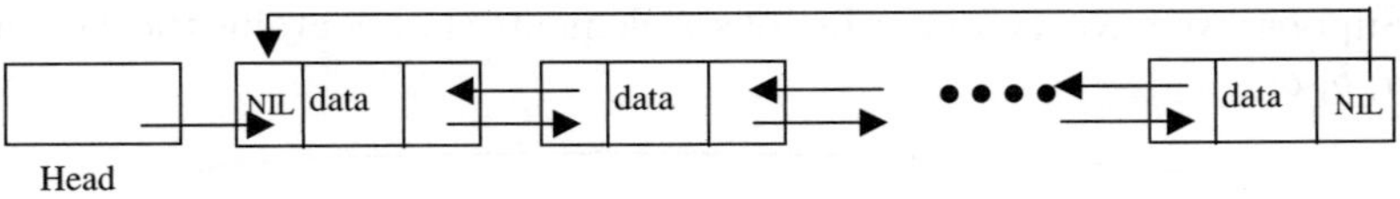

Fig. 6.7. The general structure of a doubly circular queue.

The insertions in the queue are made at the position immediately after the element in the queue with equal or higher priority.

The dequeue operation returns the highest priority element (the one closest to the front).

It can be seen that priority queues combine the properties of queues (LIFO) and ordered lists (by priority). High priority elements are retrieved before lower priority elements in a priority queue while among elements having the *same* priority, LIFO is the rule used.

Priority queues find application in many different areas. For example, priority queues can be used by the CPU scheduler component of an operating system to allow higher priority jobs to run before lower priority ones.

Exercises

Beginner's Exercises

1. Compute the value of f and g in the following code fragment and correct the illegal statements, if there are any.

```
int a = 3;
int b = 7;
int c;
int *f;
int *g;

f = &a;
g = &b
g = a;
c = f;
. . .
```

2. Define an ADT that describes an airline reservation system.
3. Describe how you could implement a linked list using an array.

4. Suppose we have a circular list of six elements that contains the elements *a*, *b*, *c*.

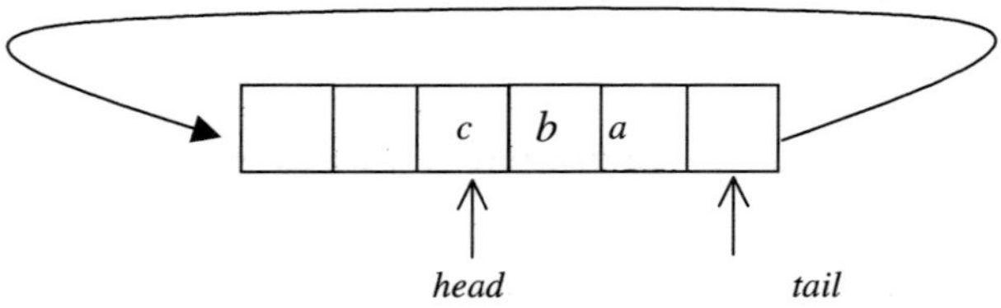

Show the state of the queue after each of the following operations are performed.

Dequeue(Q);
Dequeue(Q);
Enqueue(*d*, Q);
Enqueue(*e*, Q);
Dequeue(Q);
Enqueue(*a*, Q);
Enqueue(*b*, Q);
Dequeue(Q);
Dequeue(Q);

Intermediate Exercises

5. Define a queue to describe the simulation of a line at the cashier of a supermarket. Assume that we have a single queue of customers and 20 cashiers. When a cashier becomes available, the person at the front of the line is removed and it is served. A customer takes 5 minutes to be served. Every 2 minutes a new customer arrives at the line. Compute how many customers have been served before the queue contains 50 customers in line.
6. Give the complete implementation of the linked list ADT using pointers and structs.
7. Give the pseudocode for the Dequeue operation using linked lists.

Advanced Exercises

8. Propose an alternative solution, other than the one used in Sec. 6.7, to the problem of distinguishing between a full queue and an empty one in a circular queue.
9. Implement the priority queue ADT. Use your implementation to develop a job scheduling algorithm.

Chapter 7

Lists

RUNHE HUANG* and JIANHUA MA†

Hosei University, Japan
**rhuang@k.hosei.ac.jp*
†*jianhua@k.hosei.ac.jp*

In this chapter, two kinds of linked lists are introduced, i.e. singly linked lists and doubly linked lists. Through implementations of stacks, queues, and deques with singly linked lists and doubly linked lists, we study or review other data structures as well. Taking student data as an example, we provide readers many functions and two complete source programs in C.

7.1. Introduction

In this section, we introduce some basic concepts related to lists so as to make you understand what is a structure and how to define a structure, what is a node and how to define a node, what is a link and what is a linked list.

First, let us explain what is a structure.

> A structure is a collection of elements each of which can be of different types.

Taking student data as an example and assuming it includes student name, student identity number, and student height, we can define student data as a structure as shown below rather than as individual separated data items.

```
typedef    struct s_data{
           char student_name[14];
           int student_ID;
           float student_height;
}STUDENT_DATA;
```

As we can see that student name has a data type of **char**, student identity number has a data type of **int**, and student height has a data type of **float**. The structure, **STUDENT_DATA**, is a collection of three different types of data elements. Now, we can use **STUDENT_DATA** as a variable type to define variables. **studentA** and ***pstudent_data** are variables that are of **STUDENT_DATA** type.

```
STUDENT_DATA studentA, *pstudent_data;
```

It is possible to create arrays of structures since a structure is a data object. An array of a structure is declared by preceding the array name with the structure **typedef** name.

```
STUDENT_DATA student[36];
```

Indexing into an array is not as efficient as using a pointer to an array by assigning the pointer to the base of the array as follows.

```
STUDENT_DATA student[36], *pstudent_data;
        pstudent_data = (STUDENT_DATA*)
                        malloc(sizeof (STUDENT_DATA));
        pstudent_data = &student[0];        //base = &student[0];
```

As we can see that one of the disadvantages of using an array of structures is that the size of the array has to be fixed as shown in Fig. 7.1. When the number of structures to be used is somehow uncertain or may be changing dynamically during runtime, there is a difficulty to allocate memory to an array. The solution to this problem is to use a linked list.

What is a linked list?

> A linked list is a chain of self-referential structures that are linked from one to another.

Taking the same example of student data, we can define the structure of student data in a linked list as follows.

```
typedef  struct s_data{
         char student_name[14];
         int student_ID;
         float student_height;
         struct s_data *next;
} STUDENT_DATA;
```

Where, **next** is a pointer, it is also a so-called link or a reference. Since the structure, **s_data**, contains the pointer **(next)** to the instance of itself, it is usually called as a self-referential structure. Different from an array of structure, a linked list is able to allocate memory for new structures

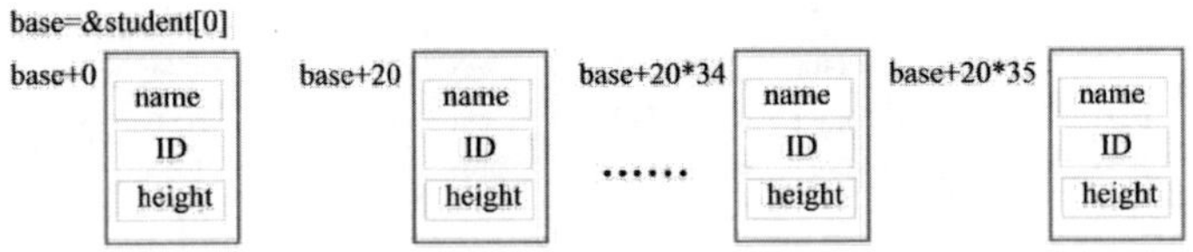

Fig. 7.1. An array of structures in memory.

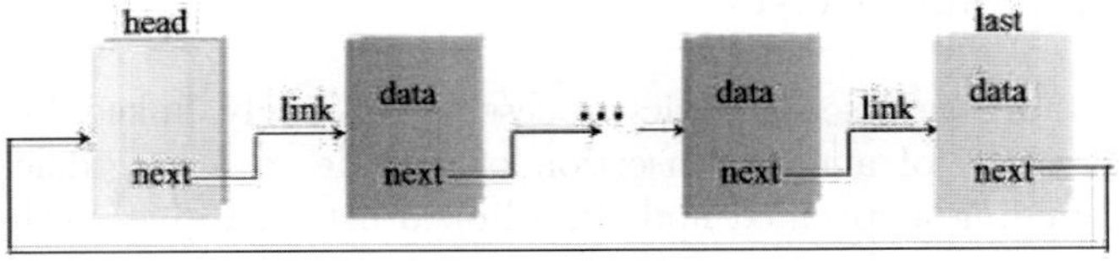

Fig. 7.2. A linked list.

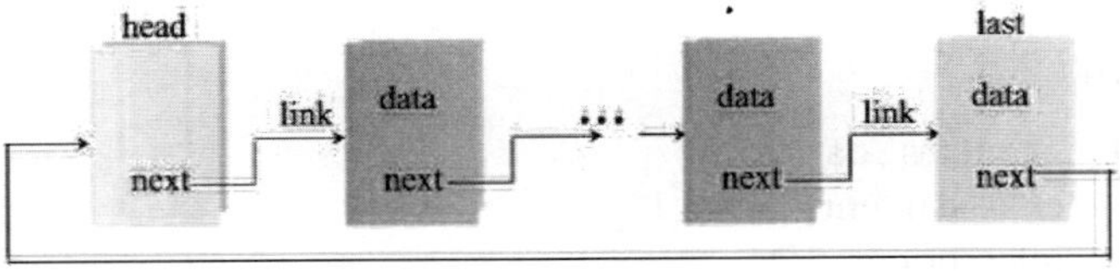

Fig. 7.3. A circular linked list.

as needed using the runtime library routine *mallloc()* and *calloc()* in C. Obviously, the advantages of a linked list over an array of structures are that it can grow and shrink in size and provide flexibility of rearranging the items efficiently.

In a linked list, each structure contains data items and a reference/references to the next structure/structures in the list. Such a structure is called a **node**. If every node in a linked list has only one link to the next node and the last node has a null next reference, which indicates the termination of the list, the linked list is called as a singly linked list as shown in Fig. 7.2.

If the last node has a link to the head node instead of a null reference, the linked list is called as a circular linked list as shown in Fig. 7.3.

If every node has two links, one is to the next node and the other is to the preceding node in the list. The linked list is called as a doubly linked list. For a doubly linked list, traversals are in either direction. The ending node in either direction has a link to null reference as shown in Fig. 7.4.

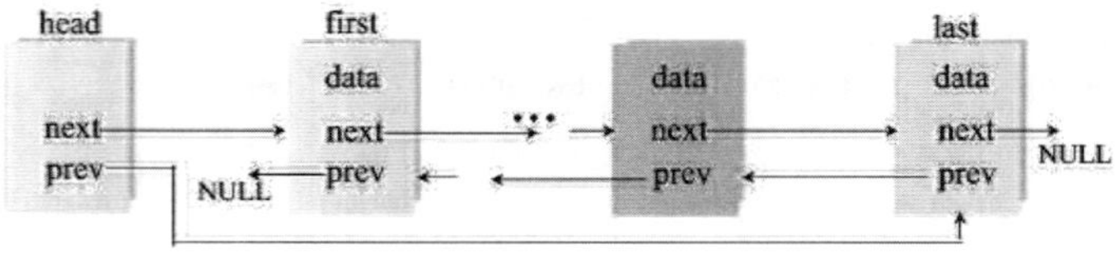

Fig. 7.4. A doubly linked list.

7.2. Singly Linked Lists

In this session, we discuss basic processing on singly linked lists, which includes creation of a node, insertion of a node to a list, deletion of a node, and finding a specified node in a linked list, and gives each function and implementation in C, and finally provides a complete source code of an example in Appendix 7.1. Let us take student data as an example again and define STUDENT_DATA structure in the file, **st_data.h**. For implementation convenience, all necessary global declarations, library files and header files are included in the file, **header.h**.

st_data.h

```
typedef   struct s_data{
          char student_name[14];
          int student_ID;
          float student_height;
          struct s_data *next;
}STUDENT_DATA;
```

header.h

```
#include <stdio.h>
#include <stdlib>
#include <malloc.h>
#include "st_data.h"
static STUDENT_DATA *head;
```

To create a singly linked list node, it is in fact to allocate memory for a node structure using *malloc()* and return a pointer to this memory area. The link **(next)** of the node initially points to a null reference.

```
#include "header.h"
STUDENT_DATA *create_a_node() {
      STUDENT_DATA *p;
```

```
4.      p = (STUDENT_DATA *)malloc(sizeof(STUDENT_DATA));
5.      if (p == NULL) {
6.          printf("create_a_list_of_student_data: failed.¥n");
7.          exit(1);
8.      }
9.      p->next = NULL;
10.     return p;
11. }
```

Where, line 3 declares **p** as a STUDENT_DATA structure pointer, line 4 allocates memory to the node **p**, lines 5–8 check if the node **p** is correctly created, line 9 assigns a NULL reference to the link of the node **p**, and line 10 returns the pointer **p** to the allocated memory area.

To add a node, insert a node at the end of a singly linked list. That is to say, after creating a new node, the task is to find the last node and assign the new node to the link **(next)** of the last node, thus, the newly added node becomes the last node instead. If the last node is not found then the new node should be both the first node and the last node of the singly linked list. In such a case, the new node is assigned to the link of the head node. The head node is initially assigned with a null reference when the singly linked list is still empty (there is no any other nodes except the head node) or points to the first node when the singly linked list is not empty.

```
1. #include "header.h"
2. STUDENT_DATA *add_a_node(STUDENT_DATA *new) {
3.      STUDENT_DATA *p;
4.      for (p = head; p->next != NULL; p = p->next)
5.          ;
6.      p->next = new;
7. }
```

Where, lines 4 and 5 continue searching until it finds the last node, line 6 assigns the new node to the link of the last node or to the head node if the singly linked list is empty.

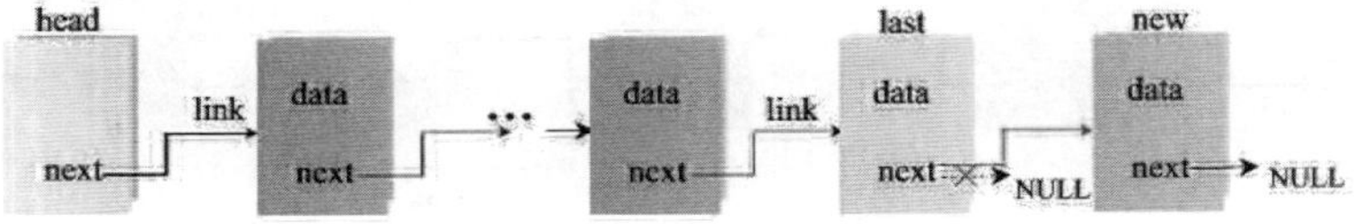

Fig. 7.5. Add a node at the end.

To insert a node after a specified node, first find the specified node and then assign the new node to the link of the specified node. At the same time, the new node has to be linked to the succeeding node of the specified node. That is to say, the succeeding node of the specified node is assigned to the link of the new node. If the specified node is not found, the insertion operation fails and exits from the insertion function.

```
1.  #include "header.h"
2.  void insert_a_node_after(STUDENT_DATA *new,
    STUDENT_DATA *node_x) {
3.  if (new == NULL || node_x == NULL || new == node_x ||
        node_x->next == new) {
4.      printf("Bad arguments¥n");
5.      return;
6.    }
7.    if (node_x->next == NULL)   /* check if it is the last node */
8.      add_a_node(new);
9.    else {
10.       new->next = node_x->next;   /*add link_a*/
11.        node_x->next = new;   /* change link_b to link_c*/
12.    }
13. }
```

Where, lines 3–6 check if the parameters for the function are proper, lines 7 and 8 check if the specified node is the last node, line 8 calls the function, **add_a_node**, since the specified node is the last node. Lines 9–12 insert the new node after the specified node by adding **link_a** and changing **link_b** to **link_c** as shown in Fig. 7.6.

To delete a node, find the proceeding node (for example, **node_*x***) of the node (for example, **node_*y***) to be deleted, change the link of **node_*x*** so that it points to the succeeding node of **node_*y***, delete the link of **node_*y***, and finally free the memory used by **node_*y***.

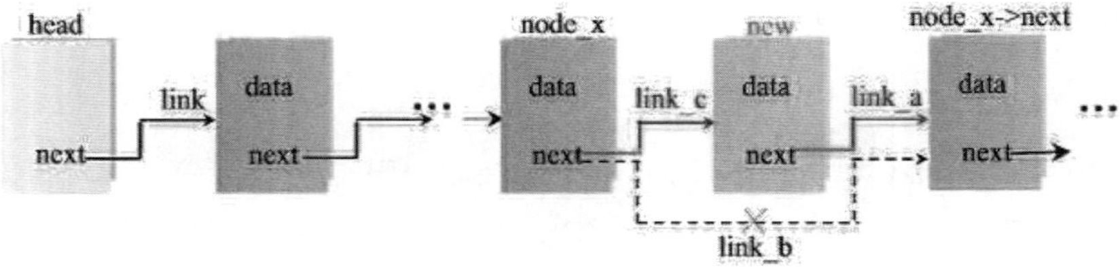

Fig. 7.6. Insert a node.

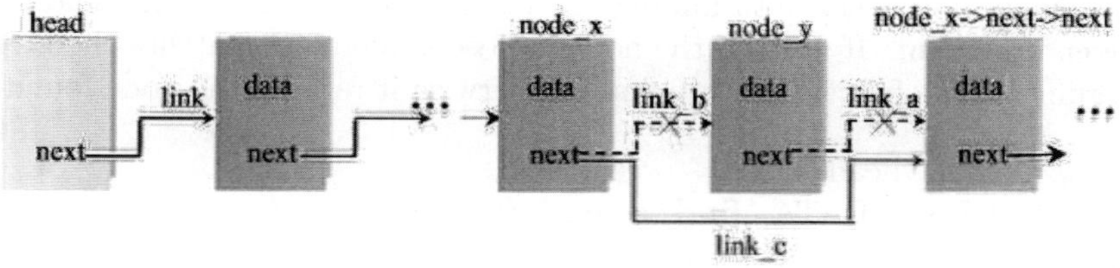

Fig. 7.7. Delete a node.

```
1.  #include "header.h"
2.  void delete_a_node(STUDENT_DATA *node_y) {
3.     STUDENT_DATA *p;
4.     if (node_y == head->next) /* head is the node proceeding
          node_y */
5.        head->next = node_y->next;
6.     else { /* find the node p proceeding node_y */
7.        for (p = head; ((p != NULL) &&(p->next != node_y));
             p = p->next)
8.         ;
9.        if (p == NULL){ /* check if node p exists */
10.        printf("Failure: can not find node_y!");
11.        return;
12.       }
13.       p->next = p->next->next;
           /* delete two links (link_a and link_b) and add one link
             link_c */
15.    }
16.    free(node_y);
17. }
```

Where, line 4 checks if **node_*y*** is the first node (the one after head node), line 5 changes the link of the head node so that it points to the succeeding node of **node_*y*** if **node_*y*** is the first node, lines 7 and 8 continue to search until the proceeding node, **node_*x***, is found lines 9–11 check if the proceeding node exists and terminates the function if it does not exist, otherwise the link of the proceeding node is changed by deleting **link_a** and **link_b** and adding **link_c** in line 13, and line 16 frees memory space used by **node_*y***.

To find a node, search for the node based on one of its data fields in the structure of node as a search key. Let us take student ID as a search key in the student data structure. Searching for node is to traverse the singly linked list until finding one node whose student ID matches the given argument. If none of the nodes whose student ID matches the given argument, the function returns null, otherwise it returns the node found.

```
1.  #include "header.h"
2.  STUDENT_DATA *find_a_node(int id){
3.     STUDENT_DATA *p;
4.     for( p = head; p != NULL; p = p->next )
5.        if (p->student_ID == id)
6.           return p;
7.     return NULL;
```

Where, line 4 goes through the list, lines 5 and 6 return the found node whose **student_ID** matches the given argument **id**, and line 7 returns null reference if there is no matching node.

To traverse a singly linked list, it is to go through and display data items of each node in the linked list. Assuming that we would like to print out student data of all students, the function below allows you to do that.

```
1. #include "header.h"
2. void traverse_list(){
3.   STUDENT_DATA *p;
4.   for (p = head; p != NULL; p = p->next){
5.     printf("student name = %s, student ID %d, student height %f.¥n",
       p->student_name, p->student_ID, student_height);
6.   }
7. }
```

Where, lines 4–6 show that a node pointer starts from head, advances to the next node in each step, and prints out three data items of each node until the node pointer points to null reference, which means reaching the end of the singly linked list.

The complete source program of an example that does the testing of all functions introduced in this section is provided in Appendix 7.1 at the end of this Chapter. This program reads records in data file **record.dat** (that is given in Appendix 7.3) and adds each record one by one to the end of the singly linked list. You can insert a new record to the list after any node (in the main() function of the program we insert a new record after head node but you replace head node by any other node), and delete any node in the singly linked list (in the main() function of the program we delete the new node but you can replace the new node by any other specified node). The program also provides finding ID and name functions that you can test.

7.2.1. *Implementing Stacks with Singly Linked Lists*

A stack is an object container of objects (data items) that are inserted and removed according to the **last-in-first-out** principle. There are basic five operations on a stack, which are stack initialization, empty stack check, full stack check, pushing an item onto and popping an item off. There are also various implementations of stacks. This section first recalls how to implement a stack with an array and then move on to implementing stacks with singly linked lists.

Array implementation of a stack is to use an array to hold stack items and a counter to indicate the total number of items in the stack. Now let us define array size, item's data type, and stack structure in a file, **stack.h**. Five basic operations on a stack can be defined in the stack ADT interface in a file, **operation.h**, as below.

stack.h

```
typedef int ITEM_type;
#define MAXSIZE 10
typedef struct stack{
    int top;
    ITEM_type stack_array[MAXSIZE];
}STACK;
static STACK *stack;
```

operation.h

```
void stack_initialize()
void stack_push(ITEM_type)
ITEM_type stack_pop( )
int stack_empty()
int stack_full()
```

As for the five operations on a stack, **stack_initialize()** is to initialize the stack to be empty, **stack_empty()** is to check if the stack is empty, **stack_full()** is to check if the stack is full, **stack_push()** is to push an item onto the stack, and **stack_pop()** is to pop an item off the stack. Their implementations in C are given below.

```
void stack_initialize(){
    stack->top = 0;
}
int stack_empty(){
    return (stack->top <= 0);
}
```

```
int stack_full(){
    return (stack->top >= MAXSIZE);
}

void stack_push(ITEM_type item){
    if (stack_full() != 0)
        printf("the stack is full!");
    else
        stack->stack_array[stack->top++] = item;
}
ITEM_type stack_pop(){
    if (stack_empty() != 0)
        printf("the stack is empty!");
    else
        return stack->stack_array[--stack->top];
}
```

As we can see that the problem for implementing stacks with arrays is that we have to fix the size of an array and it is not possible to change the defined size during runtime. Now, let us introduce how to implement a stack with a singly linked list. Instead of using an array, we can hold the stack items in each node of a singly linked list in which the size of the list can be dynamically changing, either shrinking or growing, during runtime. One does not need to worry about whether predefined size is enough or too big. Stack node structure in a singly linked list can be defined as follows in a file, **stack_node.h**.

```
typedef int ITEM_type;
#define MAXSIZE 10
typedef struct stack_node {
        ITEM_type item;
        struct stack_node * next;
}STACK_NODE;
static STACK_NODE *head;
```

Operations on the stack using a singly linked list (we also call it as linked stack) becomes processing nodes of the list. Pushing a data item onto the stack corresponds to the process of inserting a node as the first and popping a data item off the stack corresponds to the process of deleting the first node. Of course, at first, we need to initialize the singly linked list to be an empty list, that is to say, the list has only head node at beginning. When inserting an item, it is necessary to make a node with the given item. Both functions of initializing the linked list and making a node are given

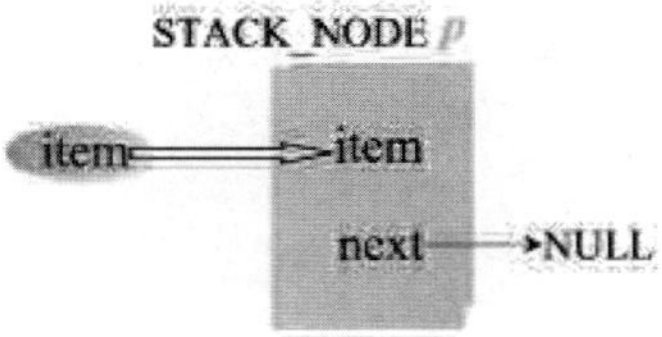

Fig. 7.8. Make a stack node.

below. The functions presented below need to include **stack_node.h** file by adding **#include "stack_node.h"**.

```
void stack_initialize() {
    head = (STACK_NODE*)malloc(sizeof (STACK_NODE));
    if (head == NULL) {
       printf("run out of memory!.¥n");
       exit(1);     }
    head->next = NULL;
}

STACK_NODE *make_a_node(ITEM_type item) {
    STACK_NODE *p;
    p = (STACK_NODE *)malloc(sizeof (STACK_NODE));
    if (p == NULL) {
       printf("run out of memory!¥n");
       exit(1);     }
    p->item = item;
    p->next = NULL;
    return p;
}
```

To push an item onto a linked stack is to create a node with the given item and insert the node at the front of the linked list. The function, **push_a_node()**, is given below.

```
#include "stack_node.h"
void push_a_node(ITEM_type item){
  STACK_NODE *new;
  new = make_a_node(item);
  if(new == NULL)
    pritf("Failure: push a nonexistent node!");
  else if (head->next == NULL)
    head->next = new;     /* add link_a*/
```

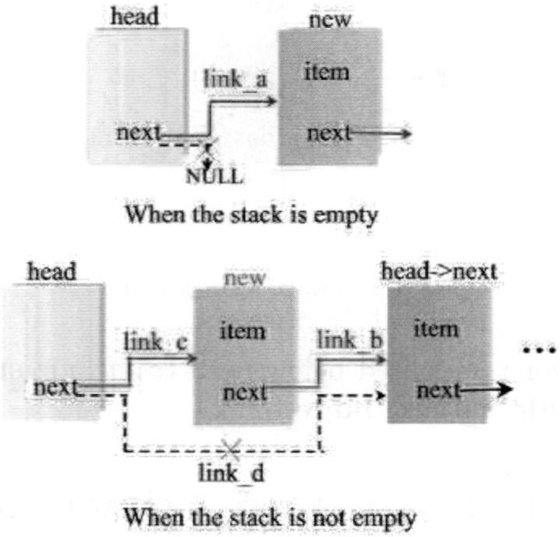

Fig. 7.9. Pushing a node onto a stack.

```
  else {
    new->next = head->next;         /* add link_b*/
    head->next = new;       /* add link_C*/
}
```

When the linked list is empty, the process of inserting a node is only to add a link **(link_a)** from the head node to the new node. When the linked list is not empty, apart from adding a link between the head node and the new node, it is also necessary to add a link from the new node to its succeeding node, that is, the previous first node, and to delete the link between the head node and the previous first node. Fig. 7.9 shows the two cases.

To pop an item off a linked stack is to find the first node, output the item contained in the node, delete the node, and release memory. The process of deleting a node is to add a link from the head node to the previous second node. Of course, after the deletion, the previous second node becomes the current first node. When the stack is empty, there is nothing to pop off as shown in Fig. 7.10.

```
ITEM_type pop_a_node(){
    STACK_NODE *first;
    ITEM_type item;
    if (head->next == NULL)
        printf("empty stack!");
    else {
        first = head->next;       /* find the first node */
```

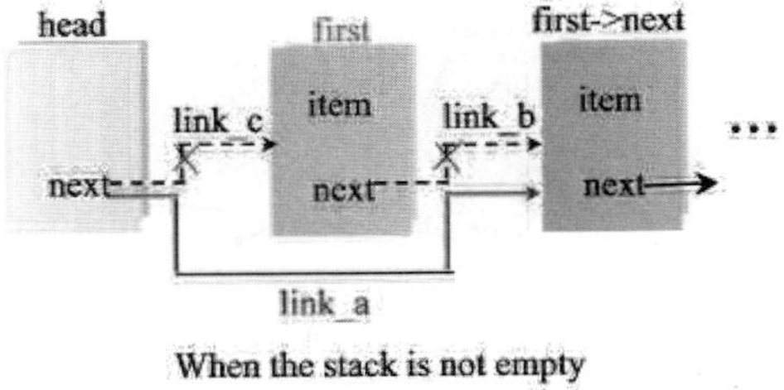

Fig. 7.10. Popping an item off.

```
        item = first->item;   /* get the item */
        head->next = first->next;   /* add like_a*/
        free(first);
    return item;
  }
```

7.2.2. *Implementing Queues with Singly Linked Lists*

This section will discuss how to implement queues with singly linked lists. At first, we will take a look at how a queue is implemented using an array. A queue is a container of objects that are inserted and removed according to the **first-in-first-out** principle. Objects can be inserted at any time but only the object that has been in the queue longest may be removed. Array implementation of a queue is to use an array to hold the items, a counter to count the number of total items in the queue and two indices to keep track of the front and the rear of the queue. A data item is inserted from the rear and removed from the front. The queue structure is defined below in a file, **queue.h**, and the basic operations of the queue are defined in the queue ADT interface in a file, **operation.h**, below.

queue.h

```
typedef int ITEM_type;
#define MAXSIZE 10
typedef struct queue{
        int count;
        int head;
        int tail;
        ITEM_type queue_array[MAXSIZE];
}QUEUE;
Static QUEUE *queue;
```

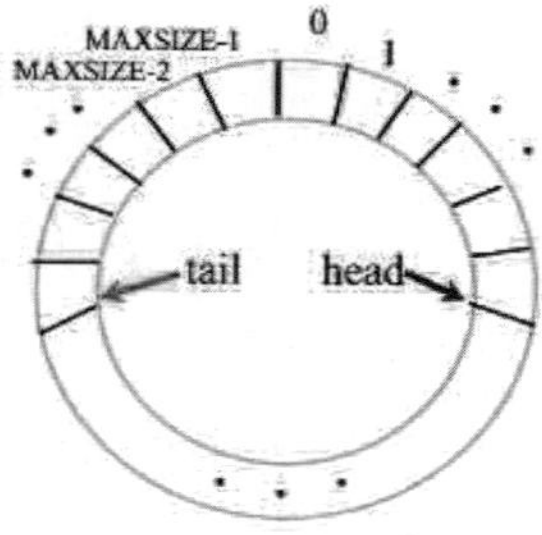

Fig. 7.11. A circular array.

operation.h

```
void queue_initialize()
void enqueue(ITEM_type)
ITEM_type dequeue( )
int queue_empty()
int queue_full()
```

As for five operations on a queue, **queue_initialize()** is to initialize the queue to be empty, **queue_empty()** is to check if the queue is empty, **queue_full()** is to check if the queue is full, **enqueue()** is to add an item onto the queue, and **dequeue()** is to delete an item from the queue.

Their implementations use a circular array. A circular array is an array that looks like a circle. The position around circle is numbered from 0 to MAXSIZE-1. Moving the indices is just the same as doing modular arithmetic like a circular clock face. When a count is increased to be over MAXSIZE-1, it starts over again at 0 as shown in Fig. 7.11. Then we have,

```
queue->tail = (queue->tail + 1)%MAXSIZE;
queue->head = (queue->head + 1)%MAXSIZE;
```

Such a queue is also called a circular queue from the implementation view of point.

Five functions that operate on a queue using a circular array in C are given below.

```
void queue_initialize(){
    queue->count = 0;
    queue->head = 0;
    queue->tail = 0;
}
```

```
int queue_empty(){
    return ( queue->count<= 0);
}
int queue_full(){
  return (queue->count >= MAXSIZE);
}

void enqueue(ITEM_type item){
 if (queue_full() != 0)
    printf("the queue is full!");
 else {
 queue->count++;
    queue->tail = (queue->tail + 1)%MAXSIZE;
    queue->queue_array[queue->tail] = item;
 }
}

ITEM_type dequeue(){
  ITEM_type item;
  if (queue_empty() != 0)
     printf("the queue is empty!");
  else {
   queue->count–;
   item = queue->queue->array[queue->head];
   queue->head = (queue->head + 1)%MAXSIZE;
   return item;
  }
}
```

Let us now turn to how to implement a queue with a singly linked list. Instead of using an array, we can hold items of the queue in nodes of a singly linked list. It is sometimes called linked queue. The first thing to do is to define the queue node structure as shown in the file, **queue_node.h**, below.

```
typedef int ITEM_type;
#define MAXSIZE 10
typedef struct queue_node {
       ITEM_type item;
       struct queue_node *next;
}QUEUE_NODE;

static QUEUE_NODE *head;
static QUEUE_NODE *tail;
```

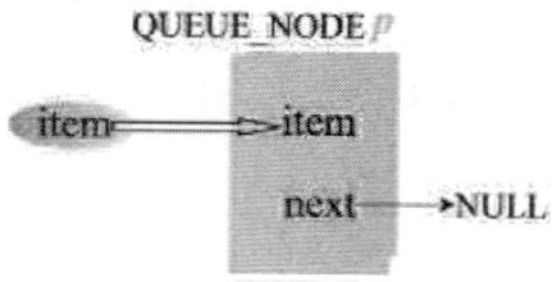

Fig. 7.12. Make a queue node.

Operations on a linked queue become the processing of nodes in a singly linked list, which is very similar to the operations on a linked stack. The differences are that to enqueue an item to the linked queue is to add the item to the end of the list as the last node, and to dequeue an item is to delete the first node that contains the item. When adding an item to the linked queue, it is necessary to make a node with the given item as shown in Fig. 7.12. The function (**make_a_node()**) below that is mirror to the one given in Sec. 7.2.2 makes possible to process an item directly by making a new node with the given item.

```
QUEUE_NODE *make_a_node(ITEM_type item) {
    QUEUE_NODE *p;
    p = (QUEUE_NODE *)malloc(sizeof (QUEUE_NODE));
    if (p == NULL) {
        printf("run out of memory!¥n");
        exit(1);
    }
    p->item = item;
    p->next = NULL;
    return p;
}
```

To initialize a linked queue is to allocate memory for the head node and the tail node and let both head and tail nodes point to the NULL reference.

```
#include "queue_node.h"
void queue_initialize() {
    head = (QUEUE_NODE *)malloc(sizeof (QUEUE_NODE));
    tail = (QUEUE_NODE *)malloc(sizeof (QUEUE_NODE));
    if ((head == NULL) || (tail == NULL)) {
        printf("run out of memory!¥n");
        exit(1);
    }
    head->next = NULL;
    tail->next = NULL;
}
```

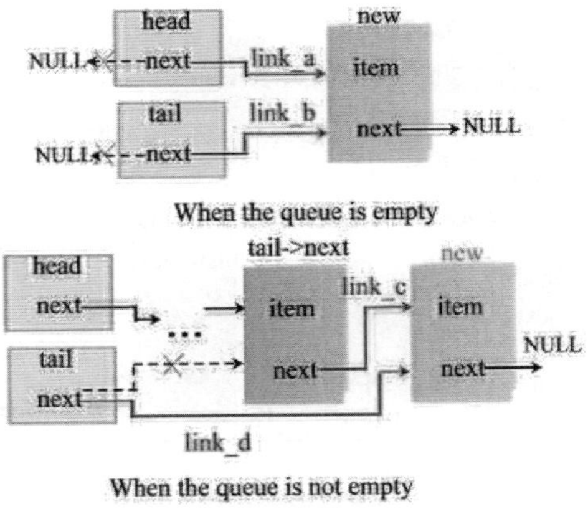

Fig. 7.13. Adding a node onto a queue.

To enqueue an item to a link queue is to create a node with the given item and insert the node at the end of the list. There are two possible cases: one is when the linked queue is empty and another is when the linked queue is not empty as shown in Fig. 7.13. In the former case, after inserting a new node with the given item, both head and tail nodes point to the new node while in the latter case, the new node is inserted as the current last node. The previous last node has a linked to the new node and the link of the tail node is also changed to point the new node. These two cases are illustrated in the figure below.

```
#include "queue_node.h"
void enqueue(ITEM_type item){
  QUEUE_NODE *new;
  new = make_a_node(item);
  if(new == NULL)
    pritf("Failure: push a nonexistent node!");
  else if (head->next == NULL)
    head->next = new;      /* add link_a*/
    tail->next = new;      /* add link_b*/
  } else {
    tail->next->next = new;      /* add link_c*/
    tail->next = new;      /* add link_d*/
  }
}
```

To delete an item from a link queue is to find the first node, get the item contained in the node, delete the node, and release memory. If the queue

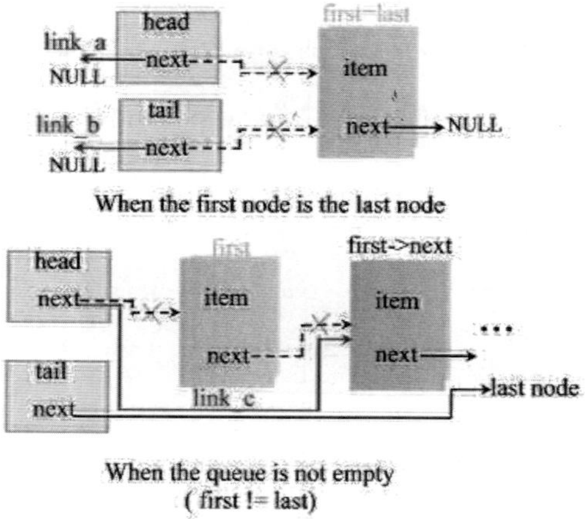

Fig. 7.14. Deleting a node from a queue.

is empty, the function prints out a message like "empty queue!", otherwise the function continues to process the first node. When the first node is also the last node, after deletion of the first node, the linked queue becomes empty such that both the head node and the tail nodes point to a NULL reference. Otherwise the head node points to the previous second node and the link of the tail node remains the same as shown in Fig. 7.14.

The function, dequeue() that implements deletion of an item from the linked queue is given below.

```
#include "queue_node.h"
ITEM_type dequeue(){
    QUEUE_NODE *first;
    ITEM_type item;

    if (head->next == NULL)
        printf("empty queue!");
    else {
        first = head->next;        /* find the first node */
        item = first->item;   /* get the item */
        if (first->next == NULL)   /* check if first is last node*/
            tail->next = NULL;   /* add link_b*/
        head->next = first->next;   /* add link_c or link_a */
        free(first);
    return item;
}
```

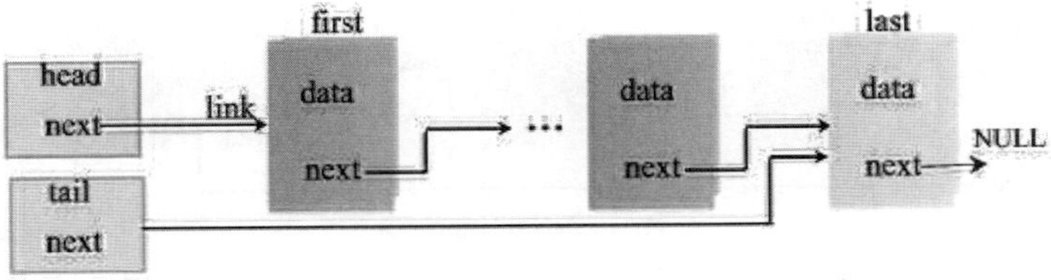

Fig. 7.15. A double-ended linked list.

7.2.3. *Double-Ended Linked Lists*

A double-ended list is similar to a singly linked list discussed earlier, but it has one additional reference (tail) to the last node as well as to the first node as shown in Fig. 7.15. With additional link to the last node, a double-ended linked list is able to insert a new node directly at the end of the list without finding the last node by iterating through the entire list as in a single-ended list. Therefore, it is efficient to insert a new node at the end of the list.

In a single-ended list, inserting a node at the end of the list requires $O(n)$ comparisons. Where, n is the total number of items in the list the following loop is used to find the last node.

```
for (p = head; p->next != NULL; p = p->next)
```

While in a double-ended list, inserting a node at the end of the list involves changing only one or two references without requiring any comparisons. It takes $O(1)$ time.

```
tail->next->next = node;
        tail->next = node;
```

Besides the insertion of a node at the end of the list is more efficient, other operations on the double-end linked list are completely the same as the operations on a single-end linked list. Below, we only present the operation of inserting an item to a double-end linked list.

To insert an item to a double-end linked list becomes quite simple. It can be seen from the source code of the function below.

```
void add_node_at_end(STUDENT_DATA *new) {
      if(new == NULL)
        printf("Failure: push a nonexistent node!");
      else if (head->next == NULL) {
                head->next = new;
```

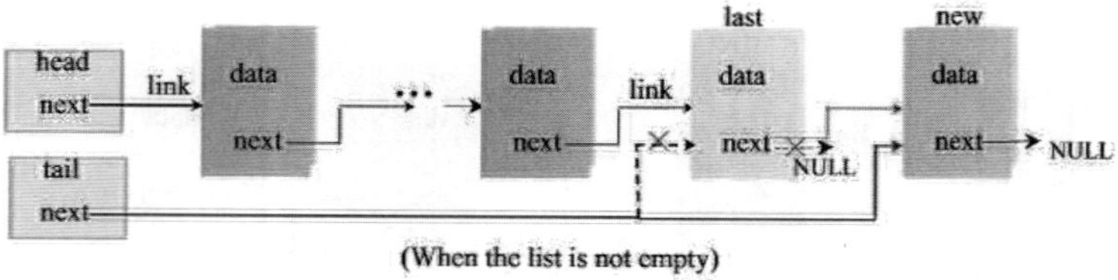

Fig. 7.16. Add a node at the end.

```
            tail->next = new;
            return;
          else{
            tail->next->next = new;
            tail->next = new;
      }
}
```

7.3. Doubly Linked Lists

7.3.1. *Doubly Linked Lists Processing: Insertion, Deletion and Traversal*

In a doubly linked list, each node has two links, one link to its previous node and another link to its next node. Thus in the definition of a node structure, one more pointer, **prev**, is added into the node structure, the rest is the same. Of course, at the end of a direction, there is an ending node. Here, we specify that the first node and the last node are the ending nodes in each direction, respectively. It is efficient to have head and tail nodes that point to the first node and the last node, respectively. In this section, we still take STUDENT_DATA as an example to discuss how to process doubly linked lists. The STUDENT_DATA node structure for a doubly linked list is defined in the file, **st_data.h**, all necessary global declarations library files, and header files are included in the file, **header.h**. We will discuss five operations as given in the file, **operation.h**, on a doubly linked list.

header.h

```
#include <stdio.h>
#include <stdlib>
#include <malloc.h>
#include "st_data.h"
static STUDENT_DATA *head;
```

– Create a list node
– Add a node to the end of a list
– Insert a node in the middle of a list
– Remove a node from a list

st_data.h

```
typedef struct s_data{
        char student_name[14];
        int student_ID;
        float student_height;
        struct s_data *next;
        struct s_data *prev;
}STUDENT_DATA;
```

In the following, we describe each operation, define each function and give their implementations in C and finally provide you a complete source code of an example that can test each function. The source program is given in Appendix 7.2.

To create a doubly linked list node, is to allocate memory for the node structure defined in the file "**st_data.h**" and to return a pointer to this memory area. The node has two pointers **(next)** and **(prev)** to a null reference, respectively.

```
#include "header.h"
STUDENT_DATA *create_a_node() {
    STUDENT_DATA *p;
    p = (STUDENT_DATA *)malloc(sizeof (STUDENT_DATA));
    if (p == NULL) {
        printf("Failed: run out of memory!¥n");
        exit(1);
    }
    p->next = NULL;
    p->prev = NULL;
    return p;
}
```

To add a node to a doubly linked list, insert the node at the end of the list as shown in Fig. 7.17. Since there is a link of the head node, which is directly linked to the last node, searching for the last node is not necessary. If the list is empty, both links of the head node are linked to the new node as shown in lines 4 and 5. Otherwise the link, **prev**, of the head node is changed to point to the new node, the previous last node points to the new

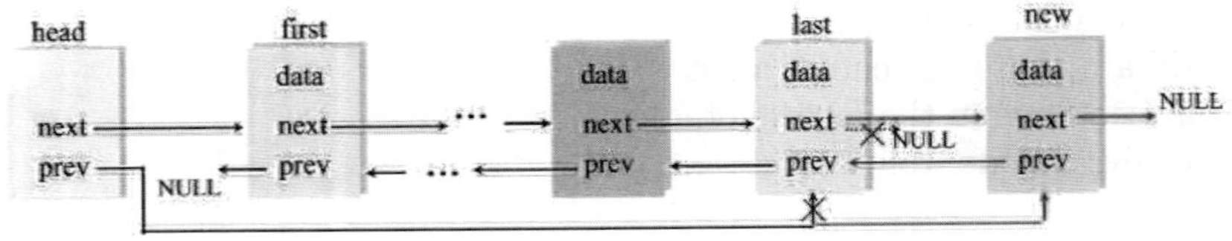

Fig. 7.17. Add a node at the end.

node, and the new node becomes current last node as seen in lines 8, 9, and 10 below.

```
1.  #include "header.h"
2.  void add_node_to_end(STUDENT_DATA *new){
3.      if (head->prev == NULL) {
4.          head->next = new;
5.          head->prev = new;
6.      }
7.      else{
8.         head->prev->next = new;
9.         new->prev = head->prev;
10.        head->prev = new;
11.     }
12. }
```

To insert a node to a doubly linked list, insert a node to a specified location in the list. It is normally to insert a node after a specified node. First it is necessary to find the specified node in the list, and then insert the new node after it. Instead of changing two links in a singly linked list, insertion of a node after a specified node in a doubly linked list has to change four links. The function that inserts a node, **node_y** after the node, **node_x**, is given below. As we can see that if the specified node, **node_x**, is the last node, insertion of the node, **node_y**, becomes insertion of a node to the end of the list. Thus, it can simply call the function, **add_node_to_end()**, which was just described above. If the specified node, **node_x**, is the head node, then the special handling for the link, **prev**, of the head is necessary. That is both links of the head node have to point to the new node, **node_y**.

```
#include "header.h"
void insert_node_after(STUDENT_DATA *node_y,
                       STUDENT_DATA *node_x){
    if (node_y == NULL|| node_x == NULL||
          node_y == node_x || node_x->next == node_y) {
```

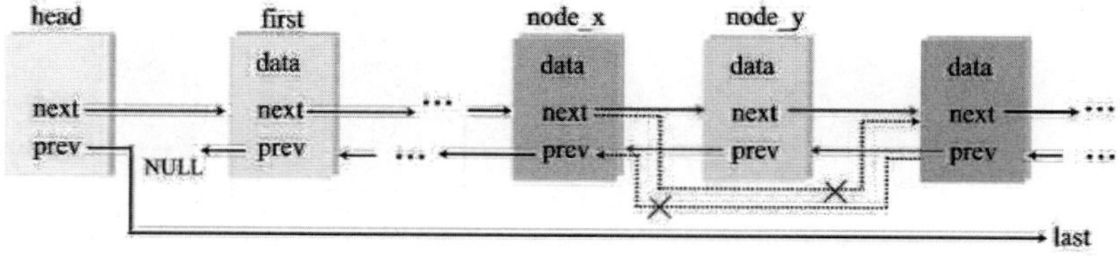

Fig. 7.18. Insert a node.

```
        printf("insert_a_node_after:bad arguments¥n");
        return;
      }
    if (node_x->next == NULL)              /* node_x is the last node*/
          add_node_to_end(node_y);
    else if (node_x == head) {              /* node_x is head node*/
          node_y->next = node_x->next;
          node_x->next->prev = node_y;
          node_y->prev = NULL;
          node_x->next = node_y;
    } else {                                 /* node_x is in the list */
          node_y->next = node_x->next;
          node_x->next->prev = node_y;
          node_y->prev = node_x;
          node_x->next = node_y;
    }
}
```

To delete a node from a doubly linked list, find the proceeding node **(node_x)** of the node **(node_y)** to be deleted, delete **node_y** and free up the memory used by the deleted node, **node_y**. If the node to be deleted is the first node or the last node, the handling of two links of the head node is necessary. Otherwise in the situation as shown in Fig. 7.19, deletion of the node in the list (neither the first node nor the last node) is simply to add two new links and free the deleted node.

```
#include "header.h"
void delete_a_node(STUDENT_DATA *node_y){
  if (head->next == node_y){  /*first node */
      node_y->next->prev = NULL;
      head->next = node_y->next;
      free(node_y);
  }
```

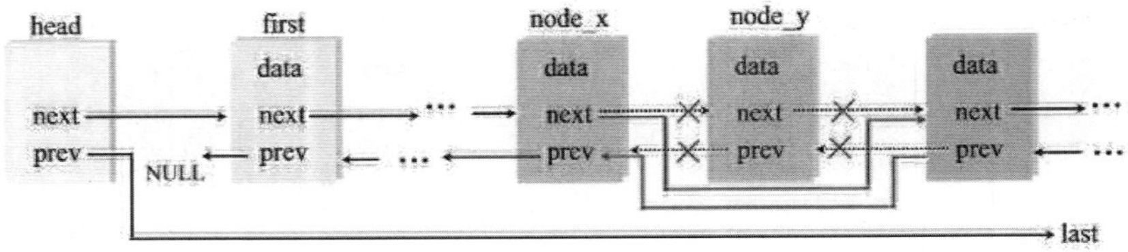

Fig. 7.19. Delete a node.

```
    else if (head->prev == node_y) {   /*last node */
        node_y->prev->next = NULL;
        head->prev = node_y->prev;
        free(node_y);
    }
    else{   /*middle node*/
        node_y->prev->next = node_y->next;
        node_y->next->prev = node_y->prev;
        free(node_y);
    }
}
```

Traversing forward through a doubly linked list is the same as the traverse through a singly linked list. Traversing backward through a doubly linked list, is similar but starts at the last node in the list.

```
#include "header.h"
void traverse_forward(){
    STUDENT_DATA *p;
    for (p = head; p != NULL; p = p->next)
        printf("student ID = %d¥n", p->student_ID);
}

void traverse_backward(){
    STUDENT_DATA *p;
    for (p = head; p != NULL; p = p->prev)
        printf("student ID = %d¥n", p->student_ID);
}
```

The complete source program of an example that does the testing of all functions introduced in the section is provided in Appendix 7.2 at the end of this Chapter. This program reads records in data file **record.dat** (that is given in Appendix 7.3) and adds each record one by one to the end of the singly linked list. You can insert a new record to the list after any node (in the program we insert a new record after the first node but you can replace the first node by any other node), and delete any record in the doubly linked list (in the program we delete the new node but you can replace the new node by any other specified node). The traverse forward and backward functions print the student ID which they traverse.

7.3.2. *Implementing Deques with Doubly Linked Lists*

In this section, we will introduce double-ended queues and operations on a double-ended queue. A double-ended queue is the extension of a queue, which is also called a deque. A deque data structure allows insertion and deletion at both the front and the rear of a queue. A deque node structure is defined in a file, **deque_node.h**.

deque_node.h.

```
typedef int ITEM_type;
#define MAXSIZE 10
typedef struct deque_node     {
        ITEM_type item;
        struct deque_node *next;
        struct deque_node *prev;
}DEQUE_NODE;

static DEQUE_NODE *head;
```

The basic operations of a deque described in this section are insertion and deletion of a DEQUE_NODE at both ends of a doubly linked list. The function, **make_a_node()**, makes it possible to process an item directly by making a new node with the given item as shown in Fig. 7.20. The processing of a deque becomes the processing of nodes in a doubly linked list. Readers may find the functions presented here are quite similar to the functions in the last section.

To make a new node with a given item, allocate memory space for a deque node and assign the given item to the node's item field and set null reference to both links of the deque node, and then return the allocated memory location to the node pointer.

```
#include "deque_node.h"
DEQUE_NODE *make_a_node(ITEM_type item) {
   DEQUE_NODE *p;
   p = (DEQUE_NODE *)malloc(sizeof (DEQUE_NODE));
   if (p == NULL) {
```

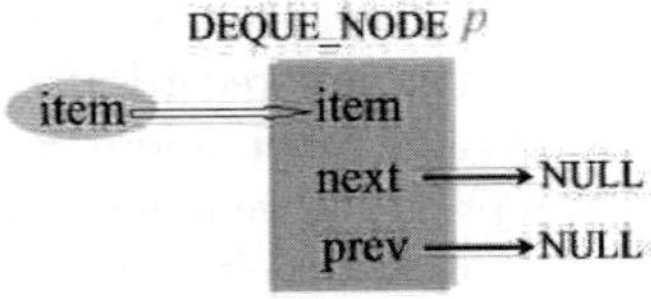

Fig. 7.20. Make a deque node.

```
        printf("run out of memory!.¥n");
        exit(1);
    }
    p->item = item;
    p->next = NULL;
    p->prev = NULL;
    return p;
}
```

Before carrying on operations on a deque, we have to initialize it, that is to say, the head node of a doubly linked list at the beginning is allocated with memory and point to the null reference. The function, **deque_initialize()**, is presented below.

```
#include "deque_node.h"
void deque_initialize() {
    head = (DEQUE_NODE *)malloc(sizeof (DEQUE_NODE));
    if (head == NULL) {
        printf("run out of memory!.¥n");
        exit(1);
    }
    head->next = NULL;
    head->prev = NULL;
}
```

The function, **deque_add_at_front()**, is to create a new node with the given data item and insert the node at the front of the deque, that is insert the new node after the head node as shown in Fig. 7.21.

The function checks whether the deque is empty or not. In the case of empty, the inserted new node is the last node as well. Thus both links of the head node, **next** and **prev**, point to the new node.

```
#include "deque_node.h"
void deque_add_at_front(ITEM_type item){
    DEQUE_NODE *new_node;
```

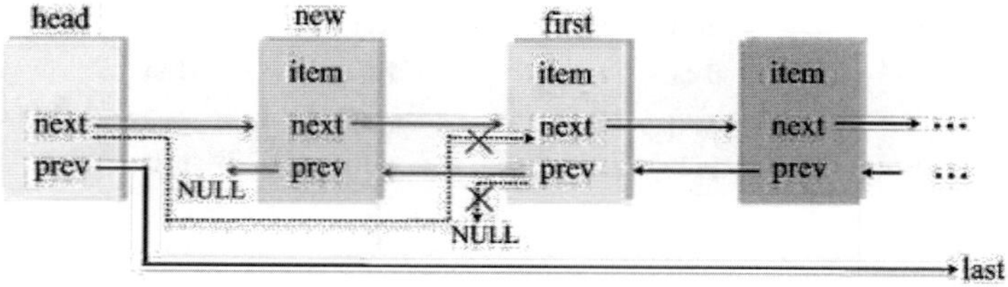

Fig. 7.21. Insert a node at the front.

```
    new_node = make_a_node(item);
    if(new_node == NULL)
        printf("Failed: push a nonexistent node!¥n");
    else if (head -> next == NULL) {
        head->next = new_node;
        head->prev = new_node;
        return;
    }
    else {
        new_node ->next = head -> next;
        new_node ->prev = NULL;
        head->next->prev = new_node;
        head->next = new_node;
    }
}
```

We can also add a data item from the end of a deque as shown in Fig. 7.22. The function, **deque_add_at_rear()**, allows a new node with the given item to be inserted at the rear of the deque. When the deque is empty, the new node is processed in the same way as it is in the function, **deque_add_at_front()**.

```
#include "deque_node.h"
void deque_add_at_rear(ITEM_type item){
    DEQUE_NODE *new_node;
    new_node=make_a_node(item);
    if(new_node == NULL)
        printf("Failed: push a nonexistent node!¥n");
    else if (head -> next == NULL) {
        head->next = new_node;
        head->prev = new_node;
        return;
    }
```

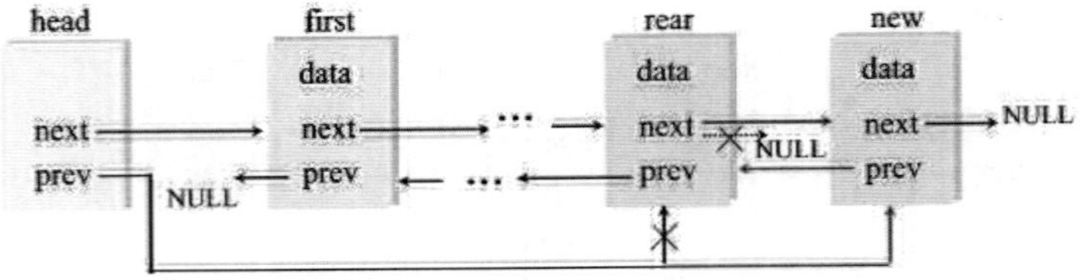

Fig. 7.22. Insert a node at the rear.

```
    else {
        new_node->prev = head->prev;
        head->prev->next = new_node;
        head->prev = new_node;
      }
}
```

There are two ways to delete a node from a deque. We can delete a node at the front or a node at the rear as shown in Fig. 7.23. Since the head node has a link pointing to the first node and a link pointing to the last node, these two versions of deleting a node are efficient in a deque. The function, **deque_add_at_front()**, is to delete the first node. If the first node is the last node as well, the deletion process becomes free the first node and let both the **next** and **prev** links of the head node point to the null reference. Otherwise the **prev** link remains the same and the **next** link points to the previous second node. Thus the previous second node becomes the current first node. The **prev** link of the current first node has to be set with the null reference.

```
#include "deque_node.h"
void deque_delete_at_front(ITEM_type item){
    DEQUE_NODE *front_node;
    if (head->next == NULL){
        printf("empty dequeue!");
        exit(1);
      }
    else if (head->prev == head->next) {/*last node */
        head->next = NULL;
        head->prev = NULL;
        free(head->next);
    }
    else {
```

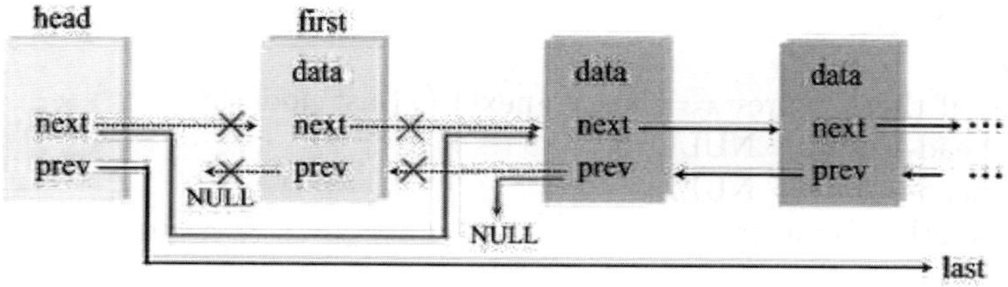

Fig. 7.23. Delete a node at the front.

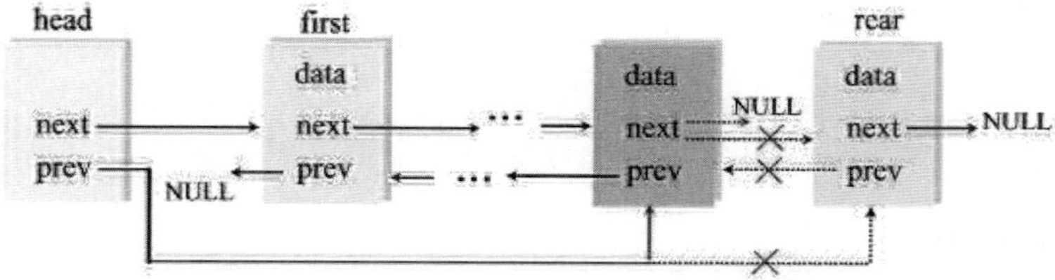

Fig. 7.24. Delete a node at the rear.

```
        front_node = head->next;
        head->next->prev = NULL;
        head->next = head->next->next;
        free(front_node);
    }
}
```

In the function, **deque_add_at_rear()**, when the last node is the first node, it means after a deletion, the deque becomes an empty deque such that both the **prev** and **next** links of the head node have to point to the null reference. Otherwise it frees the previous last node and the node that is preceding the previous last node becomes the current last node. The **prev** link of the head node is changed to point to the current last node and the **next** link of the current last node is set with the null reference.

```
#include "deque_node.h"
void deque_delete_at_rear(ITEM_type item){
    DEQUE_NODE *rear_node;
    if (head->next == NULL){
        printf("empty dequeue!");
```

```
        exit(1);
    }
    else if (head->prev == head->next) {/*last node */
      head->next = NULL;
      head->prev = NULL;
      free(head->next);
    }
    else {
      rear_node = head->prev;
      head->prev = rear_node>prev;
      rear_node->prev->next = NULL;
      free(rear_node);
    }
}
```

References

1. R. Sedgewick, *Algorithms in C*, Addison-Wesley, 1990.
2. M. A. Weiss, *Data Structures and Algorithm Analysis in C*, Second Edition, Addison-Wesley, 1997.
3. R. Kruse, C. L. Tondo and B. Leung, *Data Structures and Program Design in C*, Second Edition, Prentice-Hall, 1997.
4. M. T. Goodrich and R. Tamassia, *Data Structures and Algorithms in JAVA*, John Wiley, 1998.

Appendix 7.1.

The Source Program in C of Implementation of a Singly Linked List

```
/* Implementation of a singly linked list */
/* slist.c */

#include
#include
#include
#include
#define MAXLEN 10
static STUDENT_DATA *head;

typedef struct s_data{
```

```
 int student_ID;
 char student_name[14];
 float student_height;
 struct s_data *next;
}STUDENT_DATA;

STUDENT_DATA *create_a_node();
void add_a_node_end(struct s_data *new);
void insert_a_node_after(struct s_data  *new, struct s_data *node_x);
void delete_a_node(STUDENT_DATA *node_y);
STUDENT_DATA *find_a_node_ID(int  id);
STUDENT_DATA *find_a_node_name(char name);
void print();

main (){
  int i,ID;
  char name[10];
  STUDENT_DATA *p,*new,*tmp1,*tmp2;
  FILE *fp;

  new=(STUDENT_DATA *)malloc(sizeof(STUDENT_DATA));
  if ((fp=fopen("record","r"))==NULL)  exit(0);

  for (i=0;istudent_ID,p->student_name,&p->student_height);
   add_a_node_end(p);
    }

  print(head);
  printf ("Please input the new element:");
  scanf (" %d %s %f",&new->student_ID,new->student_name,
         &new->student_height);

  insert_a_node_after(new,head);
  print(head);

  delete_a_node(new);
  print(head);

  tmp1=(STUDENT_DATA *)malloc(sizeof(STUDENT_DATA));
  printf("Please input the ID:");
  scanf("%d",&ID);
  tmp1=find_a_node_ID(ID);
  printf(" %d %s %f\n",tmp1->student_ID,tmp1->student_name,
         tmp1->student_height);
  tmp2=(STUDENT_DATA *)malloc(sizeof(STUDENT_DATA));
```

```
  printf("Please input student name:");
  scanf("%s",&name);
  tmp2=find_a_node_name(name);
  printf(" %d %s %f\n",tmp2->student_ID,tmp2->student_name,
         tmp2->student_height);

  fclose(fp);
}

STUDENT_DATA *create_a_node() {
  STUDENT_DATA *p;
  p = (STUDENT_DATA *)malloc(sizeof (STUDENT_DATA ));

  if (p == NULL){
    printf("Failed: run out of memory!\n");
    exit(1);
  }
  p ->next = NULL;
  return p;
}

void add_a_node_end(STUDENT_DATA *new){
  STUDENT_DATA *p;

  for (p = head; p->next != NULL; p = p->next)
     ;
  p->next = new;
}

void insert_a_node_after(STUDENT_DATA *new, STUDENT_DATA *node_x){
  if (new == NULL|| node_x == NULL|| new == node_x
      || node_x ->next == new )      {
    printf("Bad arguments\n");
    return;
  }

  if(node_x->next == NULL)  /* check if it is the last node */
    add_a_node_end(new);
  else{
    new->next =  node_x->next;  /* add link_a*/
    node_x->next = new;  /* change link_b to link_c*/
  }
}

void delete_a_node(STUDENT_DATA *node_y){
  STUDENT_DATA *p;
```

```
  if (node_y == head->next)  /* head is the node proceeding node_y */
     head->next = node_y->next;
  else{   /* find the node p proceeding node_y */
   for (p=head; ((p != NULL) &&(p->next != node_y)); p = p->next)
 ;
   if (p == NULL){   /* check if node p exists */
     printf("Failure: can not find node_y!");
     return;
   }
   p->next = p->next->next;
    /* delete two links (link_a and link_b) and add one link link_c*/
  }
  free(node_y);
}


STUDENT_DATA *find_a_node_ID(int  id){
  STUDENT_DATA *p;
  for( p=head; p != NULL; p = p->next )
    if ( p->student_ID == id)
      return p;
  return NULL;
}

STUDENT_DATA *find_a_node_name(char name){
  STUDENT_DATA *p;
    for( p=head; p != NULL; p = p->next )
      if (strcmp( p->student_name, name)==0)
        return p;
  return NULL;
  }

void print(STUDENT_DATA *head)
{
  STUDENT_DATA *p;
  if (head!=NULL)
    {
    printf("Now these records are:\n");
    for ( p=head;p!=NULL;p=p->next)
    printf(" %d %s %f\n",p->student_ID,p->student_name,
           p->student_height);
    }
   else
     printf("\n It is a null list!\n");

}
```

Appendix 7.2.

The Source Program in C of Implementation of a Doubly Linked List

```
/* Implementation of a doubly linked list */
/* dlist.c */

#include
#include
#include
#define MAXLEN 5

typedef  struct s_data{
  int student_ID;
  char student_name[14];
  float student_height;
  struct s_data *next;
  struct s_data *prev;
}STUDENT_DATA;

STUDENT_DATA *create_a_node();
void add_a_node_to_end(STUDENT_DATA *node);
void insert_a_node_after(STUDENT_DATA *node_y,STUDENT_DATA *node_x);
void delete_a_node(STUDENT_DATA *node);
void traverse_forward();
void traverse_backward();
void print();

static STUDENT_DATA *head;

main(){
  int i,ID;
  STUDENT_DATA *p,*new,*tmp;
  FILE *fp;

  head=(STUDENT_DATA *)malloc(sizeof(STUDENT_DATA));
  head->next = NULL;
  head->prev = NULL;

  new=(STUDENT_DATA *)malloc(sizeof(STUDENT_DATA));
  tmp=(STUDENT_DATA *)malloc(sizeof(STUDENT_DATA));
  if ((fp=fopen("record","r"))==NULL)  exit(0);

  for (i=0;istudent_ID,p->student_name,&p->student_height);
```

```
    add_a_node_to_end(p);
   }
   print(head);

   tmp=head->next;
   printf ("Please input the new element:");
   scanf (" %d %s %f",&new->student_ID,new->student_name,
          &new->student_height);
   insert_a_node_after (new,tmp);
   print(head);

   delete_a_node(new);
   print(head);

   traverse_forward();
   traverse_backward();

   fclose(fp);
}

STUDENT_DATA *create_a_node() {
  STUDENT_DATA *p;
  p = (STUDENT_DATA *)malloc(sizeof (STUDENT_DATA ));

  if (p == NULL) {
    printf("Failed: run out of memory! \n");
    exit(1);
   }
   p->next = NULL;
   p->prev = NULL;
   return p;
}

void add_a_node_to_end(STUDENT_DATA *node){
 if (head->prev == NULL) {
     head->next = node;
     head->prev = node;
 }
 else{
     head->prev->next = node;
     node->prev = head->prev;
     head->prev = node;
 }
}

void insert_a_node_after(STUDENT_DATA *node_y, STUDENT_DATA *node_x){
```

```
  if  (node_y == NULL|| node_x == NULL|| node_y == node_x ||
       node_x ->next == node_y )       {
    printf("insert_a_node_after:bad arguments\n");
    return;
  }
  if  (node_x->next == NULL)
    add_a_node_to_end(node_y);
  else if (node_x == head)
    {
      node_y->next = node_x->next;
      node_x->next->prev = node_y;
      node_y->prev = NULL;
      node_x->next = node_y;
    }
  else{
    node_y ->next = node_x->next;
    node_x ->next->prev = node_y;
    node_y ->prev = node_x;
    node_x ->next = node_y;
  }
}

void delete_a_node(STUDENT_DATA *node_y){
  STUDENT_DATA *p;
  if (node_y== head){  /*head node*/
    printf("attempt to delete a head node!");
    return;
  }
  else if  (head->next == node_y){  /*first  node */
    node_y->next->prev = NULL;
    head->next = node_y->next;
    free(node_y);
  }
  else if  (head->prev == node_y) {  /*last  node */
    node_y->prev->next = NULL;
    head->prev = node_y->prev;
    free(node_y);
  }
  else{  /*middle node*/
    node_y->prev->next = node_y->next;
    node_y->next->prev = node_y->prev;
    free(node_y);
  }
}

void traverse_forward(){
```

```
  STUDENT_DATA *p;

  for (p = head; p!=NULL; p= p->next)
    printf("student ID = %d \n", p->student_ID);
}

void traverse_backward(){
  STUDENT_DATA *p;

  for (p = head; p!=NULL; p=p->prev)
    printf("student ID = %d \n", p->student_ID);
}

void print(STUDENT_DATA *head)
{
  STUDENT_DATA *p;
  if (head!=NULL)
    {
    printf("Now these records are:\n");
    for ( p=head;p!=NULL;p=p->next)
    printf(" %d %s %f\n",p->student_ID,p->student_name,
           p->student_height);
    }
   else
     printf("\n It is a null doubly linked list!\n");
}
```

Appendix 7.3.

Record.dat

```
950127 camel 1.60
950136 liapi 1.75
  950150 muzhi 1.55
  950152 totoh 1.60
950176 zhaoc 1.80
```

Exercises

Beginner's Exercises

1. What is a structure?
2. What is a self-referential structure?

3. What is a link in a linked list?
4. What is a linked stack?
5. What is a linked queue?
6. What are the advantages of using a linked list over using an array?

Intermediate Exercises

7. Define a TEACHER_DATA structure with teacher's name, course name and number of students in the teacher's class.
8. Define a STUDENT_DATA structure with student's name, number of courses taken and birth date including year, month and day.
9. Insert a group of 10 students' data to a singly linked list. Traverse the list and print out the student data.
10. Write a function to exchange arbitrary two nodes in a singly linked list.
11. Write a function that concatenates two singly linked lists into a singly linked double-ended list.
12. Write a function that converts the singly linked double-ended list into a doubly linked double-ended list.

Advanced Exercises

13. Insert a group of 10 students' data to a singly linked list and calculate the average age of the students.
14. Write a function to arrange a singly linked list of student data in ascending order according to student's age.
15. Write an algorithm to check correspondence of parentheses in expressions with three types of parenthesis and implement the algorithm with a linked stack. For example, an expression is as follow:

$$\{x + (h - (j - (k - [l - n])))^{*}c - [(d + e)]\}/(y - [a + b])$$

16. Write an algorithm that can copy input sequence (Hint: using linked stack).
17. Write an algorithm that can reverse input sequence (Hint: using linked queue).
18. Write an algorithm to implement a reverse Polish calculator using a linked stack. In a reverse Polish calculator, the operands (numbers) are entered before the operation (+, -, *, /) is specified. Therefore, the operands are pushed onto a linked stack. When an operation is performed, it pops its operands from the linked stack and pushes its result back onto the linked stack. For example,

$$35 + 2/ \qquad \text{means} \qquad (3 * 5)/(1 + 2)$$

The figure below shows each state of the linked stack in each step. As it can be seen that a reverse Polish calculator is that any expression, no matter how complicated, can be specified without the use of parentheses.

Chapter 8

Searching

TIMOTHY K. SHIH
Tamkang University, Taiwan
tshih@cs.tku.edu.tw

8.1. Introduction

In our previous discussion of lists, stacks, and queues, the purposes of these structures are designed to store data, which should be retrieved for frequent usage. Information retrieval is one of the interesting issues in computer engineering and computer science. The challenges of information retrieval include the efficiency of storage usage, as well as the computation speed, which is important for fast retrieval. Searching means to retrieve a record of data from a structure or from a database, which may contain hundreds or even several millions of records. The storage structure of these records is the essential factor, which affects the speed of search. However, a good searching strategy also influences the speed, even on the same underlying storage structure. In this chapter, we will discuss the strategies, which can be used for information retrieval on different storage structures.

What is the purpose of searching? It is to find the information for a particular application. For instance, in a bank account, the information will be the balance of the account. But, based on what information does a search program perform. That is, what information does the program seek in order to find out the correct balance? Of course, it is the account number of the bank customer. In a search strategy, *records* and *keys* are the fundamental concepts. A record is an aggregation of information, which can be represented by an abstract type (discussed in Chapter 2). A key is an element of the record, which will identify the record. Usually, each key in a storage structure or a database is unique. For instance, the account number of bank customers cannot be duplicated. But, the content of records may include similar or the same information. For example, a person and his father can have separate accounts in the same bank. But, the father and the son may have the same address. A record should contain sufficient fields in order to hold necessary information. The following is a simplified record of a bank account:

Account number: integer number
Password: string
Name: string
Address: long string
Telephone number: integer number or string
Additional telephone number: integer number of string
Balance: float point number

Note that, it is not necessary for the bank application program to fill information in each record. For instance, the additional telephone number of the above record is optional. However, the key field (i.e. the account number) should always contain correct information.

The storage structure discussed in previous chapters (e.g. linked lists, or array) can be used to store records. Each record of a linked list or an array of records may contain the detailed information of a bank account. Linked lists and arrays are some of the fundamental structures to hold records. However, in this book, other sophisticated structures, such as binary trees, B-trees and graphs, can be used as well. In this chapter, we will discuss search strategies based on linked lists and arrays. Other search mechanisms for the particular structures will be discussed in each individual chapter.

Almost all programming languages have an implementation of the array data type. An array is a sequential collection of atomic elements or compound elements. Each element has an index. The index can identify an element, which is a similar concept to keys of a storage structure. However, index usually represents the physical address of an element. But, keys represent a logical address. Indices are sequential since memory (i.e. RAM) locations are continuous. Keys may or may not be sequential. If an array is implemented in a computer memory, the search strategy can be sequential or via some dynamic mechanism. In addition to array, linked lists can be used to store a sequence of atomic or compounded elements. Usually, linked lists are implemented in computer memory. And, an access strategy of linked lists should be sequential.

Another aspect of searching relates to the storage devices used to store information records. If the records are only stored in computer memory (i.e. RAM), the strategy is an *internal search.* If the records are stored completely or partially in hard disks, tapes or CD ROMs, the mechanism is an *external search.* In this chapter, we only discuss internal search. However, some of the methods can be used in external search as well.

8.2. Sequential Search

The simplest search strategy is the sequential search mechanism. Imagine that, there is a pile of photos from which you want to search for a picture. You can start from the first photo until you find the one, or search till the last photo (the photo is missing). The strategy is sequential. When you are looking for the picture, you are making a *comparison* between a photo and the picture in your mind. Comparison of sequential search can be on a single key, or on a compounded key (includes several search criteria). In a sequential storage structure, there are two indices, the first and the last indices, of which the boundary of maximal search is formed. In addition, a sequential search strategy needs to maintain a *current index*, which represents the position of the current comparison (i.e. to the photo you are looking at). In this chapter, we present the algorithms of searching. It is relatively easy to implement the algorithm in any programming language. The algorithm of sequential search follows:

```
Precondition: first is the first index of the storage structure
              last is the last index of the storage structure
              current is an index variable
              key is the search key to the target record
Postcondition: target is the index points to the record found.
               Or, target = −1 if the record is not found
Algorithm:
    Initial step: set current = first
    Search step: repeat {
                   If key == retrieve_key(current) then
                       Set target = current
                       Exit
                   Set current = next(current)
                   } until current == −1
                 If current · −1 then
                   Print "record found", retrieve_record(target)
                 Else
                   Print "record not found"
```

The sequential search algorithm firstly set the initial value of the current index (i.e. **current**). It is necessary to know that, in any iteration process, such as the for-loop statement, the repeat-until statement, etc., there are three important factors to watch out. They are the initial process, the incremental process, and the termination process. The search algorithm sets **current** to **first** for the initial process, uses a next function to increase the index value, and checks the termination process with the "**current** == −**1**" condition. Note that, in the algorithm, the "==" sign means to compare its left operand to its right operand, and to return a Boolean value. The next function returns a "−**1**" if the iteration is out of the storage boundary. The function call retrieve_key(**current**) takes an index and returns a key associated with the index. Similarly, the function call retrieve_record(**target**) takes an index and returns the record of the index. If there is record found in the storage structure, the record is printed; otherwise, the algorithm prints an error message.

8.2.1. *Search on Linked List*

The implementation of the sequential search depends on the underlying storage structure. It is possible to implement the algorithm using any type of structure, as long as the search process visits each record sequentially. But, we only present the implementation using linked list and array. Other structures are associated with their own searching strategy, which may not be sequential as well. The implementation using linked list uses the following mechanisms. Since linked lists are using pointers in a language such as C^{++}, indices are pointers. The next function can be implemented by updating the return value to point to the next record. However, the next function should be able to access the "**last**" value in order to check with the storage boundary. The retrieve_key function takes the pointer of a record, and returns the key of the record. Usually, it will use the membership function of the abstract data type associated with the record. The retrieve_record function uses the same strategy. But, the function returns a compound value of the entire record. The Print function, as a method of the abstract type, should be able to output the compound value. An example of a linked list is illustrated in Fig. 8.1:

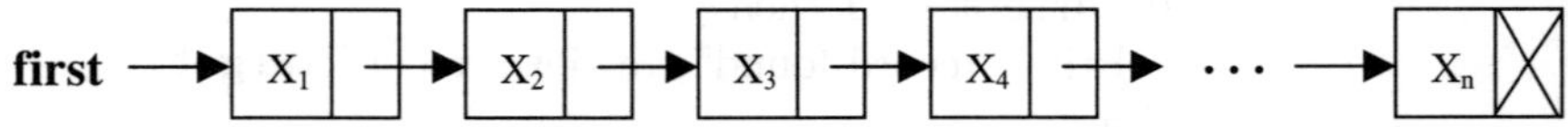

Fig. 8.1. A linked list.

0	1	2	3	4		n-1
X_1	X_2	X_3	X_4	X_5	...	X_n

Fig. 8.2. An array.

8.2.2. *Search on Array*

On the other hand, the sequential search implementation can be on an array. In this case, the next function can be an update of the **current** index. Since all of the indices are implemented using array indices, which are integers, it is relatively easier to trace or debug the program. The retrieve_key function can be replaced by an access to a record of array element. Similarly, the retrieve_record function gets values of the record. The algorithm used for array and for linked list should be the same. But, the implementation can be different.

The linked list implementation and the array implementation of the sequential search algorithm use the same strategy — sequential access of each record. However, it is not necessary for a search to be sequential, if array is used as a random access memory. However, if array is used as fast search storage, some preconditions should be established. In the next section, we discuss one of the faster search algorithms. An example of an array is illustrated in Fig. 8.2.

8.3. Binary Search

Suppose that, in your hand, you have a deck of student ID cards. And you want to search for a student. The worst case is you need to look at the cards one by one sequentially until the last student is found. This is sequential search. However, it is possible that you randomly look at some cards. If you are lucky, the student can be found in just a second. However, the random search mechanism does not guarantee you to find the student immediately. One of the methods that you can use to improve your luck but still perform reasonably is the *Binary Search* strategy. When you are checking a dictionary for a word, you assume it is in a location of the dictionary. Then, depending on where you tried, you will search forward or backward one or several times, until the word is found. The reason for searching forward and backward is that the words in a dictionary are sorted according to the alphabetical order. Conclusively, if we want such a fast search algorithm, two preconditions need to be established. First, the records should be sorted. Sorting algorithms will be discussed in Chapter 5.

Second, we need to "guess" for the starting point and decide which way to "guess" for the next search point, if necessary. In the following sections, we discuss the binary search algorithm. One condition to implement the binary search algorithm is the storage structure used should allow random access to every element. Therefore, linked list is not a suitable storage. Array is used for binary search.

8.3.1. *Binary Search Algorithm*

In Chapter 1, we discussed the concept of *recursion*. Recursion is a concept, which applies the same method to solve a problem, within a stepwise-decomposed domain, to find the solution. The process to find a student in a deck of ID cards can be recursively solved. Think about this. If the student number to be searched is smaller than the card picked, you do not need to care about the cards after the card has been currently selected. The deck of cards, before the card selected, may contain the target. The same procedure can be used to search the new deck of cards.

In order to realize such a search strategy, we need to have a boundary for search. Assuming that, a list of storage records is sorted. And we use **first** and **last** to bind the boundary, the recursive algorithm of binary search algorithm follows:

Precondition: **sorted_array** is an array of sorted records
first is the first index of the sorted array
last is the last index of the sorted array
current is an index variable
key is the search key to the target record
Postcondition: **target** is the index points to the record found.
Or, **target** = **−1** if the record is not found
Algorithm: **recursive_bs(first, last)**
Search step:
if **first** ≤ **last** {
current = (**first** + **last**) / 2
if **key** == **retrieve_key(current)** then
Return **current**
else if **key** > **retrieve_key(current)** then
Return **recursive_bs**(**current** + 1, **last**)
Else
Return **recursive_bs**(**first**, **current** − 1)
}
else Return **−1**

```
Algorithm: binary_search
    Step: target = recursive_bs(first, last)
          If target ≠ −1 then
              Print "record found", retrieve_record(target)
          Else
              Print "record not found"
```

The recursive algorithm (i.e. **recursive_bs**) takes two parameters. Note that, in a programming language that supports recursion, each function call will maintain a local variable space, such as the two parameters passed to the function. Recursion in a run-time environment is implemented by using a stack. That is, each call to the function has its own space. Therefore, the **first** and the **last** variables of each function call have different values.

The position, which we "guess" is the middle of the sorted array. If the key is found, we return the position. Otherwise, the right or the left side of the array is searched depending on whether the key is greater than or less than the current value found. The recursive function is called by another function. If the return value indicates a useful target position, the record is printed. Otherwise, the error message is printed.

Recursive function is natural since it reflects the definition of functions. For instance, the factorial function is defined recursively. However, in a procedural programming language, which use for-loop or while-loop statements for iterative computing, it is easier to think and code iteratively. Moreover, recursive programming takes stack space in memory, as each call to the recursive function allocates a new local parameter space. In general, iterative programming is faster for commercial computers. In the following algorithm, we present an iterative version of the binary search algorithm:

```
Algorithm: iterative_bs
    Search step:
        While first ≤ last {
            current = (first + last) / 2
            if key == retrieve_key(current) then
                Return current
            else if key > retrieve_key(current) then
                first = current + 1
            Else
                last = current − 1
        }
    Return −1
```

Algorithm: **binary_search**
Step: **target** = **iterative_bs**
If **target** $\neq -1$ then
Print "record found", retrieve_record(**target**)
Else
Print "record not found"

The iterative version does not use parameters. However, the **first** and the **last** variables of the array indices will be changed if necessary. The two versions of algorithms can be implemented in any programming language, except that the recursive version needs to run on a language, which supports recursion. The two versions produce the same result for the same array. They also perform the same search sequence. In the following example, suppose we want to search for the record with a key of 9, the content of the record, "Jason" will be returned. And the search order is presented as shown in Table 8.1.

The values of indices of the iteration is shown in Table 8.2.

The search example takes three iterations to find "Jason". It is the worst cast of such a process. If the record we want to search is "Mary", we will find that in the first iteration. In general, binary search is faster than sequential search. If we use sequential search, it takes six steps to find "Jason" and five steps to find "Mary". In the following section, we should have an analysis of the two algorithms.

8.4. Analysis

When one analyzes an algorithm, in general, we talk about the average behavior of the algorithm. However, there are three cases for the analysis.

Table 8.1.

Array Index	1	2	3	4	5	6	7	8	9
Key	−26	−5	−2	0	4	9	28	59	99
Content	Tim	Nina	Tom	John	Mary	Jason	George	Alex	Jason
Search Order					1	3	2		

Table 8.2.

First	1	6	6
Last	9	9	6
Current	5	7	6

The *best case* is the lucky situation, of which the algorithm finds its solution in the shortest time. The *average case* is the one we are working on, which means on the average, how many steps the algorithm may take to complete the job. The *worst case* is, of course, the longest time for the algorithm to find the solution.

In a sequential search, if there are n elements in the storage structure, the worst case of search is that n steps are taken. Of course, the best case is that only 1 step is taken. But, what about the average case? Theoretically, the element could be in the first position, the second position, or, the nth position. Thus, the average case should take an average of all of these possible positions:

$$(1 + 2 + 3 + \cdots + (n - 1) + n)/n = (n + 1)/2$$

Consequently, the sequential search is an algorithm of time complexity of $O(n)$. The binary search algorithm is analyzed in the similar manner. If we are lucky, the middle of the search array contains the target record. Then, the best case is 1 step. The binary search algorithm uses a strategy to divide the array into two parts each time to guess the solution. But, how many times can we divide an array of n elements? The *halving function* is defined by $H(n)$ = *the number of times that* n *can be divided by two, stopping when the result is less than one.* And, $H(n) = \lfloor \log_2 n \rfloor + 1$. It turns out that $H(n)$ is nearly equal to the base 2 logarithm of n. The worst case of binary search is, therefore, equal to $O(\log_2 n)$. The analysis of average case is tedious. But, the average case of binary search has the time complexity same as the worst case, which is $O(\log_2 n)$. conclusively, we say that binary search is an algorithm of time complexity that equals $O(\log_2 n)$.

8.4.1. *The Comparison Trees*

Search algorithms use comparisons to identify the target as well as to decide the next position of search. The comparison process can be visualized, in order to have a better understanding of the search efficiency. According to the example presented in Sec. 8.3.1, and the sequential search algorithm that compares the equality of a target to the key, the comparison tree of sequential search can be drawn as shown in Fig. 8.3.

Note that, each comparison results in the equal (to the left tree) or the unequal (to the right tree) situation. A box representing the target record is found, and the circle representing the record is not found. For a sequential search, the worst case will result when one searches toward the end of the search tree. The binary search uses the equality comparison, as well as the inequality comparisons (i.e. the $\leq$ and the $\geq$ operators).

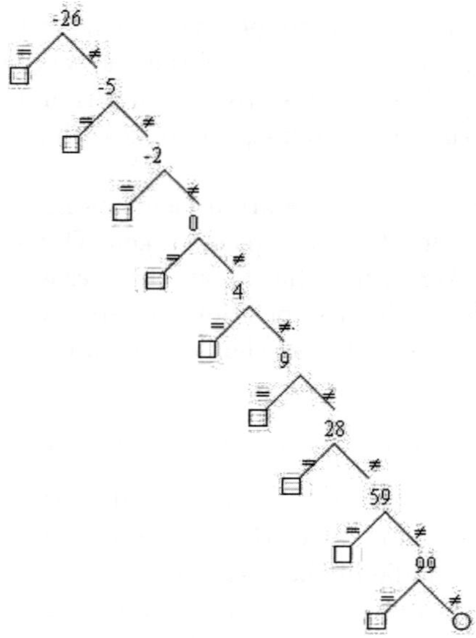

Fig. 8.3. The comparison tree of sequential search.

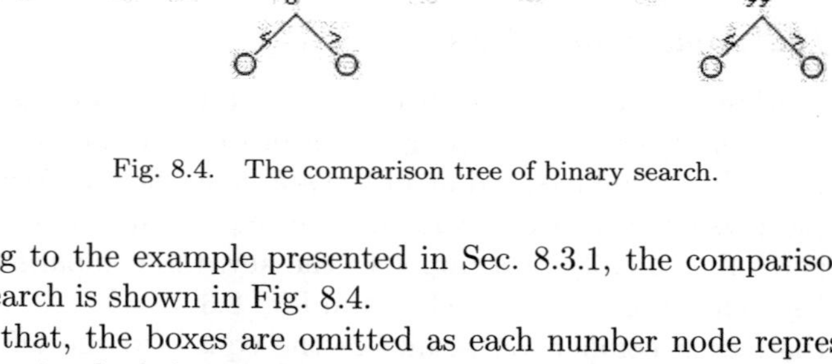

Fig. 8.4. The comparison tree of binary search.

According to the example presented in Sec. 8.3.1, the comparison tree of binary search is shown in Fig. 8.4.

Note that, the boxes are omitted as each number node represents the success retrieval of the number. From the visualized search trees, we can see that binary search algorithm performs better than sequential search in general. However, binary search requires to use array, and the data records should be sorted. On the other hand, sequential search does not have these restrictions.

8.5. Fibonacci Search

Binary search is faster than sequential search. But, is there a search algorithm faster than binary search? It is proven that, the best possible time complexity of search n objects will be $O(\log_2 n)$. However, within this restriction, we may improve the efficiency of the search algorithm. In the binary search algorithm, we use a division operator, which is time consuming. One way to improve the efficiency is to replace the division by a shift operator. Based on the integer representation used in many commercial computers, a right-shift operation will divide and truncate an integer, which is used as the index of the search array. On the other hand, it is possible to use the subtraction operator, if the programming language does not support the shift operator. Fibonacci search uses such a strategy. We have set this as an exercise problem. The Fibonacci search algorithm is very similar to binary search. However, it will perform better since subtraction is faster than division.

Exercises

Beginner's Exercises

1. Write a program, input a number, n, and read from a disk file of n records. A record can take a format similar to the one discussed in Sec. 8.1. Store these records in a linked list. Write a sequential search function, which accepts a key and prints the corresponding record or displays an error message if the record is not found.
2. Write a program using an array of n records, which is filled with sorted records. The sorting order is according to the key of each record. Write a binary search function, which accepts a key and prints the corresponding record or displays an error message if the record is not found.
3. A sorted array F with data $2, 6, 9, 11, 13, 18, 20, 25, 26, 28$. Please show how the following binary search algorithm works to find "9" from the input array F.

```
procedure BINSRCH(F , n , i , k)
    front ← 1 ; rear ← n
        while 1 <= n do
            m ← ⌊front + rear)/2 ⌋
            case
            : k > k_m : front ← m + 1          //look in upper half
            : k = k_m : i ← m ; return
```

: k < k_m : rear ← m − 1 *//look in lower half*
end
end
i ← 0 *//no record with key k*
end BINSRCH

4. Assume that there is an array with indices and keys shown below.

Array Index	1	2	3	4	5	6	7	8	9	10	11	12	13	14	15	16	17	18
Key	−26	−5	−2	0	7	11	13	24	35	39	44	46	52	55	59	67	72	79

Please show the sequence of compared keys when using binary search algorithm to search the key "−2."

Intermediate Exercises

5. Revise Exercise 2, by adding a counter before each of the comparison statement, to count the number of comparisons used. Write a program to invoke the binary search function, with all of the keys of the records as parameters on iterations. Summarize the number of comparisons used and find how many times in average, the comparison is made to retrieve all records.
6. The time complexity of binary search is ________.

Advanced Exercises

7. The Fibonacci number is defined as the following:

$$f(0) = 1$$
$$f(1) = 1$$
$$f(n) = f(n-1) + f(n-2), \text{ if } n > 1$$

Revise the binary search algorithm, using subtraction to replace the division operator. Use the concept of Fibonacci number.
8. On an ordered file with keys (1, 2, 3, 4, 5, 6, 7, 8, 9, 10, 11, 12, 13, 14, 15, 16), use Fibonacci search to determine the number of key comparisons made while searching the keys "7" and "10." (Note: Fibonacci number $F_5 = 5$, $F_6 = 8$, $F_7 = 13$.)

Chapter 9

Sorting

QUN JIN

Waseda University, Japan

jin@waseda.jp

In this chapter, we discuss sorting algorithms. We begin by introducing three basic sorting methods: Selection Sort, Insertion Sort and Bubble Sort. These methods are easy to understand and easy to program, but they are not very efficient. We then discuss three more efficient sorting methods: Quick Sort, Heap Sort and Merge Sort, and briefly describe two more improved sorting methods: Shell Sort and Radix Sort. Finally, we give the performance comparison of all these sorting methods.

9.1. Basic Sorting

First, let us consider what sorting is. Sorting is an operation that arranges the data in some appropriate order according to some key. We have many examples in our daily life. An English dictionary is a good example, in which all words are arranged in alphabetic order. A phone directory is another one, in which phone numbers are listed in some order.

There are two kinds of sorting algorithms: *Internal Sort* and *External Sort.* Algorithms for sorting data collections that fit into main memory (for example, an array in C language) are called *internal sorting.* Selection Sort, Insertion Sort, Bubble Sort, Quick Sort and Heap Sort are internal sorting. On the other hand, algorithms for sorting data collections from tape or disk are called *external sorting.* Merge Sort is external sorting.

Now let us see how to sort a collection of data. Before discussing the basic ideas of sorting algorithms, we have to describe some general terminologies.

Data compositions: files of records containing keys.

File: collection of records.

Record: collection of fields.

Field: collection of characters.

Key: uniquely identifies a record in a file, used to control the sort.

The basic sorting operations that arrange the data in a specific order according to a specific key are *comparison* and *exchange*. That is, compare two items of the data and exchange their places in the data if they are not in the proper order by the specific key.

9.1.1. *Selection Sort*

Selection Sort is one of the simplest algorithms. The basic idea is to first select successive elements in the ascending order and place them into their proper position. Then find the smallest element from the array, and exchange it with the first element. Find the second smallest element, and exchange it with the second element; and so on. Repeat these procedures until the data is sorted in the proper order.

The following program is an example of implementation in C language for Selection Sort.

```
void selection_sort(int array[], int n)
{
 int i, j, min, tmp;
 for (i = 0; i < n; i++) {
  min = i;
  for (j = i + 1; j < n; j++) {
   if (array[j] < array[min]) min = j;
  }
  tmp = array[min];
  array[min] = array[i];
  array[i] = tmp;
 }
}
```

For each i from 1 to $n-1$, it compares array[i] with array [$i+1$], ..., array [n], and exchanges array [i] with the smallest one of them.

Quiz: Generate an array of 10 random integers, and write a complete C program using Selection Sort to sort the array into increasing order.

[Hint: Refer to the Web Page or CD-ROM to see the sorting process.]

9.1.2. *Insertion Sort*

Insertion Sort is almost as simple as Selection Sort, but a little more flexible. The basic idea is to sort a collection of records by inserting them into an already sorted file. The procedure can be described as follows. First, take elements one by one, and then insert the element in its proper position among those already taken and sorted in a new collection; repeat these processes until all elements are taken and sorted in the proper order.

The following program is an example implementation of the above sorting procedure.

```
void insertion_sort(int array[], int n)
{
 int i, j, tmp;
 for (i = 1; i < n; i++) {
  tmp = array[i];
  for (j = i; array[j - 1]>tmp; j--) {
   array[j] = array[j - 1];
  }
  array[j] = tmp;
 }
}
```

For each i from 2 to n, the elements array[1], ..., array $[i]$ are sorted by placing array $[i]$ into its proper position among the sorted list of elements in array [1], ..., array $[i-1]$.

Quiz: Generate an array of 10 random integers, and write a complete C program using Insertion Sort to sort the array into increasing order.

[Hint: Refer to the Web Page or CD-ROM to see the sorting process.]

9.1.3. *Bubble Sort*

The third elementary sorting algorithm introduced here is called Bubble Sort. The basic idea of this algorithm is to let greater elements "*bubble*" to the right-hand side of the sorted file (or array). The sorting process is given as follows. First, compare two elements in the neighbor. If they are not in the proper order, exchange them (that is, swap them). Therefore, the greatest element "bubbles" to the most right. Next, compare two elements in the neighbor, except the greatest one or greater ones that have already been sorted on the right. If they are not in order, exchange them (swap), so that a greater element "bubbles" to the right. Repeat the above processes until all elements are sorted in the proper order.

We show an example implementation in C language for Bubble Sort below.

```
void bubble_sort(int array[], int n)
{
 int i, j, tmp;
 for (i = n; i > 0; i--) {
  for (j = 1; j < i; j++) {
   if (array[j - 1]>array[j]) {
    tmp = array[j - 1];
    array[j - 1] = array[j];
    array[j] = tmp;
   }
  }
 }
}
```

During one pass, an element will be continuously moved to the right-hand side if it is larger than its right neighbor until it encounters a larger element. Then the larger element will be compared with its right neighbor, and moved to the right-hand side if it is larger. On completion of the first pass, the largest element reaches the right end of the array. On the second pass, the second largest element is put into the second position to the right end, and so on.

Quiz: Generate an array of 10 random integers, and write a complete C program using Bubble Sort to sort the array into increasing order.

[Hint: Refer to the Web Page or CD-ROM to see the sorting process.]

9.2. Quick Sort

Invented in 1960 by C. A. R. Hoare, Quick Sort is one of the most popular sorting algorithms that have been well investigated. It has been greatly improved since then. Quick Sort is quite easy to be implemented, and has a good average performance ($N \log N$), but not very stable. The performance in the worst case is N^*N.

The basic idea of Quick Sort is to apply the so-called "*divide-and-conquer*" paradigm, which works based on the mechanism to partition the file into two parts, then recursively sort the parts independently. The detailed procedures are as follows: First choose a pivotal (central) element (for example, first, last or middle element). Elements on either side are then moved so that the elements on one side of the pivot are smaller and

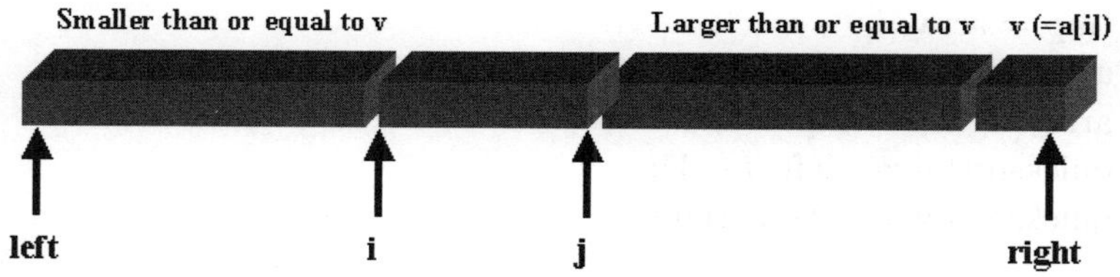

Fig. 9.1. Basic algorithm for Quick Sort.

those on the other side are larger. Apply the above procedures to the two parts until the whole file is sorted in the proper order.

The core part of the basic algorithm is given below.

```
quicksort(int array[], int left, int right) {
        int i;
  if (right > left) {
        i = partition(left, right);
        quicksort(array, left, i - 1);
        quicksort(array, i + 1, right);
        }
        }
```

where partition (left, right) makes the following conditions hold: when the element array[i] is placed in its final place, all elements of array[left], ..., array[$i-1$] are smaller than or equal to array[i], and all elements of array[$i+1$], ..., array[right] are larger than or equal to array[i]. That is, array[j] $<=$ array[i] for $j < i$ and array[j] $>=$ array[i] for $j > i$, as shown in Fig. 9.1.

A full implementation for Quick Sort in C language is given as follows.

```
quicksort(int array[], int left, int right) {
  int v, i, j, tmp;
  if (right > left) {
    v = array[right]; i = left -1; j = right;
    for (; ;) {
      while (array[++i] < v);
      while (array[--j] > v);
      if (i >= j) break;
      tmp = array[i];
      array[i] = array[j];
      array[j] = tmp;
    }
```

```
    tmp = array[i];
    array[i] = array[right];
    array[right] = tmp;
    quicksort(array, left, i − 1);
    quicksort(array, i + 1, right)
  }
}
```

In this sample program, the variable v holds the current value of the "partitioning elements" array[right] and i and j are the left and right scan pointers, respectively. Quick Sort may be implemented without the recursive approach. The nonrecursive implementation for Quick Sort is given below, by using the stack.

```
quicksort(int array[], int n) {
  int i, left, right;
  left = 1; right = n; stackinit( );
  for (;;) {
    while (right > left) {
          i = partition(array, left, right);
      if (i-left > right-i) {
        push(left);
        push(i-left);
        left = i + 1;
      }
      else {
        push(i + 1);
        push(right);
        right = i − 1;
      }
    if (stackempty( )) break;
    right = pop( );
    left = pop( );
  }
}
```

Quiz: Generate an array of 10 random integers, and write a complete C program using Quick Sort (both Recursive and Nonrecursive versions) to sort the array into increasing order.

[Hint: Refer to the Web Page or CD-ROM to see the sorting process.]

9.3. Heap Sort

Heap Sort is an elegant and efficient sorting algorithm that has been widely used. Good performance (NlogN) is guaranteed in any case. Another advantage of Heap Sort is that no extra memory is needed in the sorting process. Comparing with Quick Sort, inner loop in Heap Sort is a bit longer, generally about twice as slow as Quick Sort on the average.

Before introducing the algorithm of Heap Sort, we firstly give a brief introduction on the so-called *Priority Queue*. Let us recall a deletion operation in a stack and a queue. It deletes the newest element from a stack, whereas it deletes the oldest element from a queue. Priority queue is a generalization of the stack and the queue, which supports the operations of inserting a new element and deleting the largest element. Application of priority queues includes simulation, numerical computation, job scheduling, etc.

Now, let us see what the heap is. Heap is a data structure to support the priority queue operations. Heap can be represented in a complete binary tree, in which every node satisfies the so-called *heap condition*: the key in each node is larger than (or equal to) the keys in its children (if available); the largest key is in the root. Heap represented as an array could be something like this: root in array[1]; children of root in array[2] and array[3]; ...; children of i in array[$2i$] and array[$2i + 1$] (parent of i in array[$i/2$]); and so on.

The basic idea of Heap Sort is simply to build a heap containing the elements to be sorted and then to remove them all in order.

The following program is a function that implements the *down heap* operation on a heap.

```
void down_heap(int array[], int n, int x)
{
 int i, v;
 v = array[x];
 while (x <= n/2) {
   i = x + x;
   if (i<n && array[i] <array[i + 1]) i++;
   if (v>=array[i]) break;
   array[x] = array[i];
   x = i;
 }
 array[x] = v;
}
```

Using the above function, we may have an example implementation for the Heap Sort.

```
void heap_sort(int array[], int n)
{
  int x, tmp;
  for (x = n/2; x >= 0; x--) {
    down_heap(array, n, x);
  }
  while (n > 0) {
    tmp = array[0];
    array[0] = array[n];
    array[n] = tmp;
    down_heap(array, --n, 0);
  }
}
```

Please note here we have assumed the *downheap* function has been modified to take the array and heap size as the first two arguments.

Quiz: Generate an array of ten random integers, and write a complete C program using Heap Sort to sort the array into increasing order.

[Hint: Refer to the Web Page or CD-ROM to see the sorting process.]

9.4. Merge Sort

Merging is the operation of combining two sorted files to make one larger sorted file, while selection, as we have seen in Quick Sort, is the operation of partitioning a file into two independent files. We might consider that selection and merging are complementary operations.

Merger Sort is one of the most common algorithms for external sorting. It has a rather good and stable performance ($N \log N$, even in the worst case), the same as Quick Sort and Heap Sort. One of its major drawbacks is that Merge Sort needs linear extra space for the merge, which means it can only sort half the memory.

Both Quick Sort and Merge Sort apply the "divide-and-conquer" paradigm. As we saw in Quick Sort, a selection procedure was followed by two recursive calls. However, for Merge Sort, two recursive calls was followed by a merging procedure, which could be described as follows: First divide the file in half; sort the two halves recursively; and then merge the two halves together while sorting them.

The following program is an example in C language for Merge Sort with two recursive calls, where we have used $b[l], \ldots, b[r]$ as an auxiliary array to manage the merging operation without sentinels.

```
mergesort(int a[], int l, int r) {
  int i, j, k, m;
  if (r > l) {
    m = (r + l)/2;
    mergesort(a, l, m);
    mergesort(a, m + 1, r);
    for (i = m + 1; i > l; i--) b[i - 1] = a[i - 1];
    for (j = m; j < r; j++) b[r + m - j] = a[j + 1];
    for (k = l; k <= r; k++)
      a[k] = (b[i] < b[j]) ? b[i++] : b[j--];
  }
}
```

A C program example without nonrecursive calls is also given below, using linked lists, in which a bottom–up approach has been applied.

```
struct node *mergesort(struct node *c) {
  int i, n;
  struct node *a, *b, *head; *todo, *t;
  head = (struct node *) malloc(sizeof *head);
  head->next = c;
  a = z;
  for (n = 1; a != head->next; n = n + n) {
    todo = head->next;
    c = head;
    while (todo != z) {
      t = todo; a = t;
      for (i = 1; i < n; i++) t = t->next;
      b = t->next;
      t->next = z;
      t = b;
      for (i = 1; i < n; i++) t = t->next;
      todo = t->next;
      t->next = z;
      c->next = merge(a, b);
      for (i = 1; i <= n + n; i++) c = c->next;
    }
```

```
  }
  return head->next;
}
```

Quiz: Generate an array of 10 random integers, and write a complete C program using Merge Sort (both Recursive and Non-recursive versions) to sort the array into increasing order.

[Hint: Refer to the Web Page or CD-ROM to see the sorting process.]

9.5. Shell Sort

Shell Sort is basically an improvement of Insertion Sort. As we have seen before, Insertion Sort is slow since it compares and exchanges only elements in neighbor. Shell Sort solves this problem by allowing comparison and exchange of elements that are far apart to gain speed. The detailed procedure is given as follows: First take every hth element to form a new collection of elements and sort them (using Insertion Sort), which is called h-sort; Then choose a new h with a smaller value, for example, calculated by $h_i+1 = 3^* h_i+1$, or $h_i = (h_i+1-1)/3$; $h_0 = 1$, thus, we have a sequence [. . . , 1093, 364, 121, 40, 13, 4, 1]; Repeat until $h = 1$, then the file will be sorted in the proper order.

An implementation in C language for Shell Sort is given below.

```
void shell_sort(int array[], int n)
{
 int i, j, k, tmp;
 for (k = 1; k < n/9; k = 3 * k + 1);
 for (; k > 0; k/ = 3) {
  for (i = k; i < n; i++) {
   j = i;
   while (j >= k && array[j - k] > array[j]) {
  tmp = array[j];
  array[j] = array[j - k];
  array[j - k] = tmp;
  j- = k;
   }
  }
 }
}
```

Quiz: Generate an array of 10 random integers, and write a complete C program using Shell Sort to sort the array into increasing order.

[Hint: Refer to the Web Page or CD-ROM to see the sorting process.]

9.6. Radix Sort

The basic idea of Radix Sort is to treat keys as numbers represented in a base-M number system, for example, $M = 2$ or some power of 2, and process with individual digits of the numbers, so that all keys with leading bit 0 appear before all keys with leading bit 1. And among the keys with leading bit 0, all keys with second bit 0 appear before all keys with second bit 1, and so forth. There are two approaches for Radix Sort: Radix Exchange Sort and Straight Radix Sort. The feature of Radix Exchange Sort is that it scans from left to right, that is, scans from the left to find a key which starts with bit 1, and scans from the right to find a key which starts with bit 0, then exchange; continue the process until the scanning pointers cross. This leads to a recursive sorting procedure that is very similar to Quick Sort. On the other hand, Straight Radix Sort, as an alternative method, scans the bits from right to left.

We show a C Program Example for Radix Exchange Sort as follows, which is very similar to the recursive implementation of Quick Sort.

```
void radixexchange(int array[], int l, int r, int b)
{
 int i, j, tmp;
 if (r > l && b >= 0) {
  i = l;
  j = r;
  while (j != i){
    while (bits(array[i], b, 1) == 0 && i < j) i++;
    while (bits(array[j], b, 1) != 0 && j > i) j--;
    tmp = array[i];
    array[i] = array[j];
    array[j] = tmp;
  }
  if (bits(array[r], b, 1) == 0) j++;
  radixexchange(array, l, j - 1, b - 1);
  radixexchange(array, j, r, b - 1);
 }
}
```

Table 9.1. Performance comparison.

Algorithms	**Performance**	**Comments**
Selection Sort	N^2	good for small and partially sorted data
Insertion Sort	N^2	good for almost sorted data
Bubble Sort	N^2	good for $N < 100$
Quick Sort	$N \log N$	excellent
Heap Sort	$N \log N$	excellent
Merge Sort	$\log N$	good for external sort
Shell Sort	$N^{1.5}$	good for medium N
Radix Sort	$N \log N$	excellent

```
unsigned bits(unsigned x, int k, int j)
{
 return (x >> k) & ~ (~ 0 << j);
}
```

Quiz: Generate an array of 10 random integers, and write a complete C program using Radix Sort to sort the array into increasing order.

[Hint: Refer to the Web Page or CD-ROM to see the sorting process.]

9.7. Comparison of Sorting Algorithms

In this section, we give a performance comparison of all these sorting algorithms described in this chapter. As shown in Table 9.1, Selection Sort, Insertion Sort and Bubble Sort have a performance of N^2. Selection Sort is good for small and partially sorted data, while Insertion Sort is good for data that are already almost sorted. On the other hand, Heap Sort is not so good for sorted data, but has a very good performance of $N \log N$. Quick Sort and Radix Sort have the same performance as Heap Sort. They are considered to be excellent among all these sorting algorithms. Bubble Sort is good for $N < 100$, and Shell Sort is considered to be good for medium N, which has a performance of $N^{1.5}$. Finally, Merge Sort has a performance of $\log N$, and is good for external sort.

References

1. R. Sedgewick, *Algorithms in C*, Addison-Wesley, 1990.
2. M. A. Weiss, *Data Structures and Algorithm Analysis in C*, Second Edition, Addison-Wesley, 1997.

3. R. Kruse, C. L. Tondo and B. Leung, *Data Structures and Program Design in C*, Second Edition, Prentice-Hall, 1997.
4. I. T. Adamson, *Data Structures and Algorithms: A First Course*, Springer, 1996.

Appendices

Appendix 9.1.1: *Example of a Complete C Program Source for Selection Sort*

```
#include <stdio.h>
#include <stdlib.h>
#define SIZE 10

void selection_sort(int array[], int n)
{
  int i, j, min, tmp;

  for (i=0; i<n; i++) {
    min = i;

    for (j=i+1; j<n; j++) {
      if (array[j] < array[min]) min = j;
    }

    tmp = array[min];
    array[min] = array[i];
    array[i] = tmp;
  }
}

main ()
{
  int i, j;
  int order[SIZE] = {25, 41, 92, 3, 60, 18, 76, 39, 54, 87};

  printf("Initial Order:\n");
  for (i=0; i<SIZE; i++) {
    printf("%d ", order[i]);
  }
  printf("\n");

  printf("Selection Sort:\n");
  selection_sort(order, SIZE);
```

```
    for (i=0; i<SIZE; i++) {
      printf("%d ", order[i]);
    }
    printf("\n");
  }
```

Appendix 9.1.2: *Example of a Complete C Program Source for Insertion Sort*

```
#include <stdio.h>
#include <stdlib.h>
#define SIZE 10

void insertion_sort(int array[], int n)
{
  int i, j, tmp;

  for (i=1; i<n; i++) {
    tmp = array[i];

    for (j=i; array[j-1]>tmp; j--) {
      array[j] = array[j-1];
    }

    array[j] = tmp;
  }
}

main ()
{
  int i, j;
  int order[SIZE] = {25, 41, 92, 3, 60, 18, 76, 39, 54, 87};

  printf("Initial Order:\n");
  for (i=0; i<SIZE; i++) {
    printf("%d ", order[i]);
  }
  printf("\n");

  printf("Insertion Sort:\n");
  insertion_sort(order, SIZE);

  for (i=0; i<SIZE; i++) {
```

```
    printf("%d ", order[i]);
  }
  printf("\n");
}
```

Appendix 9.1.3: *Example of a Complete C Program Source for Bubble Sort*

```
#include <stdio.h>
#include <stdlib.h>
#define SIZE 10

void bubble_sort(int array[], int n)
{
  int i, j, tmp;

  for (i=n; i>0; i--) {
    for (j=1; j<i; j++) {

      if (array[j-1]>array[j]) {
tmp = array[j-1];
array[j-1] = array[j];
array[j] = tmp;
      }

    }
  }
}

main ()
{
  int i, j;
  int order[SIZE] = {25, 41, 92, 3, 60, 18, 76, 39, 54, 87};

  printf("Initial Order:\n");
  for (i=0; i<SIZE; i++) {
    printf("%d ", order[i]);
  }
  printf("\n");

  printf("Bubble Sort:\n");
  bubble_sort(order, SIZE);
```

```
  for (i=0; i<SIZE; i++) {
    printf("%d ", order[i]);
  }
  printf("\n");
}
```

Appendix 9.2.1: *Example of a Complete C Program Source for Quick Sort*

1. Recursive Quick Sort

```
#include <stdio.h>
#include <stdlib.h>
#define SIZE 10

void printArray(int[]);

void quick_sort_r(int array[], int l, int r)
{
  int i, j, v, tmp;

  if (l < r) {
    v = array[r];
    i = l-1;
    j = r;

    while (1) {
      while (array[++i] < v);
      while (array[--j] > v);

      if (i>=j) break;

      tmp = array[i];
      array[i] = array[j];
      array[j] = tmp;

      printArray(array);
    }

    tmp = array[i];
    array[i] = array[r];
    array[r] = tmp;
    printArray(array);
```

```
    quick_sort_r(array, l, i-1);
    quick_sort_r(array, i+1, r);
  }
}


void printArray(int a[])
{
  int i;

  for (i=0; i<SIZE; i++){
    printf("%d ", a[i]);
  }
  printf("\n");
}

main ()
{
  int i, j;
  int order[SIZE] = {25, 41, 92, 3, 60, 18, 76, 39, 54, 87};

  printf("Initial Order:\n");
  printArray(order);

  printf("Quick Sort:\n");
  quick_sort_r(order, 0, SIZE-1);

  printArray(order);
}
```

2. Nonrecursive Quick Sort

```
#include <stdio.h>
#include <stdlib.h>
#define SIZE 10
#define MAX 100

void push(int);
int pop();
void stackinit();
int stackempty();

int stack[MAX];
```

```
void printArray(int a[])
{
  int i;

  for (i=0; i<SIZE; i++){
    printf("%d ", a[i]);
  }
  printf("\n");
}

void quick_sort(int array[], int n)
{
  int i, j, v, tmp, l=1, r=n;

  stackinit();

  while (1) {
    while (l < r) {
      v = array[r];
      i = l-2;
      j = r;

      while (1) {
while (array[++i] < v);
while (array[--j] > v);

if (i>=j) break;

tmp = array[i];
array[i] = array[j];
array[j] = tmp;

printArray(array);
      }

      tmp = array[i];
      array[i] = array[r];
      array[r] = tmp;
      printArray(array);
      if (r-i < i-l) {
push(l);
push(i-1);
l = i+1;
      } else {
push(i+1);
push(r);
```

```
r = i-1;
      }
    }

    if (stackempty()) break;

    r = pop();
    l = pop();
  }
}

void push(int x)
{
  int i;

  for (i=0; i<MAX; i++) {
    if (stack[i] == 0) {
      stack[i] = x;
      return;
    }
  }
}

int pop()
{
  int i, v;

  for (i=0; i<MAX; i++) {
    if (stack[i] == 0 && i>0) {
      v = stack[i-1];
      stack[i-1] = 0;
      return v;
    }
  }

  return NULL;
}

void stackinit()
{
  int i;

  for (i=0; i<MAX; i++){
    stack[i] = 0;
  }
}
```

```
int stackempty()
{
  if (stack[0] == 0) return 1;
  else return 0;
}

main ()
{
  int i, j;
  int order[SIZE] = {25, 41, 92, 3, 60, 18, 76, 39, 54, 87};

  printf("Initial Order:\n");
  printArray(order);

  printf("Quick Sort:\n");
  quick_sort(order, SIZE-1);

  printArray(order);
}
```

Appendix 9.3.1: *Example of a Complete C Program Source for Heap Sort*

```
#include <stdio.h>
#include <stdlib.h>
#define SIZE 10

void down_heap(int[], int, int);

void heap_sort(int array[], int n)
{
  int x, tmp;

  for (x=n/2; x>=0; x--) {
    down_heap(array, n, x);
  }

  while (n>0) {
    tmp = array[0];
    array[0] = array[n];
    array[n] = tmp;

    down_heap(array, --n, 0);
  }
}
```

```
void down_heap(int array[], int n, int x)
{
  int i, v;
  v = array[x];

  while (x <= n/2) {
    i = x+x;
    if (i<n && array[i]<array[i+1]) i++;

    if (v>=array[i]) break;

    array[x] = array[i];
    x = i;
  }

  array[x] = v;
}

main ()
{
  int i, j;
  int order[SIZE] = {25, 41, 92, 3, 60, 18, 76, 39, 54, 87};

  printf("Initial Order:\n");
  for (i=0; i<SIZE; i++) {
    printf("%d ", order[i]);
  }
  printf("\n");

  printf("Heap Sort:\n");
  heap_sort(order, SIZE-1);

  for (i=0; i<SIZE; i++) {
    printf("%d ", order[i]);
  }
  printf("\n");
}
```

Appendix 9.4.1: *Example of a Complete C Program Source for Merge Sort*

1. Recursive Merge Sort

```
#include <stdio.h>
#include <stdlib.h>
```

```
#define SIZE 10

void printArray(int a[])
{
  int i;

  for (i=0; i<SIZE; i++){
    printf("%d ", a[i]);
  }
  printf("\n");
}

void merge_sort_r(int array[], int l, int r)
{
  int i, j, u, v, tmp[r];

  if (l<r) {
    v = (l+r)/2;
    merge_sort_r(array, l, v);
    merge_sort_r(array, v+1, r);

    for (i=v+1; i>l; i--) tmp[i-1] = array[i-1];
    for (j=v; j<r; j++) tmp[r+v-j] = array[j+1];

    for (u=l; u<=r; u++) {
      if (tmp[i] < tmp[j]) {
array[u] = tmp[i++];
      } else {
array[u] = tmp[j--];
      }
    }
    printArray(array);
  }
}

main ()
{
  int i, j;
  int order[SIZE] = {25, 41, 92, 3, 60, 18, 76, 39, 54, 87};

  printf("Initial Order:\n");
  printArray(order);

  printf("Merge Sort:\n");
  merge_sort_r(order, 0, SIZE-1);
```

```
  printArray(order);
}
```

2. Nonrecursive Merge Sort

```
#include <stdio.h>
#include <stdlib.h>
#define SIZE 10

struct node *tail;

struct node *merge(struct node *, struct node *);

struct node *merge_sort(struct node *c)
{
  int i, n;
  struct node *a, *b, *head, *todo, *t;

  head = (struct node *)malloc(sizeof (struct node *));
  head->next = c;
  tail->next = tail;
  a = tail;

  for (n=1; a != head->next; n=n+n) {
    todo = head->next;
    c = head;

    while (todo != tail) {
      t = todo;
      a = t;

      for (i=1; i<n; i++) t = t->next;
      b = t->next;
      t->next = tail;
      t = b;
      for (i=1; i<n; i++) t = t->next;
      todo = t->next;
      t->next = tail;
      c->next = merge(a, b);
      for (i=1; i<=n+n; i++) c = c->next;
    }
  }
  return head->next;
}
```

```
struct node *merge(struct node *a, struct node *b)
{
  struct node *c = tail;

  do
    if (a->key <= b->key) {
      c->next = a;
      c = a;
      c = a->next;

    } else {
      c->next = b;
      c = b;
      b = b->next;

    }
  while (c != tail);

  c = tail->next;
  tail->next = tail;

  return c;
}

void print_stack(struct node *c) {
  while (c != tail) {
    printf("%d ", c->key);
    c = c->next;
  }
  printf("\n");
}
```

Appendix 9.5.1: *Example of a Complete C Program Source for Shell Sort*

```
#include <stdio.h>
#include <stdlib.h>
#define SIZE 10

void shell_sort(int array[], int n)
{
  int i, j, k, tmp;

  for (k=1; k < n/9; k=3*k+1);
```

```
  for (; k>0; k/=3) {
    for (i=k; i<n; i++) {
      j = i;

      while (j>=k && array[j-k] > array[j]) {
tmp = array[j];
array[j] = array[j-k];
array[j-k] = tmp;

j -= k;
      }
    }
  }
}

main ()
{
  int i, j;
  int order[SIZE] = {25, 41, 92, 3, 60, 18, 76, 39, 54, 87};

  printf("Initial Order:\n");
  for (i=0; i<SIZE; i++) {
    printf("%d ", order[i]);
  }
  printf("\n");

  printf("Shell Sort:\n");
  shell_sort(order, SIZE);

  for (i=0; i<SIZE; i++) {
    printf("%d ", order[i]);
  }
  printf("\n");
}
```

Appendix 9.6.1: *Example of a Complete C Program Source for Radix Sort*

```
#include <stdio.h>
#include <stdlib.h>
#define SIZE 10

unsigned bits(unsigned, int, int);

void radixexchange(int array[], int l, int r, int b)
```

```
{
  int i, j, tmp;

  if (r>l && b>=0) {
    i = l;
    j = r;

    while (j != i){
      while (bits(array[i], b, 1) == 0 && i<j) i++;
      while (bits(array[j], b, 1) != 0 && j>i) j--;

      tmp = array[i];
      array[i] = array[j];
      array[j] = tmp;
    }

    if (bits(array[r], b, 1) == 0) j++;
    radixexchange(array, l, j-1, b-1);
    radixexchange(array, j, r, b-1);
  }
}

unsigned bits(unsigned x, int k, int j)
{
  return (x>>k) & ~(~0<<j);
}

main ()
{
  int i, j;
  int order[SIZE] = {25, 41, 92, 3, 60, 18, 76, 39, 54, 87};

  printf("Initial Order:\n");
  for (i=0; i<SIZE; i++) {
    printf("%d ", order[i]);
  }
  printf("\n");

  printf("Radix Sorting...\n");
  radixexchange(order, 0, SIZE-1, 30);

  for (i=0; i<SIZE; i++) {
    printf("%d ", order[i]);
  }
  printf("\n");
}
```

Exercises

Beginner's Exercises

1. Generate an array of 20 random integers. Use Selection Sort to sort the array into increasing order.
2. Use Insertion Sort to sort the array created in Exercise 1 into increasing order.
3. Use Bubble Sort to sort the array created in Exercise 1 into increasing order.
4. Use the recursive Quick Sort to sort the array created in Exercise 1 into increasing order. Output the array before and after sort.
5. Use Heap Sort to sort the array created in Exercise 1 into increasing order.
6. Use the recursive Merge Sort to sort the array created in Exercise 1 into increasing order. Output the array before and after sort.
7. Use Shell Sort to sort the array created in Exercise 1 into increasing order.
8. Use Radix Exchange Sort to sort the array created in Exercise 1 into increasing order.

Intermediate Exercises

9. Write a C program using Selection Sort to sort the following string in alphabetic order.

   AMULTIMEDIACOURSE

10. Use Insertion Sort to sort the string in Exercise 9.
11. Use Bubble Sort to sort the string in Exercise 9.
12. Use Quick Sort to sort the string in Exercise 9.
13. Use Heap Sort to sort the string in Exercise 9.
14. Use Merge Sort to sort the string in Exercise 9.
15. Use Shell Sort to sort the string in Exercise 9.
16. Use Radix Exchange Sort to sort the string in Exercise 9.

Advanced Exercises

17. Use the nonrecursive Quick Sort to sort the array created in Exercise 1 into increasing order. Compare the output of the recursive Quick Sort in Exercise 4.
18. Use the nonrecursive Merge Sort to sort the array created in Exercise 1 into increasing order. Compare the output of the recursive Merge Sort in Exercise 6.

19. Generate an array of 1000 random integers. Use Selection Sort, Insertion Sort, Bubble Sort, Quick Sort, Heap Sort, Merge Sort, Shell Sort, and Radix Sort to sort the array into increasing order. And compare their execution time.

Chapter 10

Tables

C. R. DOW
Feng Chia University, Taiwan
crdow@fcu.edu.tw

10.1. Introduction

In Chapter 4, we showed the problem of searching a list to find a specific entry and discussed two well-known searching algorithms: sequential search and binary search. By using key comparisons alone, we can complete a binary search of n items in fewer than $\log(n)$ comparisons. In this chapter, we begin with normal rectangular arrays, and then extend to the study of hash tables which can break the $\log(n)$ barrier of binary search. The average time complexity of hashing is bounded by a constant that does not depend on the size of the table.

10.2. Rectangular Arrays

Nearly all high-level languages provide convenient schemes to access rectangular arrays, so the programmer generally does not have to worry about the implementation details of rectangular arrays. Computer storage is practically arranged in a contiguous sequence, so for every access to a rectangular array, the computer converts the location to a position along a line. In this section, we will talk about the details of the ordering process (see Fig. 10.1).

10.2.1. *Row-Major and Column-Major Ordering*

The normal way to read a rectangular array is from left to right of each row or from top to bottom of each column. We can read the entries of the

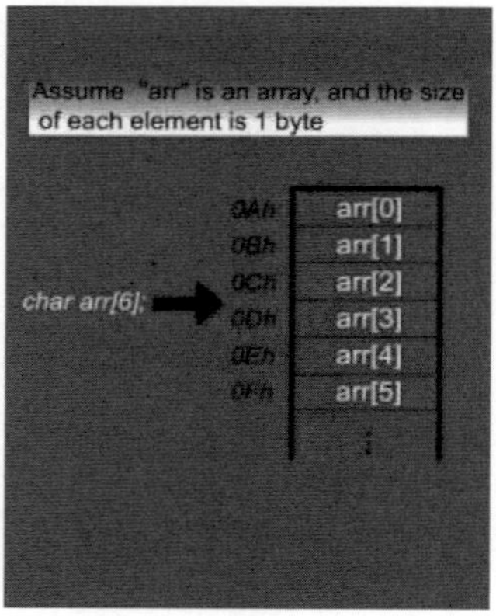

Fig. 10.1. Contiguous sequence.

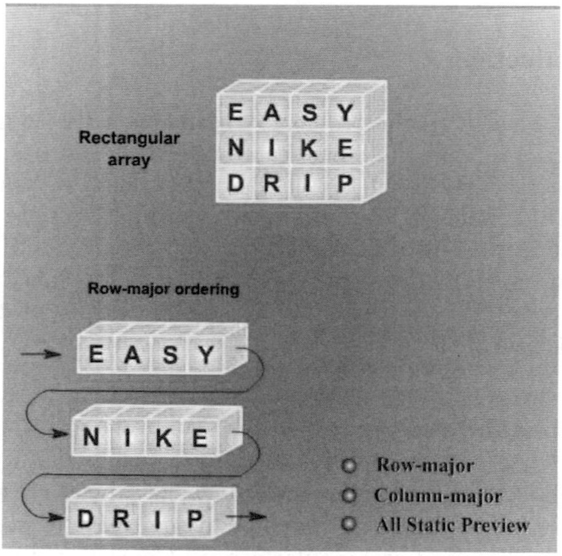

Fig. 10.2. Row- and column-major ordering.

first row from left to right, then read the entries of the second row, and so on until the last row has been read. Most systems store a rectangular array with the order, called **row-major ordering** (see Fig. 10.2). Similarly, if a rectangular array is read from top to bottom of each column, this method is called **column-major ordering** (see Fig. 10.2).

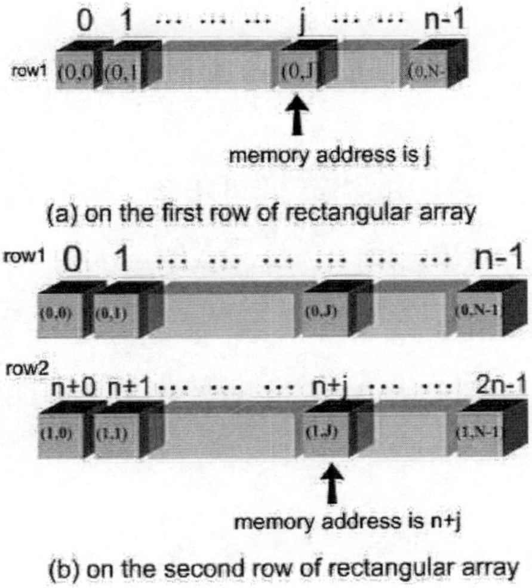

Fig. 10.3. Indexing rectangular arrays.

10.2.2. *Indexing Rectangular Arrays*

In general, an index (i, j) is translated into a memory address where the corresponding entry of the array will be stored. A formula for the calculation can be derived as follows. Suppose we use row-major ordering and the rows are numbered from 0 to $m-1$ and the columns from 0 to $n-1$. Thus, the array will have mn positions, and the range is from 0 to $mn-1$. With this information, we can define a formula to convert an index to a position. On the first row, (0, 0) goes to position 0, (0, j) goes to position j, and (0, $n-1$) goes to position $n-1$ as shown in Fig. 10.3(a).

On the second row, the first entry of the second row, (1, 0), comes after (0, $n-1$), and it goes into position n (see Fig. 10.3(b)). Also, we can see that (1, j) goes to position $n+j$ and (2, j) goes to position $2n+j$, so the formula is

$$\textit{Entry } (i, j) \textit{ goes to position } ni + j\,.$$

The above formula, which gives the sequential location of an array entry, is called an ***index function***. According to this function, we can calculate the memory position accurately.

10.2.3. *Variation: An Access Table*

Although calculating the index function of a rectangular array is simple, it might be not very efficient on some small machines to do multiplication. Thus, we can use the following method to eliminate the multiplications.

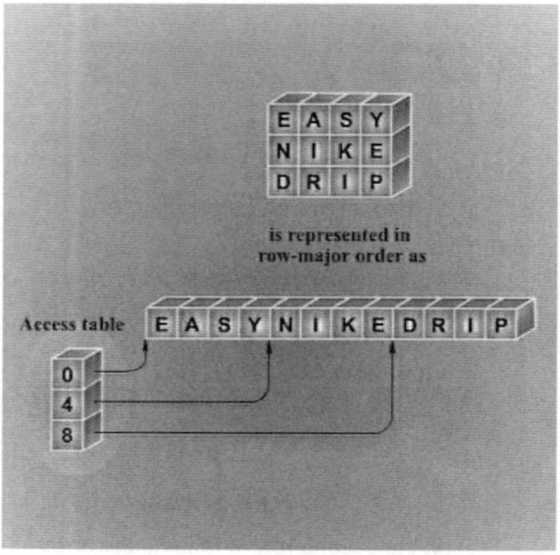

Fig. 10.4. Access table for a rectangular array.

Assume the size of a rectangular array is m^*n. This method is to keep an auxiliary array, a part of the multiplication table for n. The array will contain the values

$$0, n, 2n, 3n, \ldots, (m-1)n$$

We can use the small array to keep a reference to each column of the rectangular array. It will be calculated only once, and it can also be calculated by addition on the small machine. The array is normally much smaller than the rectangular array, so that it can be placed in memory permanently without wasting too much space.

This auxiliary table provides an example of an ***access table*** (see Fig. 10.4). In general, an access table, also called access vector, is an auxiliary array used to find data stored somewhere else.

10.3. Tables of Various Shapes

We may not store data into every position of a rectangle array. If we define a matrix to be an array of numbers, then some of the positions will be 0 or no data, such as tri-diagonal matrix, lower triangular matrix, etc. Several matrix examples are shown in Fig. 10.5. In this section, we study schemes to implement tables of various shapes to eliminate unused space in a rectangular array.

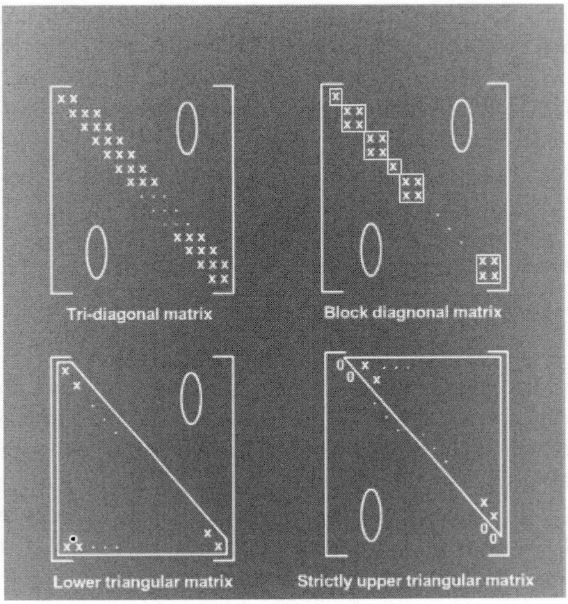

Fig. 10.5. Matrices of various shapes.

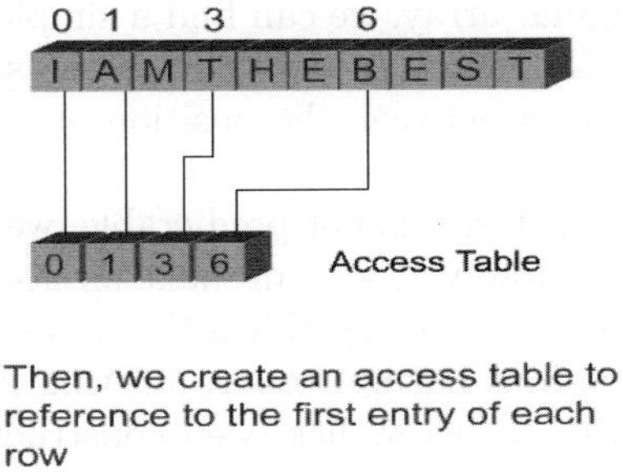

Fig. 10.6. Contiguous implementation of a triangular table.

10.3.1. *Triangular Tables*

As shown in Fig. 10.6, all indices (i, j) of the lower triangular table are required to satisfy $i >= j$. A triangular table can be implemented in a contiguous array by sliding each row out after the one above it (please press the "play it" button in Fig. 10.6). To create the index function, we assume the rows and the columns are numbered starting from 0. We know the end of each row will be the start of the next row. Clearly, there is no entry before row 0, and only one entry of row 0 precedes row 1. For row 2 there are 1 + 2 = 3 preceding entries (one entry of row 0 and two entries of row 1), and for row i there are

$$1 + 2 + \cdots + i = \frac{1}{2}i(i+1)$$

entries. Thus, the entry (i, j) of the triangle matrix is

$$\frac{1}{2}i(i+1) + j$$

As we did for rectangular arrays in Sec. 10.2, we can avert multiplications and divisions by setting up an access table. Each entry of the access table makes a reference to the start position of each row in the triangular table. The access table will be calculated only once at the beginning of the program, and it will be used again and again. Notice that even the initial calculation of the access table requires only addition but not multiplication or division to calculate its entries in the following order.

$$0, 1, 1+2, (1+2)+3, \ldots$$

10.3.2. *Jagged Tables*

In an ordinary rectangular array, we can find a simple formula to calculate the position, because the length of each row is the same. For the case of jagged tables, the relation between the position of a row and its length is unpredictable.

Since the length of each row is not predictable, we cannot find an index function to describe it. However, we can make an access table to reference elements of the jagged table. To establish the access table, we must construct the jagged table in a natural order, starting from 0 and beginning with its first row. After each row has been constructed, the index of the first unused position of the continuous storage is entered as the next entry in the access table. Figure 10.7 shows an example of using the access table for jagged table.

10.3.3. *Inverted Tables*

Multiple access tables can be referred to a single table of records by several different keys forthwith. In some situations, we may need to display different information sorted by different keys. For example, if a telephone company wants to publish a telephone book, the records must be sorted

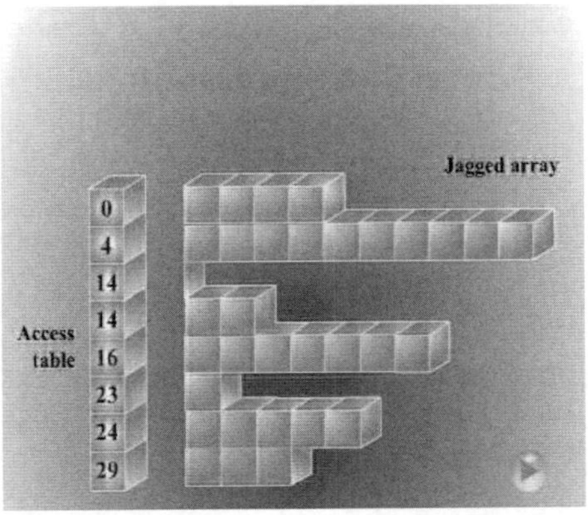

Fig. 10.7. Access table for jagged table.

alphabetically by the name of the subscriber. But to process long-distance charges, the accounts must be sorted by telephone number. To do routine maintenance, the company also needs to sort its subscribers by address, so that a repairman may work on several lines with one trip. Therefore, the telephone company may need three copies of its records, one sorted by name, one sorted by number and one sorted by address. Notice that keeping three same data records would be wasteful of storage space. And if we want to update data, we must update all the copies of records and this may cause erroneous and unpredictable information for the user.

The multiple sets of records can be avoided by using an access table. We can even find the records by any of the three keys. Before the access table is created, the index of records is required. According to the index number, we can replace data with the index number in the access table. Thus, the table size can be reduced and it will not waste too much storage space. Figure 10.8 shows an example of multikey access table for an inverted table.

10.4. The Symbol Table Abstract Data Type

Previously, we studied several index functions used to locate entries in tables, and then we converted them to access tables, which were arrays used for the same purpose as index functions. The analogy between functions and table lookup is very close. If we use a function, an argument needs to be given to calculate a corresponding value; if we use a table, we start with an index and look up a corresponding value from the table.

Index	Name	Address	Phone
1	Hill,Thomas M.	New York Ave. #317	4589123
2	Baker, John S.	20 Ash Street	2373124
3	Roberts, L. B.	42 Maple Street	4879437
4	King, Barbara	New York Ave. #181	2457983
5	Royal,Thomas M.	39 King Street	6784331
6	Forest, Carolyn	High Towers #102	4934122
7	Bloody, Mary	17 Maple Street	2345672

Access Tables

Name	Address	Phone
2	7	7
7	2	2
6	5	4
1	3	1
4	6	3
3	4	6
7	1	5

Fig. 10.8. Multikey access tables: an inverted table.

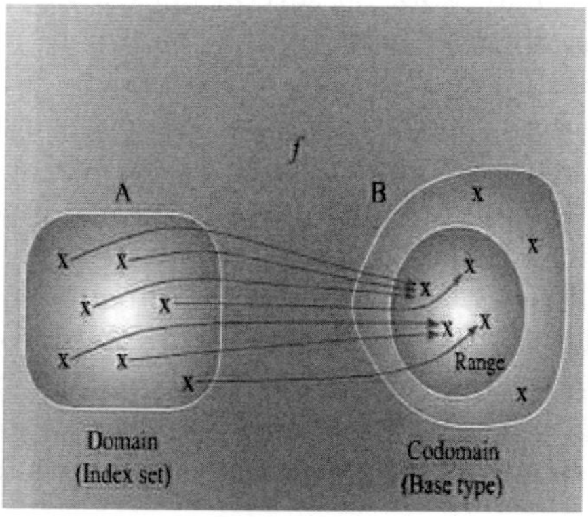

Fig. 10.9. The domain, codomain and range of a function.

10.4.1. *Functions and Tables*

Let us start from the definition of a function (see Fig. 10.9). In mathematics, a function is defined in terms of two sets and an accordance from elements of the first set to elements of the second set. If f is a function from set A to set B, then f assigns to each element of A a unique element of B. The set A is called the ***domain*** of f, and the set B is called the ***codomain*** of f.

Table access begins with an index and uses the table to look up a corresponding value. Thus, we call the domain of a table the ***index set***, and the codomain of a table the ***base type*** or ***value type***. For instance, we may have the array declaration:

int array[n] ;

Then the index set is the set of integers between 0 and $n - 1$, and the base type is the set of integers.

10.4.2. *An Abstract Data Type*

Before we define the table as a new abstract data type, let us summarize what we know. If we have a table with index set I and base type T, the table is a function from I into T and with the following operations.

(1) Table access: Given an index argument in I, we can find a corresponding value in T.
(2) Table assignment: Modify the value at a specified index in I to a new value.

These two operations can be easily implemented by the C language or some other languages. Comparing with another abstract data type, *list*, an element can be inserted into the list or removed from it. There is no reason why we cannot allow the possibility of further operations. Thus, various operations for the table are defined as follows.

(3) Creation: Set up a new function.
(4) Insertion: Add a new element x to the index set I and define a corresponding value of the function at x.
(5) Deletion: Delete an element x from the index set I and confine the function to the resulting smaller domain.
(6) Clearing: Remove all elements from the index set I, so there is no remaining domain.

The fifth operation might be hard to implement in C, because we cannot directly remove any element from an array. However, we may find some ways to overcome it. Anyway, we should always be careful to write a program and never allow our thinking to be limited by the restrictions of a particular language.

10.4.3. *Comparisons*

The abstract data types of list and table can be compared as follows. In the view of mathematics, the construction for a list is the sequence, and for a table it is the set and the function. Sequences have an implicit order: a first element, a second, and so on. However, sets and functions have no order and they can be accessed with any element of a table by index. Thus, information retrieval from a list naturally invokes a search. The time required to search a list generally depends on how many elements the list has, but the time for accessing a table does not depend on the number of elements in the table. For this reason, table access is significantly faster than list searching in many applications.

Finally, we should clarify the difference between table and array. In general, we shall use table as we have defined it previously and restrict the term "array" to mean the programming feature available in most high-level languages and used for implementing both tables and contiguous lists.

10.5. Static Hashing

10.5.1. *Hashing Function*

When we use a hash function for inserting the data (a key, value pair) into the hash table, there are three rules that must be considered. First of all, the hash function should be easy and quick to compute, otherwise too much time is wasted to put data into the table. Second, the hash function should achieve an even distribution of all data (keys), i.e. all data should be evenly distributed across the table. Third, if the hash function is evaluates the same data many times, the same result should be returned. Thus, the data (value) can be retrieved (by key) without failure.

Therefore, a selection of hash function is very important. If we know the types of the data, we can select a hash function that will be more efficient. Unfortunately, we usually do not know the types of the data, so we can use three normal methods to set up a hash function.

Truncation

It means to take only part of the key as the index. For example, if the keys are more than two-digit integers and the hash table has 100 entries (the index is 0∼99), the hash function can use the last two digits of the key as the index. For instance, the data with the key, 12345 will be put into the 45th entry of the table.

Folding

It means to partition the key into many parts and then evaluate the sum of the parts. For the above example, the key 12345 can be divided into three parts: 1, 23 and 45. The sum of the three parts is $1 + 23 + 45 = 69$, so we can put the data into the 69th entry of the table. However, if the sum is larger than the number of entries, the hash function can use the last two digits as the index, just like the truncation hash function described above.

Modular Arithmetic

It means to divide the key by the size of the index entries, and take the remainder as the result. For the above example, the key 12345 can be divided by the number of entries 100, i.e. $12345/100 = 123\ldots45$, the remainder 45 will be treated as the index of the table.

Sometimes, the key is not an integer number, therefore the hash function must convert the key to an integer. In the C example of Fig. 10.10, the key is a string, so we can add the values of the characters (a string is a set of characters) as the key.

```
int string2integer(char *key)
{
    int ikey = 0;
    while (*key)
         ikey += *(key++);
    return ikey;
}

/* function: hash, using an integer as key */
int hash (int key)
{
    // some hash function implementation
    return key & TABLE_ENTRIES_NUMBER;
    // modular arithmetic implementation
}

/* function: hash, using a string as key */
int stringHash (char *key)
{
    int ikey = string2integer(key);
    return hash(ikey);
}
```

Fig. 10.10. Hashing by using a character string.

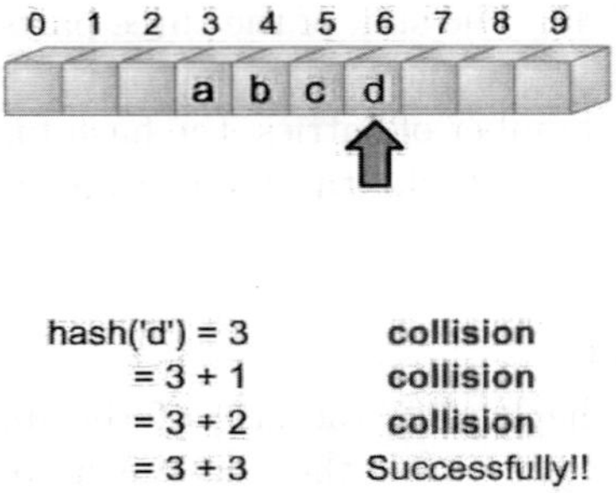

Fig. 10.11. Linear probing.

10.5.2. *Collision Resolution with Open Addressing*

In the previous section, we have described the hash function. In some situations, different keys may be mapped to the same index. Therefore, we will describe in this section a number of methods to resolve this collision.

Linear Probing

The simplest method to resolve the collision is to search the first empty entry of the table. Of course, the starting entry of search depends on the index returned by the hash function. When the starting entry is not empty, this method will sequentially search the next entry until it reaches an empty entry. If the entry is at the end of the table, its next entry will be the first entry of the table. An example of this scheme is shown in Fig. 10.11.

The problem of linear probing happens when the table becomes about half full, there is a trend toward clustering; that is, there are many long strings of nonempty entries in the table. Consider the example in Fig. 10.12, the color position means a filled entry. In the first situation, if we insert a data with a key 'a' (denoted as DATA(a)), the linear probing will search two times (the 'b' entry is empty). In the next situation, we insert DATA(a) again, this method will be wasted four times. For the last situation, it will search five times. If we discuss the average times of inserting DATA(a), DATA(b), DATA(c) and DATA(d) in these three situations:

Situation 1:

$$\Big(\underset{\text{DATA(a)}}{\underline{2}} + \underset{\text{DATA(b)}}{\underline{1}} + \underset{\text{DATA(c)}}{\underline{2}} + \underset{\text{DATA(d)}}{\underline{1}}\Big) \;/\; 4 = 1.5 \text{ times}$$

Situation 2:

$$\Big(\underset{\text{DATA(a)}}{4} + \underset{\text{DATA(b)}}{3} + \underset{\text{DATA(c)}}{\underline{2}} + \underset{\text{DATA(d)}}{\underline{1}}\Big) \;/\; 4 = 2.5 \text{ times}$$

Clustering

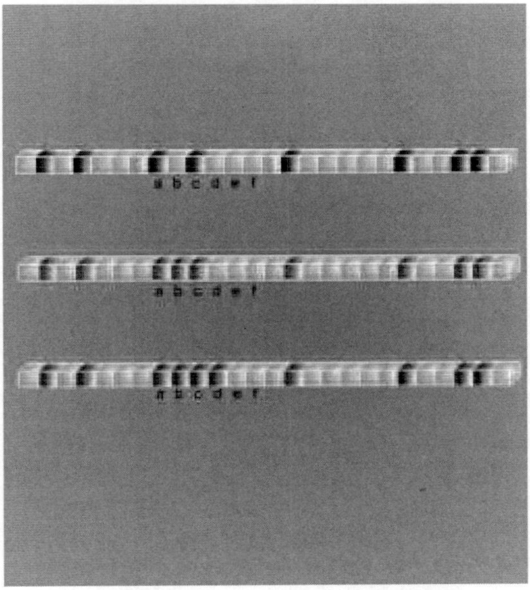

Fig. 10.12. Clustering.

Situation 3:

(	5	+	4	+	3	+	2	)	/	4	=	3.5 times
	DATA(a)		DATA(b)		DATA(c)		DATA(d)					

Just like the name, linear probing, the average overhead of searching an empty entry is also linear, i.e. $O(n)$ for the clustering situation.

Rehashing and Increment Functions

In order to resolve the problem of linear probing, we can provide more than one hash function. When a collision occurs, another hash function could be used (see Fig. 10.13). This method is called rehashing and an increment function is derived from this method. We treat the second hash function as an increment function instead of a hash function, that is, when a collision occurs, the other increment function is evaluated and the result is determined as the distance to move from the first hash position (see Fig. 10.14). Thus, we wish to design an increment function that depends on the key and can avoid clustering.

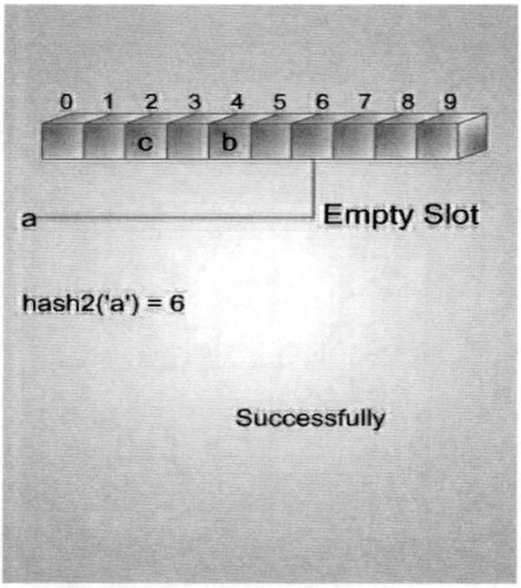

Fig. 10.13. Rehashing.

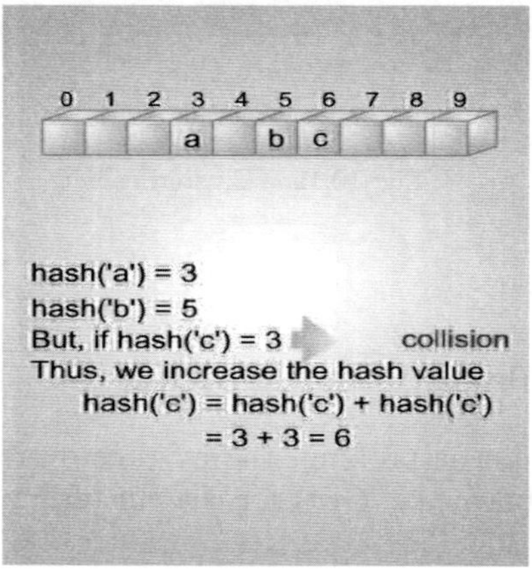

Fig. 10.14. Increment function.

Key-Dependent Increments

As just mentioned, we can design an increment function that depends on the key. For instance, the key can be truncated to a single character and use its code as the increment. In C, we might write

$$\text{increment} = {}^{*}\text{key}\,; \quad //\text{or} \quad \text{increment} = \text{key}[0]\,;$$

Quadratic Probing

If the hash function is **h** and increment function is $\mathbf{i^2}$, the method probes the table at locations $h+1$, $h+4$, $h+9$, i.e. at location $h+i^2$ (%HASHSIZE) when there is a collision. In Fig. 10.14, we can use the $f(i) = i^2$ as the increment function.

Furthermore, how to select an appropriate HASHSIZE is very important. In general, we use a prime number for HASHSIZE to achieve better performance.

Random Probing

This method uses a random number as the increment. Of course, the random number must be the same each time when we retrieve the same value (namely by the same key) from the table or put the same value into the table. This is a very simple way to reach the goal, if we use the same seed and the same sequence value, the random number will be the same. The seed and sequence values can be obtained based on the portion of the key values.

10.5.3. *Collision Resolution by Chaining*

Up to this section we only use the contiguous storage to store the data (the key and value), but the fixed-size storage is not good when the number of data records keep changing. On the contrary, it is more appropriate for random access and refers to random positions. An example is illustrated in Fig. 10.15 and in the following we will describe the advantages and disadvantages of the chaining scheme.

Advantages of Chaining

Space Saving and Overflow

The first advantage of chaining is space saving. If we use a contiguous storage, we need to maintain a large size of storage to avoid overflow. That is, if we put data into a table and there is no space, we may need to renew a larger array and reinsert the data (old data in table and new data not inserted yet). It is inefficient because of reconstructing (renew) and copying (reinsert) operations. On the contrary, the chaining skill will use a pointer to refer to the next data that has the same key (collision occurred), so the original storage does not need a large space to avoid overflow.

Collision Resolution

The second advantage is that when the collision occurs, we do not use any function to deal with it. We only use a pointer to refer to the new data

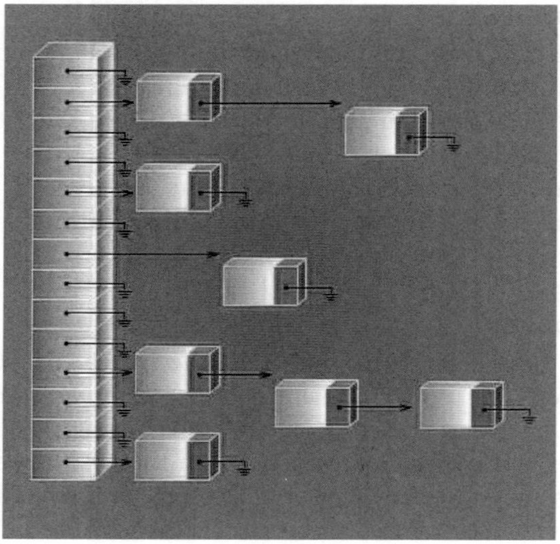

Fig. 10.15. Collision resolution by chaining.

and use a single hash address as a linked list to chain the collision data. Clustering is no problem at all, because keys with distinct hash addresses always go to distinct lists. Figure 10.15 illustrates this situation.

Deletion

Finally, deletion becomes a quick and easy means for a chained hash table. The deletion operation does the same way as deletion from a linked list.

Disadvantages of Chaining

Because the chaining structure has to remain a reference as a pointer to refer the next data that contains the same key, the structure is larger than the entry of static table (used in previous sections). Another problem is that when the chain is too long, to retrieve the final entry of this chain is too slow.

10.6. Dynamic Hashing

Motivation for Dynamic Hashing

The skill mentioned in last section is not efficient for the situation where the number of data records is substantially changed according to the time, e.g. DBMS. Because the skill uses a static array to maintain the table, the

identifiers	binary representation
A0	100 000
A1	100 001
B0	101 000
B1	101 001
C0	110 000
C1	110 001
C2	110 010
C3	110 011

Fig. 10.16. The presentation of every letter.

array may need to store the data or take the entry as a linked list header (chaining). Regardless of which situation, if the array is too large, the space could be wasted; but if the array is too small, an overflow will occur frequently (open address). If the chain is too long, it will reconstruct a new hash table and rehash the table so it is very inefficient. That is, the goal of dynamic hashing (or say extendable hashing) is to remain the fast random access of the traditional hash function and extend the function and make it easy to dynamically and efficiently adjust the space of hash table.

10.6.1. *Dynamic Hashing Using Directories*

In this section, we will use an example to describe the principle. We assume the key data is two letters and each letter is represented by three bits. An example is shown in Fig. 10.16. At the beginning of initiation, we put the data (the key) into a four entry table, every entry can save two keys. We use the last two bits as the key and determine which entry the data should be saved in. Then, we put the keys A0, B0, C2, A1, B1 and C3 into the table. Based on the last two bits of the key, A0 and B0 are put into the same entry, A1 and B1 are put into the same entry, and C2 and C3 are put into the distinct entry separately.

Now, we insert a new data C5 into the table. Since the last two bits of C5 is equal to the last two bits of A1 and B1 and every entry can only save two keys, we will branch the entry into two entries and use the last three bits to determine which one should be saved in which entry. As shown in Fig. 10.17, if we insert a new data again, it will perform the same procedure as before.

In this example, two issues are observed. First, the time of access entry is dependent of the bits of the key. Second, if the partition of the key word is leaned, the partition of the table is also leaned.

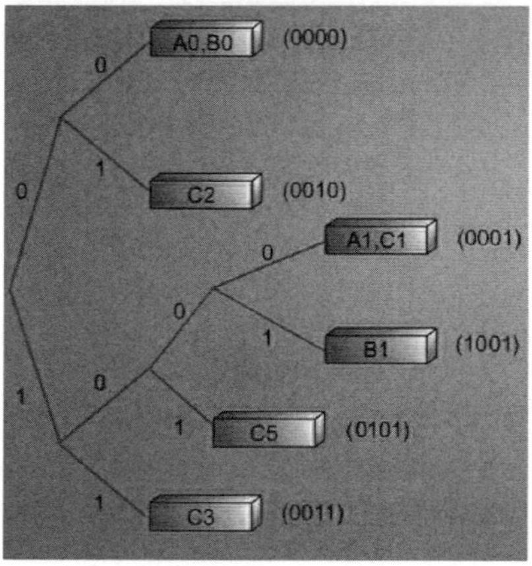

Fig. 10.17. An insertion example.

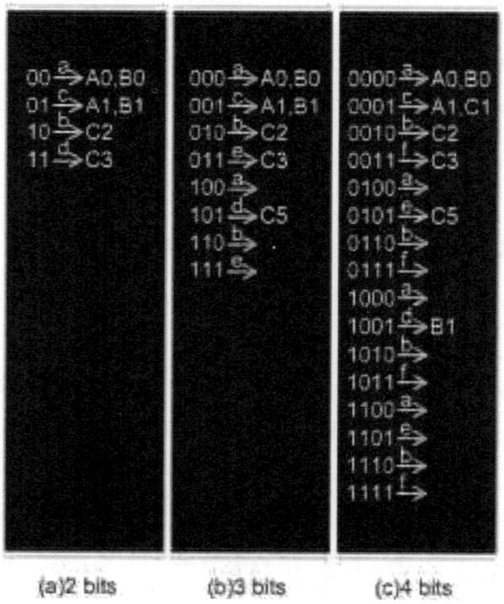

Fig. 10.18. Directory.

In order to avoid waiting too long to search the long list, each entry can be mapped to a directory, as shown in Fig. 10.18. Each subfigure of Fig. 10.18 corresponds to each subfigure of Fig. 10.17. Notice that the directory is a pointer table. If we need k bits to substitute the key, the directories will have 2^k entries.

In Fig. 10.18(a), because we only use two bits to represent four keys, the directories also need only four entries. When inserting C5, C5's last two bits equal A1 and B1 (01), but the entry (01) has two pointers (pointing to A1 and B1). Thus, the directory must be extended as shown in Fig. 10.18(b), where C5 would be put into entry 101. Finally, we put C1 into table, the last three bit is 001 and equals to A1 and B1, and the entry 001 has two pointers to indicate A1 and B1's pointers, so we need to extend this table again, as shown in Fig. 10.18(c). Although the last three bits are the same (001), the last four bits of A1 and C1 are the same (0001). However, B1 is (1001), so B1 will be put into the 1001th entry.

Using this approach, the directory will be dynamically extended or shrunk. Unfortunately, if these keys do not distribute uniformly, the directory will become very large and most of the entries will be empty, as shown in Fig. 10.18(c). To avoid this situation, we may convert the bits into a random order and it can be performed by some hash functions.

10.6.2. *Directory-Less Dynamic Hashing*

In the previous section, we need a directory to place the pointers of the data. In this section, we assume that there is a large memory that is big enough to store all records, then we can eliminate the directory.

When an overflow occurs, we need to increase the memory space, but this will waste too much memory. To avoid the overflow, we only add one page and rehash the table. As shown in Fig. 10.19, when we insert a new

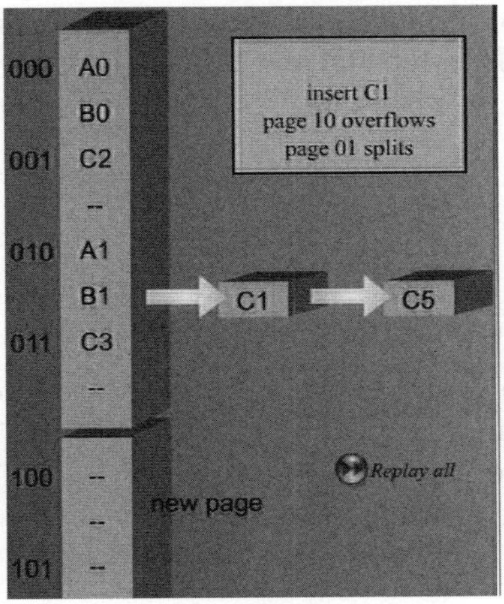

Fig. 10.19. A directory-less hashing example.

data C5 the table will be extended. Despite rehashing, the new page is empty. Once again, if we insert a value C1 again, the same situation occurs and the new page will still be empty. So this approach can avoid creating many new pages (two times to the original one). Sometimes, the new page is still empty, i.e. the new page is not effective.

The general method to deal with overflow problem is one of the traditional rehash functions, just like the open addressing.

10.7. Conclusions

In this chapter, we described the table of various shapes, including triangular tables, jagged tables and inverted tables, in the former sections. And we also described the technique to implement the abstract data type of the table. In the later sections, we focused on the data retrieval from the table. So we explained many hashing functions, such as static hashing (truncation, folding, modular, etc.) and dynamic hashing (using directories and directoryless), and approaches of collision resolution, such as open addressing (linear probing, quadratic probing, etc.) and chaining.

Exercises

Beginner's Exercises

Multiple-choice questions

1. Suppose there is integer array M (5,8), the address of M (0,0), M (0,3) and M (1,2) are 100,106 and 120, respectively. What is the address of M (4,5)?
   (a) 174
   (b) 164
   (c) 168
   (d) 186
   (e) None of above.
2. Assume each integer takes one memory location to store. Consider the array declaration: var A : array[1..5, 20..25 ,10..15] of integer. Assume the array is stored in row-major order. If A[4,25,15] is stored in location 1999, what is the location of A[2,25,15]?
   (a) 2005
   (b) 1931
   (c) 1927
   (d) 2000
   (e) None of above.

3. Assume that A is an n^*n matrix with $A(i, j) = 0$, for $i + j \geqq n + 2$. What are the maximum number nonzero elements in A?
   (a) $n^*(n + 1)/2$
   (b) $n^*(n - 1)/2$
   (c) n^2
   (d) $n^2/2$
   (e) None of above.

4. Which is not a method of setting up a hash function?
   (a) Truncation
   (b) Modular Arithmetic
   (c) Chaining
   (d) Folding
   (e) None of above.

5. Consider the symbol table of an assembler, which data structure will make the searching faster (assume the number of symbols is greater than 50).
   (a) Sorted array
   (b) Hashing table
   (c) Binary search tree
   (d) Unsorted array
   (e) Linked list.

6. A hash table contains 1000 slots, indexed from 1 to 1000. The elements stored in the table have keys that range in value from 1 to 99999. Which, if any, of the following hash functions would work correctly?
   (a) key MOD 1000
   (b) (key – 1) MOD 1000
   (c) (key + 1) MOD 999
   (d) (key MOD 1000) + 1
   (e) None of above.

7. Which is not the method of resolving collision when handling hashing operations?
   (a) Linear probing
   (b) Quadratic probing
   (c) Random probing
   (d) Rehashing
   (e) None of above.

8. Consider the following four-digit employee numbers: 9614, 1825 Find the two-digit hash address of each number using the midsquare method. The address are

(a) 14,06
(b) 30,06
(c) 28,15
(d) 28,30
(e) None of above.

9. Continue from 8. Find the two-digit hash address of each number using the folding method without reversing (shift folding). The address are

   (a) 61,82
   (b) 10,43
   (c) 14,25
   (d) 96,18
   (e) None of above.

10. Which is not the application of using hashing function?

   (a) Data searching
   (b) Data store
   (c) Security
   (d) Data compression
   (e) None of above.

Yes–no questions

1. If a rectangular array is read from top to bottom of each column, this method is called row-major ordering.
2. We can use triangular tables, jagged tables and inverted tables to eliminate unused space in a rectangular array.
3. If f is a function from set A to set B, then f assigns to each element of A a unique element of B. The set A is called the codomain of f, and the set B is called the domain of f.
4. The time required to search a list generally does not depend on how many elements the list has, but the time for accessing a table depends on the number of elements in the table. For this reason, table access is significantly slower than list searching in many applications.
5. A selection of hash function is very important. If we know the types of the data, we can select a hash function that will be more efficient. Furthermore, we always know the types of the data, so we can set up a hash function easily.
6. We can provide more than one hash function to resolve the clustering problem of linear probing. When a collision occurs, another hash function could be used. This method is called rehashing and an increment function is derived from this method.

7. The chaining skill uses a pointer to refer to the next data, which has the same key (collision occurred), so the origin storage does not need a large space to avoid overflow. When the chain is long, it is easy to retrieve the final entry of this chain.
8. The goal of dynamic hashing (or say extendable hashing) is to remain the fast random access of the traditional hash function and extend the function and make it not difficult to dynamically and efficiently adjust the space of hash table.
9. In the method of dynamic hashing using directories, the directory is a pointer table. If we need n bits to substitute the key, the directories will have 2^{n+1} entries.
10. We can find out that the space utilization for directory-less dynamic hashing is not good, because some extra pages are empty and yet overflow pages are being used.

Intermediate Exercises

11. Write a program that will create and print out a lower triangular table. The input is a number N (e.g. 4) and the table will look like the following.

    1 0 0 0
    2 3 0 0
    4 5 6 0
    7 8 9 10

1. Please design a hash function that can be used to save a character into a hash table (array) and this hash function should be used to do the searching. (Please use the linear probing technique to solve the collision problem.)
2. Please design a hash function that can be used to save an integer into a hash table (array) and this hash function should be used to do the searching. (Please use the chaining technique to solve the collision problem.)

Advanced Exercises

14. A **lower triangular matrix** is a square array in which all entries above the main diagonal are 0. Describe the modifications necessary to use the access table method to store a lower triangular matrix.
15. In extendable hashing, given a directory of size d, suppose two pointers point to the same page. How many low-order bits do all identifiers

share in common? If four pointers point to the same page, how many bits do the identifiers have in common?

16. Prove that in directory-based dynamic hashing a page can be pointed at by a number of pointers that is a power of 2.
17. Devise a simple, easy-to-calculate hash function for mapping three-letter words to integers between 0 and $n-1$, inclusive. Find the values of your function on the words

    POP LOP RET ACK RER EET SET JET BAT BAD BED

    for $n = 11, 15, 19$. Try for as few collisions as possible.
18. Based on Exercise 17, write a program that can insert these words (PAL, LAP, etc.) into a table, using the tree structure and arrays as show in Figs. 10.17 and 10.18, respectively.

Chapter 11

Binary Trees

SANGWOOK KIM

Kyungpook National University, Korea
swkim@cs.knu.ac.kr

We can represent any tree as a binary tree. Binary trees are an important type of tree structure. In this chapter, we study binary tree as data structure using the linked list for their implementation. Binary tree is a valuable data structure for a range of applications in computer science.

11.1. Binary Tree

In this section, we study the definition of the binary tree that can illustrate the behavior of some algorithms like sorting and searching. Especially, we have used comparison trees showing the comparison keys in searching.

11.1.1. *Definition and Properties*

A binary tree is different from a tree. Binary trees have characteristics that any node can have at most two branches. Thus, we distinguish between the subtree on the *left* and the subtree on the *right* for binary trees. Also a binary tree may have zero nodes.

Definition. A *binary tree* is either empty, or it consists of a *root* and two disjoint binary trees called the *left subtree* and *the right subtree.*

Before we consider general characteristics of binary tree, we can construct small binary trees by recursion.

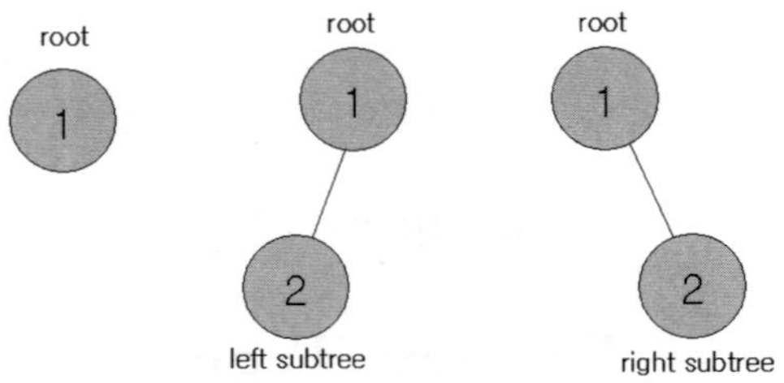

Fig. 11.1. A binary tree with one node and two different binary trees with two nodes.

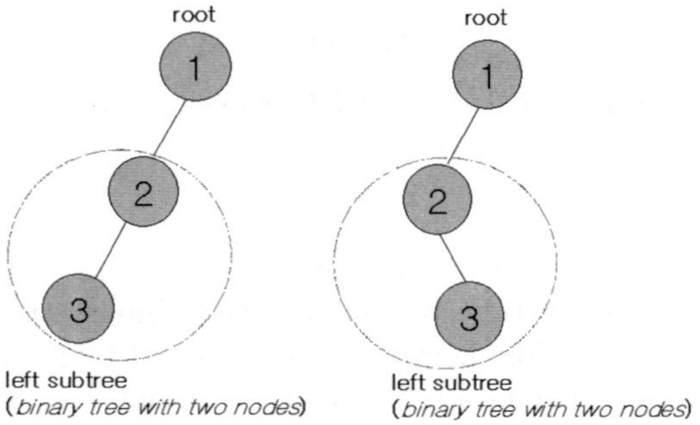

Fig. 11.2. Binary trees with two nodes in left subtrees.

(1) If the number of nodes is zero, there is an empty binary tree.
(2) If the number of nodes is one, there is only a binary tree with root node that both left and right subtrees are empty.
(3) If the number of nodes is two, one node on the tree is the root and another is in a subtree. In this case, one of the left and the right subtrees must be empty, and the other subtrees have exactly one node. Thus we have two different binary trees with two nodes.
In the binary tree, since the left and right are important, binary trees with two nodes in Fig. 11.1 are different from each other.
(4) If the number of nodes is three, one of three nodes is the root and other two nodes will be one of the following.
   (i) Two node in left subtrees and empty in right subtree: In this case, we have two binary trees as Fig. 11.2, since there are two binary trees with two nodes and only one empty tree.
   (ii) Empty in left subtree and two nodes in right subtree: In this case, we have two more binary trees as in Fig. 11.3.

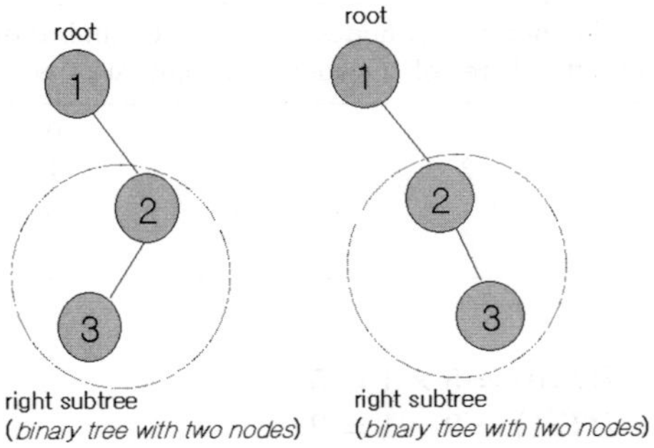

Fig. 11.3. Binary trees with two nodes in right subtrees.

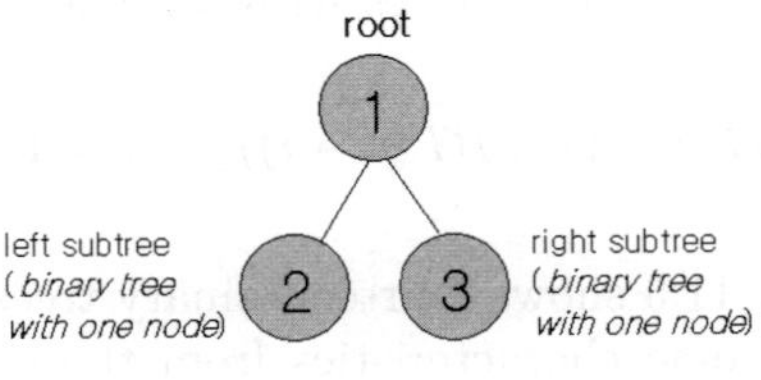

Fig. 11.4. Binary trees with one node in left subtrees and one node in right subtree.

(iii) One node in left subtrees and one node in right subtree: In this case, we have one binary tree as in Fig. 11.4, since the left and right subtrees both have one node, and there is only one binary tree with one node.

We already knew that when there are three nodes, we construct five binary trees with three nodes.

And now, if there are many nodes, how many binary trees can we construct? Let n be the number of nodes and $BT(n)$ be the number of binary trees to be constructed. From the above observation, $BT(1) = 1$, $BT(2) = 2$ and $BT(3) = 5$.

If $n = 4$, $BT(4)$ is calculated as follows.
After one node is selected as root node, there are four cases according to the number of nodes in the left (and right) subtree of the root as follows.
In case 1, the number of binary trees with three nodes in left subtree is five and the number of binary trees with zero node in right subtree is one as we know. In case 2, the number of binary trees with two nodes in left subtree is two and the number of binary trees with one node in right subtree is one. The cases 3 and 4 are the same. Thus we can obtain the following.

	The number of nodes in left subtree of the root	The number of nodes in right subtree of the root
Case 1	3	0
Case 2	2	1
Case 3	1	2
Case 4	0	3

In case 1, $BT(3) \times BT(0) = 5 \times 1 = 5$
In case 2, $BT(2) \times BT(1) = 2 \times 1 = 2$
In case 3, $BT(1) \times BT(2) = 1 \times 2 = 2$
In case 4, $BT(0) \times BT(3) = 1 \times 5 = 5$

Thus, $BT(4) = 5 + 2 + 2 + 5 = 14$. Also $BT(5) = 42$, and $BT(6) = 132$. Generally, the number of binary trees with n nodes is

$$BT(n) = \sum_{i=1}^{n}(BT(i-1) \times BT(n-i)), \quad n = 1 \text{ and } BT(0) = 1\,.$$

For an example, Fig. 11.5 shows fourteen binary trees with four nodes.

We can observe some characteristics from the construction of binary trees for n nodes. There are $n-1$ nodes, $n-2$ nodes, $\ldots, 1$, and 0 node in left (and right) subtree. These numbers of nodes determine the depth d of binary tree.

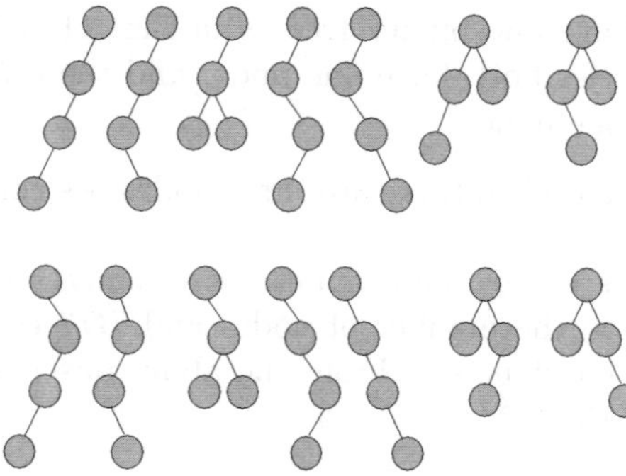

Fig. 11.5. Fourteen binary trees with four nodes.

Suppose that the root of a binary tree has level 0. Since the root is the only node on level $l = 0$, the maximum number of nodes on level $l = 0$ is $2^l = 20 = 1$. Thus, the maximum number of nodes on level l is computed as follows.

For level $l = 0$, $2^0 = 1$.
For level $l = 1$, $2^1 = 2$.
For level $l = 2$, $2^2 = 4$.
....
For level $l = i$, 2^i.

The maximum number of nodes on level i is two times the maximum number of nodes on level $i - 1$ (or 2^i). Finally, the maximum number of nodes on the level l of a binary tree is 2^l nodes, $l \geq 0$.

Also, if we use the maximum number of nodes on the level l ($l \geq 0$) of a binary tree, we can know the maximum number of nodes in a binary tree of depth d. That is as follows.

Maximum number of nodes in a binary tree of depth d

$$= \sum_{l=0}^{d-1} (\text{maximum number of nodes on level } l)$$

$$= \sum_{l=0}^{d-1} 2^l = 2^d - 1$$

where $d \geq 1$.

Definition. If a binary tree of depth d has $2^d - 1$ nodes, it is a *full binary tree* of depth d, $d \geq 1$.

The number of $2^d - 1$ nodes is the maximum number of nodes in a binary tree of depth d. For the full binary tree starting with the root on the level 0 in Fig. 11.6, the depth is 4 and the number of maximum nodes is 15.

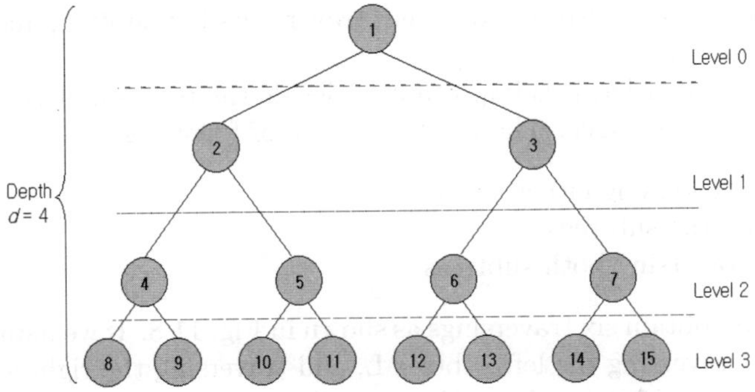

Fig. 11.6. Full binary tree of depth 4 and 15 nodes.

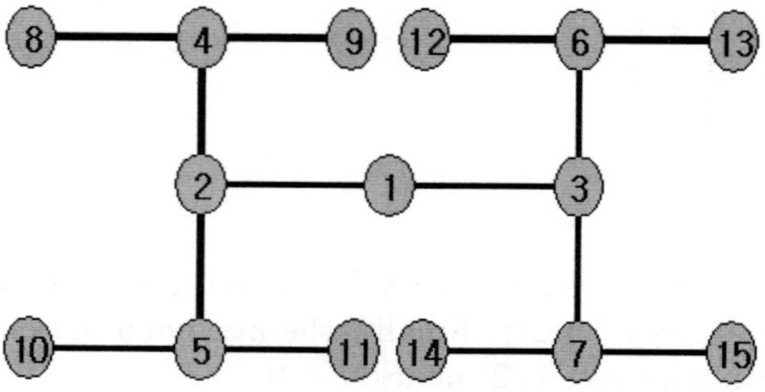

Fig. 11.7. An example of VLSI circuit design using full binary tree with 15 nodes.

Definition. A binary tree with n nodes and depth d is *complete* iff its nodes have correspondence to the nodes numbered from 1 to n in the full binary tree of depth d.

This binary tree can apply to various fields as VLSI design, computer network structure and algorithm design in computer science. Figure 11.7 shows an example for VLSI circuit design using a binary tree. Some applications of a binary tree will be shown in this chapter.

11.1.2. *Traversal of Binary Tree*

There are many operations to be performed on a binary tree. One of them is the *traversing* binary tree. This traversing tree is important and there are many applications in computer science. Traversing tree is to visit each node in the tree exactly once. We can obtain an ordered sequence of nodes for a tree as a result by traversing a tree. However, we obtain some different order of nodes according to the way of traversing a binary tree. At a given binary tree, we can visit a node itself, traverse its left subtree, and traverse its right subtree.

In traversal order, it is important to decide the position of visiting node itself in the binary tree. The position is one of following.

(1) *before* traversing either subtrees
(2) *between* the subtrees
(3) *after* traversing both subtrees

Thus we can obtain six traversings as shown in Fig. 11.8. If we name visiting a node V, traversing the left subtree L, and traversing the right subtree R, we can rewrite six traversing orders as follows.

V L R L V R L R V V R L R V L R L V

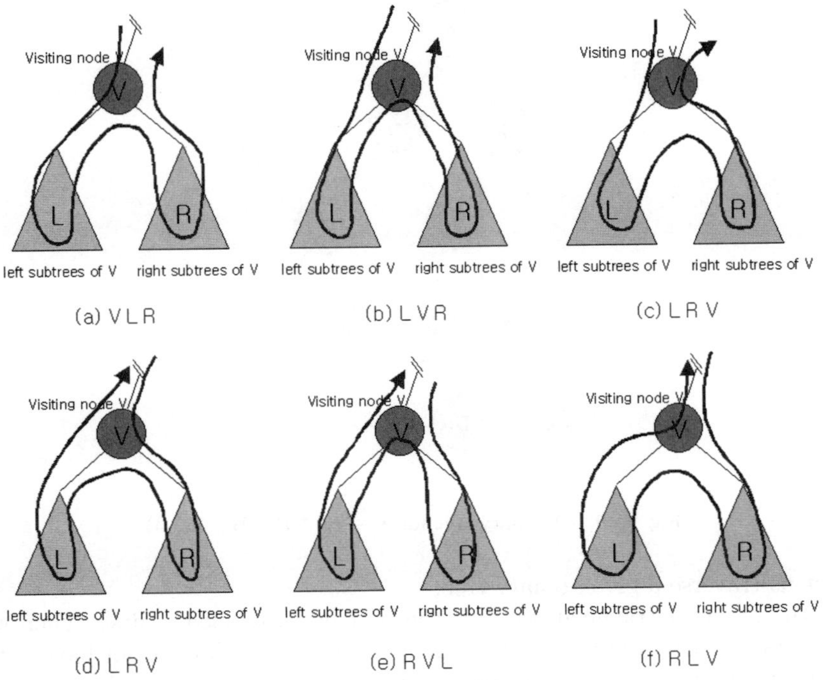

Fig. 11.8. Six examples of traversing of binary tree.

As traversing, we can visit all the nodes of the binary tree in turn. Since traversing left subtree and traversing right subtree is symmetric, we can reduce these six to three by traversing left subtree before right subtree as $V\ L\ R$, $L\ V\ R$ and $L\ R\ V$ only.

According to the position of visited node, we call these *preorder*, *inorder* and *postorder*, respectively. These are named according to the turn at which the given node is visited.

- *Preorder traversal* (VLR): the node is visited before the subtrees.
- *Inorder traversal* (LVR): the node is visited between the subtrees.
- *Postorder* (LRV): the node is visited after both of the subtrees.

As an example, consider the binary tree of Fig. 11.9 to represent arithmetic expression X + (C * D / B – 3 ^ 4). This binary tree contains an arithmetic expression with some operators and operands. These binary operators are add (+), multiply (*), minus (–), divide (/) and power (^), and operands are 3, 4, B, C, D and X. For each node that contains an operator, its left subtree gives the left operand, and its right subtree gives the right operand.

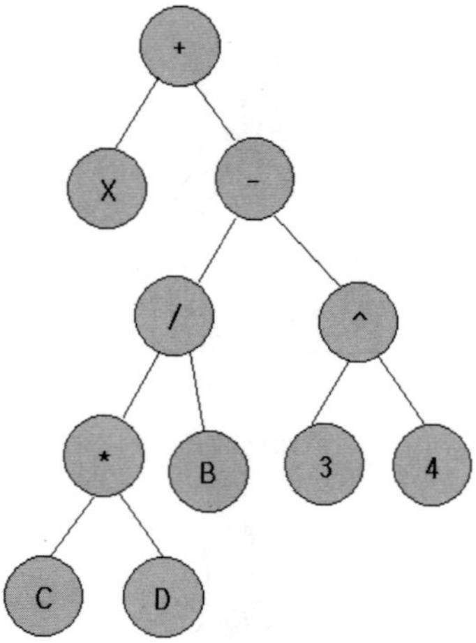

Fig. 11.9. A binary tree for X + (C * D / B – 3 ^ 4).

Let us traverse a given binary tree.
In the preorder traversal, we visit the root node, labeled + first. Then we traverse the left subtree. We visit node X, since node X does not have both left and right subtrees in the given binary tree. And we move the traversal to the right subtree of the root where we can find some nodes labeled –, /, ^, *, B, 3, 4, C, and D. At this point, we must traverse this subtree using the preorder method. We visit the root, labeled –, of this subtree, and then traverse the left subtree of node –. Again, we visit root node /, and then traverse the left subtree of node /. Node * is visited. Continuously, we traverse the left subtree of node *, then we visit node C. Since both left and right subtrees of node C are empty, we cannot traverse both subtrees of node C. Thus we visit node D in the right subtree of node *. After visiting node D, node B is visited. Since we have traversed the left subtree of node –, we traverse the right subtree of node –. Node ^ is visited, and then node 3 in left subtree and node 4 in right subtree are visited. Thus we visit the nodes in the order +, X, –, /, *, C, D, B, ^, 3 and 4 by the preorder traversal of the binary tree.

In the inorder traversal, we traverse the left subtree of the root node +. We visit the node labeled X first, and then visit the root node +. Next we move the traversal to the right subtree of node +. In the right subtree of node +, we must traverse it using inorder method. We must traverse the left subtree of node – before visiting node –. Its root of left subtree of node – is node /, and has the left subtree containing nodes *, C, D and B. Since node * is root, after visiting node C, we visit node * and node D in order. Also since node / is root of nodes *, C and D, we visit node / and node B in order. Since the left subtree of node – has visited, node – is visited. At this point, we move the traversal to the right subtree of node –. Since the root of the right subtree of node – is node ^, we must visit node ^ after visiting node 3, and visit node 4 in order. Thus we visit the nodes in the order X, +, C, *, D, /, B, –, 3, ^, and 4 by the inorder traversal of the binary tree.

In the postorder traversal, before visiting node itself, we traverse both the left and right subtrees of each node first. By this postorder traversal, the root of a binary tree is always visited lastly. We visit the node labeled X first. Then we move the traversal to the right subtree of node +. In the right subtree of node +, we must traverse it using postorder method. We must traverse the left subtree of node – before visiting right subtree of node –. Its root of left subtree of node – is node /, and has the left subtree containing nodes *, C, D and B. Before visiting node *, we must visit nodes C and D in order. Also after node B is visited, node / is visited. At this point, we move the traversal to the right subtree of node –. Since the root of the right subtree of node – is node ^, we must visit nodes 3 and 4 in order first. After visiting nodes 3 and 4, we visit node ^, and then we must visit node – and + in order. Thus we visit the nodes in the order X, C, D, *, B, /, 3, 4, ^, – and + by the inorder traversal of the binary tree.

Finally, we obtain the traversal result on the binary tree in Fig. 11.9 as follow.

- Preorder: + X – / * C D B ^ 3 4
- Inorder: X + C * D / B – 3 ^ 4
- Postorder: X C D * B / 3 4 ^ – +

The arithmetic expression containing unary or binary operator can be represented by a binary tree. A binary tree traversal can be applied to the *compiler.* When compiler recognizes an arithmetic expression, it represents traversal order for arithmetic expression and generates object codes according to the evaluation. As you see, the traversing result decides the operator precedence for arithmetic expression according to the evaluation direction. Now we define the expression tree.

Definition. An *expression tree* is the binary tree, which consists of simple operands and operators of an expression. The leaves of a binary tree contain simple operands and the interior nodes contain the operators. For each binary operator, the left subtree contains all the simple operands and operators in the left operand of the given operator, and the right subtree contains everything in the right operand. For a unary operator, one of the two subtrees will be empty.

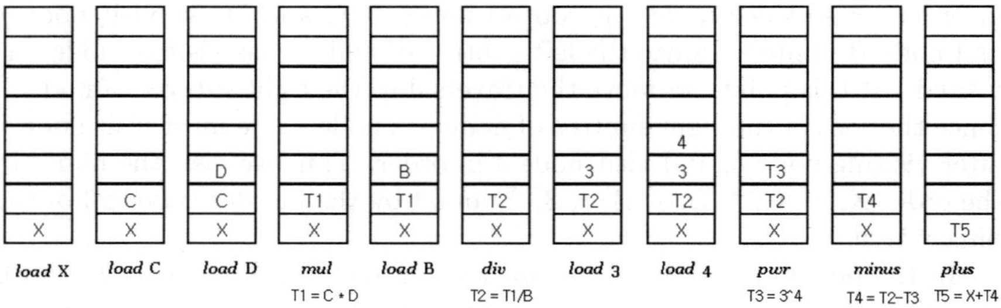

Fig. 11.10. An evaluation of expression tree for X + (C * D / B – 3 ^ 4).

For an example of code generation of the expression tree in Fig. 11.9, the compiler to use one address instruction format can generate following object code (pseudo code) based on evaluation of postorder traversal.

...
load X
load C
load D
mul
load B
div
load 3
load 4
pwr
minus
plus
...

Figure 11.10 shows the evaluation sequence of example object code to be generated by compiler. Also the binary tree is very useful and efficient for searching and sorting.

11.1.3. *Implementation of Binary Trees*

We study the implementation of a binary tree to perform what we have studied before including data structure for a binary tree, traversal functions and main function. Also, we create the function for an example of the code generation and evaluation of a binary tree in Fig. 11.9.

We must represent mathematical definition as an abstract data type. If binary tree is specified as an abstract data type, we manipulate some

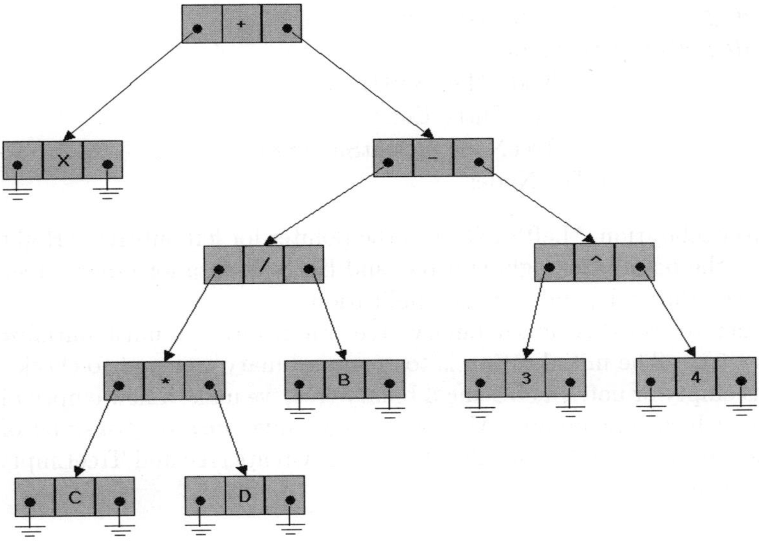

Fig. 11.11. A linked binary tree.

operations to be performed on this binary tree. Also we must add reference to the way in which binary trees will be implemented in memory. Thus we use linked representation for easy use, and also reference to keys or the way in which they are ordered.

Linked implementation uses storage to be formed of two fields of data and pointer. Since a binary tree is constructed in linked structures, all the nodes are linked in storage dynamically. In order to find the tree in storage, we need a special pointer. The name for this pointer is root, since this pointer points to the root of the tree. Using this pointer, we recognize easily an empty binary tree as if root = ***null***. We assign its root pointer to ***null*** to create a new empty binary tree. Figure 11.11 is the linked binary tree of Fig. 11.9. As you see, the difference between them is that linked binary tree has ***null*** links explicitly.

(1) Declaration of data structure for a binary tree

For linked implementation of the binary tree, we construct its data structure and each node in a binary tree.

In a binary tree, each node has three fields; left subtree, right subtree and data. As with linked lists, we use two types to define a binary tree in syntax of C programming language. Two ***struct*** are as follows.

```
typedef struct treenode TreeNode;
typedef struct treenode{
                TreeNode *LeftSubTree;
                    TreeEntry Entry;
                    TreeNode *RightSubTree;
                } TreeNode;
```

In this declaration, *LeftSubTree is the pointer for left subtree, *RightSubTree is the pointer for right subtree, and Entry is data for binary tree. The type TreeEnrty depends on the application.
In order to use this linked binary tree practically, we must initialize the binary tree. The initialization is to create a binary tree and to check if the tree is empty or not. In creating a binary tree, we make a new empty binary tree to which root points. Also we obtain value ***true*** or ***false*** according as the tree is empty or not. Two functions, CreateTree and TreeEmpty, are built easily.

(2) Traversal function

In order to make functions to traverse a linked binary tree we have studied three traversal methods, preorder, inorder and postorder. In each of the three methods, we use recursion. It is easy. We assume that we have the root to be a pointer to the root of the tree and another function Visit that visits a node according to the request of each node. Three functions, Preorder, Inorder and Postorder, are as follows. The Preorder function visits each node of the tree in preorder. The result is preorder sequence of nodes that have been performed on every entry in the binary tree. There are some related functions for preorder in exercise and solution.

```
/* Visiting each node of the binary tree in preorder sequence. */
void Preorder(TreeNode *CurrentNode)
{
        if (CurrentNode)
        {
                Visit(CurrentNode->Entry);
                Preorder(CurrentNode->LeftSubTree);
                Preorder(CurrentNode->RightSubTree);
        }
}
```

The Inorder function visits each node of the binary tree in inorder. The result is inorder sequences of nodes that have been performed on every entry in the binary tree.

```
/* Visiting each node of the binary tree in inorder sequence. */
void Inorder(TreeNode *CurrentNode)
{
        if (CurrentNode)
        {
                Inorder(CurrentNode->LeftSubTree);
                Visit(CurrentNode->Entry);
                Inorder(CurrentNode->RightSubTree);
        }
}
```

The Postorder function visits each node of the tree in postorder. The result is postorder sequences of nodes that have been performed on every entry in the binary tree.

```
/* Visiting each node of the binary tree in postorder sequence. */
void Postorder(TreeNode *CurrentNode)
{
        if (CurrentNode)
        {
                Postorder(CurrentNode->LeftSubTree);
                Postorder(CurrentNode->RightSubTree);
                Visit(CurrentNode->Entry);
        }
}
```

(3) Evaluation function for an expression tree

This function evaluates the expression by making a left to right scan, stacking operand, and evaluating operators popping proper operands and then placing the result into the stack. The following is evaluation function.

```
void Evaluation(TreeNode *CurrentNode)
{
    if (CurrentNode)
      {
          Evaluation(CurrentNode->LeftSubTree);
          Evaluation(CurrentNode->RightSubTree);
          switch(CurrentNode->Entry)
          {
            case each operator x:
                  Pop the proper number of operands for operator
                  x from stack;
```

```
                Perform the operation x and store the result onto the
                stack;
            default: push(CurrentNode->Entry);
            }
    }
}
```

(4) Main function

In order to use some implementation functions for a linked binary tree, we call these functions by main function.

In the main function, we assume that we have root to be a pointer to the root of the tree. The function InitialTree( ) makes a binary tree, and functions Preorder(root), Postorder(root), and Inorder(root) are used to traverse a binary tree. The function Evaluation(root) is used for the application of expression tree of an example.

```
void main( )
{
        root = (TreeNode*) malloc(sizeof(treenode));
        InitialTree( );
        Preorder(root);
        Postorder(root);
        Inorder(root);
        Evaluation(root);
}
```

11.2. Binary Search Trees

Since there may be an ordered list of nodes that consists of lists, records or files, the use of a binary search tree is important to manipulate it efficiently. We may use nodes of the tree to look up information, add, delete, or change. So, we want to make it into a binary search tree with the list or file of nodes. It is difficult to manipulate sequential ordered nodes to be efficient, for example, sequential search time is slow rather than binary search. Therefore, we try to construct them into a tree efficiently.

In this section, we study the binary search tree to have some issues. One of them is an implementation for ordered lists in which we can search quickly, and another is insertion and deletions quickly in ordered list.

11.2.1. *Definition*

We can use a binary search tree to solve the problems efficiently. So we can make comparison trees showing the progress of binary search by moving node either left or right. If the target key is smaller than the one in the current node in the tree, moving is left. If the target key is larger than the one in the current node in the tree, moving is right. Thus concept of the target *key* is very important in binary search.

Definition. A *binary search tree* is a binary tree. This binary tree is either empty or in which every node contains a key and satisfies the following properties:

(1) The key in the left subtree of a node (if any) is less than the key in its parent node.
(2) The key in the right subtree of a node (if any) is greater than the key in its parent node.
(3) The left and right subtrees of the root are the binary search tree.

This definition always assumes that not more than two entries may have equal keys in a binary search tree. If this definition allows entries with equal keys, it must be changed. From this definition, we can see that a binary search tree has the ordering relative to the key in the root node of the binary tree. Also each subtree is another binary search tree recursively.

After examining the root of the tree, either left or right subtree of root is moved with order relation, and then for each subtree, the same process is performed recursively. However, the binary search must not have equal keys. All the keys in the left subtree must be smaller than the key of the root, and those in the right subtree must be greater than the key of the root. Figure 11.12 shows the definition of a binary search tree, since *values* (L) $<$ *key* (N) $<$ *values* (R).

Figure 11.13 is an example of a binary search tree, since the values in the left subtree are smaller than the key value of the root, and those in the right subtree are greater than that of the root. If we use this binary search tree, we can search or sort listed data efficiently. However, the keys in a binary search tree must be the sorted list.

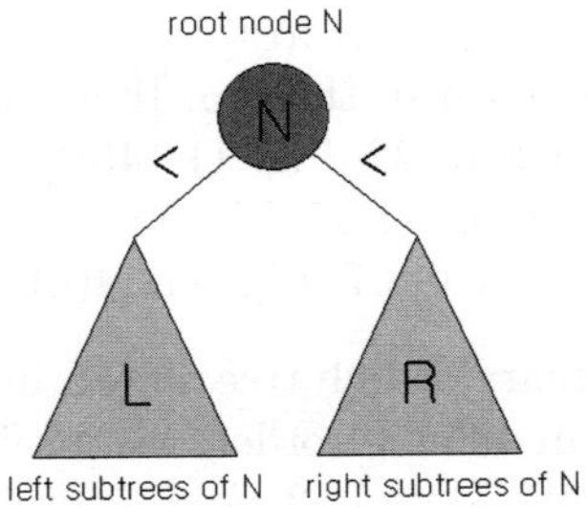

Fig. 11.12. The definition of a binary search tree.

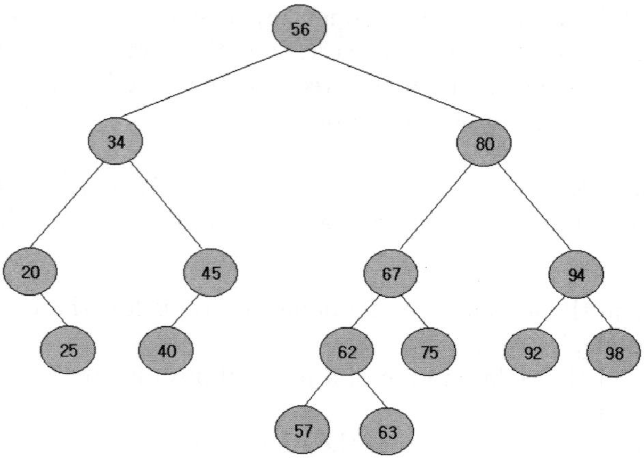

Fig. 11.13. An example of a binary search tree.

11.2.2. *Insertion into a Binary Search Tree*

We shall extend the operation for a binary search tree. The operations as *insertion* or *deletion* to be manipulated are useful for searching and sorting lists. First, we study the important operation to insert a new node into a binary search tree. When the insertion operation is performed, the keys remain properly ordered. This means that the resulting tree after insertion of node into binary search tree must satisfy the definition of a binary search tree. Let us consider an example to insert a node into a binary search tree. We want to insert the keys 56, 24, 45, 67, 3, 79, 60 into an initial empty tree in given order. The insertion process is as follows:

(1) For the first 56 to be inserted, it is the root of the binary search tree [Fig. 11.14(a)].
(2) For 24, since it is less than 56, it goes to the left of 56 [Fig. 11.14(b)].
(3) For 45, after comparing it to 56, it goes to left, and then comparing it to 24 and goes to left [Fig. 11.14(c)].
(4) For 67, it goes to the right of the root [Fig. 11.14(d)].
(5) For 3, it goes to the left of 24 [Fig. 11.14(e)].
(6) For 79, it goes to the right of 67 [Fig. 11.14(f)].
(7) For 60, it goes to the left of 67 [Fig. 11.14(g)].

Finally, we obtain the binary search tree shown in Fig. 11.14.

When we insert keys in different order, we obtain different binary search trees. Also if we insert the keys 1, 2, 3, 4, 5 or 10, 9, 8, 7, 5 in order, a chain is produced as Fig. 11.15.

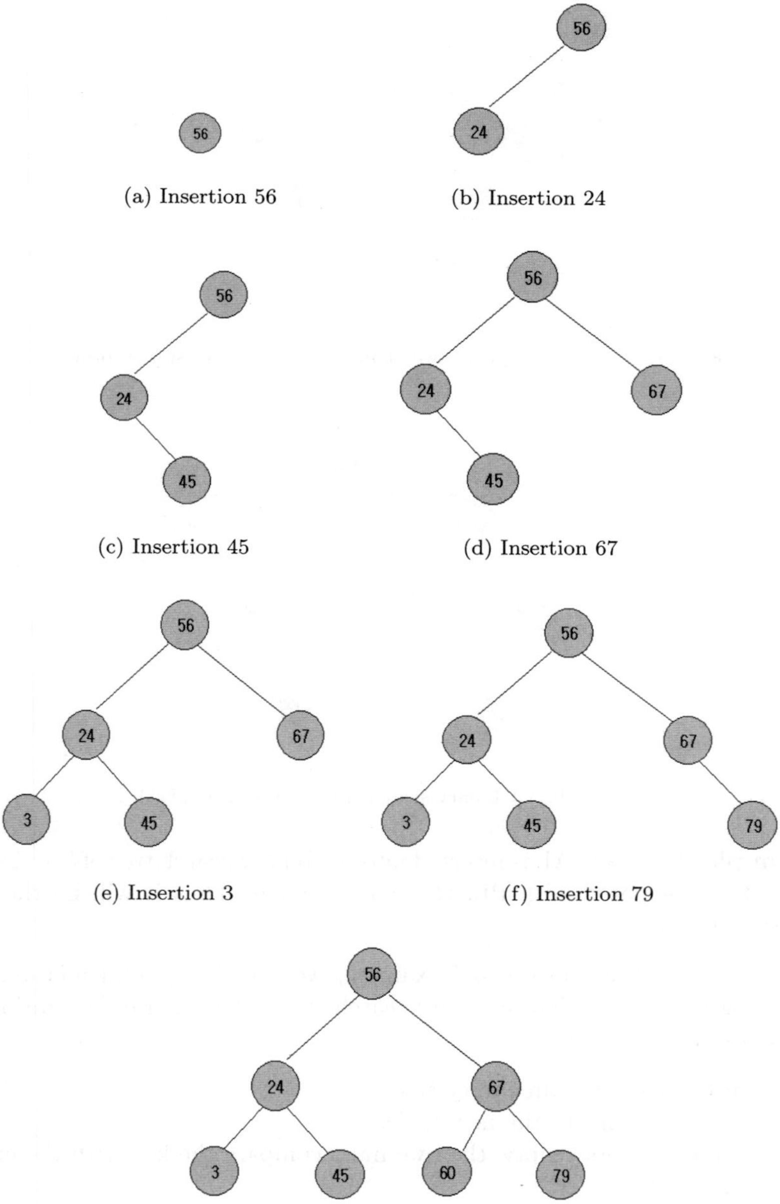

(a) Insertion 56
(b) Insertion 24
(c) Insertion 45
(d) Insertion 67
(e) Insertion 3
(f) Insertion 79
(g) Insertion 60

Fig. 11.14. An example of insertion into a binary search tree.

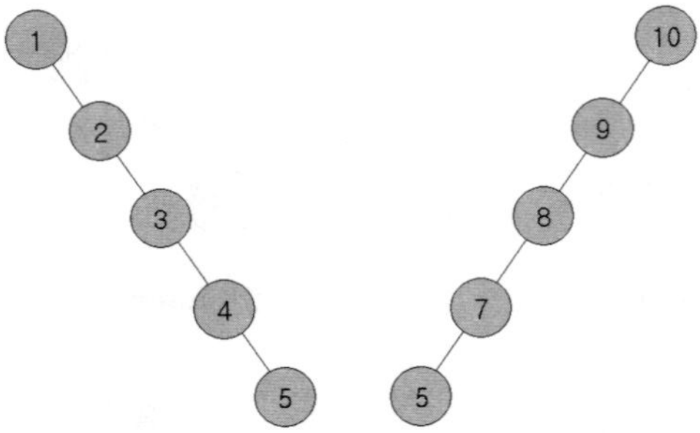

Fig. 11.15. An example of two chains by insertion of special order.

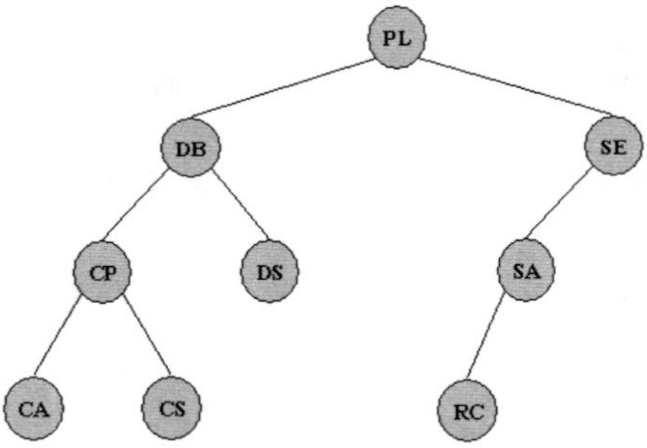

Fig. 11.16. A binary search tree for insertion of AL.

Example. If the key AL is inserted into the binary search tree of Fig. 11.16, the AL is compared with PL, DB, CP, and CA. Thus it will be the left subtree of CA.

Now, from the above small example, we use the general method for inserting a new node into a binary search tree. The general description of methods is as follows:

(1) Insert a node into an empty tree.
(2) Make root point to the new node.
(3) If the tree is not empty, then we must compare the key with the entry in the root.
    (i) If the key is less, then it must be inserted into the left subtree of the root.
    (ii) If the key it is greater, then it must be inserted into the right subtree of the root.

(iii) If the keys are equal, then we have duplicate key in the tree. Thus we must perform another task.

We must describe this insertion method by using recursion, since the same insertion method must be performed on the left or right subtree, after doing at the root. However, for the duplicate key, a new key is inserted on the right side of existing entry. If we traverse the tree, the entries with duplicate keys are visited in same order in which they were inserted.

From the above description, we can write a function using abstract data type and functions declared previously. The following is the recursive insertion function in syntax of C programming language.

```
/* Insertion Function.
input : Entry to be inserted.
output : Tree with inserted Entry.
Method : Using search and insertion algorithm of binary search tree. */

TreeNode* Insert(TreeNode *node, Enter key)
{
        // if node is NULL, creating new node.
        if (node == NULL)
        {
                node = (TreeNode*) malloc(sizeof(treenode));
                node->Entry = key;
                node->LeftSubTree = NULL;
                node->RightSubTree = NULL;
        }
        else
        {
                // Entry is less than insertion key
                if (node->Entry < key)
                {
                    // Move to right subtree.
                    node->RightSubTree =
                    Insert(node->RightSubTree, key);
                }
                //Entry is greater than key.
                else if (node->Entry > key)
                {
                      // Move to left subtree.
                      node->LeftSubTree = Insert(node->LeftSubTree,
                                                            key);
                }
```

```
                    else
                    {
                      printf("exist already \n");
                      }
        }
  return node;
}
```

This function is performed with Search, since comparisons of keys are performed in the same order. Function of searching always finds the first entry that was inserted with a given key. Insert function has the same performance as that of Search.

11.2.3. *Deletion from a Binary Search Tree*

We obtained a method that inserts a new node into the binary search tree. Now we study a method that deletes a node from the binary search tree. Two methods can be used to create and to update the binary search tree easily.

Figure 11.17 shows an example for simple deletion from a binary search tree. As shown in Fig. 11.17(a), the deletion of leaf node is simple. This process replaces the link to the deleted node by ***null***. Also deletion of the node with only one subtree is simple as in Fig. 11.17(b). The process adjusts the link from the parent of the deleted node to point to its subtree. However, deletion of the node with two subtrees nonempty is more complicated as Fig. 11.17(c).

In this case, the problem is that the parent of the deleted node points to specific subtrees. What shall we do with the other subtree?

One solution is to replace the node with the greatest key in the left subtree in place of the deleted node, and then connect the remaining left subtree and the right subtree to that node. Another is to replace the node with the least key in the right subtree in place of the deleted node, and then connect the remaining right subtree and the left subtree to that node. Figure 11.18 shows this process for deletion of the node with two subtrees nonempty from a binary search tree.

It is important to find the node with the least key in the right subtree (the node with the greatest key in the left subtree). Since all keys in the left subtree are less than every key of the right subtree, it must be the rightmost node of left subtree (or leftmost node of the right subtree) of the deleted node.

Example. If the root PL is deleted from the binary search tree of Fig. 11.16, two binary search trees are obtained as in Fig. 11.19.

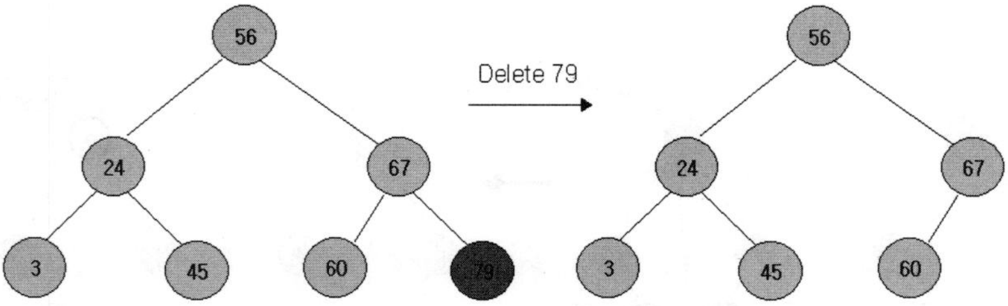

(a) Deletion of a leaf node

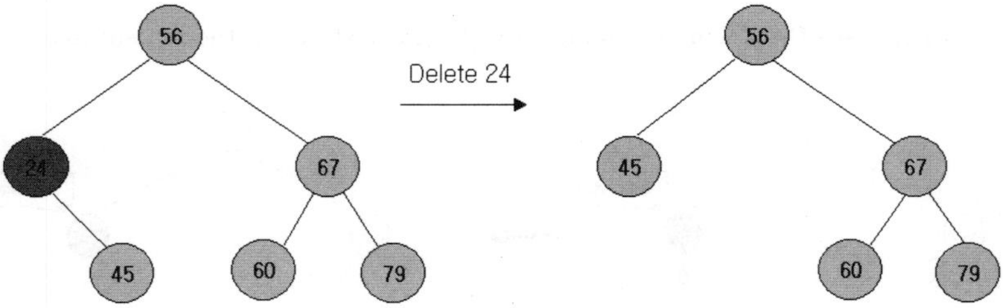

(b) Deletion of the node with only one subtree

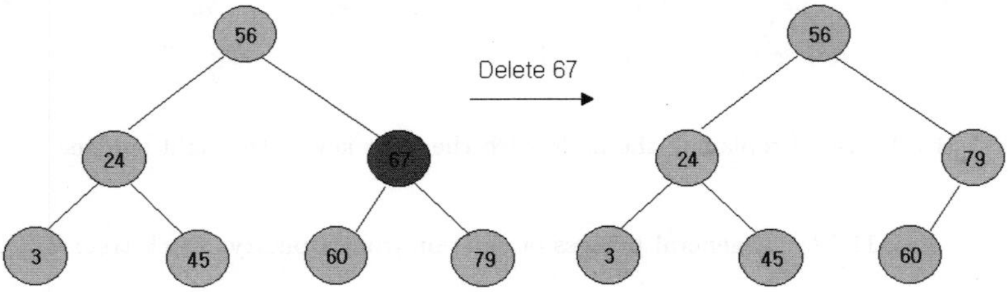

(c) Deletion of the node with two subtree

Fig. 11.17. An example of deletion from a binary search tree.

From the previous examples, we create the implementing process for deletion of a node from a binary search tree. The general description for implementation is as follows.

(1) If a node to be deleted is a leaf node, link to the deleted node by ***null***.
(2) If a node to be deleted has one subtree only, adjust the link from the parent of the deleted node to point to its subtree.
(3) If a node to be deleted has two subtree:

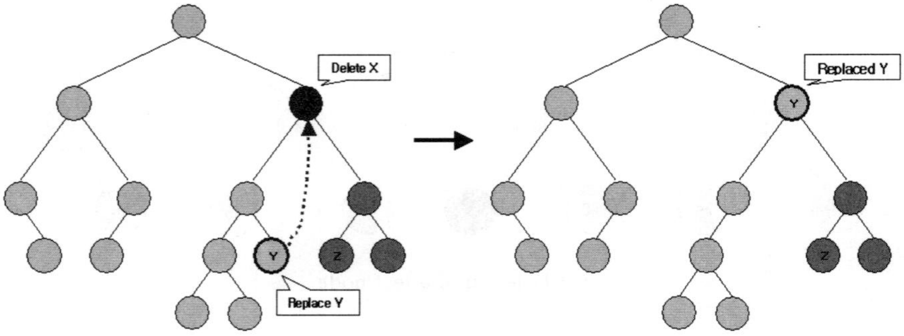

(a) A case of replacing the node with the greatest key in the left subtree

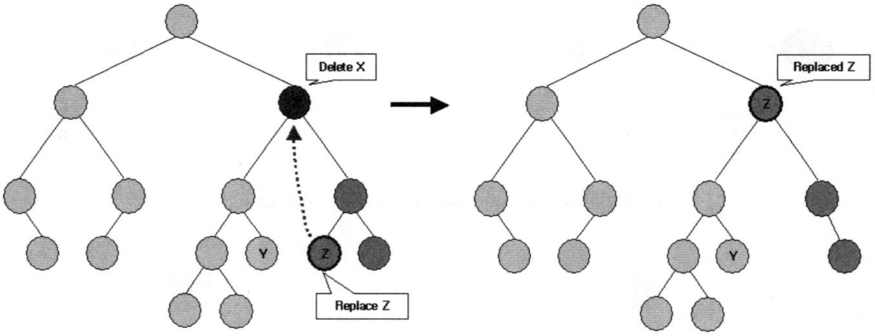

(b) A case of replacing the node with the least key in the right subtree

Fig. 11.18. A general process of deletion from a binary search tree.

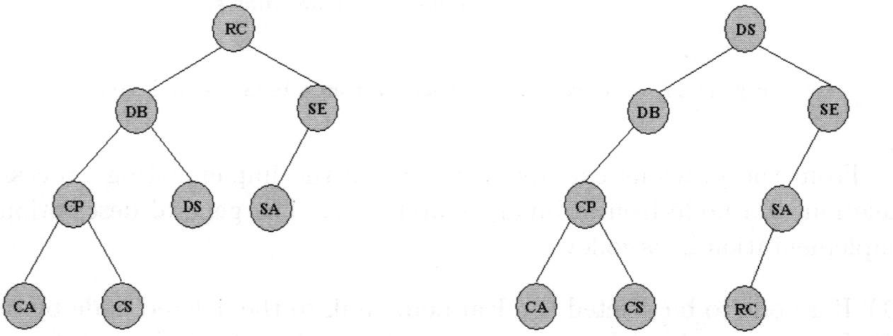

Fig. 11.19. Two binary search trees from deletion of node PL of Fig. 11.16.

(i) Find the node with the greatest key in the left subtree (or the least key in the right subtree).
(ii) Replace the node found into node to be deleted.
(iii) Adjust pointers to parent node, left and right subtree.

We create the function to implement deletion of a node from a binary search tree based on this description. This function is based on replacing the node with the greatest key in the left subtree into a node to be deleted. The function is as follows.

```
/* Deletion Function.
input: Entry of node to be deleted
output: New tree with deleted node */

void Delete (TreeNode *node, TreeNode *parent, Enter key)
{
        // Finding key
        if (node != NULL && node->Entry != key)
        {
                parent = node;
                if (node->Entry < key)
                        Delete(node->RightSubTree, parent, key);
                else
                        Delete(node->LeftSubTree, parent, key);
        }

        else {
        // If key is exist or not.
        if (node != NULL)
        {
               // Rebuild tree. A node has both left and right subtree.
                if (node->LeftSubTree != NULL &&
                     node->RightSubTree != NULL)
                {
                        // One subtree or no subtree
                        // Save the greatest key value from
                           LeftSubTree
                        TreeNode *tmp = node->LeftSubTree;
                        TreeNode *tmp2 = node;   // Parent of tmp
                        // Finding the greatest key value
                        while (tmp->RightSubTree != NULL)
                        {
```

```
                        tmp2 = tmp;
                        tmp = tmp->RightSubTree;
                    }
                    // The greatest key value is Entry value of
                       deleted node.
                    node->Entry = tmp->Entry;
                    node = tmp;
                    parent = tmp2;
                }

                // Adjust pointers of remaining tree.
                TreeNode *tmp3;
                if (node->LeftSubTree == NULL)
                    tmp3 = node->RightSubTree;
                else
                    tmp3 = node->LeftSubTree;
                // If a node is root, remaining tree is root.
                if (node == root)
                    root = tmp3;
                else
                {
                    // Remaining tree is subtree of parent.
                    if (node == parent->LeftSubTree)
                        parent->LeftSubTree = tmp3;
                    else
                        parent->RightSubTree = tmp3;
                }
            }
        }
}
```

The Delete is the function name to delete a node from the tree. TreeNode *node is the current node, TreeNode *parent is the parent of the current node, and Enter key is the key to be deleted. After this function, we obtain another binary search tree that a specified node has been deleted from the binary search tree. This function uses the calling parameter as a pointer to the node to be deleted.

11.2.4. *Search of a Binary Search Tree*

We apply a binary search tree to search an entry with a particular target key. It is an important operation for binary search tree.

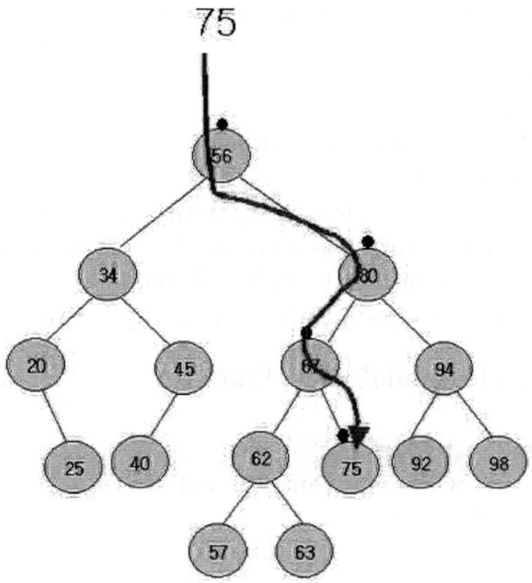

Fig. 11.20. An example of searching a binary search tree.

For example, let us search the value 75 in the binary search tree of Fig. 11.20. In order to search for the target, it is compared with the key at the root of the tree first. If the target equals to the key, then searching is finished since we found the target. If the target is not found (not equal), searching is repeated in the left subtree or the right subtree. So the process is as follows.

(1) We first compare 75 with the key of the root, 56.
(2) Since 75 are greater than 56 in orders, next we compare 75 with 80 in the right subtree.
(3) Since 75 are less than 80, we compare 75 with 67 in the left subtree.
(4) Finally, since 75 are greater, we find the target 75 in the right subtree.

Figure 11.20 shows this process to search for a tree. Small dots on node 56, 80, 67 and 75 present the node to be compared with target. The arrowed line is the direction of move. The search of a binary search tree is repetition of comparisons and move in the tree. If the key is found, the function finishes searching the tree. However, if the key is not found, the function finishes if it meets an empty subtree.

Now, from the above small example, we make the general function to search for a target in a binary search tree using recursion. If an entry in tree has a key equal to target, then the return value points to such a node, otherwise the function returns ***null***. Thus recursive function to search a tree is simple as follows.

```
/* Search Function.
input: Entry value of Node to be searched
output: Pointer to a Node
Method: Compare current node's Entry with input key. If the key is equal
to current node Entry, return the pointer. If key is greater than current
node Entry, change the pointer to right subtree.
If key is less than current node Entry, change the pointer to left subtree.*/

TreeNode* Search(TreeNode* node, Enter key)
{
        if (node != NULL) {
                // while node entry is not NULL.
                if (node)
                {
                        // If Entry is equal to key, return node pointer.
                        if (node->Entry == key) return node;
                        // If Entry is less, move to right subtree.
                        else if (node->Entry < key)
                                node = Search(node->RightSubTree,
                                        key);
                        // If Entry is greater, move to left subtree
                        else
                                node = Search(node->LeftSubTree,
                                        key);
                }
        }
        return node;
}
```

Since this function Search is based on binary search, that has the same comparison ($O(\log n)$) if it is applied to same tree. We can say that this performance is better than other methods, since log n grows slowly as n increases.

11.2.5. *Implementation of a Binary Search Tree*

In order to implement a binary search tree, we need an empty binary tree, nodes already in order and tree insertion and comparison algorithm. Also we use the abstract data type and functions of a binary tree.

We have already made a ***typedef*** and functions for a binary tree. For the practical implementation using a binary tree, we can change the specifications and parameters in the abstract data type of a binary tree.

Followings are functions for declarations, output and main for insertion, deletion and searching of binary search tree in C programming language syntax.

```
#include <stdio.h>
#include <stdlib.h>

// Abstract Data Type of Binary tree

typedef int Enter;
typedef struct treenode TreeNode;
typedef struct treenode{
            TreeNode *LeftSubTree;
            Enter Entry;
            TreeNode *RightSubTree;
} TreeNode;

// root is global variable of Tree.
TreeNode *root = NULL;
//
// Function declaration of insertion, deletion and search
// Declaration of preorder function for output tree entry value by
   preorder traversing to
// confirm correct insertion, deletion or search.
//
// Main function
int main( )
{
            int choice;
            Enter key;

            while(1) {
                        printf("Select (1)Insert (2)Delete (3)Search
                                  (4)View (5)Exit : ");
                        scanf("%d", &choice);
                        switch(choice)
                        {
                                  case 1:
                                            printf ("Key : ");
                                            scanf ("%d", &key);
                                            root = Insert(root, key);
```

```
                        break;
                case 2:
                        printf ("Key : ");
                        scanf ("%d", &key);
                        Delete(root, NULL,key);
                        break;
                case 3:
                        printf ("Key : ");
                        scanf ("%d", &key);
                        TreeNode *node = Search(root,
                                                    key);
                        break;
                case 4:
                        preorder(root);
                        printf ("\n");
                        break;
                default:
                        break;
            }
            if (choice == 5)
                break;
        }
return 0;
}
```

11.3. An AVL Tree and Balancing Height

In this section, we study the *AVL tree.* In practical application, there are many searches, insertions and deletions in a tree with n nodes. However, since we do not know order n and the tree may not be balanced, we need considerable time to manipulate a tree with n nodes. Thus in order to optimize search times, we keep the tree balancing at all times. An AVL tree has $O(\log n)$ in the worst case to manipulate searches, insertions and deletions in a tree with n nodes.

11.3.1. *Definition*

In *complete binary tree* with node n, we know already that the left and right subtrees of any node have the same height. In this section, we try to make a search tree that the height of every left and right subtree never differs by more than 1 by changing a search tree.

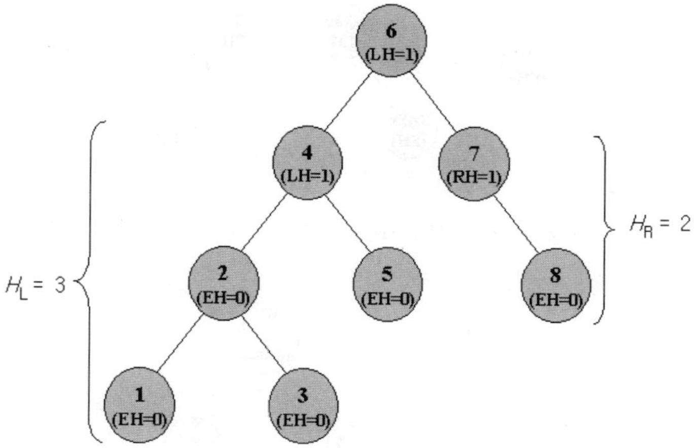

Fig. 11.21. An example of an AVL tree.

Definition. An *AVL tree* is a binary search tree that is either empty or that consists of two AVL subtree, left and right subtrees, whose heights differ by no more than 1 as follow.

$$|H_{\mathrm{L}} - H_{\mathrm{R}}| = 1$$

H_{L} is the *height* of the left subtree and H_{R} is the *height* of the right subtree.

Figure 11.21 shows an example of AVL trees to satisfy the definition. In Fig. 11.21, LH, RH and EH is a *balance factor* that means a *left-high* node, a *right-high* node and *equal*, respectively. LH $= 1$ of root 6 means that left subtree of root 6 has height 1 more than its right subtree. RH $= 1$ of node 7 means that its right subtree has height 1 more than left subtree. EH $= 0$ is same height.

In Fig. 11.21, since the height of the left subtree (root is 4) is 3 and the height of the right subtree (root is 7) is 2, $|H_{\mathrm{L}} - H_{\mathrm{R}}| = 1$. Since both subtrees (of 4 and 7) are balanced, the tree is balanced. In the left subtree (root is 4), it is balanced because the height of its subtree differs by only 1. Also since its subtrees (root 2 and 5) are balanced, this subtree is a balanced tree. Right subtree (root 7) is balanced, because the height of its subtree differs by only 1. Continuing this, we create a tree balance.

Example. Figure 11.22 shows the AVL tree with only one node or two nodes.

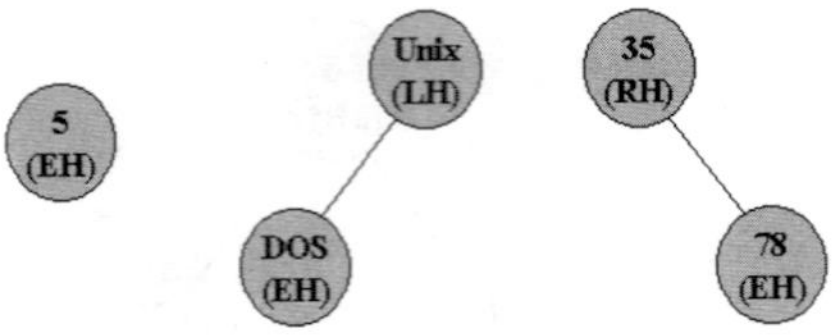

Fig. 11.22. AVL trees with one or two nodes.

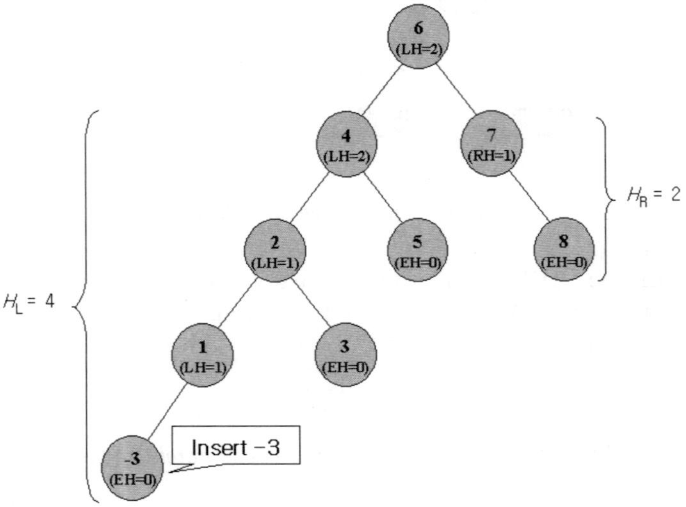

Fig. 11.23. A tree with $|H_L - H_R| \geq 2$ after insertion of new node into an AVL tree.

11.3.2. *Insertion into an AVL tree*

As a binary tree, we can insert a new node x into an AVL tree, keeping the tree balanced in any case. It means that we must insert new node x without changing the height of the subtree. Thus, it is important that the height (balance) of the root must not be changed. When we insert a new node x, the height of the root may increase. Thus, we must adjust the balance factor of the root to keep an AVL condition $|H_L - H_R| \leq 1$.

Figure 11.23 shows a tree to insert new node with –3 into an AVL tree of Fig. 11.21. This tree is not an AVL tree, because the height of the left subtree is two more than right subtree. Also balance factors are changed. In order to keep balance of an AVL tree, we must rebuild the tree. This rebuilding is called *rotation*.

Rotations

If $|H_L - H_R| \geq 2$, by inserting a node, we must rebuild the tree to maintain its balance. There are three considerations to restore balance.

- After a new node is inserted into the AVL tree, if $H_R - H_L \geq 2$, we rotate the AVL tree to left to keep the condition $|H_L - H_R| \leq 1$. By a left rotation, the balance must be restored.
- However, after a new node is inserted into the AVL tree, if $H_L - H_R \geq 2$, we rotate the AVL tree to right to keep the condition $|H_L - H_R| \leq 1$. By a right rotation, the balance must be restored.
- If the insertion makes $|H_L - H_R| \leq 1$, we do nothing.

From three considerations, we can describe the methods to rebuild the tree to become an AVL tree.

Single rotation

This is the case of $H_R - H_L \geq 2$ at root 3 and node 5 of Fig. 11.24(a). The node 5 is right higher, since the right height of the node 5 is 3 ($H_R = 3$) and left height of the node 5 is 1 ($H_L = 1$), that is, $H_R - H_L \geq 2$. Thus, we must rotate the tree to the left to be an AVL tree. It is called *the left rotation*. If $H_R - H_L \geq 2$ at two or more nodes in the tree, left rotation is performed with respect to the closest parent of the new node that a balance factor (RH or LH) was 2.

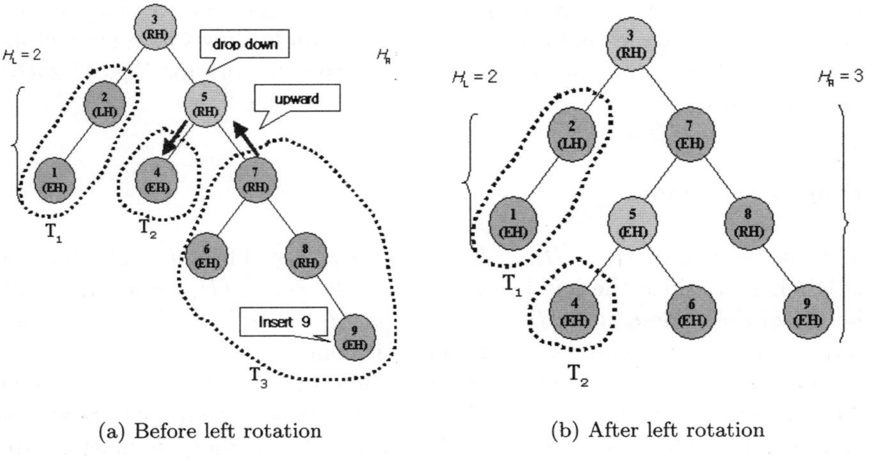

(a) Before left rotation

(b) After left rotation

Fig. 11.24. Restoring balance by a left rotation in case of right higher.

Bal. Factor Node No.	1	2	3	4	5	6	7	8	9
RH			②		②		1	1	
LH		1							
EH	0			0		0			0

Bal. Factor Node No.	1	2	3	4	5	6	7	8	9
RH			1					1	
LH		1							
EH	0			0	0	0	0		0

Figure 11.24 shows the *left rotation* in case of $H_{\text{R}} - H_{\text{L}} \geq 2$, where node 3 is the root of the tree, and node 5 is the root of its right subtree. Although $H_{\text{R}} - H_{\text{L}} \geq 2$ at both the root 3 and node 5, left rotation is performed at the node 5. The action of the left rotation at the node 5 is as follows.

(1) Rotate node 7 upward to the node 5.
(2) Drop node 5 down into the left subtree of node 7.
(3) Link the node 6 to the right subtree of node 5. The key of the node 6 is between key of nodes 5 and 7.

By the left rotation, although the height has increased by the insertion of a node, the height of resulting tree decreases by 1. Also the balance factors must be changed appropriately. Following tables show change of the balance factors. The circled number in the entry is the balance factor of the node that the balance is broken at. The first table shows balance factors for Fig. 11.24(a), and the second shows balance factors for Fig. 11.24(b) after left rotation.

Double rotations

This is the case of $H_{\text{L}} - H_{\text{R}} \geq 2$ at node 8 of Fig. 11.25(a). The node 8 is left higher, since the left height of the node 8 is 3 ($H_{\text{L}} = 3$) and right height of the node 8 is 1 ($H_{\text{R}} = 1$), that is, $H_{\text{L}} - H_{\text{R}} \geq 2$. Thus, we must rotate the tree to be an AVL tree, but it is complicated.

Since the left subtree of node 8 is left higher, first we have to move node 7 to the place of the node 5 as in Fig. 11.25(b). However, since the new tree is still right higher (the subtree with root 8 is left higher), it must rotate to the right to balance as Fig. 11.25(c). Figure 11.25 shows that the tree is balanced by the first left rotation and the second right rotation. It is

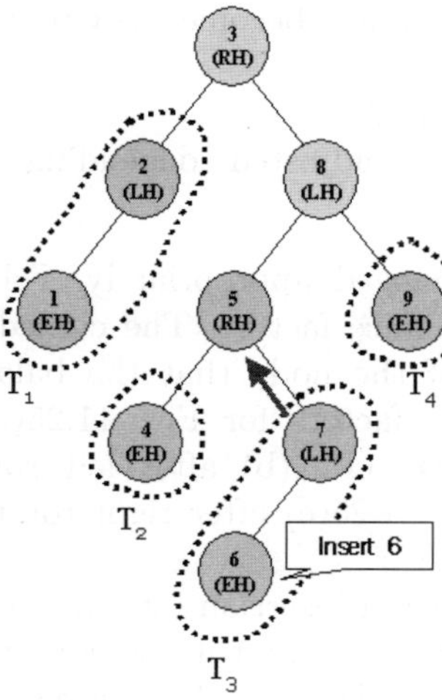

(a) Before right rotation

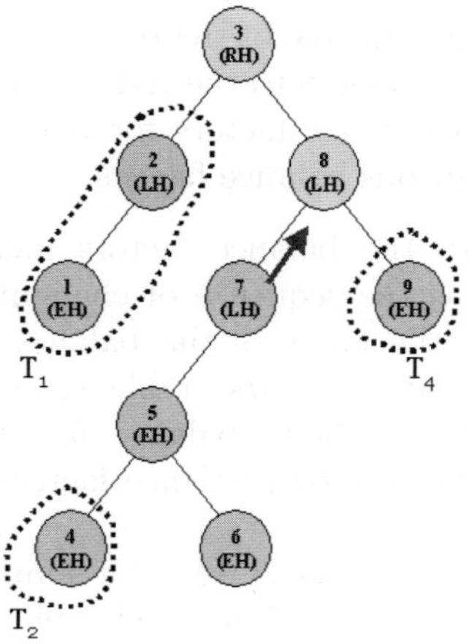

(b) After first right rotation

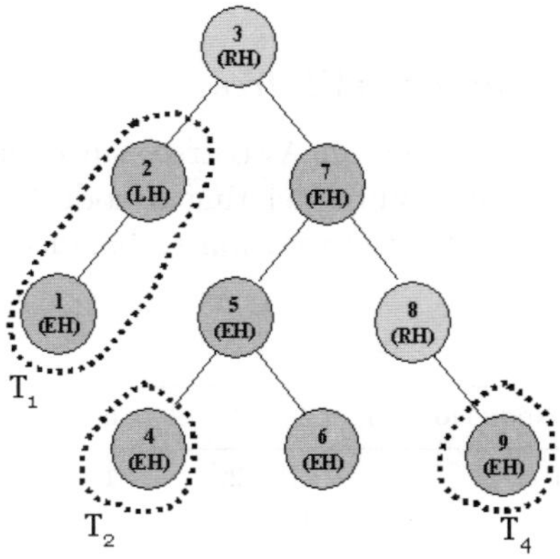

(c) After second left rotation (double rotation).

Fig. 11.25. An AVL tree balancing by double rotation in case of left higher.

called *double rotation*. For the tree of Fig. 11.25, double rotation performs as follows.

(1) By left rotating the subtree with root 5, node 7 becomes its root.
(2) Link node 7 to the left subtree of node 8.
(3) Link node 5 to the left subtree of node 7, and then link the node 6 to the right subtree of node 5.

(4) By right rotating the tree with root 8, node 7 becomes new root of the right subtree of the root 3.
(5) Link node 8 to the right subtree of node 7.
(6) All balance factors for nodes are newly adjusted, depending on the previous balance factors.

Also the balance factors must be changed appropriately. Following tables is the sequence of changing the balance factors. The circled number in the entry is the balance factor of the node that the balance is broken at. The first table shows balance factors for Fig. 11.25(a) and the second shows balance factors for Fig. 11.24(b) after left rotation. Final table shows balance factors for Fig. 11.25(c) after right rotation of Fig. 11.25(b).

Now, Fig. 11.26 shows a simple example of insertion into an AVL tree using rotation. Multimedia player receives stream with various objects from server, and renders the scene graph. Figure 11.26 receives various multimedia objects *text*, *image*, *video*, *animation*, *audio*, *graphic*, *geometric* and *h.263* in turn.

11.3.3. *Deletion from an AVL tree*

If we try to delete a node from an AVL tree, since the height is changed, the balance must be kept. While deleting a node from an AVL tree, we can use the same concept for the rotation to balance the tree as inserting a node.

Bal. Factor Node No.	1	2	3	4	5	6	7	8	9
RH			**②**		**1**				
LH		**1**					**1**	**②**	
EH	**0**			**0**		**0**			**0**

Bal. Factor Node No.	1	2	3	4	5	6	7	8	9
RH			**②**						
LH		**1**					**②**	**②**	
EH	**0**			**0**	**0**	**0**			**0**

Bal. Factor Node No.	1	2	3	4	5	6	7	8	9
RH			**1**					**1**	
LH		**1**							
EH	**0**			**0**	**0**	**0**	**0**		**0**

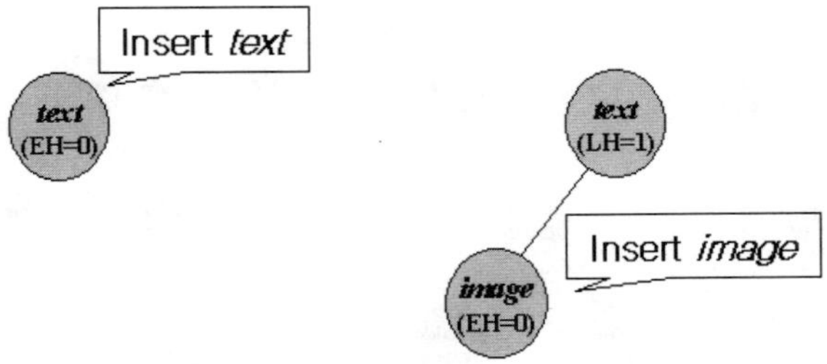

(a) Insertion of node *text* and *image* into AVL tree

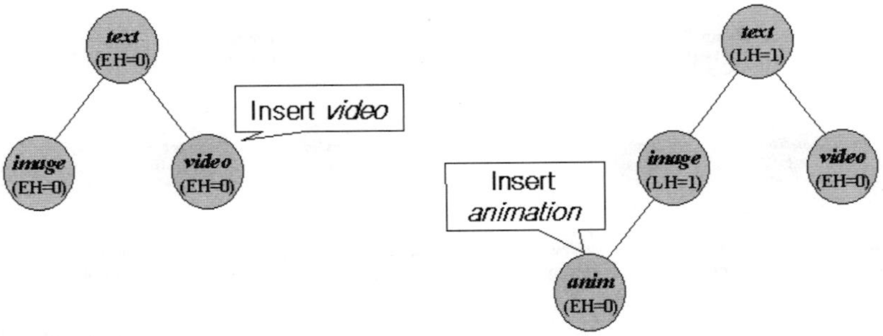

(b) Insertion of node *video* and *animation* into AVL tree

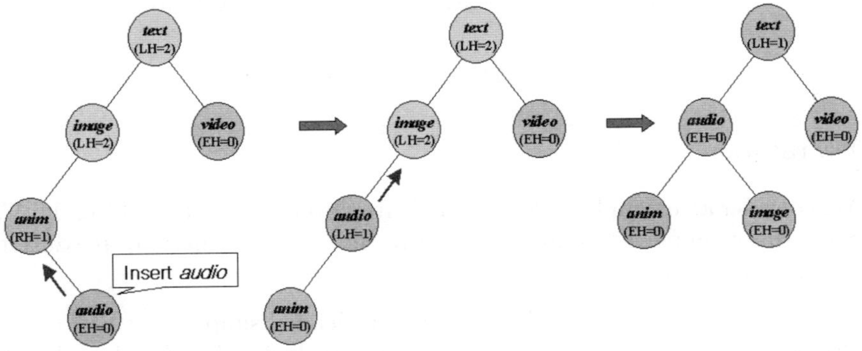

(c) Insertion of node *audio* and AVL tree after double rotation

Fig. 11.26. The insertion of multimedia object into an AVL tree using rotation.

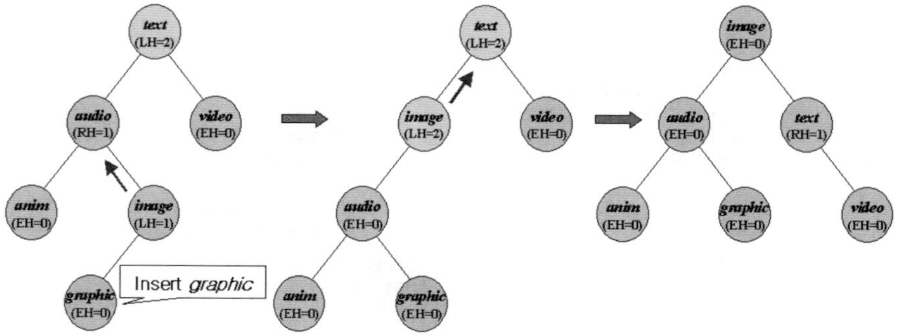

(d) Insertion of node *graphic* and AVL tree after double rotation

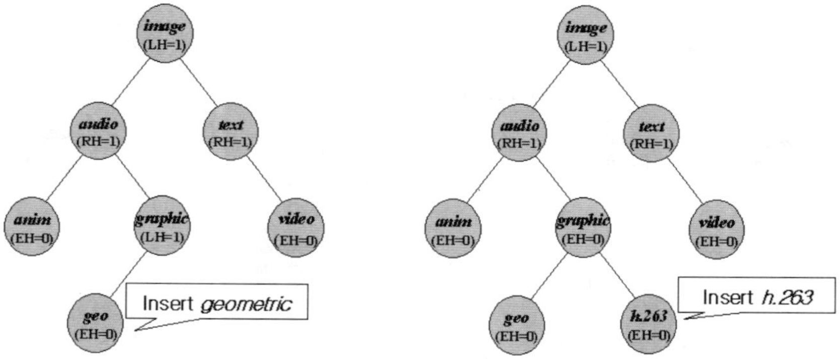

(e) Insertion of node *geometric* and *sound* into AVL tree

Fig. 11.26. (*Continued*)

No rotation

We consider an example to delete a node from simple AVL tree of Fig. 11.27. Since this example is too simple and keeps the balance of an AVL tree during the deletion, it does not have any rotations.

(1) If a node is the leaf as the node 2, it is deleted simply.
(2) If a node has at most one subtree as the node 8, it is deleted, and then the single node 9 is linked to the node 7.
(3) If the node to be deleted has two subtrees as the node 3, its deletion is more complicated. In this case, we find the immediate predecessor node 2 of the node 3 under the *inorder* traverse, and then link parent node 7 of node 3 to the immediate predecessor node 2. We delete node 3.

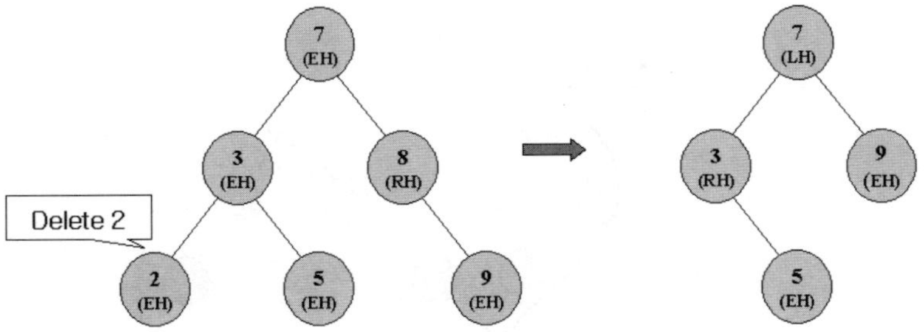

(a) Deletion of leaf node 2 in an AVL tree

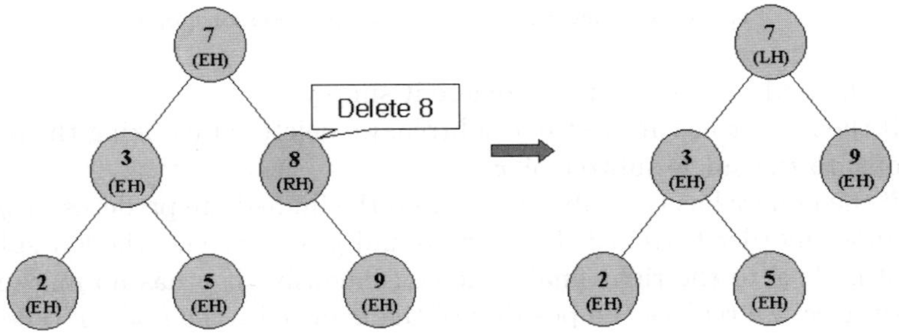

(b) Deletion of node with one subtree in an AVL tree

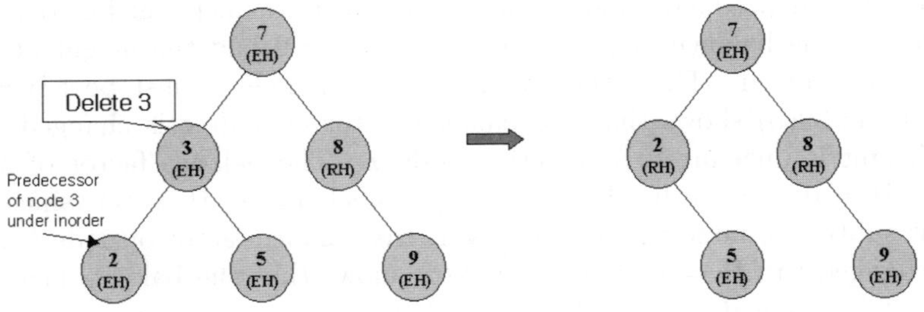

(c) Deletion of node with two subtrees in an AVL tree

Fig. 11.27. An example to delete a node from simple AVL tree.

From the above examples, we can make the general description to delete a node from an AVL tree. Although the left or right subtree is shortened by deleting, if the height of a tree is unchanged or $|H_L - H_R| \le 1$, the tree is not rebuilt. For any node x in an AVL tree, its deletion is performed as follows.

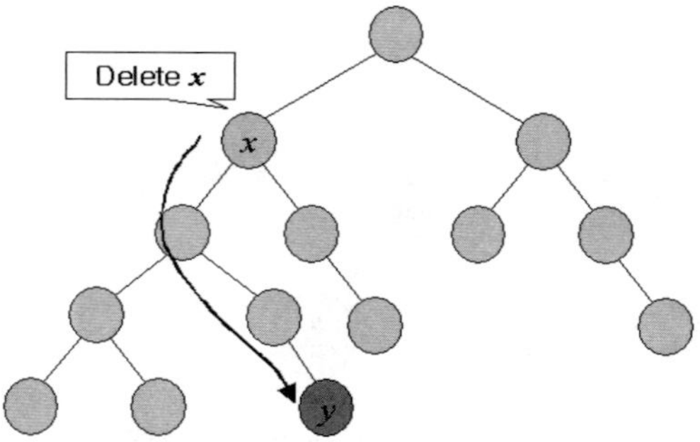

Fig. 11.28. Finding the immediate predecessor y of x.

(1) If the node x is the leaf, we delete it simply.
(2) If the node x has at most one subtree, we delete x by linking the parent of x to the single subtree of x.
(3) If the node x has two subtrees, we find the immediate predecessor y of x under inorder traversal. In order to find y, we traverse the left subtree of node x to the right final node continuously. If y has no more right subtree, we replace the position of the node x by the node y. Then we delete former y in the tree. Figure 11.28 shows this.

Figure 11.29 shows that the tree is not rebuilt. Figure 11.29(a) shows that both balance factor and the height of node t are unchanged by deleting node x. The balance factor of node t is EH $= 0$ and the height of tree T_1 is unchanged. Thus, the balance factor of node t must be EH $= 0$. Figure 11.29(b) shows that the balance factor of node t is changed, but its height is unchanged by deleting node x. The balance factor of node t is EH $= 0$ and the height of tree T_1 is unchanged. However, since the right subtree of node t is reduced by 1, the balance factor of node t must be changed to LH $= 1$. Figure 11.29(c) shows that the balance factor of node t is changed, also its height is changed by deleting node x. Since balance factor of node t is RH $= 1$ and the height of tree T_2 is reduced by 1, the balance factor of node t must be changed to EH $= 0$.

We consider another example to delete a node from the larger AVL tree. Its deletion is very complicated, since this example may not keep the balance of an AVL tree during the deletion. This has some rotations.

Rotation

By the deletion of the node x, since the height of the subtree rooted at x may be reduced by 1 or not, we must trace the balance factor for the

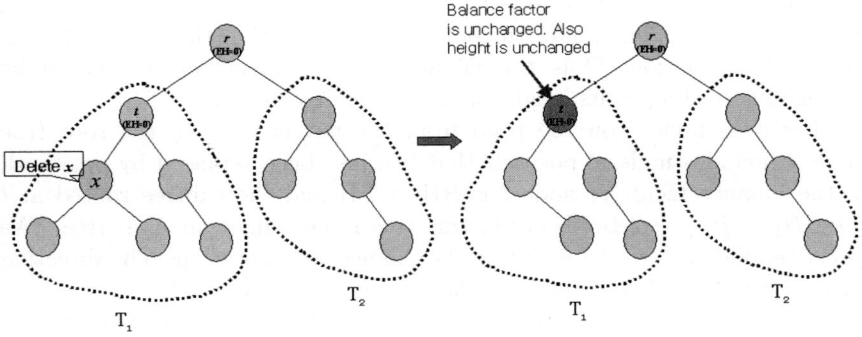

(a) Both balance factor and height are unchanged

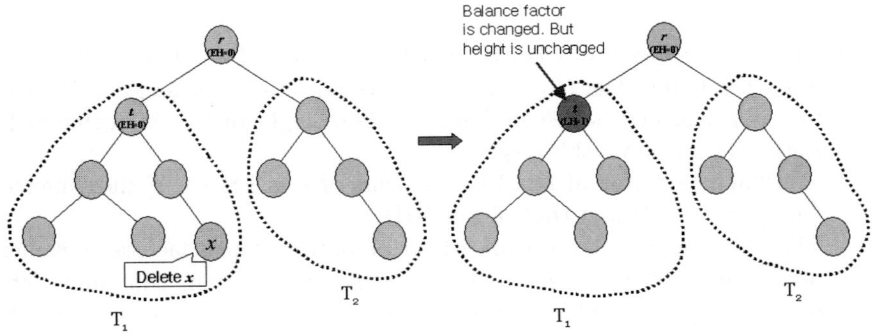

(b) Balance factor is changed, but height is unchanged

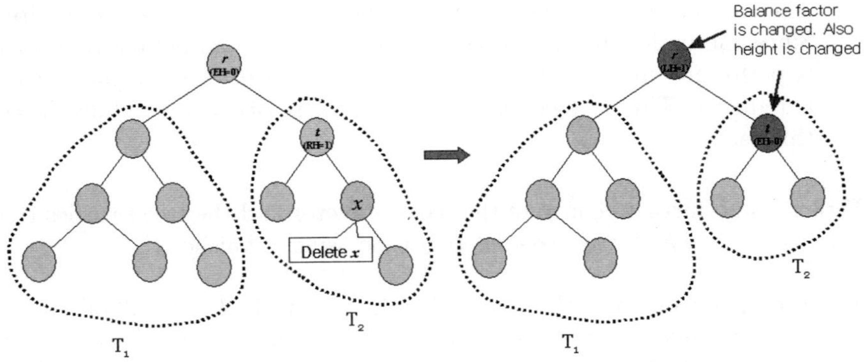

(c) Both balance factor and height are changed

Fig. 11.29. The deletion of node x without rotation.

change of height for each node t on the path from the parent of x to the root in the tree. The node t includes node of position that has just been replaced by deletion. Thus, the balance factor of the current node t can be changed according to its height of the left or right subtree.

For each node t on the path from the parent of x to the root (the node t includes node of position that has just been replaced by deletion), if the balance factor of node t is RH or LH and the subtree rooted at t has $|H_{\mathrm{L}} - H_{\mathrm{R}}| \geq 2$ by deleting, this tree is no longer an AVL tree. We must rebuild the tree to maintain its balance with rotation. The direction of rotation depends on which height of subtree was reduced.

In the deletion with rotation, we have single and double rotations according to the balance factor of each t and s, where s is the root of the taller subtree of t. While the tree has $|H_{\mathrm{L}} - H_{\mathrm{R}}| \geq 2$ at node t and s, the direction of rotation is determined according to following cases.

(1) The balance factor of t is LH (or RH) and that of s is EH:
Since the node t has $H_{\mathrm{R}} - H_{\mathrm{L}} \geq 2$ by the deletion, the single left rotation is performed to restore balance. The height of tree is unchanged. Figure 11.30 shows this case.

(2) The balance factor of t is LH and that of s is LH (or if the balance factor of t is RH and that of s is RH):
The case means that the direction of both balance factors is same. Since the node t has $H_{\mathrm{R}} - H_{\mathrm{L}} \geq 2$ by the deletion, the single left rotation is performed to restore balance. The height of tree is reduced. Figure 11.31 shows this case.

(3) The balance factor of t is RH and that of s is LH (or if the balance factor of t is LH and that of s is RH):
The case means that the direction of both balance factors is opposite. Since the node t has $H_{\mathrm{R}} - H_{\mathrm{L}} \geq 2$ by the deletion, double rotations is performed in order s and t to restore balance. The height of tree is reduced. The balance factor of new root is EH. Figure 11.32 shows this case.

If there is no further change of the balance factor and the tree satisfies the condition of an AVL tree, the deletion processing is finished.

Example. Given the AVL tree as in Fig. 11.33. In Fig. 11.33(a), if we try to delete node 11, we place the immediate predecessor node 10 into the position of node 11 as Fig. 11.33(b). Since the node 10 of Fig. 11.33(b) has the right higher subtree, we rotate node 10 to the left as shown in Fig. 11.33(c). The height of Fig. 11.33(c) is 4 and left higher at the node 9.

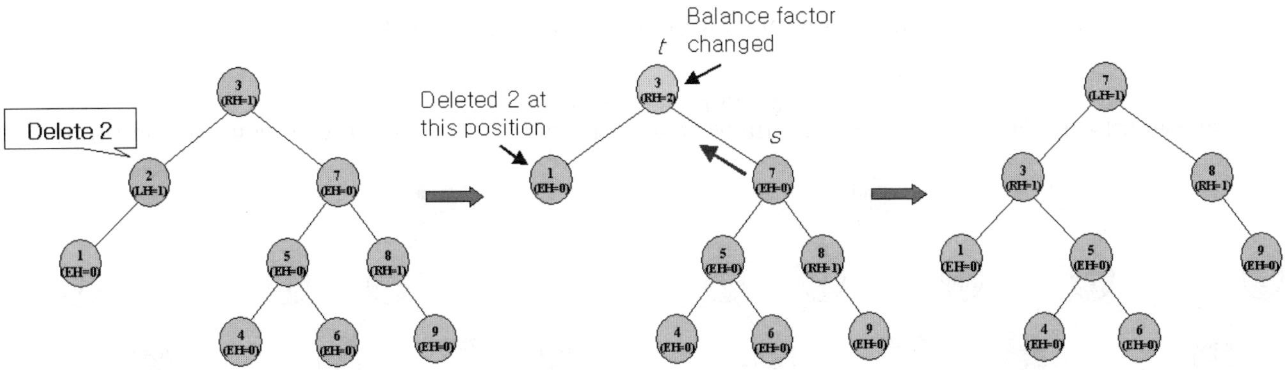

(a) Delete node 2 from an AVL tree

(b) RH = 2 at t and EH = 0 at s
(t has $|H_{\mathrm{L}} - H_{\mathrm{R}}| \geq 2$)

(c) After left rotation

Fig. 11.30. The left rotation when t is RH and s is EH.

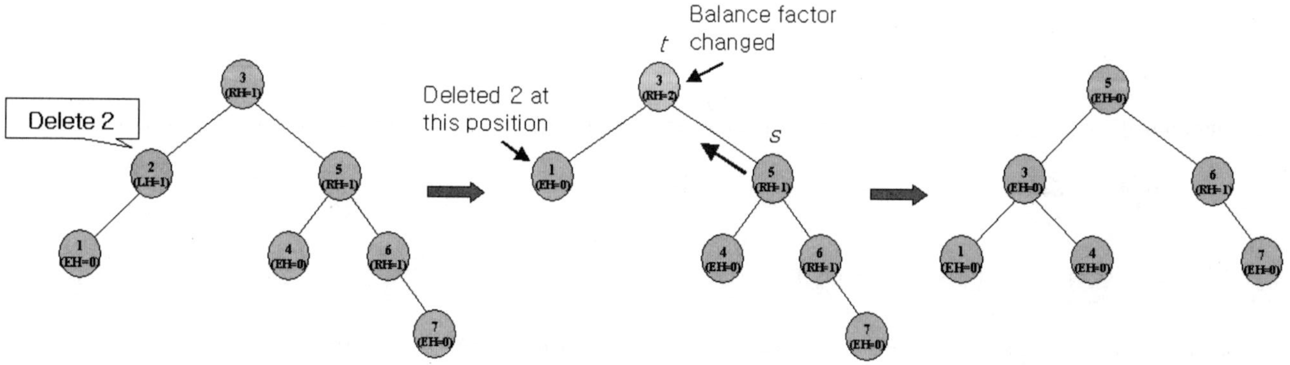

(a) Delete node 2 from an AVL tree

(b) RH = 2 at t and RH = 1 at s (t has $|H_{\mathrm{L}} - H_{\mathrm{R}}| \geq 2$)

(c) After left rotation

Fig. 11.31. The left rotation when t is RH and s is RH.

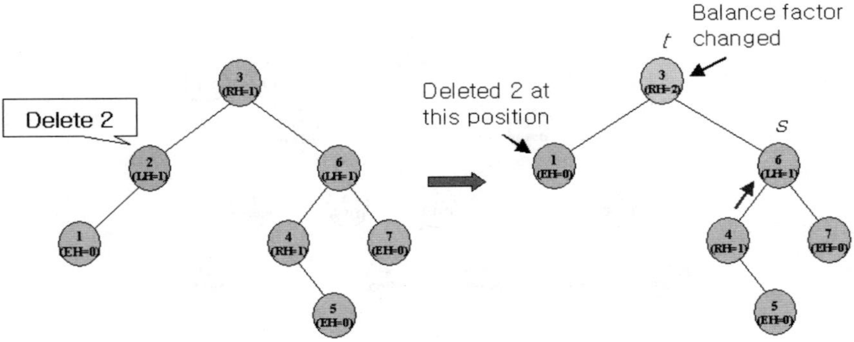

(a) Delete node 2 from an AVL tree

(b) RH = 2 at t and LH = 1 at s (t has $|H_{\mathrm{L}} - H_{\mathrm{R}}| \geq 2$)

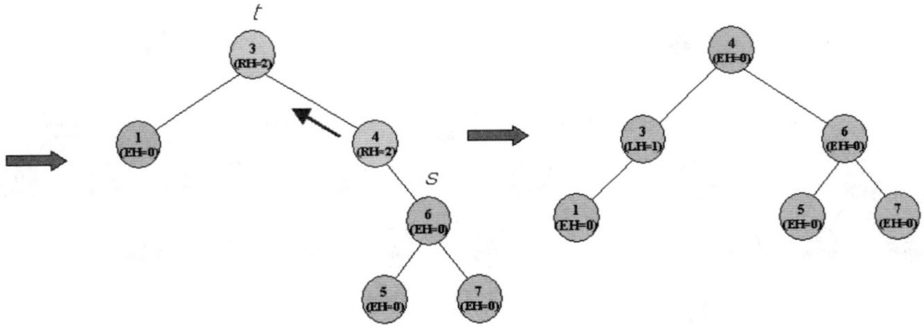

(c) RH = 2 at t and RH = 2 at s (t or s have $|H_{\mathrm{L}} - H_{\mathrm{R}}| \geq 2$)

(d) After double rotation

Fig. 11.32. The double rotations when t is RH and s is LH.

We rotate the node 7 to the left, and then to the right as shown in (d) and (e) of Fig. 11.33.

11.3.4. *Implementation of an AVL tree*

From actions and cases of an AVL tree, we can implement functions for the left and right rotations to balance it. For the practical implementation using, we need the abstract data type, and also use an AVL tree with nodes already in order, tree insertion and comparison algorithm. There are functions in C programming language syntax in Appendix for the left and right rotations while insertion into and deletion from an AVL tree.

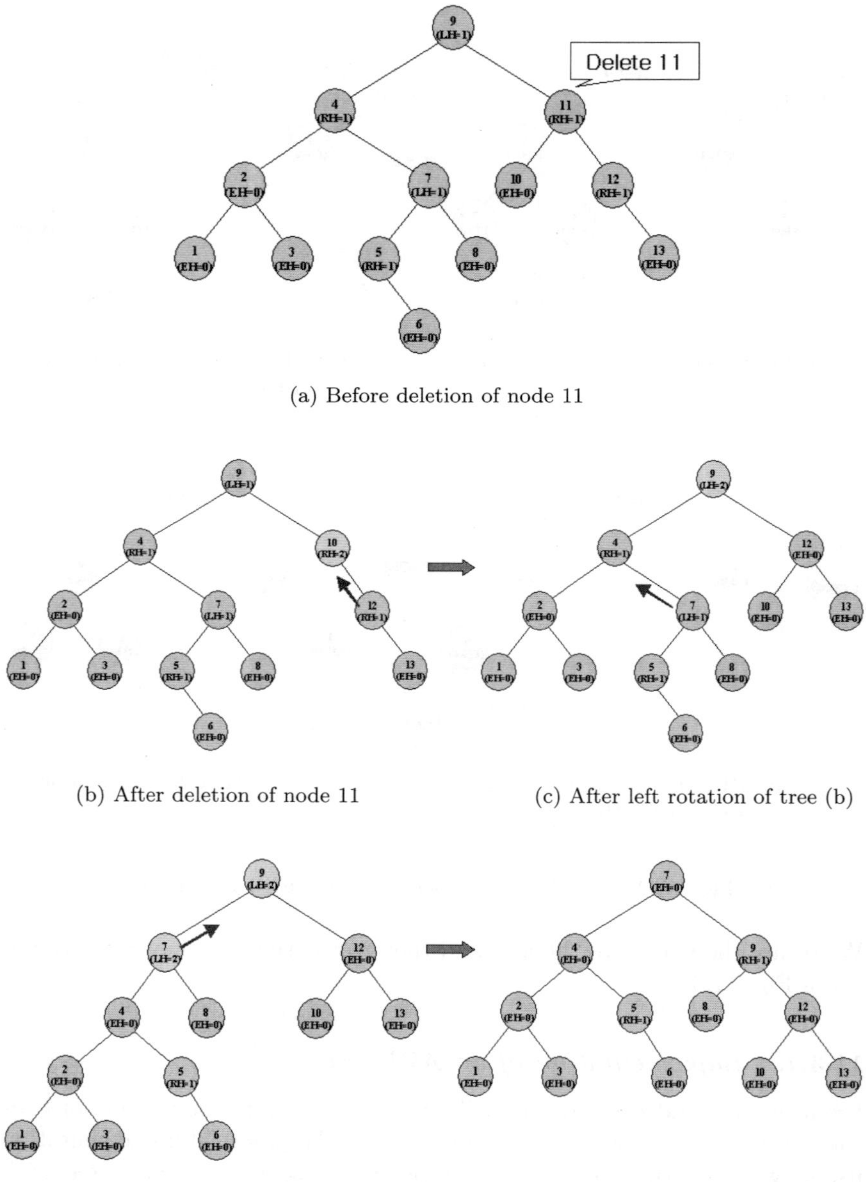

(a) Before deletion of node 11

(b) After deletion of node 11

(c) After left rotation of tree (b)

(d) After left rotation of tree (c)

(e) After right rotation of tree (d)

Fig. 11.33. An example to delete a node from a complicated AVL tree.

Appendix

```
#include < stdio.h >
#include < stdio.h >

// Declaration of integer entry
typedef int Enter;

typedef struct avltreenode AVLTreeNode;
typedef struct avltreenode{
          AVLTreeNode *LeftSubTree;
          Enter Entry;
          AVLTreeNode *RightSubTree;
          int Balance;
} AVLTreeNode;

AVLTreeNode *root = NULL;

// Output of tree entry using traversing in preorder
void preorder(AVLTreeNode *CurrentNode)
{
        if (CurrentNode)
        {
printf ("%d,%d\n",CurrentNode->Entry, CurrentNode->Balance);
        preorder(CurrentNode->LeftSubTree);
        preorder(CurrentNode->RightSubTree);
        }
}

void Insert(Enter key)
{
      //Current node and its parent node in searching
         AVLTreeNode *CurrentNode, *ParentNode;
      //New creating node for insertion
         AVLTreeNode *NewNode;
      //Unbalanced node and its parent
         AVLTreeNode *UnbalanceNode, *UnbalanceParentNode;
      //Temporary node pointer for rotation
         AVLTreeNode *tmp, *tmp2;

      // If direction = +1: insertion into a left subtree
      // If direction = -1: insertion into a right subtree
      // direction is added to balance value to check tree is balance or
            unbalance. //
```

```
// If root is NULL, function finishes.
    int direction;
    if (root == NULL)
    {
            root = (AVLTreeNode*)malloc(sizeof (avltreenode));
            root->Entry = key;
            root->LeftSubTree = NULL;
            root->RightSubTree = NULL;
            root->Balance = 0;
            return;
    }

    // Initialize.
    UnbalanceNode = root;
    UnbalanceParentNode = NULL;
    CurrentNode = root;
    ParentNode = NULL;

    // Searching tree.
    while (CurrentNode)
    {

    // If the balance factor of current node is +1 or –1, save that
       node. //
       // The node has possibility to be unbalanced node. //
              if (CurrentNode->Balance)
              {
                     UnbalanceNode = CurrentNode;
                     UnbalanceParentNode = ParentNode;
              }
              ParentNode = CurrentNode;

              // Checking if the current node is equal to inserting
                 node.
       // If equal, finishes.
              if (key == CurrentNode->Entry) return;

              // Move to the left when key is less than.
              else if (key < CurrentNode->Entry)
                     CurrentNode =
                            CurrentNode->LeftSubTree;

              // Move to the right when key is greater than.
              else
```

```
                    CurrentNode =
                         CurrentNode->RightSubTree;
    }

    // Create new node and put the value.
    NewNode = (AVLTreeNode*) malloc(sizeof (avltreenode));
    NewNode->Entry = key;
    NewNode->LeftSubTree = NULL;
    NewNode->RightSubTree = NULL;
    NewNode->Balance = 0;

// Compare it with parent node, and then decides left subtree or right
   subtree.
    if (key < ParentNode->Entry)
          ParentNode->LeftSubTree = NewNode;
    else
          ParentNode->RightSubTree = NewNode;

  // According to the unbalanced node, decide to move to the left or
     right.
    if (key < UnbalanceNode->Entry)
    {
          CurrentNode = UnbalanceNode->LeftSubTree;
          tmp = CurrentNode;
          direction = 1;
    }
    else
    {
           CurrentNode = UnbalanceNode->RightSubTree;
           tmp = CurrentNode;
           direction = -1;
    }

// Set balance factors of nodes on the path from the current node to the
   new
// creating node.

    while (CurrentNode != NewNode)
    {
           if (key < CurrentNode->Entry)
           {
                  CurrentNode->Balance = 1;
                  CurrentNode =
```

```
                                CurrentNode->LeftSubTree;
                }
                else
                {
                        CurrentNode->Balance = -1;
                        CurrentNode =
                                CurrentNode->RightSubTree;
                }
        }
```

// Checking if balance factor of unbalance node is 0 (or when adding direction to it). If it is balanced, function finishes. //

```
    if (UnbalanceNode->Balance == 0 || UnbalanceNode->Balance +
            direction == 0)
        {
            UnbalanceNode->Balance += direction;
            return;
        }

        // Move to the left.
        if (direction == 1)
        {
                // Move the node pointer and set balance factor newly.
                if (tmp->Balance == 1) //Single Right Rotation
                {
                UnbalanceNode->LeftSubTree= tmp->RightSubTree;
                        tmp->RightSubTree = UnbalanceNode;
                        UnbalanceNode->Balance = 0;
                        tmp->Balance = 0;
                }
                else // Double Rotation
                {
                        tmp2 = tmp->RightSubTree;
                        tmp->RightSubTree = tmp2->LeftSubTree;
                UnbalanceNode->LeftSubTree=tmp2-RightSubTree;
                        tmp2->LeftSubTree = tmp;
                        tmp2->RightSubTree = UnbalanceNode;
                        if (tmp2->Balance == 1)
                        {
                                UnbalanceNode->Balance = -1;
                                tmp->Balance = 0;
                        }
```

```
                else if (tmp2->Balance == -1)
                {
                        UnbalanceNode->Balance = 0;
                        tmp->Balance = 1;
                }
                else
                {
                        UnbalanceNode->Balance = 0;
                        tmp->Balance = 0;
                }
                tmp2->Balance = 0;
                tmp = tmp2;
        }
}

// Move to the right.
else
{
        // Move the node pointer and set balance factor newly.
        if(tmp->Balance == -1) // Single Left Rotation
        {
        UnbalanceNode->RightSubTree= tmp->LeftSubTree;
                tmp->LeftSubTree = UnbalanceNode;
                UnbalanceNode->Balance = 0;
                tmp->Balance = 0;
        }
        else // Double Rotation
        {
                tmp2 = tmp->LeftSubTree;
                tmp->LeftSubTree = tmp2->RightSubTree;
        UnbalanceNode->RightSubTree=tmp2-LeftSubTree;
                tmp2->RightSubTree = tmp;
                tmp2->LeftSubTree = UnbalanceNode;
                if (tmp2->Balance == 1)
                {
                        UnbalanceNode->Balance = 1;
                        tmp->Balance = 0;
                }
                else if (tmp2->Balance == -1)
                {
                        UnbalanceNode->Balance = 0;
                        tmp->Balance = -1;
```

```
                    }
                    else
                    {
                            UnbalanceNode->Balance = 0;
                            tmp->Balance = 0;
                    }
                    tmp2->Balance = 0;
                    tmp = tmp2;
            }
        }
// If parent of unbalanced node is NULL, the subtree of unbalanced node
becomes root. It means that tmp is root. //
        if (UnbalanceParentNode == NULL) root = tmp;
// The subtree of unbalanced node becomes the subtree of parent of the
unbalanced node. It means that tmp becomes the subtree of parent of the
unbalanced node. //
    else if(UnbalanceNode==UnbalanceParentNode->LeftSubTree)
                UnbalanceParentNode->LeftSubTree = tmp;
        else
                UnbalanceParentNode->RightSubTree = tmp;
}

/*Search Func.
input : Entry value of Node to be search.
output : Node pointer
*/
AVLTreeNode* Search(Enter key)
{
        if (root != NULL){
                AVLTreeNode *node = root;
                // While node is not NULL.
                while (node)
                {
                        // If Entry = key, return node pointer.
                        if (node->Entry == key)
                                return node;

                        //If Entry < key, move to the right.
                        else if (node->Entry < key)
                                node = node->RightSubTree;
                        // If Entry > key, move to the left.
                        else
```

```
                                node = node->LeftSubTree;
                }
        }
        return NULL;
}

/*
 Delete Func.
 input : Entry of Node to be deleted
 output : Deleted tree.
*/
void Delete(Enter key)
{

    // Selected current node and its parent node
        AVLTreeNode *CurrentNode, *ParentNode;
    // Unbalanced node and its parent
        AVLTreeNode *UnbalanceNode, *UnbalanceParentNode;
    // Temporary node pointer
        AVLTreeNode *tmp, *tmp2;
    // Save nodes on the path from the root to the node to be deleted
        AVLTreeNode *SaveNode[100];

// Save direction of each node on the path from the root to the node to
be deleted (–1 or +1) //
        int Path[100];
        int NodeCount = 0; // Save the number of SaveNode
        int PathCount = 0; // Save the number of Path
        int i; // Loop iterations

        // Initialize.
        CurrentNode = root;
        ParentNode = NULL;

        // Finding the key.
        while (CurrentNode != NULL && CurrentNode->Entry !=
                key)
        {
                ParentNode = CurrentNode;

          // Save the node on the path while searching.
                SaveNode[NodeCount++] = CurrentNode;
                if (CurrentNode->Entry < key){
                        CurrentNode =
```

```
                    CurrentNode->RightSubTree;
               Path[PathCount++]=-1;
                    // Save the direction.
          }
          else {
               CurrentNode =
                    CurrentNode->LeftSubTree;
               Path[PathCount++] = 1;
                    // Save the direction.
          }
}
SaveNode[NodeCount++] = CurrentNode;
// If the key exists.
if (CurrentNode != NULL)
{
     // Case of the leaf node
     if (CurrentNode->LeftSubTree == NULL &&
          CurrentNode->RightSubTree == NULL)
     {
      //Root only exists in the tree.
          if (PathCount == 0)
          {
               root = NULL;
          }
          // Disconnect from the parent of node.
          else if (Path[PathCount-1] == -1)
               ParentNode->RightSubTree =
                    NULL;
          else if (Path[PathCount-1] == 1)
               ParentNode->LeftSubTree =
                    NULL;
     }
// If it exists in left of current node, copy the maximum value in left
subtree into current node.//
     else if (CurrentNode->LeftSubTree != NULL)
     {
// to save the maximum value in the LeftSubTree.//
          tmp = CurrentNode->LeftSubTree;
          tmp2 = CurrentNode;// parent of tmp
          Path[PathCount++] = 1;
          SaveNode[NodeCount++] = tmp;
```

```
                    // Finding the maximum value
                    while (tmp->RightSubTree != NULL)
                    {
                            SaveNode[NodeCount++] = tmp;
                            tmp2 = tmp;
                            tmp = tmp->RightSubTree;
                            Path[PathCount++] = -1;
                    }
    // The maximum value is Entry value to have been deleted.//
                    CurrentNode->Entry = tmp->Entry;
                    tmp->Balance = 0;

// If the node with maximum value is not leaf, it has one subtree only.
If it has no subtree, disconnect it. //
                if (Path[PathCount-1] == -1)
                {
                        if (tmp->LeftSubTree != NULL)
                tmp2->RightSubTree = tmp->LeftSubTree;
                        else
                        tmp2->RightSubTree = NULL;
                }
                else
                {
                        if (tmp->RightSubTree != NULL)
                tmp2->LeftSubTree = tmp->RightSubTree;
                        else
                            tmp2->LeftSubTree = NULL;
                }
        }
        else if (CurrentNode->RightSubTree != NULL)
        {
    // Save minimum value in the RightSubTree
                tmp = CurrentNode->RightSubTree;
                tmp2 = CurrentNode;//tmp 의 parent
                Path[PathCount++] = -1;
    // The minimum value is the Entry of deleted node.//
                SaveNode[NodeCount++] = tmp;
      // Search the minimum value.//
                while (tmp->LeftSubTree != NULL)
                {
                        SaveNode[NodeCount++] = tmp;
```

```
                        tmp2 = tmp;
                        tmp = tmp->LeftSubTree;
                        Path[PathCount++] = 1;
                }
                CurrentNode->Entry = tmp->Entry;
                tmp->Balance = 0;

// If the node with maximum value is not leaf, it has one subtree only.
If it has no subtree, disconnect it. //
                if (Path[PathCount-1] == -1)
                {
                        if (tmp->LeftSubTree != NULL)
                tmp2->RightSubTree = tmp->LeftSubTree;
                        else
                        tmp2->RightSubTree = NULL;
                }
                else
                {
                        if (tmp->RightSubTree != NULL)
                tmp2->LeftSubTree = tmp->RightSubTree;
                                else
                        tmp2->LeftSubTree = NULL;
                }
        }

        // There are two more nodes to have been searched.//
        if (NodeCount > 1){
                preorder(root);
                printf ("\n");

        // Search the already searched nodes from end reversly.//
                for (i = NodeCount - 2; i >= 0; i--)
                {
        // Change the balance factor of previous node. //
                        if (SaveNode[i+1]->Balance == 0)
                        {
          // Set the balance factor
                        SaveNode[i]->Balance += -Path[i];
                                // Unbalanced with +2 or -2
                        if (SaveNode[i]->Balance == 2 ||
                                SaveNode[i]->Balance == -2)
                                {
                        // Save parent of unbalance node. //
```

```
if(I !=0 && SaveNode[i–1] != NULL)
UnbalanceParentNode=SaveNode[i–1];
else
UnbalanceParentNode = NULL;
// Save the unbalanced node.
UnbalanceNode = SaveNode[i];
// Balance is +2. Left is unbalance.
if (SaveNode[i]->Balance == 2) {
// Save to rotate. //
tmp = UnbalanceNode->LeftSubTree;
// Single Right Rotation
if (tmp->Balance >= 0) {
// Set the balance factor. //
if (tmp->RightSubTree) {
UnbalanceNode->Balance =1-tmp->RightSubTree->Balance;
tmp->Balance = –1 + tmp->RightSubTree->Balance;
}
else
{
UnbalanceNode->Balance = 0;
tmp->Balance = 0;
}
// rotate
UnbalanceNode->LeftSubTree = tmp->RightSubTree;
tmp->RightSubTree = UnbalanceNode;
}
else // Double Rotation
{
// rotate
tmp2 = tmp->RightSubTree;
tmp->RightSubTree = tmp2->LeftSubTree;
UnbalanceNode->LeftSubTree = tmp2->RightSubTree;
tmp2->LeftSubTree = tmp;
tmp2->RightSubTree = UnbalanceNode;
//Set the balance factor.
if (tmp2->Balance == 1)
{
UnbalanceNode->Balance = –1;
tmp->Balance = 0;
}
else if (tmp2->Balance == –1)
{
```

```
UnbalanceNode->Balance = 0;
tmp->Balance = 1;
}
else
{
UnbalanceNode->Balance = 0;
tmp->Balance = 0;
}
tmp2->Balance = 0;
tmp = tmp2;
}
}
// Balance is -2. Right is unbalance.
else if (SaveNode[i]->Balance == -2)
{
// Save to rotate.
tmp = UnbalanceNode->RightSubTree;
if (tmp->Balance<= 0) // Single Left Rotation
{
// Set the balance factor.
if (tmp->LeftSubTree)
{
UnbalanceNode->Balance = -1 - tmp->LeftSubTree->Balance;
tmp->Balance = 1 + tmp->LeftSubTree->Balance;
}
else
{
UnbalanceNode->Balance = 0;
tmp->Balance = 0;
}
// Rotate.
UnbalanceNode->RightSubTree = tmp->LeftSubTree;
tmp->LeftSubTree = UnbalanceNode;
}
else // Double Rotation
{
tmp2 = tmp->LeftSubTree;
tmp->LeftSubTree = tmp2->RightSubTree;
UnbalanceNode->RightSubTree = tmp2->LeftSubTree;
tmp2->RightSubTree = tmp;
tmp2->LeftSubTree = UnbalanceNode;
// Set the balance factor.
```

```
                    if (tmp2->Balance == 1)
                                  {
                UnbalanceNode->Balance = 1;
                    tmp->Balance = 0;
                                  }
                    else if (tmp2->Balance == -1)
                         {
                    UnbalanceNode->Balance = 0;
                         tmp->Balance = -1;
                         }
                    else
                         {
                UnbalanceNode->Balance = 0;
                    tmp->Balance = 0;
                         }
                    tmp2->Balance = 0;
                    tmp = tmp2;
                         }
                    }
// If parent of unbalanced node is NULL, its subtree is root. tmp
becomes the root. //
      if (UnbalanceParentNode == NULL) root = tmp;
      else if (UnbalanceNode ==
            UnbalanceParentNode->LeftSubTree)
               UnbalanceParentNode->LeftSubTree = tmp;
                    else
               UnbalanceParentNode->RightSubTree = tmp;
                         }
                    }
               }
          }
          free (SaveNode[NodeCount-1]);
      }
  }

      void main( )
      {
        int choice;
            Enter key;
            while (1){
            printf ("Select(1) Insert(2)Delete(3)Search(4)View
                   (5)Exit : ");
```

```
            scanf ("%d", &choice);
            switch(choice)
            {
                case 1:
                        printf ("Key : ");
                        scanf("%d", &key);
                        Insert(key);
                        break;
                case 2:
                        printf ("Key : ");
                        scanf ("%d", &key);
                        Delete(key);
                        break;
                case 3:
                        printf ("Key : ");
                        scanf ("%d", &key);
                        Search(key);
                        break;
                case 4:
                        preorder(root);
                        printf ("\n");
                        break;
                default:
                        break;
            }
            if (choice == 5)
                break;
        }
}
```

Exercises

Beginner's Review Exercises

A. Fill in the blank of each statement.

1. A binary tree is a tree in which no node can have more than ( ) subtrees.
2. The height of a binary tree can be related to the ( ) of nodes in the tree.
3. If the height, H, of a binary tree is given, the maximum number, N(max), of nodes in the tree can be calculated as ( ).

4. The ( ) for a binary tree visits each node of the tree once in predetermined sequence.
5. The traversal method is called ( ), since all nodes in same level are visited before proceeding to the next level.
6. We can traverse a binary tree in six different sequences. Only three of standard sequences are called preorder, inorder, and ( ).
7. In the ( )traversal, the left subtree is visited first, and then the root and the right subtree are visited in order.
8. In the postorder traversal, the ( ) is visited first, and then the right subtree and the root are visited in order.
9. The ( ) of a binary tree is the difference in height between its left and right subtrees.
10. A binary tree is balanced if the heights of its subtrees differ by no ( ) and its subtrees are also balanced.
11. The inorder traversal of a binary search tree produces an ( ).
12. The ( ) node in the binary search tree is the smallest value, and the rightmost node is the ( ).
13. The ( ) of a node in a binary search tree goes down to the left or right subtree, comparing with the values of node until a subtree has a null.
14. An ( ) tree is a search tree in which the heights of the subtrees differ by no more than 1.
15. When a new node is coming into the taller subtree of the root and its height has increased more than 2, we must rebuild the tree to keep balance of tree. The rebuilding is called ( ).
16. The ( ) is that the height of the right subtree is higher than other in AVL tree.
17. When we delete a node from AVL tree, if the node has at most ( ) subtrees, we delete it by linking its parent to its single subtree.

B. Answer yes or no.

1. In the preorder traversal, the root node is visited first, and then the right subtree and the left subtree are visited in order. ( )
2. If the root level is 0 in a binary tree, the maximum number of nodes in level 3 is 8. ( )
3. The tree is balanced if its balance factor is 2 and its subtrees are also balanced. ( )
4. If the height, H, of a binary tree is given, the minimum number, N(min), of nodes in the tree can be calculated as (N(min) $= H$). ( )
5. All items in the left subtree of a binary search tree are less than the root. ( )

6. All items in the right subtree of the binary search tree are greater than or equal to the root. (   )
7. Each subtree in the binary search tree is itself a binary search tree. (   )
8. When we delete a node from AVL tree, if the node is the root, we delete it directly. (   )
9. We must balance a changed tree by double rotation: first the left subtree to the left and then the out of balance node to the right. (   )
10. When we insert a new node into an AVL tree, we need not check the balance of each node. (   )

C. Answer the following.

1. How many different binary trees can be made from three nodes with the key values 1, 2, and 3?
2. What is the maximum number of nodes on level 4 in a binary tree? What is the maximum number of nodes in a binary tree of depth 4?
3. If the number of nodes of degree 2 in a binary tree is 7, what is the number of nodes of degree 0? And what is the minimum number of nodes of a complete binary tree of depth 4?
4. What is the maximum number of nodes in the Nth level of a binary tree?
5. Draw a complete binary tree to level 3, if root has level 0.
6. Draw a binary tree whose preorder sequence is $ABCDEFGHI$ and inorder sequence is $BCAEDGHFI$?
7. Draw expression tree for the expression 56 * 42 / 2 + 67 –6 * 12.
8. Find a binary tree whose preorder and inorder traversal creates the same result.
9. For the expression tree of Fig. 11.34. Traverse by preorder, inorder and postorder respectively.
10. Find the infix, prefix and postfix expressions in the expression tree given in Fig. 11.34.
11. If there is a binary tree that the left subtree contains M nodes and the right subtree contains N nodes, For each of preorder, inorder and postorder traversal, how many nodes are visited before the root node of the tree is visited?
12. For the binary search tree of Fig. 11.35,
    (a) What is the height of above tree?
    (b) What is the height of each node 5 and 7.
    (c) If the level of root node is 0, what nodes are on level 2?
    (d) Which levels have the maximum number of nodes that they could contain?

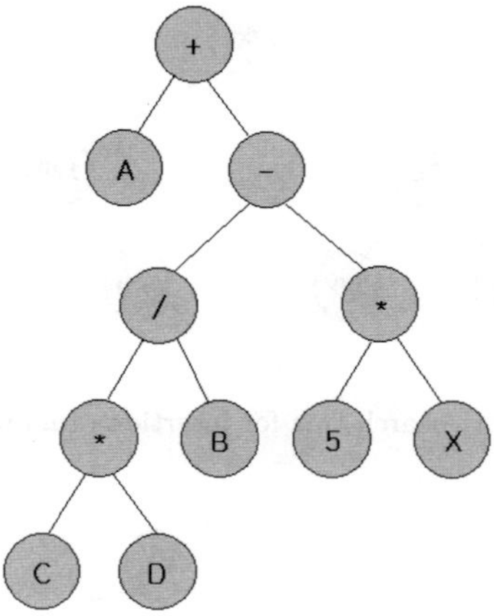

Fig. 11.34. An expression tree.

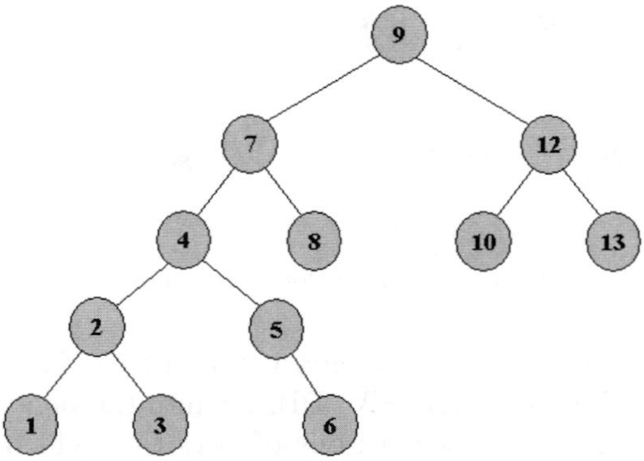

Fig. 11.35. A binary search tree.

(e) List nodes on the path for searching node 6 in the binary search tree.
(f) Show the subtrees of node 4.
(g) Show the linked list representation of this tree.

13. If root node has level 0, how many ancestors does a node of a binary search tree have?
14. What is the maximum height of a binary search tree with N nodes?
15. Draw the immediate steps that insert the keys 14, 150, 54, 66, 39, 22, –5, 2 and 17 into an initially empty binary search tree.

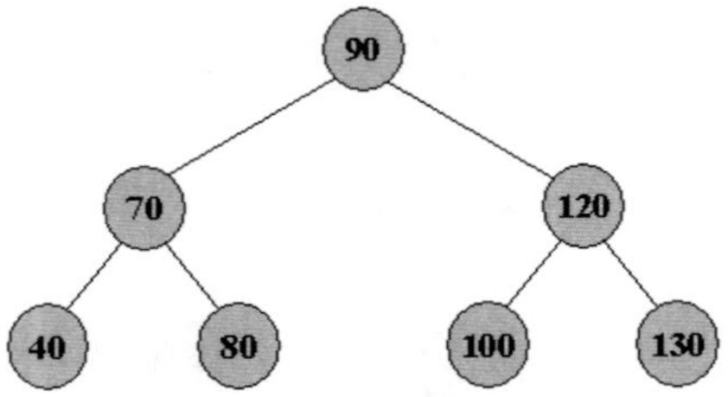

Fig. 11.36. A binary search tree for insertion of number 50, 60 and 110.

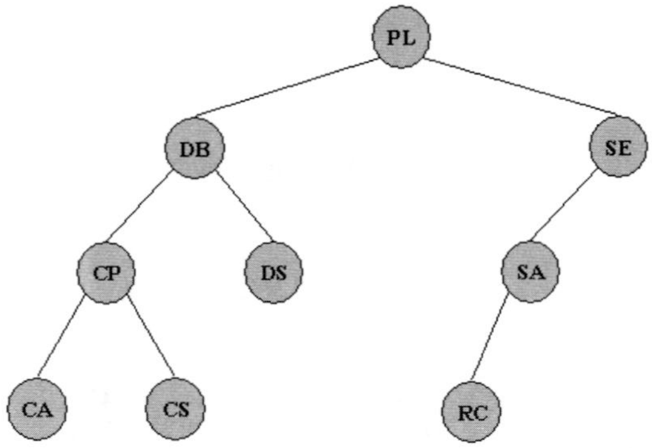

Fig. 11.37. A binary search tree for insertion of AL, CV, DB, FS.

16. Insert 50, 60 and 110 into the binary search tree of Fig. 11.36.
17. Insert each of the keys AL, CV, DB, FS into the binary search tree of Fig. 11.37. Show the comparisons of keys that will be made in each case.
18. Delete root node from the binary search tree of Fig. 11.37. Draw the result tree.
19. Balance the tree of Fig. 11.38.
20. Delete the node containing 60 from the binary search tree in Fig. 11.38.
21. Draw the resulting tree of inserting 42, 51, 14, –5, 90, 23, 36 and 63 into an initially empty AVL tree.
22. Insert the keys to build them into an AVL tree in the order shown in each of the followings.

    (a) CS112, CS123, CS345, CS563, CS666, CS800
    (b) CS100, CS999, CS222, CS800, CS300, CS777, CS342
    (c) DB01, PL03, CS01, MM03, CA02, AL05, SE01, AI03

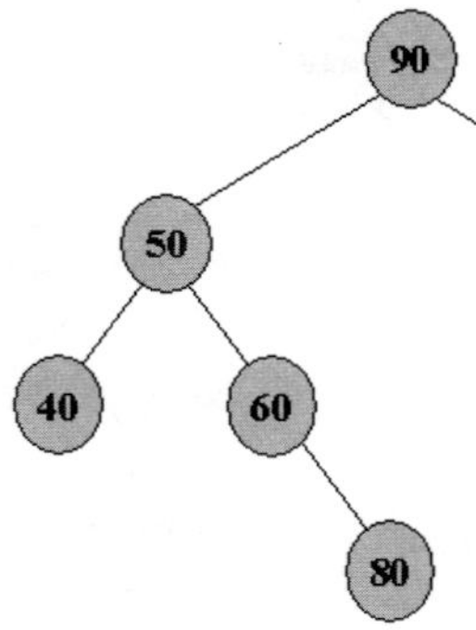

Fig. 11.38. A given tree for balancing.

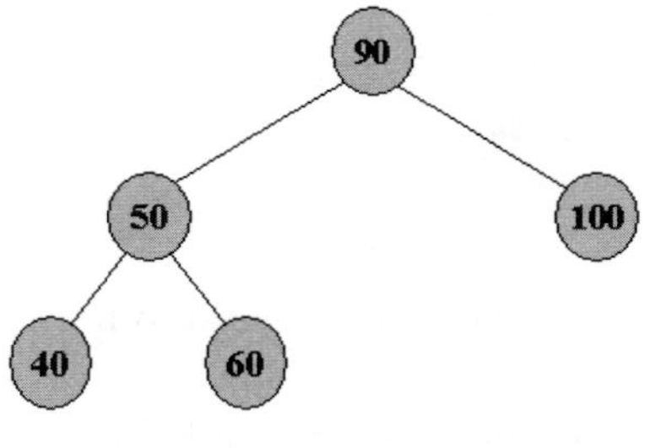

Fig. 11.39. An simple AVL tree for insertion of number 20.

23. Insert 20 into the AVL tree of Fig. 11.39. The resulting tree must be an AVL tree. What is the balance factor in the resulting tree? And insert 90 into the given tree.
24. Delete each of the following keys in AVL tree of Fig. 11.40.
    (a) com120
    (b) com10
    (c) com580
    (d) com65
25. What is the balance factor of the tree in Fig. 11.40.

Intermediate Programming Exercises

1. We need a function in C syntax to initialize a binary search tree from another one. Write a function in C syntax, CopyBinTree, to copy a binary search tree from another one.

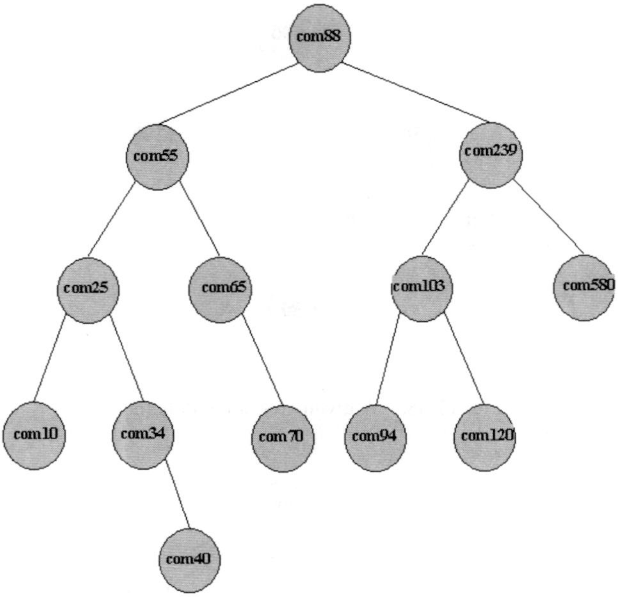

Fig. 11.40. A complicated AVL tree.

2. Write a simple function in C for each of followings.
   (1) Counting the number of leaves in a binary tree.
   (2) Finding a leaf node of a binary tree.
   (3) Postorder traversal without recursion.
   (4) Finding the smallest node in a binary search tree.
   (5) Computing the height of an AVL tree.
   (6) Checking if a tree is an AVL tree or not.
3. Write a C program to evaluate any expressions written in *postfix* expression. Also write a C program to convert any expressions written in *postfix* expression to *infix* expression.
4. Write an entire C program to manipulate a course for students. Write and use several functions as follows.
   (1) A function, ReadStuName, to read lists of student name, course name and professor name from a text file.
   (2) A function, InsertAVL, to insert them into an AVL tree.
   (3) A function, UserInf, for a simple user interface.
   (4) A function, SearchName, to search the specified name.
   (5) A function, InsertNewName, to insert a new name into an AVL tree.

(6) A function, DeleteName, to delete an existing name from an AVL tree.
(7) A function, ListEntries, to list the student name, course, professor name.

Once the program has been written, test and execute your program with at least 15 students names.

Advanced Interactive Exercises

1. If e is an expression with binary operators and operands, the conventional way of writing e is called *infix* form. In this chapter, why do we represent this form into expression tree? We are using the *infix* form in the programming languages. How does the compiler recognize the operator precedence of expression?
2. Suppose that a binary tree has the preorder sequence $GFDABEC$ and the postorder sequence $ABDCEFG$. Can you draw the binary tree? If you cannot draw the binary tree, explain the reason. And also if inorder sequence is given, can you draw the binary tree?
3. We can implement a tree by linked list. However, we implement a tree by various types. Don't you think it is too difficult to handle the pointer in linked list representation of a complicate tree? If you implement a tree by other representations, by which one can you implement?
4. We can obtain same binary search tree by inserting in different order. For an example, if we inset the keys in either of the order 56, 24, 45, 67, 3, 79, 60 and 56, 67, 60, 79, 24, 3, 45, we can obtain a tree of Fig. 11.41. Why is the resulting tree same, even though the order is not the same? Are there other possible orders for this same tree? From two orders in example, why is 56 first? Can you obtain the same tree in insertion in either of the order 3, 24, 45, 67, 56, 79, 60 and 56, 67, 60, 79, 24, 3, 45. If not, explain the reason.

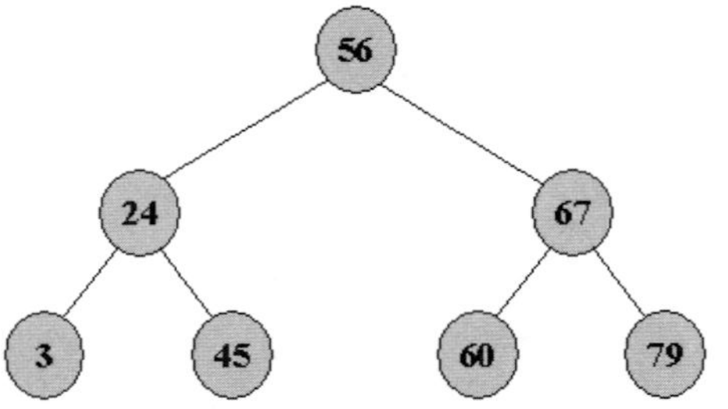

Fig. 11.41. A resulting binary search tree on inserting in different order.

5. If you insert the keys $3, 3, \ldots, 3$ into an initially empty binary tree, can you build the binary tree? If you can build a tree, what is the form of this tree? Is this tree a binary tree? Why? If you insert another 3 in this tree, which position does new 3 locate? If we search targets 3 or 5 in this tree, what do you think about efficiency for searching in each case?
6. For an AVL tree at rooted p, if the balance factor of p is not equal and the shorter subtree is shortened by insertion, what has happened in this tree? Do you already know this is not an AVL tree? At this point, what do we do for this tree? If you rotate this tree, explain the reason. Also how do you decide the direction of rotation? Let q be the root of the taller subtree of p. If the balance factors of p and q are opposite, why do we have a double rotation in order q, p? Also what is the balance factor of p and q respectively?

Chapter 12

Graph Algorithms

GENOVEFFA TORTORA* and RITA FRANCESE†

University of Salerno, Italy

**jentor@unisa.it*

†francese@unisa.it

Graph theory has originally been developed for solving mathematical problems, and, nowadays, graphs are the most widely used data structure. The purpose of this chapter is to illustrate some of the most important graph algorithms.

12.1. Introduction

Graphs belong to the mathematical tradition: they were first introduced by Euler in 1736. Since then, thanks to their structural richness, graphs have been largely employed for formulating and solving a large variety of engineering and science problems. Electronics, project management, chemistry, and genetics are some examples of fields where they have been used. For underlining the generality of graphs, it is important to point out that trees and lists are special cases of this data structure.

In this chapter we will focus on some of the most interesting graph algorithms. Firstly, in Sec. 12.2 we give some basic concepts on graphs and describe how graphs are represented on a computer. In Sec. 12.3 we discuss two algorithms for searching a graph. In Sec. 12.4 we show how to obtain a topological sort and in Sec. 12.5 we describe how to determine the strongly connected components of a graph. Section 12.6 examines how to solve the minimum spanning tree problem and, finally, in Sec. 12.7 we conclude by discussing the most known shortest path algorithms.

12.2. Graphs and Their Representations

Basic Definitions

Now we present the mathematical definition of graph.

> **Definition**
> A graph $G = (V, E)$ consists of two sets called the set of vertices V and the set of edges E. V is a finite not empty set of items named *vertices* or *nodes*. An edge in E is a pair of vertices in V.

Graph theory can be applied to several human activity areas. As shown in Fig. 12.1, graphs can be, for example, employed to represent:

- a road map, where cities and roads are denoted, respectively, by vertices and edges
- a chemical molecule, where atoms and links are denoted, respectively, by vertices and edges.

If the edges are ordered pairs, i.e. $(u, v) \neq (v, u)$ the graph is ***directed***, otherwise it is ***undirected***, i.e. (u, v) and (v, u) are considered the same edge. Figure 12.2(a) shows an undirected graph $G = (V, E)$, where $V = \{a, b, c, d, e, f\}$ and $E = \{(a, d), (a, b), (a, e), (a, f), (b, e), (b, d), (b, c), (c, d), (d, e), (f, e)\}$. Undirected graphs connect vertices, with no consideration about directions. For example, a map of streets in a town is an undirected graph, but a map of streets that shows the postman's route is a directed graph. Each undirected graph can be represented by a directed graph by associating two directed edges to each undirected edge.

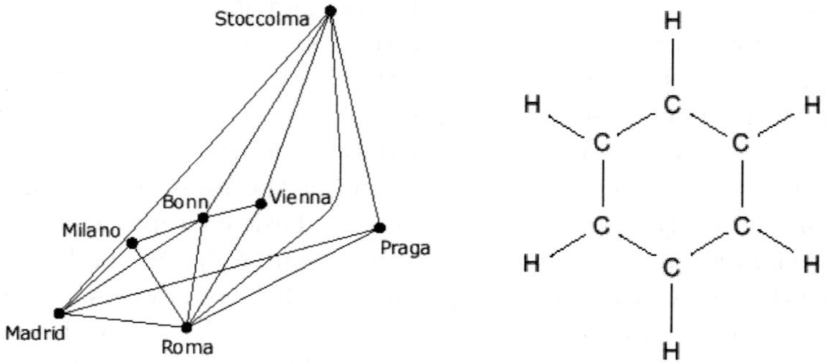

Fig. 12.1. Two applications of the graph model.

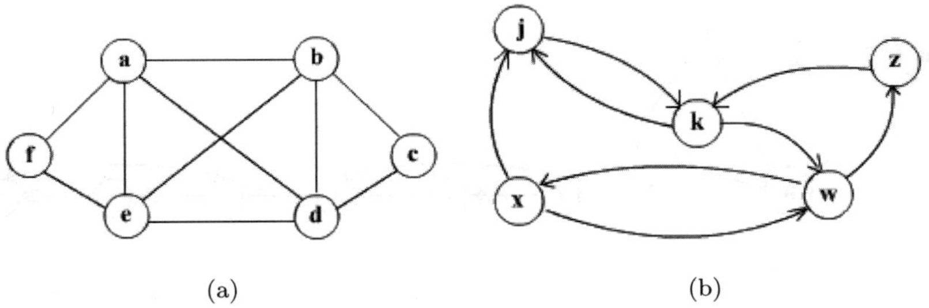

Fig. 12.2. Undirected and directed graphs.

Figure 12.2(b) depicts a directed graph $G = (V, E)$, where $V = (j, k, w, x, z)$ and $E = \{(j, k), (k, j), (k, w), (w, x\}, (w, z), (x, j), (x, w), (z, k)\}$.

Let (u, v) be an edge in a directed graph $G = (V, E)$. We say that the edge (u, v) is ***incident from*** the vertex u or ***leaves*** the vertex u and is ***incident to*** the vertex v or ***enters*** the vertex v. As an example, in Fig. 12.2(b) the edge (x, j) is incident from the vertex x and incident to the vertex j. If G is an undirected graph then we say that (u, v) is ***incident on*** both the vertices u and v. We say that a vertex u is ***adjacent*** to a vertex v if there exists an edge (u, v) in E. As an example, we have that the vertex a is adjacent to the vertex f in Fig. 12.2(a). The adjacency relationship is symmetric if the graph is undirected. In a directed graph we can have that u is adjacent to v and the vice versa does not hold. As an example, we have in Fig. 12.2(b) that x is adjacent to j, but j is not adjacent to x. The number of vertices adjacent to a vertex v in an undirected graph is called ***degree*** of v. The degree of the vertex a in Fig. 12.2(a) is 4. In a directed graph we name ***out-degree*** the number of vertices incident from vertex u and ***in-degree*** the number of vertices incident to the vertex u.

A ***path*** is a sequence of distinct vertices $(V_0, \ldots, V_n)$ such that each V_i is adjacent to V_{i+1}, for each i in $[0, \ldots, n]$. The ***length*** of this path is n. V_0 and V_n are, respectively, called the ***source*** and the ***target*** vertices. In Fig. 12.2(b) we have a path (j, k, w, x) of length 3.

A *cycle* is a path $(V_0, \ldots, V_n)$ containing at least three vertices and such that $V_0 = V_n$. In Fig. 12.3 the path (f, g, e, f) forms a cycle.

A directed acyclic graph (DAG) G is a directed graph containing no cycles.

We say that a graph is ***connected*** if there is a path between any pair of vertices. The graph depicted in Fig. 12.4 is connected.

We say that a graph $G = (V, E)$ is ***weighted*** if each edge in E has a *weight*. In the road map example, weights represent distances between cities. Figure 12.5 shows an example of weighted graph.

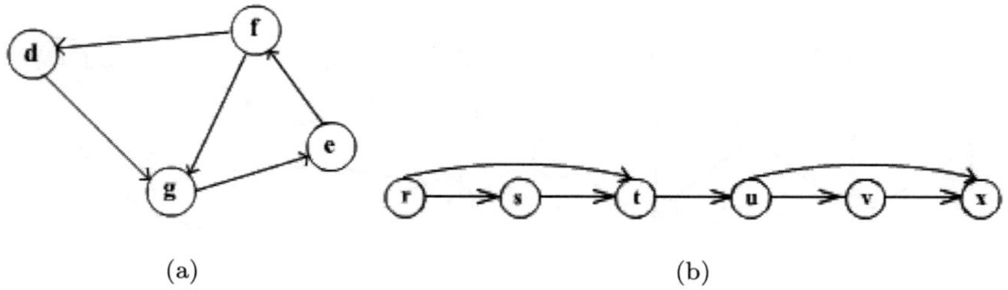

Fig. 12.3. Cyclic and acyclic graphs.

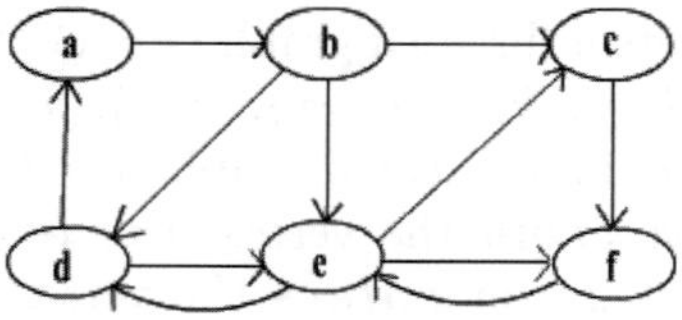

Fig. 12.4. A connected graph.

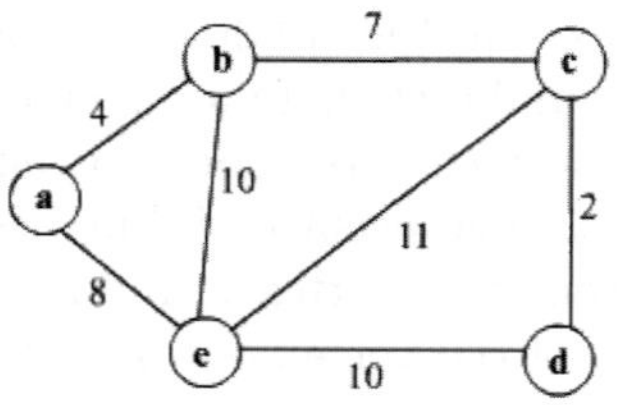

Fig. 12.5. A weighted graph.

Graph Representations

There exist several kinds of representations for graphs. The most commonly used are the *adjacency matrix* and the *adjacency lists*.

In the former case, given a graph $G = (V, E)$, we number its vertices from 1 to $|V|$ and represent G by a $|V|x|V|$ ***adjacency matrix*** A of 0's and 1's, where

$$A(i,j) = \begin{cases} 1 & \text{if } (i,j) \in E \\ 0 & \text{otherwise} \end{cases}$$

for i, j in $[1, \ldots, |V|]$.

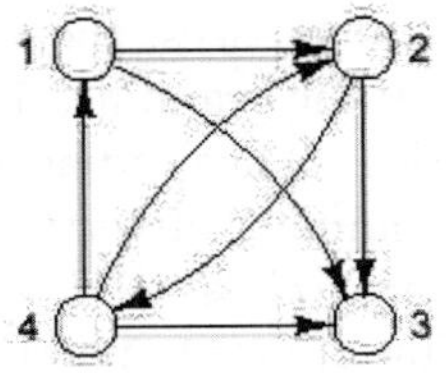

	1	2	3	4
1	0	1	1	0
2	0	0	1	1
3	0	0	0	0
4	1	1	1	0

Fig. 12.6. A directed graph and its adjacency matrix.

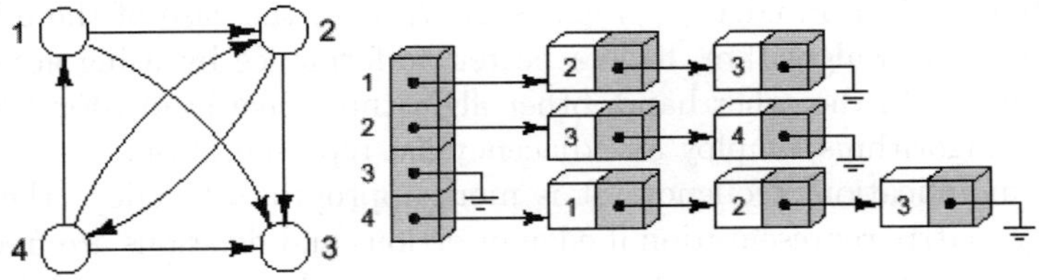

Fig. 12.7. A directed graph and its adjacency lists.

Figure 12.6 shows an example of adjacency matrix.

If G is a weighted graph, for each (i, j) in E, $A(i, j) = w(i, j)$, the weight of the edge (i, j). This representation is very convenient if there is the need to test the existence of an edge. The required time in this case is fixed and does not depend on either $|V|$ nor $|E|$. On the other hand, the adjacency matrix requires an $O(|V|x|V|)$ storage space, even if the number of edges is smaller, namely $O(|V|)$.

An alternative representation for graphs is in terms of ***adjacency lists***. Given a graph $G = (V, E)$, its representation by adjacency lists consists in associating to each vertex v in V the list of the vertices adjacent to v. The graph is represented by $|V|$ adjacency lists. Thus, for each vertex v in V its adjacency lists $ListArr[v]$ contains pointers to the vertices adjacent to v. If G is a weighted graph, then the weight $w(v, u)$ is stored together with the vertex u in the adjacency list of v. An example of adjacency list representation of a graph is given in Fig. 12.6.

If G is a directed graph, the sum of the lengths of the lists in $ListArr$ is $|E|$, because each edge (u, v) appears only in $ListArr[u]$. If G is undirected, the sum of the lengths of the lists in $ListArr$ is $|2E|$, because each edge (u, v) appears in both the adjacency lists of u and v. Thus, the amount of memory required by this representation is $O(|V| + |E|)$.

When we have to choose how to represent a graph, we should take into account the following aspects:

- The number of vertices. If a graph has 100 vertices, the corresponding adjacency matrix contains 10,000 entries. If the graph has 1,000 vertices, the adjacency matrix has 1,000,000 entries. Thus, adjacency matrices could not be used for graphs with a large number of vertices.
- The graph density. If a graph is sparse, i.e. $|E| \ll |V|^2$, the adjacency relationship holds between a small fraction of vertex pairs. As a consequence, adjacency lists require a reasonable amount of memory and are more appropriate. On the contrary, if a graph is dense, i.e. $|E| \approx |V|^2$, the adjacency matrix representation is more advantageous.
- The algorithm to be implemented. As an example, algorithms that repeatedly ask if an edge (i, j) exists in G, as in the case of the all-pairs shortest path algorithm, have a better performance by using adjacency matrices. On the other hand, other algorithms, like Depth-First-Search based algorithms, employ an adjacency list representation.
- The modification frequency. It is more appropriate to adopt the adjacency matrix representation if edge insertions and deletions are frequent. On the contrary, we should choose adjacency lists when modifications involve the attributes of a vertex or an edge, such as the size, weight or color.

12.3. Graph Algorithms for Search

Searching a graph consists in exploring, following an appropriate strategy, all the nodes and edges of a graph. Let us present two strategies that are usually considered: the Breadth-First-Search and the depth-first-search.

12.3.1. *Breadth-First-Search*

Because of its simplicity, Breadth-First-Search (BFS) is a searching algorithm largely adopted by many important algorithms, such as the Dijkstra's and Prim's ones.

Given a graph $G = (V, E)$ and a vertex s in V, called source, BFS determines all the vertices reachable from s as follows: first, it searches all the nodes that are reachable from s by an edge. Next, it searches all the nodes reachable from the source by two edges. In general, all the vertices at distance k from s are visited before the vertices at distance $k + 1$.

The algorithm colors each vertex white, gray or black. At first, all vertices are white to denote that they have not been visited yet. The first time a vertex m is reached, it is colored black or gray. It is colored black if all the adjacent vertices have been discovered, otherwise gray. Thus, gray vertices have adjacent vertices white colored. BFS constructs a BFS tree.

This tree initially contains only the root (the source). Each time a new vertex m is reached when the algorithm examines the adjacency lists of a vertex n, the edge (n, m) and the node m are added to the BFS tree and we say that n is the predecessor of m in the BFS tree.

The graph representation that is adopted is the adjacency lists. Additional data structures are exploited:

- *color*$[n]$, storing the color of each vertex n.
- *pred*$[n]$, storing the predecessor of each vertex n. Given a vertex n, the predecessor of n is a vertex m that has been already visited if n has been discovered during the scanning of the adjacency list of m. If n has no predecessor or n is the source then *pred[n]* $= NULL$
- $d[n]$, storing the distance from the source s to a vertex n.
- a FIFO queue Q, storing the set of the gray vertices.

```
Procedure BFS(G,s)
begin
for each vertex n in V[G] - {s}
      begin
          color[n] = white
          d[n] = infinity
          pred[n] = NULL
      end
color[s] = gray
d[s] = 0
pred[s] = NULL
INIT(Q); ADDQ(Q, s)
while (!ISEMPTY(Q))
      begin
          n = DEL(Q)
          for each m in the adjacency lists of n
              if color[m] = white then
                    begin
                        color[m] = gray
                        d[m] = d[n] + 1
                        pred[m] = n
                        ADDQ(Q, m)
                    end
          color[n] = black
      end
end
```

Description

Lines 1–4 initialize the arrays *color*, d and *pred* to white, infinity and NULL, respectively.
Lines 5 indicates that the source s has been visited and paints s gray. Lines 6 and 7 set $d[s]$ to 0 and $pred(s)$ to NULL, respectively.
Line 8 initializes the queue Q that contains the gray vertices and adds the vertex s to it.
Lines 9–16 are executed until the gray vertex queue is empty.
Line 10 extracts and erases the vertex n from Q.
The for loop of lines 11–16 consider each vertex m in the adjacency list of n: if m is white it means that it is searched for the first time. Thus, the algorithm discover m by executing lines 13–16 that set its color to gray, its distance to $d[n] + 1$, its predecessor to n, and places m at the tail of the queue Q. When the adjacency lists of all n have been entirely examined, the algorithm executes line 17 that paints n black.

Figure 12.8 shows a series of screendumps of the Breadth-First-Search animation of the Internet version of the Growing Book, describing how BFS works on an undirected graph. The distance from the source s is written inside the vertices. In particular, Fig. 12.8(a) depicts the result of the initialization. In Fig. 12.8(b) the vertices adjacent to s have been identified and added to Q. In Fig. 12.8(c) s is blackened because all its adjacent vertices have been visited. s is deleted from Q and the vertices adjacent to w, the head vertex of Q, are reached and added to Q, as shown in Fig. 12.8(d). Figures 12.8(e)–12.8(i) depict the successive iterations of the loop in lines 9–18. Figure 12.8(l) shows the final result.

Analysis

The running time of BFS is linear in the size of the adjacency lists of G, i.e. $O(V + E)$. In fact, the initialization phase takes $\Theta(V)$ time. The queue operations require $O(V)$ total time because the ADDQ and DELQ functions take $O(1)$ time, and each vertex is added to the queue at most once, and removed from the queue at most once. Each time a vertex is extracted from Q, its adjacency list is scanned. This operation is performed for at most all the vertices in G. The sum of the lengths of all the adjacency lists is $\Theta(E)$, and, as a consequence, the total time for scanning the adjacency lists is $O(E)$.

12.3.2. *Depth-First-Search*

The Depth-First-Search (DFS) algorithm corresponds, for many aspects, to a preorder traversal on a tree. The visit starts from a node that has

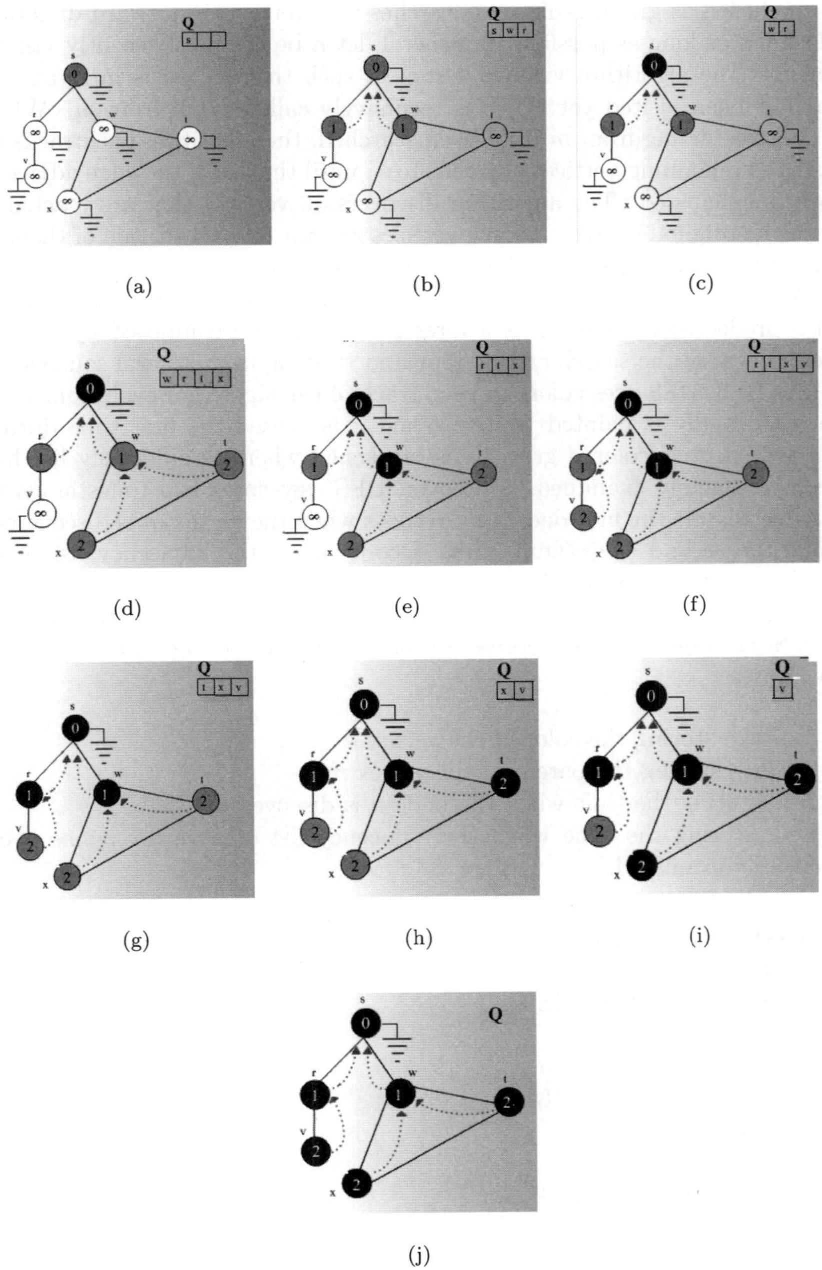

Fig. 12.8. Screendumps of the Breadth-First-Search animation.

been chosen as graph radix and searches new vertices in forward direction (deeper), as long as possible. In general, let n be the most recently visited vertex. The algorithm visits a vertex m such that (n, m) is in E and m has not been visited yet. DFS is recursively called again from m. When all paths starting from m have been searched, the algorithm backtracks to visit the remaining vertices adjacent to n, until the list of the edge adjacent to it is exhausted. The algorithm discovers all vertices that are reachable from the original source. If some vertices remain unreached, one of them is selected as new source and the visit restarts from it.

We saw that BFS predecessor subgraph is a tree. On the contrary, the DFS predecessor subgraph is a forest, i.e. it can be composed by several trees, because the search can be repeated starting from several sources.

As BFS, DFS uses colors to keep track of the algorithm evolution: each vertex initially is painted white. When it is visited the first time during the search, it is colored gray. It is blackened when its adjacency list has been completely examined. Moreover, DFS associates two timestamps to each vertex m: the first one, $d[m]$, records when the vertex m is discovered, while the second timestamp, $f[m]$, records when the adjacency list of m has been entirely explored.

An algorithm for the Depth-First-Search of a graph is given below. It uses an adjacency list representation and the following additional data structures:

- $color[n]$, storing the color of the vertex n.
- $pred[n]$, storing the parent of the vertex n.
- $d[n]$, storing the time when the node n is discovered.
- $f[n]$, storing the time when the adjacency list of a vertex n has been entirely examined.

Procedure DFS(G)

```
 begin
    for each vertex n in V
      begin
            color[n] = white
            pred[n] = NULL
      end
 time = 0
 for each vertex n in V
        if color[n] = white
        then DFS − Visit(n)
 end
```

```
Procedure DFS-Visit(n)
  begin
1. color[n] = gray
2. time = time + 1; d[n] = time
3. for each m adjacent to n
4.          if color[m] = white
            then
             begin
5.                pred[m] = n
6.                DFS-Visit(m)
             end
7. color[n] = black
8. time = time + 1; f[n] = time
  end
```

Description

Lines 1–3 set the color and the parent of each vertex to white and NULL, respectively. Line 4 initializes the global time counter to 0. Lines 5–7 consider each vertex in V in order to verify if there exists a white vertex. If a white vertex is found, the *DFS-Visit* procedure is called to visit all the vertices reachable from it.

The recursive Procedure DFS-Visit works as follows.
Line 1 paints n gray.
Line 2 increments the global variable time and records time when n has been discovered in $d[n]$. Lines 3–6 examine each vertex m adjacent to n and, if m is white, visit it recursively. Lines 7–8 paint n black (its adjacency list has been examined) and record the finishing time in $f[n]$.

Figure 12.9 shows a sequence of screendumps of the DFS animation presented in the Internet version of the Growing Book. The timestamps $d[n]$ and $f[n]$ are shown above the vertices. Let us suppose that the first node to be investigated is s. $color[s]$ is white and DFS-visit(s) is called. $color[s]$ is set to gray (see Fig. 12.9(b)) and the discovered time $d[s]$ is set to 1. w is in the adjacency list of s and its color is white. Thus, $pred[w]$ is set to s, see the dotted line between w an s in Fig. 12.9(c) and a call of DFS-Visit (w) occurs. $color[w]$ is set to gray, $d[w]$ is set to 2 and DFS-visit is called again on the vertex x in the adjacency list of w. x is painted gray and there does not exist a white vertex in its adjacency lists. Next, as shown in Fig. 12.9(f), $d[x]$ is set to 3, x is colored black, signaling that its adjacency list has been entirely examined and the finish time $f[x]$ is set to 4.

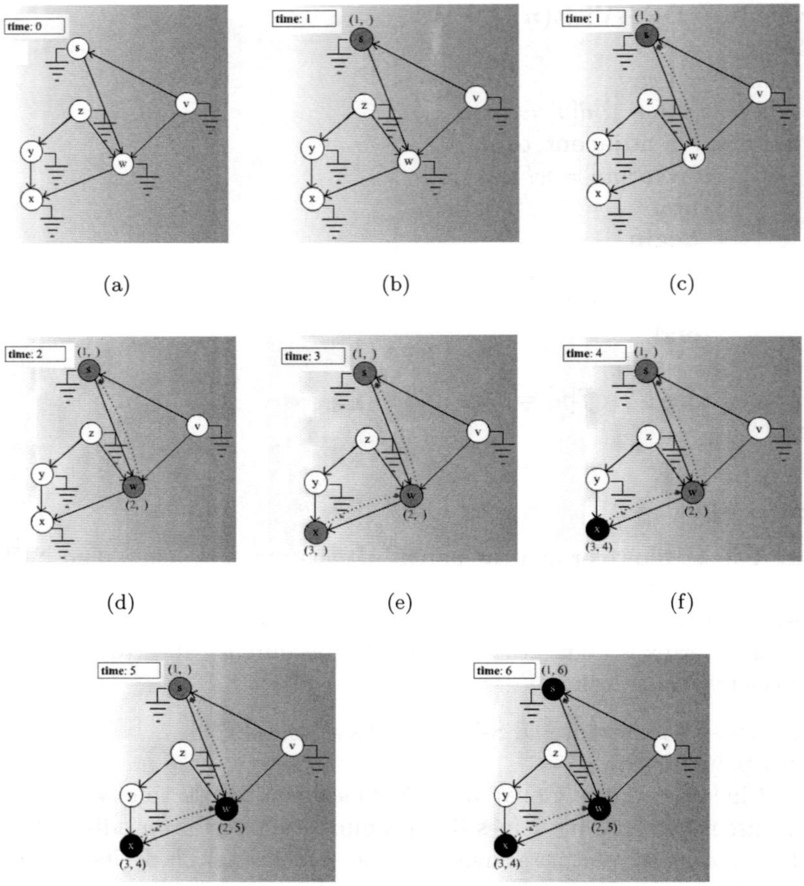

(a) (b) (c)

(d) (e) (f)

(g) (h)

Fig. 12.9. Screendumps of the Depth-First-Search animation.

Similarly, as depicted in Figs. 12.9(g) and 12.9(h), the process ends for both w and s that are painted black. This example is limited to only one source and we have shown how to search all the vertices reachable from the vertex s. The algorithm proceeds by considering the remaining white vertices.

Analysis

The running time of the DFS is $\Theta(|V|+|E|)$. In fact, let us observe that the loop on lines 1–3 of DFS takes $\Theta(V)$ time; the lines 5–7 of DFS take $\Theta(|V|)$

time. The procedure *DFS-Visit* is called only once on a given vertex n, since n is colored black the first time DFS-Visit(n) is called. The running time of the procedure *DFS-Visit* is $\Theta(|E|)$, calculated considering that

- the for loop is executed a number of times proportional to the size of the adjacency lists of n
- the sum of the lengths of all the adjacency lists is $\Theta(E)$.

12.4. Graph Algorithms for Topological Sort

Let G be a directed graph with no cycles (DAG). A ***topological order*** of G is a sequential ordering of all the vertices in G such that, for all vertices v and w in G, if there exists an edge from v to w, then v precedes w in the sequential ordering. There may be multiple sorts. In fact, 10, 7, 4, 5, 9, 3, 1, 6, 3, 8 and 7, 10, 4, 5, 9, 3, 1, 6, 2, 8 are both topological sorts of the DAG shown in Fig. 12.10. This happens because 10 is not related to 7 and both can come first in the ordering. The main use of a topological sort is to indicate the order of events, i.e. what should happen first. As an example, we can consider the graph in Fig. 12.10 as the representation of courses (vertices) and their priorities (edges). Thus, a depth-first topological order represents an admissible examination sequence.

The following simple algorithm shows how Depth-First-Search can be employed for obtaining a topological sort of a graph. The algorithm provides as output a linked list storing the vertex ordering.

Procedure Topological-Sort(G)

1. *Call DFS(G) to compute f(v), the finish time for each vertex.*
2. *As each vertex is finished insert it onto the front of the list.*
3. *Return the list.*

The procedure DFS computes the finish time $f[n]$ for each vertex n in V. Vertices are added to the list when finish. Thus, to obtain an increasing

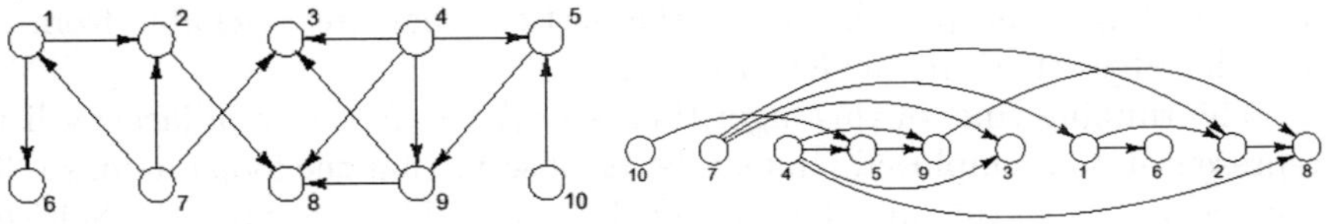

Fig. 12.10. A directed graph with no directed cycles and its depth-first topological ordering.

ordering they have to be added to the front of the list. The time is $O(|V|+|E|)$, the time required by DFS.

12.5. Strongly Connected Components

In this section we decompose a graph $G = (V, E)$ into its strongly connected components. We can determine if G is connected by running BFS or DFS and checking if some vertex has not been reached. This is performed in $O(|V|^2)$ or in $O(|E|)$ depending on whether an adjacency matrix or adjacency lists have been chosen for the representation of G.

A ***strongly connected component*** of a graph $G = (V, E)$ is a maximal subset W of V such that each vertex in W is reachable from each other vertex in W.

Now we illustrate an algorithm for determining the strongly connected components of a graph G that uses a DFS-Visit. BFS can be used as well. In fact, both discover all the vertices that are reachable from the source, i.e. a strongly connected component.

Procedure Strongly-Connected-Components(G)
1. **for each vertex** v **in** V **do**
    begin
2.   *color*$[n]$ = *white*
3.   *pred*$[n]$ = NULL
    end

4. **for each vertex** v **in** V **do**
5.   **if** *color*$[v]$ = *white*
6.   **then**
          begin
7.   *DFS-Visit* (v)
8.   **print** "*end of strongly connected component*"
          end

For each vertex v that has not been reached yet, the procedure DFS-Visit is called. DFS-Visit is appropriately modified, as suggested in Exercise 4, for providing as output the list of the vertices that are reachable from v and the edges that are incident to them.

The running time of this algorithm is $\Theta(|V| + |E|)$ if an adjacency list representation is employed. In fact, let us observe that the loop on lines 1–3 take $\Theta(|V|)$ time; the lines 4–6 take $\Theta(|V|)$ time. The procedure *DFS-Visit* is called only once on a given vertex v, since v is colored black the first time DFS-Visit(v) is called. The running time of the procedure *DFS-visit* is $\Theta(|E|)$.

12.6. Minimum Spanning Tree

Given a connected undirected weighted graph $G = (V, E)$, a ***spanning tree*** is an undirected tree connecting all vertices in V. The *minimum spanning tree* T for G is a spanning tree such that the sum of the edge weights has the minimum value.

Our goal is to find the minimum spanning tree for G and, to this aim, we give some preliminary definitions.

Given an undirected graph $G = (V, E)$:

- A *cut* $(V', V - V')$ is a partition of V.
- An edge (n, m) is said to *cross* the cut $(V', V - V')$ if n is in V' and m is in $V - V'$ or vice versa, n is in $V - V'$ and m in V'.
- A cut is said to *respect* a set of edges E_1 if no edge in E_1 crosses the cut.
- If an edge crossing a cut has the minimum weight among all the edges crossing that cut, then it is called *light edge.*
- Given a subset E_1 of edges which is a subset of some minimum spanning tree for G, an edge (n, m) in E is said to be a *safe edge* for E_1 if it can be added to E_1 and E_1 is still a subset of some minimum spanning tree for G.

How can we recognize safe edges? As described in Sec. 23 of [5], the answer is provided by the following theorem:

Theorem (*Safe Edge*)
Given a connected undirected weighted graph $G = (V, E)$, let E_1 be a subset of E contained in a minimum spanning tree for G, let $(V', V - V')$ be a cut of G respecting E_1, and let (n, m) be a light edge crossing $(V', V - V')$. Then, (n, m) is *safe* for E_1.

12.6.1. *Prim's Algorithm*

Prim's algorithm is one of the most known algorithms for finding a minimum spanning tree for a connected undirected weighted graph.

The algorithm builds a partial minimum spanning tree T, and successively adds a safe edge (u, v) and a node v to T, where u is a node in T and v is a node in V and not in T. It has the interesting property that during the execution the edges in E_1 are always forming a single tree, which is rooted in an arbitrarily chosen vertex v and grows until all the vertices in V are covered. At each step, the tree is augmented with the locally lightest edge, following a greedy strategy and, as a consequence, it applies the safe edge theorem by selecting at each step a safe edge for E_1.

The algorithm maintains for each vertex v:

- a variable $mw[v]$, containing the minimum weight of any edge connecting v to a vertex in T;
- a variable $pred[v]$, containing the parent of v in T.

During the execution, all the vertices v that are not in T are stored into a priority queue Q. The priority is determined by considering the mw values of the vertices. Thus, Q is used for selecting the edge crossing the cut having the minimum weight.

The implementation of Prim's algorithm receives as input a connected undirected graph $G = (V, E)$, a cost function w and the root r of the minimum spanning tree.

```
Procedure Prim(G,w,r)
begin

1. for each u in V do
2.        mw[u] = infinity
3. Add all the vertices in V to Q
4. mw[r] = 0
5. pred[r] = NULL
6. while (!ISEMPTY(Q))
        begin
7.          u = DELMIN(Q)
8.          for each vertex v adjacent to u do
9.                 if (v in Q) and (w(u,v) < mw[v])
                      then
                        begin
10.                        mw[v] = w(u,v)
11.                        pred[v] = u
                        end
        end
end
```

Description

Lines 1–4 set all the mw values to infinity, except $mw[r]$ that is set to 0, and add all the vertices to Q.
Line 5 initializes $pred(r)$ to null: the root has no parent.
Line 7 identifies a vertex u in Q, incident on a light edge crossing the cut $(V\text{–}Q, Q)$. Extracting u from the queue Q means adding it to the set $V\text{–}Q$ of the vertices in T.

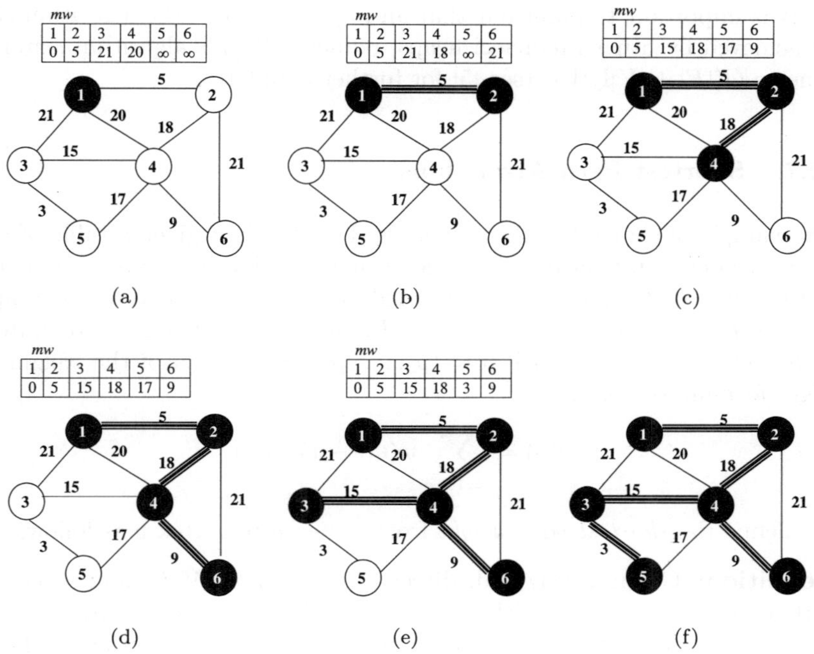

Fig. 12.11. Construction of a Minimum Spanning Tree.

Lines 8–11 update the *mw* and *pred* fields for each vertex v adjacent to u that does not belong to $V–Q$ yet.

Figure 12.11 shows an execution of this algorithm. The vertex 1 is the root of the spanning tree T. The vertices in T are colored black and the edges in T are bold. The vertices in T form a cut of the graph. At each step a new vertex and a new edge are added to T, by choosing the lightest edge crossing the cut. As an example, in Fig. 12.11(d) the algorithms adds the vertex 6 because $mw(6)$ is the minimum of $\{mw[v]$, with v in $V–T\}$.

Analysis

The running time of Prim's algorithm depends on the data structure chosen for implementing the priority queue Q. If we use a binary heap, then lines 3–4 take $O(|V|)$ time. The loop at line 6 is executed $|V|$ times. The for loop in lines 8–11 is executed $O(|E|)$ times, because $2|E|$ is the sum of the lengths of all the adjacency lists. Line 10 updates the heap key *wp*, an operation taking $O(\lg|V|)$ time in a binary heap. Thus, the total time is $O(|V|\lg|V| + |E|\lg|V|) = O(|E|\lg|V|)$.

It is important to point out that an improvement of the algorithm can be achieved by using Fibonacci heaps, reducing Prim's algorithm running time to $O(|E| + |V|\lg|V|)$ (see [5] for further details).

12.7. Shortest Path Algorithms

An example of shortest path problem is the following: given a table of the distances between adjacent cities, determine the shortest route from a city A to a city B. In a *shortest path problem*, we have an undirected graph $G = (V, E)$, a *weight function* w: $E{-}{>}R$, mapping every edge onto an item of R. The *weight* of a path $p = (p_0, \ldots, p_n)$ is the sum of the weight of edges forming the path:

$$w(p) = \sum_{i=1\ldots n} w(v(i-1), v(i))$$

We define the *shortest path weight* from vertex u to vertex v as follows:

Definition: Given a weighted, directed graph $G = (V, E)$ and a pair of vertices n, m in V for which a path exists in G, a *shortest path weight* between n and m, $\delta(m, n)$, is the minimum weight $w(p)$ of the weight of the paths from n to m, if a path from n to m exists, ∞ otherwise.

12.7.1. *Single Source Shortest Paths Problem*

In many applications we are interested in finding all the shortest paths from one vertex s, the source, to all other vertices in V. Shortest paths are represented by using a ***shortest path tree***, defined as follows.

Given a weighted, directed graph $G = (V, E)$ and a vertex s in V, construct a tree whose root is s and whose paths represent shortest paths from s to all other vertices in V, reachable from s. More formally, the problem requires to determine a directed graph $G' = (V', E')$ such that:

- G' forms a tree with root in s.
- V' is a subset of V, representing all vertices reachable from s in G.

For each vertex v in V', the unique path from s to v in G' is a shortest path from s to v in G. The algorithms we describe in the following uses an upper bound of the shortest path weight from the source s to each other vertex, the *shortest path estimate*, denoted by $d[v]$. At first, $d[v]$ is set to infinity for each vertex v in V-$\{s\}$ and $d[s]$ is set to 0.

For each edge (u, v) in E, a ***relaxation*** step is applied if a modification of the path from s to v for including u improves the shortest path estimate for v. In this case, $d[v]$ and $pred[v]$ are appropriately updated and edge (u, v) is said to be *relaxed.*

In this section we present two famous algorithms for solving the single source shortest path problem: the Dijkstra's and the Bellman–Ford algorithms.

12.7.1.1. *Dijkstra's algorithm*

Dijkstra's algorithm computes a solution to the single source shortest path problem for a weighted graph $G = (V, E)$, provided that each edge in E has a non-negative weight.

To keep track of progress, the algorithm colors each vertex white or black. At first, all vertices are white. When the shortest path from the source s to a vertex v has been found, v is blackened. That is, for every black vertex v, $d[v]$ is the weight for a shortest path from s to v. The algorithm iteratively selects the white vertex u which has the least shortest-path estimate, blackens u, and relaxes all edges leaving from u.

The graph is represented by an adjacency lists. Other data structures have been employed. In particular,

- *color*$[u]$, storing the color of the vertex u
- *pred*$[u]$, containing the parent of the vertex u
- $d[u]$, storing the shortest-path estimate for u
- Q, a priority queue on the $d[u]$ values, storing the white vertices.

```
Procedure single-source-Dijkstra(G,w,s)
begin
for each vertex u in V
    begin
        d[v] = infinity
        pred[v] = NULL
        color[v] = white
    end
d[s] = 0
Add all the vertices in V to Q
while (!=ISEMPTY(Q))
    begin
        Extract from Q the vertex u such that
            d[u] is the minimum
        color[u] = black
        for each node v adjacent to u with
                color[v] = white do
            if d[v] > d[u] + w(u, v)
```

```
                    then
                         begin
12.                        d[v] = d[u] + w(u, v)
13.                        pred[v] = u
                         end
       end
end
```

Lines 1–4 initialize the data structures: For each vertex, except the source, the color is set to *white*, $d[u]$ is set to infinity and parent to NULL.
Line 5 sets $d[u]$ to 0 for the source.
Line 6 inserts all the vertices into the priority queue.
Lines 7–13 extract the white vertex u with the smallest shortest path estimate, blackens it and relaxes all edges outgoing from it.
Lines 10–13 execute the relaxation process, decreasing $d[v]$ and setting $pred[v]$ to u.

Figure 12.12 shows an execution of the Dijkstra's algorithm. In Fig. 12.12(a) is shown the result of lines 1–5. The value of the estimate $d[v]$ is shown inside each vertex v. Each time a new vertex is selected, it is blackened. The white vertices are in the priority queue Q. The dashed edges show the predecessor. Figures 12.12(b)–12.12(g) describe the successive iterations of the loop of lines 10–13. Figure 12.12(g) shows the final values for d.

Analysis

Lines 1–4 take $O(|V|)$ time. If we implement the priority queue with a Fibonacci heap, the $|V|$ applications of the extraction from Q of the vertex with the minimum d take $O(|V|\lg|V|)$ amortized time. Each vertex v is whitened once, and the for loop of lines 10–13 examine each edge in the adjacency lists exactly once. Since the total number of edges is $|E|$, lines 10–13 are executed $|E|$ times, each one taking $O(1)$. Thus, the total running time is $O(|V|\lg|V| + |E|)$.

12.7.1.2. *Bellman–Ford algorithm*

The Bellman–Ford algorithm solves the single source shortest paths problem in the general case of a graph $G = (V, E)$ admitting edges with negative weight. If G contains a negative-weight cycle, a shortest path from s to the vertices in the cycle cannot be found. Thus, if a vertex u belongs to a negative-weight cycle, we set $\delta(s, u)$, the shortest-path weight from s to u, to $-\infty$. As shown in Fig. 12.13, since there exists the cycle (c, e, c) we

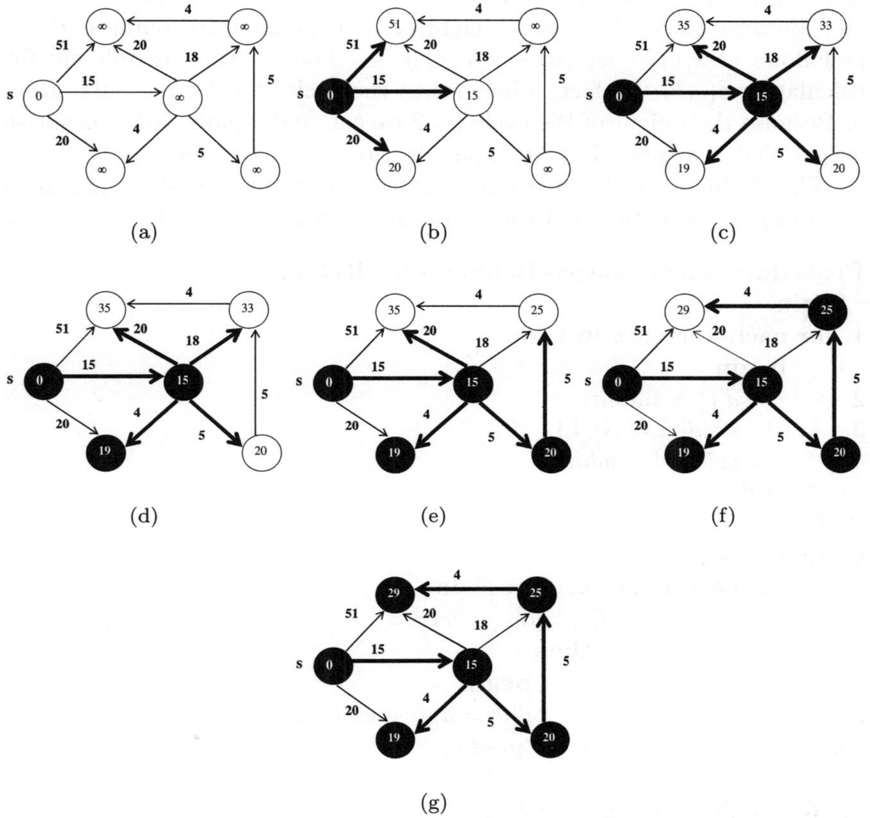

Fig. 12.12. An execution of the Dijstra's algorithm.

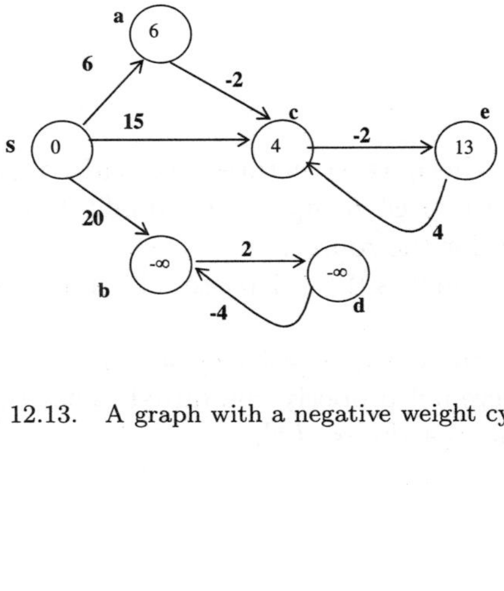

Fig. 12.13. A graph with a negative weight cycle.

have infinite paths between s and c: (s, a, c), (s, a, c, e, c), (s, a, c, e, c, e, c), etc. Because the cycle (c, e, c) weights 2, it is possible to compute $\delta(s, c)$ as follows: $\delta(s, c) = w(s, a) + w(a, c) = 4$. The situation is different for calculating $\delta(s, b)$. In fact, b belongs to the cycle (b, d, b), reachable from s. Because the weight of the cycle is –2 we can find a path with a negative weight that is arbitrarily long. Thus, $\delta(s, b) = \delta(s, d) = -\infty$.

The Bellman–Ford algorithm returns false if there exists a negative-weight cycle reachable from the source, otherwise it returns true.

```
Procedure single-source-Bellman-Ford(G,w,s)
 begin
1. for each vertex u in V do
      begin
2.        d[v] = infinity
3.        pred[v] = NULL
4.        color[v] = white
      end
5. d[s] = 0
6. for i=1 to |V| - 1 do
7.    for each edge (u,v) in E do
8.              if d[v] > d[u] + w(u,v)
                  then
                     begin
9.                   d[v] = d[u] + w(u,v)
10.                  pred[v] = u
                     end
11. for each edge (u,v) in E do
12.             if d[v] > d[u] + w(u,v)
13.                then return false
14. return true
 end
```

Description

Lines 1–4 initialize the data structures: for each vertex, except for the source, the color is set to *white*, $d[u]$ is set to infinity and parent to NULL. Line 5 sets $d[u]$ to 0 for the source.

The for loop of line 6 makes $|V| - 1$ passes. Each pass (lines 8–10) relaxes all the edges of G.

Lines 11–13 check if there is a negative cycle. In this case there exist edges in the graph that were not properly minimized. That is, there will be edges (u, v) such that $w(u, v) + d[u] < d[v]$.

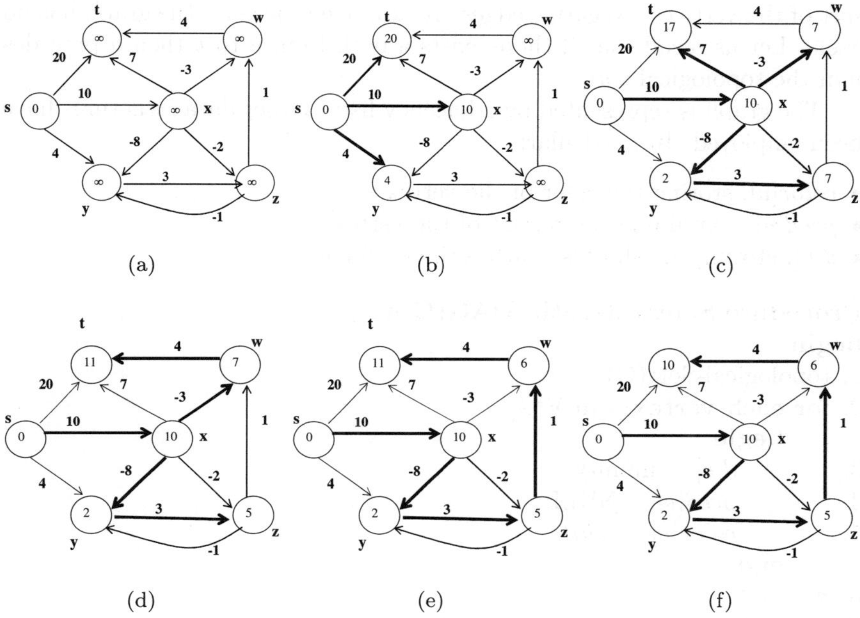

Fig. 12.14. An execution of the Bellman–Ford algorithm.

Figure 12.14 shows an execution of the procedure single-source-Bellman-Ford. In Fig. 12.14(a) is shown the results of lines 1–5. The value of the estimate $d[v]$ is shown inside each vertex v. The dashed edges show the predecessor. Figures 12.14(b)–12.14(e) describe the successive iterations of the loop of lines 7–10, where, for each step, the edges are relaxed following the order (w,t), (x,t), (x,w), (z,y), (z,w), (x,z), (y,z), (x,y), (s,t), (s,x), (s,y). Figure 12.14(f) shows the final values for the estimate d.

Analysis

The time complexity is $O(|V|\,|E|)$. In fact, lines 1–4 take $O(|V|)$ times. The for loop of lines 6–10 is executed $O(|V|)$ times. The inner loop of lines 7–10 is executed for each edge in E and takes $O(|E|)$ times. Thus, the complexity of lines 6–10 is $O(|V|\,|E|)$. Lines 11–13 take $O(|E|)$ times.

12.7.1.3. *Single-source shortest path in DAG*

Given a weighted DAG (Directed Acyclic Graph) $G = (V, E)$ we are able to solve the shortest path from a single source problem by using a topological sort of the vertices. Negative edges are admitted, because the graph has no cycle. Let us recall that if there exists a path from u to v then u precedes v in the topological sort.

The graph is represented by adjacency lists. Other data structures have been employed. In particular:

- *color*[u], storing the color of the vertex u
- *pred*[u], containing the parent of the vertex u
- $d[u]$, storing the shortest-path estimate for u

```
Procedure Shortest-path_DAG(G,w,s)
begin
1. topological-Sort(G)
2. for each vertex u in V[G]
      begin
3.        d[v] = infinity
4.        pred[v] = NULL
5.        color[v] = white
      end
6. d[s] = 0
7. for each vertex u, selected by following the
topological order do
8.        for each vertex v adjacent to u do
9.             if d[v] > d[u] + w(u, v)
                    then
                         begin
10.                      d[v] = d[u] + w(u, v)
11.                      pred[v] = u
                         end
end
```

Description

Line 1 calls the topological sort procedure on the graph G.
Lines 2–5 initialize the data structures: for each vertex, except for the source, the color is set to *white*, $d[u]$ is set to infinity and parent to NULL.
Line 5 sets $d[u]$ to 0 for the source.
Lines 7–11. For each vertex selected by following the topological ordering, the algorithm relaxes the edges that are in its adjacency lists.

Figure 12.15 shows an execution of the shortest-path-DAG algorithm. The vertex of G are topologically ordered from left to right. The node labeled s is the source. Nodes are blackened when they are visited by the algorithm and the predecessor of a node is connected to it by a shaded edge. The values of the estimate $d[\,]$ are depicted inside the

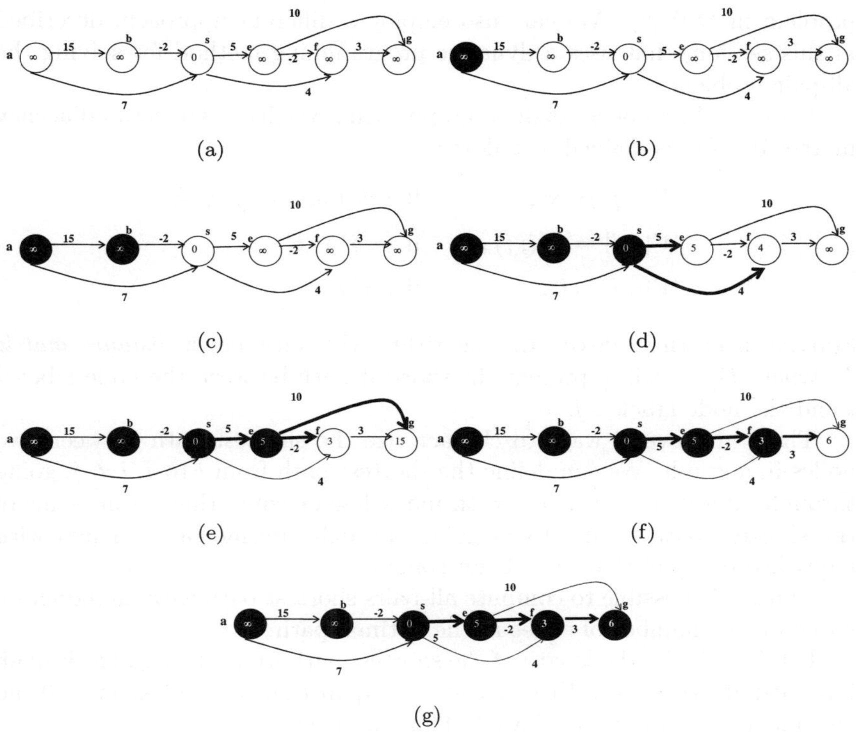

Fig. 12.15. An execution of the single-source shortest path in a DAG algorithm.

vertices. Figure 12.15(a) shows the result of the initialization of lines 2–6. Figures 12.15(b)–12.15(g) show the result of the execution of the loop in lines 8–11. The final result is given in Fig. 12.15(g).

Analysis

The topological sort of G takes $\Theta(|V| + |E|)$. In fact, lines 2–5 require $\Theta(V)$. For each vertex, the algorithm considers the edges in its adjacency lists. Thus, lines 9–11 are executed $O(|E|)$ times and take $O(1)$ time. Thus, the time complexity of the shortest-path_DAG algorithm is $\Theta(|V| + |E|)$.

12.7.2. *All-Pairs Shortest Path*

Many applications, such as computing the minimum distances between pairs of cities, require finding the shortest path between all pairs of vertices.

We can solve this problem by running the Dijkstra's algorithm $|V|$ times (once from each possible source vertex) to solve all-pairs shortest path problem in $O(|V|^3)$. We can also employ a different approach, described in this section, that uses a dynamic programming method for solving the all-pair problem.

Let $G = (V, E)$ be a weighted graph with n vertices. The nxn adjacency matrix W of G is defined as follows:

$$W[i,j] = \infty\,, \qquad \text{if } i \neq j \text{ and } (i,j) \notin E$$
$$W[i,j] = w(i,j)\,, \qquad \text{if } (i,j) \in E$$
$$W[i,j] = 0\,, \qquad \text{if } i = j$$

Starting from this matrix, the algorithm will construct a *distance matrix* D, where $D[i,j]$ will represent the shortest path between the node labeled i and the node labeled j.

There are several ways to characterize the shortest path between two nodes in a graph. We can define the shortest path from i to j, $i \neq j$, going through intermediate vertices with index less or equal than m in terms of the shortest path from i to m going through intermediate vertices with index less or equal than $m-1$, for some m.

Thus, it is possible to compute all-pairs shortest path with an induction based on the number of edges in the optimal path.

Let $D[i,j]^m$ be the length of the shortest path from i to j going through intermediate vertices with index less or equal than m. When $m = 0$, no intermediate vertices are allowed. Thus, we have

$$D[i,j]^0 = W[i,j]$$

We can recoursively define $D[i,j]^m$ in terms of $D[i,j]^{m-1}$ as follows: if we have available $D[i,j]^{m-1}$ we can generate $D[i,j]^m$ by considering m as an intermediate vertex.

$$D[i,j]^m = \min\{D[i,j]^{m-1}, D[i,m]^{m-1} + D[m,j]^{m-1}\}, m \geq 1$$

This recurrence can be solved for D^n by first computing D^1, D^2, and so on. The procedure all-pair-shortest-path computes D^n.

This procedure receives as input the adjacency matrix W and the number of vertex n, and provides as output the all-pair-shortest-path matrix D.

Procedure All-pair-shortest-path(W,D,n)
begin
1. **for** i = 1 **to** n **do**
2.   **for j = 1 to n do**
3.   D[i,j] = W[i,j]

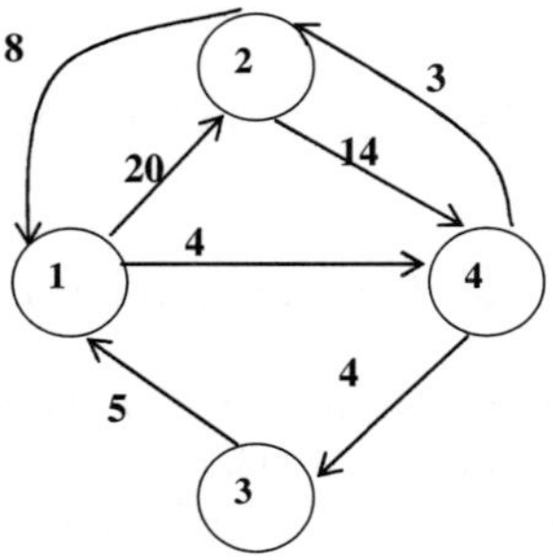

W	1	2	3	4
1	0	20	∞	4
2	8	0	∞	14
3	5	∞	0	∞
4	∞	3	4	0

Fig. 12.16. A directed graph G and its adjacency matrix W.

D^0	1	2	3	4
1	0	20	∞	4
2	8	0	∞	14
3	5	∞	0	∞
4	∞	3	4	0

D^1	1	2	3	4
1	0	20	∞	4
2	8	0	∞	12
3	5	25	0	9
4	∞	3	4	0

D^2	1	2	3	4
1	0	20	∞	4
2	8	0	∞	12
3	5	25	0	9
4	11	3	4	0

D^0	1	2	3	4
1	0	20	∞	4
2	8	0	∞	14
3	5	∞	0	∞
4	∞	3	4	0

D^0	1	2	3	4
1	0	20	∞	4
2	8	0	∞	14
3	5	∞	0	∞
4	∞	3	4	0

Fig. 12.17. An execution of the-all-pair-shortest-path procedure.

4. **for** k = 1 **to** n **do**
5.   **for** i = 1 **to** n **do**
6.   **for** j = 1 **to** n **do**
7.   D[i,j] = min {D[i,j], D[i,k] + D[k,j]}

end

Lines 1–3 initialize D^0, by copying W in D.
Lines 4–7 construct in a bottom–up way the matrix D^n: line 4 considers all paths having k as the highest vertex. Lines 5 and 6 consider all the possible pairs of vertices and for each pair line 7 computes D^k. Figure 12.17 shows an execution of this algorithm on the graph depicted in Fig. 12.16. The complexity analysis is very simple: this algorithm solves the all-pair shortest path in $O(|V|^3)$.

References

The algorithms of this chapter are adapted from [1], [5] and [9]. Further information can be found in:

1. V. A. Aho, E. J. Hopcroft and D. J. Ullman, *Data Structures and Algorithms*, Addison-Wesley, 1983.
2. R. K. Ahuja, T. L. Magnanti and J. B. Orlin, *Network Flows, Theory, Algorithms, and Applications*, Prentice Hall, NJ, 1993.
3. R. E. Bellman, "On a routing problem," *Quart. Appl. Math.* **16**, 87–90, 1958.
4. W. J. Cook, W. H. Cunningham, W. R. Pulleyblank and A. Schrijver, *Combinatorial Optimization*, 1995.
5. T. H. Cormen, C. E. Leiserson and R. L. Rivest, *Introduction to Algorithms*, Second Edition, Mc-Graw Hill, 2001.
6. E. Dijkstra, "A note on two problems in connexion with graphs," *Numerische Mathematik* **1**, 269–271, 1959.
7. E. Shimon, *Graph Algorithms*, Computer Science Press, 1979.
8. L. R. Jr. Ford, *Network Flow Theory*, Paper P-923, RAND Corporation, Santa Monica, California, 1956.
9. E. Horowitz, S. Sahni, *Fundamentals of Data Structures*, Computer Science Press, 1983.
10. R. Tarjan, *Data Structures and Network Algorithms*, Society for Industrial and Applied Mathematics, 1983.

Exercises

Beginner's Exercises

1. Define the following terms:
   Graph, directed graph, spanning tree, light edge, connected component, cycle, topological order, degree, in-degree, out-degree, path.
2. For the following graph determine:

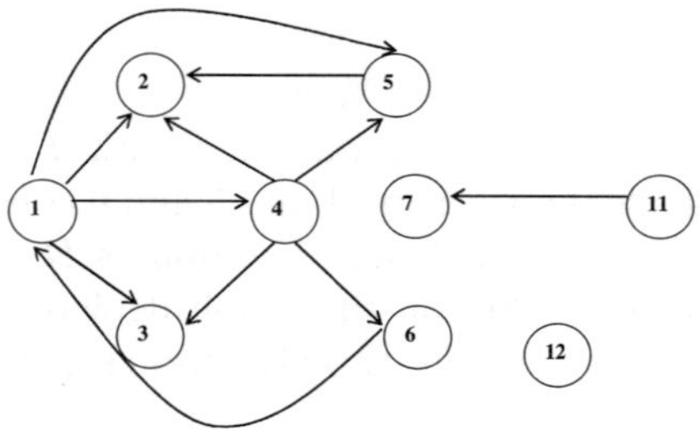

(a) Its adjacency matrix representation;
(b) Its adjacency lists representation;
(c) Its strongly connected components.

3. Use the Dijkstra's algorithm to obtain the shortest paths from the vertex 1 to all the remaining vertices of the graph in Fig. 12.16.

Intermediate Exercises

4. Rewrite the procedure DFS without using recursion. (*Hint*: Use a stack.)
5. Modify DFS — Visit in such a way that it prints the lists of the vertices v that are reachable from the source s and the edges that are incident to them.
6. Write an algorithm that determines whether or not a graph has a cycle. Your algorithm has to run in $O(|V|)$ time.

Advanced Exercises

7. Write an algorithm that for a given directed graph $G = (V, E)$ determines the transitive closure of G. If A is the adjacency matrix of G, its transitive closure A^+ is defined as follows:

$$A^+(i,j) = \begin{cases} 1 \text{ if there exists a path from } i \text{ to } j, i \neq j \\ 0 \text{ otherwise} \end{cases}$$

(*Hint* : Modify the procedure all-pair-shortest-path.)

8. Write an algorithm that determine an *Euler Circuit* in an undirected graph if it exists. (An *Euler Circuit* is a path that starts and ends at the same vertex and includes each edge once.)

Chapter 13

Analysing the Interface

STEFANO LEVIALDI

University of Rome, Italy

levialdi@dsi.uniroma1.it

Human computer interaction is often required in order to successfully design, test and refine algorithms. To support human computer interaction, we need to understand how to design the user interface. Therefore as the final chapter of this book, we introduce the concept and design principles of user interface.

13.1. Introduction

In discussing the nature and the issues that are relevant to interface design and evaluation, we will start with some recent definitions and next illustrate the "critical points" as seen by a number of authors, very active in this area of computer science, essentially falling within Human Computer Interaction. As may be remembered, this area stems from traditional Ergonomical studies but also includes cognitive and computer-based constraints and was initially named CHI, Computer Human Interaction. This acronym reminds us of the importance of the computer when compared to the human (the user); in fact a number of professional societies and International meetings fall under that name.

Only in recent years, perhaps after the 90s, that researchers and practitioners alike, discovered the importance of the user within the interface design process and also became the best judges of the quality of the implemented solutions.

A recent book (*The Humane Interface* by Jef Raskin, Addison Wesley, USA, 2000) covers a number of issues, relevant to the design and evaluation of modern interfaces exploiting the experience that the author has after being responsible for the design of the Macintosh interface and, for this reason, is strongly recommended to people wanting to learn more about interface inner workings.

An intuitive notion of interface is given in the above book, in fact we are used to working with many different programs and sometimes we do not notice they have a "front end": the interface. Other times we confuse the interface with the application itself but, luckily, when the interface is well designed (more on this later) we do not even notice there is an interface. This situation is described as working with a "transparent" interface.

In the process of designing an interface, it is very important to put the user in the correct place. When requested, he will describe his needs, his priorities, his working style: the interface should help him achieve his goals without strain — neither in the learning phase nor in the utilization phase (this is referred to as ease of learning and ease of use).

People using computers may operate in many different working domains and, more specifically, need not be computer scientists, the machine, for them, is something complex, difficult to understand and, sometimes, even hard to use. For these reasons we speak of a semantic gap between their understanding of the computer (as a machine) and what really happens when an application is run. People try to climb up towards the computer

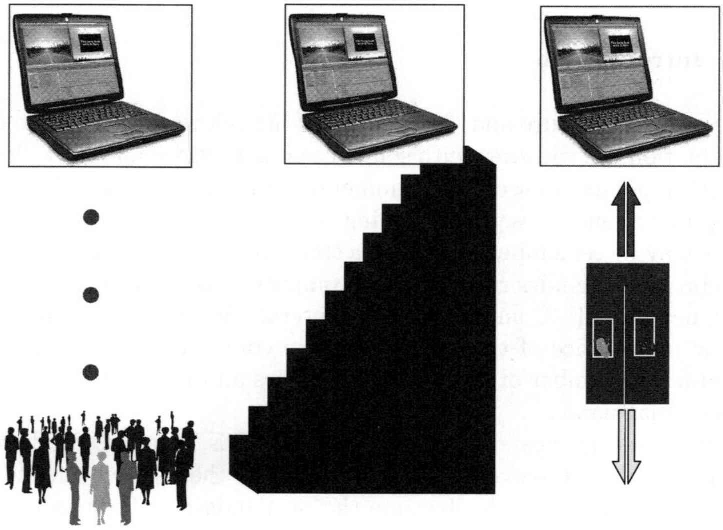

Fig. 13.1. The lift metaphor.

level, perhaps using a rope, but would much prefer a staircase in which levels of abstraction are well established.

The goal of an interface designer is to allow the user (of a given class, belonging to a specific working domain) to select (as if choosing a floor) at which level of abstraction the application should present itself.

In other words how much detail is required to understand how the system works, in which state he is currently at and how can it be operated.

The devices normally used to operate the system, the keyboard, the mouse, etc. should not be confused with the interface; they are tools that allow the user to choose which and how information must be submitted or in the case of the screen, which information will be seen.

A number of studies are continually been performed to improve the ergonomics of these devices: the shape of the mouse (recent mice exploit the thumb, the arrangement of keys on the keyboard, etc). Yet, no cognitive feature is connected to such studies which only try to relieve tiredness or discomfort from the user.

13.2. Interface Features

It is generally required that simple tasks employ simple interfaces and complex tasks may allow for more involved ones. For example, we all know how hard it is to set the clock on a VCR. Nevertheless, there is no need for such complexity, it suffices to present a window to the user where both hours and minutes are shown, to increase a value, the user would click on the top arrow and, to decrease a value, the user would click on the bottom one.

A second example shows the importance of mapping between layouts of data domains and control domains. In this case a kitchen stove has four burners and the knobs controlling them may be positioned in a number of ways, the easiest to follow by the user is the one shown on the right where there is a natural correspondence between burners and knobs.

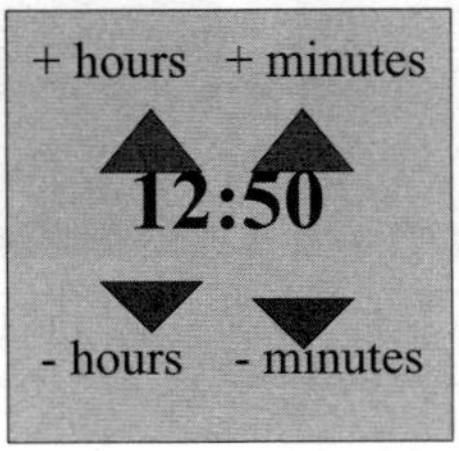

Fig. 13.2. A reasonable VCR setup window.

Another important issue is the one of exploiting a shape to indicate the function, plates imply pulling, slots inserting (filling the space) and knobs generally require pulling or turning. Moreover, door handles may indicate whether one has to push or pull.

As we have all seen and heard from the news of the 2001 election for President of the United States, many voters had difficulties with the card arrangements. In fact, the form lead them to believe that if they punched hole number 4 that meant a vote for Gore (whilst it really meant a vote for Buchanan!).

As shown below, door handles provide cues for pushing or pulling as mentioned above; yet other important clues may be provided by feedback and visibility (which is also exploited in specific screen representations). Feedback helps in deciding the correct action while visibility highlights those components on which an action may be executed [6].

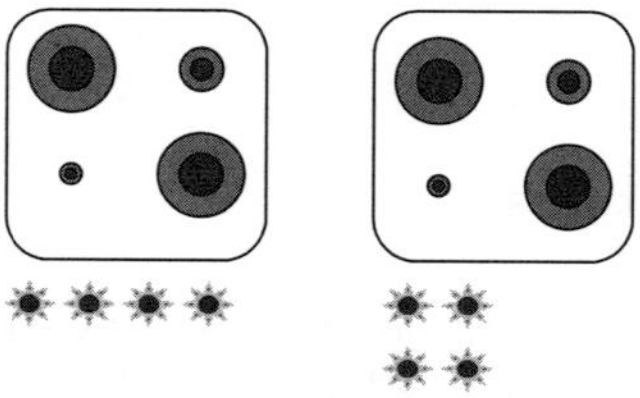

Fig. 13.3. Burners and knobs. Bad and good mappings.

Fig. 13.4. Door handles with affordance.

The correspondence between candidates and associated holes on the card were hard to follow and consequences were serious and difficult to remedy; the confusion originated on a poor mapping between the control point (the card hole) and meaning (the candidate's name).

There are two sides to the problem of designing and building interfaces:

(1) computer science issues: programming a chosen set of algorithms favoring human-program communication and control and
(2) human issues: exploiting and supporting the user's skills

Designs should cater — as much as possible — for general cases, be domain-independent and possibly exploit what has been learned in the past. In this way tested parts of an implementation may also be used in the next version of the system or even on new applications.

Broadly speaking, we have abstracted a small set of general rules: low cognitive load, few basic icons, possibility of undoing all actions, availability of backtracking, online help, etc.

The cognitive load refers to the need and deployment of human memory and of pattern recognition abilities required to perform the task with a given interface. The amount of icons is critical since too many would hinder the user instead of helping him. Naturally, a unique meaning for each icon, is also an important requirement. The generalization of the UNDO function as a recovery command, is very desirable but generally unrealistic. The online help is already available in many systems but its true benefits are not perceived since most "helps" are simply a long list of features in

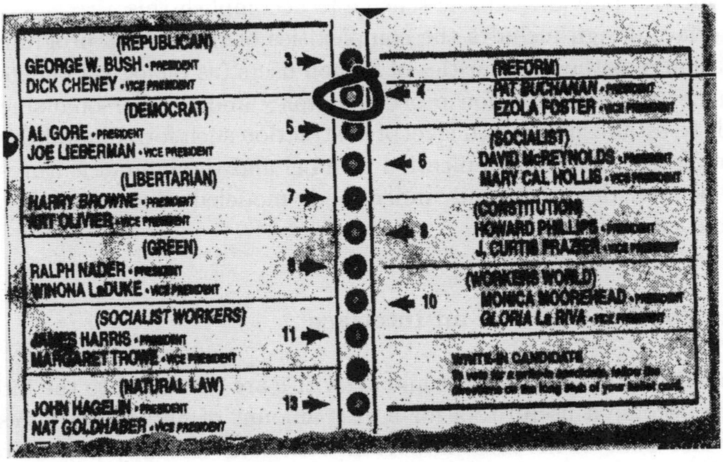

Fig. 13.5. Florida Presidential election card.

alphabetical order instead of answers to the user's questions and therefore do not provide constructive suggestions.

13.3. Formal Approaches?

Interactive computing differs from batch computing even at the basic level. A Turing machine no longer describes the time dependencies of concurrent processes that generally take place when a user sits in front of his desktop computer to perform his tasks: e-mail, word processing, database querying, printing, unzipping, etc. In fact, some computational models have been suggested like the PIE model that consider as input a series of commands, an interpretation function and the effects produced by such function. Next, properties and constraints of interactive computing are described at an abstract level so as to predict system behavior, define equivalent commands, state reachability and monotonicity.

To formalize, in the context of interface analysis and design, is a question-raiser more than an issue-solver. For instance, within the realm of documentation, we must enforce the following: to say what is implemented and to implement what is documented. This requires a high level of vision on behalf of the designers, implementers and documentors. Since documentation is presently the main information source for both users and programmers, this is the reason why the process of writing about the system should be formalized. In this way the documentation may be considered as a program for the user telling him how to proceed in unknown situations. Hyperdoc [10] provides a basic scheme to accomplish this.

Interface design includes the complexities of the human-program communication plus the peculiarities of human users (as biological beings); this fact makes the formalization process complex and cumbersome since it is difficult to establish at which level of abstraction such formal models should be formulated. The communication channel and the human features must firstly be well described and understood, modeled, documented, tested, validated and refined.

13.4. The Functions of an Interface

A number of different functions and activities are entrusted to the interface so as to become a useful tool for a vast amount of human activities. Let us here list some of the most important functions certainly not in order of importance.

One which is directly linked to the development of video games is enjoyment, i.e. the possibility of playing games but also of hacking programs, communicating with others, exploring data, composing music/poetry/essays, listening to music, draw/sketch, study, etc.

Another function is that of enabling new skills where the augmentation of human activities enables monitoring complex processes and their time evolution: this represents an empowerment. For instance controlling a super-jet may only be done via a special interface for the pilot.

Still on this list, we have delegation where the computer is left to do repetitive, dangerous, critical jobs which the human would not do as smoothly. A negative case arises when the user delegates full responsibility on incomplete tasks as when a physician may be tempted to do in some diagnostic applications.

We also have safety where we try to avoid physical contact between the user and his activity site, as in remote control operations taking place at dangerous locations (like coal mines, radioactive stations, underwater operations, etc.)

Broadly speaking, we are experiencing one of the most important and world-wide applications of the web, i.e. distance learning, also called e-learning, contract learning, chunk learning, etc. according to the teaching model. In this case we may speak of development aiming at a cultural enrichment through interactive teaching programs: arithmetic drill, road signals for car driving, language practice, self-evaluation, etc. In fact, these activities fall under the name of web-based education, or, in a wider context, global education if it is integrated with face to face learning.

A new way for doing things at one shot rather than many different stages of a job, in the past, that were done in sequence, so that for each mistake, corrections had to be done everywhere (as in a presentation, course preparation, etc.). A presentation manager (like, for instance, Power Point™) manages slides, notes, outlines, together with timings, transitions, animation, colors, backgrounds, etc.

Last but not least, we must consider computing which is what computers were made for! Integrate, plot, enhance an image, prove a theorem, compute a spacecraft trajectory, etc. are all typical computer activities and should be facilitated by a good interface (as for instance was done in Mathematica™, a well known package of mathematical applications).

13.5. Interaction History

The first interaction with a computer was through its on/off switch, then came the possibility of introducing data and next to keep up changing the data following a program request (1950–1960).

The first big revolution in terms of human–computer interactivity arrived with the light pen (which was a light-sensitive device more than

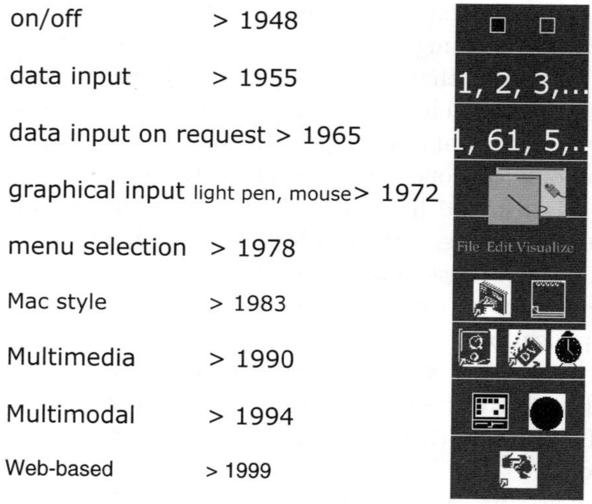

Fig. 13.6. History of human/computer interaction technology.

a light emitting one) and next the mouse which, at the beginning, was not very successful (1960–1970).

Later on came the menu selection, which ensured the correct spelling of the options, presented all the possible choices to the user (favoring memory recognition instead of recall) and needed no programming (1970–1980).

Finally, the Mac arrived (firstly called as the company, Apple) with its famous desktop metaphor (taken from the pioneering work performed at Xerox Parc (Palo Alto, California). The possibility for the layman to use a computer to fulfil his tasks (essentially an activity which may be modeled as document transformation) without having to follow a programming course, was the main asset of this system (1980–1990).

Soon arrived the different formats and devices, which could handle sounds, pictures and videos as well as text: a multitude of standards was born and wherever the standard was followed (like in European mobile telephony) a leap forward was made.

Due to the number of different functions available in most programs and to the limited amount of possibilities offered by the keyboard, modes were introduced and will continue to exist even if they are certainly error prone. Finally, because of the fast increase of web surfers, web page creators, etc. web-based systems designed for interactivity (where direct manipulation is also possible) are now continuously built. All the knowledge gained on customer requirements and on available products and services presently comes from the web.

An interface may also be described in terms of five properties. (1) Productivity may be defined as the quantity of interactions in unit time. The way in which (2) complexity can be managed, as for instance in air flight traffic control (for landing and take-off) where a single operator can handle more work (in better conditions) if he has a good user interface. (3) Reliability where programs will run many times in exactly the same way (they never get tired), in some instances they may be too inflexible. Finally, quality i.e. where programs may achieve greater quality, accuracy and reproducibility than humans, and this comes from the advances of the computer technology and not from the user interface. Security in which the interface may check the user's authority to employ certain programs, record past transactions (financial operations, etc.), perform inventory accounting, etc.

The first property is the one most commonly featured in computer-based applications yet, the interface to such applications will very likely decide whether the product is interesting, important and of any use. In fact, as it happens with humans, the first encounter between two unknown persons quickly establishes whether these two people will meet again. By analogy, we may consider the first time a user tries a product via an interface: this first encounter will be decisive, either the user will continue using the product/system (if its interface was enjoyable) or ... never again in the opposite case.

The increase in task complexity within many working domains has caused the adoption of computerized systems, which, in turn, require good interfaces to be properly handled. Finally, the property of all programs (whether related to the interface or to the application) is that they may repeat the same action(s) many thousands of times without flaw. For this reason their reliability must be very high and adequate for those tasks requiring the same sequence of actions during long periods of time.

The quality of the achieved tasks does not depend upon the interface but on that of the application program (and how well it matches the user's expectations).

As for the privacy issues, the interface may check — by a number of different techniques — the identity of the user, also offering a variety of capabilities: no access, read only, read and write.

13.6. Designing the Interface

The problem of communicating between humans (users, designers, managers and interaction experts) during interface design is very critical. In practice they should discuss and build systems, which satisfy the user requirements, and are robust and efficient from the computer science angle and exploit human abilities as monitored by the psychologist. Moreover, during regular briefing meetings, the prototype passes from a paper model to a real program through critical analysis and testing until no further refinements are needed. The main issue is to fully understand the user needs his expectations and priorities.

Using programs by means of an adequate interface may both empower the human (extending his range of operations) or make his life more boring if the required actions are repetitive, with a limited scope and without the need for any personal/creative effort.

Initially, during most of the recent past years, a first approach was used, where the whole project was in the hands of programmers. Formal systems were used to model the whole system through components and functions (even automatic tools like CASE): in the end, the results were not convincing to the users. In a second approach, the participation of psychologists (cognitive psychologists and learning theory experts) was one of the new additions to the development teams. When designing an interface for a mobile cellular phone an extensive list of items should be considered: who is the typical user, which are his real needs, how and where is the new system to be used (environment, noise, movement, etc.). The augmented and integrated development teams produced far better results.

Whenever computers had to be interconnected the problem of their compatibility has been solved by accurately matching the digital signal requirements of a machine to those of another machine. On the contrary, humans are very different from machines (luckily!) so that we need to have a better knowledge of the human to enable us to fully satisfy the human user. This technique has been called "user-centred" since it revolves around his wish list as specified by the different members of the development team. In fact sometimes users may even become coauthors of the project since they have really contributed to its definition, to its implementation and to its evaluation. As an example, of a typical program, that shows no user was involved in its development we may quote the case of the Microsoft Windows environment where to switch off such system, the user is asked to click on the start-up icon!

Sometimes machines are treated better than humans since their known limitations are well known and fully considered as well as their specific technical requirements; one wishes that humans should be treated at least as well as computers.

It is difficult to fully establish a hierarchy of design issues: which is the most important? And why?

Accruing featurism is an English name given to the activity of adding special purpose features every time a new requirement is defined or whenever a new feature becomes desirable. Generally for commercial reasons this is done to increase the value of a product, more features equals to higher value, nevertheless sometimes the reverse is true!

The problems met when testing the new interface could be hidden by local add-ons (bypassing the problems found), these new features will certainly complicate the understanding of the system, make it difficult to forecast the behavior in different cases and also provide side effects. As mentioned before, this typical activity of adding code chunks, called accruing featurism, hinders the growth of a project and sometimes may also break up its consistency.

Even if it may seem obvious, it is important to stress that the properties of the parts are not necessarily the properties of the whole. As an example within a jury, jurors may have difficulty to express their view and therefore we have an indecisive jury and vice-versa, a decisive juror may build up an indecisive jury.

In short, we must remember that the good quality of the components of an interface is no guarantee for the quality of the interface (considered as the whole).

If we consider the design process at a sufficient level of abstraction, we will be able to hide the irrelevant details. The three main partners in the design and development of interfaces are: the user, the computer (through its programs) and the designer; but as we have already seen there are other members of the designing team: the project manager, the technical author, the evaluator.

The bandwidth of human communication is given by the rate at which, in a unit of time, a quantity of information may be acquired or delivered. Generally we may use all our senses (vision, touch, hearing, smell) to acquire — in parallel — information from the environment. The amount of information that reaches our brain along time is therefore quite high. Unfortunately, machines such as computers cannot acquire (even if they may process) large amounts of information in short time intervals. For these reasons both the human user and the human designer have a wide information channel which restricts itself in order to send information to programs and to receive whatever the computer outputs.

This bandwidth difference must be compensated by a clever use of screen estate, by hierarchical layouts, by prioritizing techniques and by using a number of graphical cues which may provide the information that users require.

During the design and construction of an interface (and of its associated programs) the information comes from different sources, mainly originating at the user's side and then being analyzed by the programmer in order to fully understand the user's requests. The mental model of

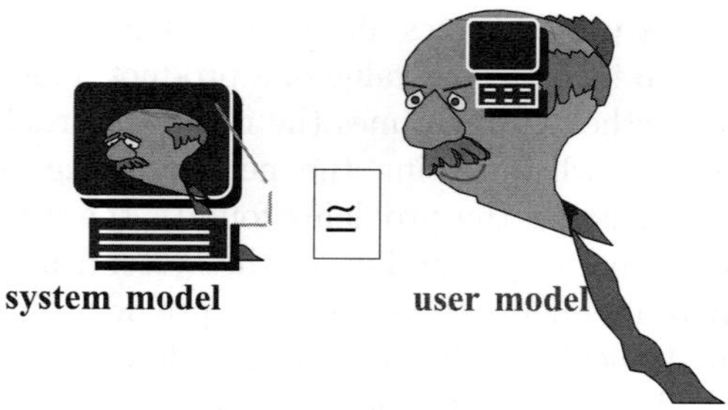

Fig. 13.7. Model matching.

the user corresponds to what the user has built in his mind to represent the system he is using and we call it the System Model. On the other hand, the designer has a model of the user, which we call the User Model, that constitutes the basis on which the program will be built to perform the interactive computing processes which will target the user's aims when using the system.

Yet mental models differ from programs in many ways: they are not equivalent, nor have the same structure, nor run at the same time, use different logical systems and may malfunction for a wide number of reasons. Nevertheless, the use of models is mandatory for enabling a good communication between users and program developers. These two models should match as closely as possible in order to allow the user to fully understand the system he is using.

If these two models were equivalent, one of them would be sufficient. The program turns useful if, in some way, it matches the mental model. In fact every computer system has been built on the basis of explicit or implicit models of the user, of his tasks, needs, expectations but generally a canonical model of the user is employed by the designer in order to implement the system.

This picture represents both models graphically, and makes explicit the matching condition as the equivalence between the models.

13.7. Interface Quality

The first and foremost condition for a good interface is coherence, i.e. that the mental model that the user will build of the system coincides (or has an extended overlap) with the user model of the programmer when building the interface. Most problems at the interface level are generated by the mismatch between these two models.

It is debatable whether it is a positive feature, for an interface, to have more ways than one to perform a given action. In fact, it may turn useful so as to accommodate different users and relative preferences but, from another point of view, the fact that the user may choose may either delay him or may favor behavioral errors.

If a vast amount of information may be handled by the interface, more knowledge may be gained as to why some events take place.

During interaction between user and system, we require predictable events, i.e. which may be foreseen; if the user has an adequate model of the system he is using then he may be able to obtain what he expects, otherwise he will believe the system behaves randomly.

Interface commands generally have a time dependency so that, each sequence of events has a meaning if performed in a given order; in many instances the results obtained differ from the expected ones, i.e. commands are generally not commutative.

Even if it may seem absurd, an interactive system based on a programmable machine may look as if it were non-deterministic. In fact, non-determinism may be perceived just because some information is not known — note-takers, diaries, calendars, transcriptions help to keep track of the user's processes. Another case of apparent randomness is when files disappear from the user's view. A program with a schedule for erasing old files should be known to the user.

The relevance of the user notation cannot be overstressed: it is through notation that users understand actions, processes and tasks according to their own experience within their working domain.

13.8. Human Issues

Some features, typical of humans, must be known so as to exploit them correctly in the interface design process. Humans shift their attention, in terms of a visual signal, every 50 ms with eye movements taking 200 ms, this allows to choose what is relevant along time. Conversely, the audio signal is captured quickly and faster than the video one.

After selection, the information is conveyed into the short term memory (STM) which is a conscious place that may manage seven objects at most. If it is unused, then its contents decay after twenty seconds; nevertheless it can be refreshed by rehearsal.

Information (data) may be stored in chunks, each one distinguishable by its name, and each chunk may also contain sub-chunks which may be processed and stored. These chunks are built by closure and the STM may be seen as a memory stack, the closure is equivalent to a pop operation.

The data (information) is transferred, after five seconds, into long term memory (LTM) which has a very high capacity and a small decay; it is generally believed that humans forget and computer memories do not, the converse is true.

For instance, our knowledge on language is contained in this memory which has interesting properties: it is associative (content driven), subjective (what we store is strongly linked with the personal experience we have gone through when recording the data) and never forgets. Yet, we may have difficulties in retrieving the information which, whenever successful, requires a tenth of a second.

Sometimes mnemonics may help in the retrieving process and this has been used in the names of commands (Ctrl+C for Control + Copy).

Since different items in memory may have the same coding (as if Hash coded) it becomes hard to recall one thing if it was recorded with two different codes, names, or in other cases two different items with the same code.

For two interactive systems, the experience of the first carries over the learning process of the second, if they are similar. The same happens when programming with a new language or when speaking a new language in terms of an older, known one. This is known as conceptual capture and is a negative effect since the new system will never be completely understood and learnt properly.

Priming is a phenomenon by means of which an idea is forced on someone like when you ask firstly to spell "shop" and then you ask "what do you do when you see a green light?" most persons would answer "stop" (by a clear vocal proximity to the word shop).

On the other hand we see a standard behavior when people panic and use a "default escape" as when there is a fire or an earthquake, for this reason we must provide a standard way to exit from an application for all applications.

Finally, there should be means for a user to recover from his mistakes so making him feel sure instead of being afraid to be trapped by the system with no possibility to recover.

Each person (user) is one of a kind: for instance, some persons regularly perform parallel processing, i.e. they handle different jobs at the same time — how can we use this? Perhaps mental processing may be viewed as an expert system: in this case the LTM may be considered as containing a body of rules with the STM as a blackboard. The number of goals is necessarily limited, we may also exploit the fact that access to rules in the LTM will increase their probability of future access.

There are many other "personal" issues like motivation, stress, play, relationship with the job, etc.: they all influence his attitudes with respect to the interface he is using, and therefore should also be taken into account during the design.

An important, very general, law of experimental psychology, due to Festinger, is known by the name of Cognitive Dissonance. It states that whichever choice a person is making (regardless of age, sex, culture, social class) the alternative chosen looks worse than the discarded one; if such choice is reversed, the positive/negative qualities will also be exchanged.

In practice, the user (with respect to the program choice he has made) may try to reduce such dissonance by adding further consonant ideas, selectively exposing himself to read positive evaluations of his choice ... (and other tricks that help) or refer to the importance of choice (his job is more significant than the program he has chosen).

In many cases, users will adapt to the choices made by the programmer/designer of the interface even if some steps appear illogical or cumbersome: in this way, unfortunately, future releases of the program will continue along the same lines without turning to more logical or simple steps that would greatly alleviate the user's mental load.

Users will take risks if they know that the system they are using will not endanger the work they have done, this will obviously be the case after they have already evaluated the consequences of their actions. If they feel the system is safe, they will behave wildly, while if the system is simple they will try complex tasks.

The interaction style of the user will depend on his attitudes (see text above) and on the system documentation; since users adapt, designers can afford to build systems far more complex than necessary.

If users test a system and are observed by behavioral scientists, they will tend to do more and better work as compared to their daily performance in the office; this is known as the Hawthorne Effect.

The user may work with an interface in different ways which we may call performances. The first one, called skill-based, runs without conscious attention or control, e.g. typing for a typist: it works only if the user's control model is an adequate representation of the interface.

The second one, called rule-based performance, may be defined as the recollection of skilled behavior patterns. Lastly, the third one, called knowledge-based, is used for an interaction which was poorly rehearsed so that rules have not been developed yet and goals must be explicitly formulated in order to work out a plan.

There are three human interaction modes that correspond to action classes: symbolic, atomic and continuous. The first one is exemplified by commands as in old systems using MSDOS and is based on textual commands that name the corresponding action.

The second class of commands is executed by pressing a key or by selecting a menu item. The input devices that constantly send a signal to the system belong to this class.

A third class of commands is frequent in video games which generally use consoles having track balls, laptop computers have finger pads that allow the user to point — on the screen — the wanted object. Also personal computers that use a mouse for interacting with objects on the screen (in a direct manipulation style) are a good example of the third class of interaction commands.

Even if this class may show overshoots or undershoots, such wrong displacements may be easily corrected with a simple and natural eye–hand coordination.

Other input possibilities are provided by soft keys, those labeled from F1 to F12 which are available on all computer keyboards. These keys allow the definition of corresponding actions (through special sequences of instructions) which will then take place when one of such keys is selected.

A real interactive system will mix all three styles. Basically, incremental interaction is based on the atomic style.

A symbolic style is supported when using a timesharing system — like in banks — ideal for mainframes. Once a command is entered, a number of operations may be entailed but only the final result will appear to the user, perhaps a receipt in a financial transaction.

The atomic-based interface requires feedback to the user, typically every stroke should provide a response (in time intervals of the order of a tenth of a second).

A continuous style needs real-time response, the cursor must follow (without leaving persistence tails on the screen) the pointing device (be it a mouse, a track ball, etc.). In some cases the user might want to perform more computer intensive operations like rotation or zooming and perhaps, on the hardware side, a coprocessor or a dedicated processor should be used.

The loss of a command submission may be recovered if the user's LTM is easily retrievable; another possibility for helping the user's memory is an automatic way for assigning names to chunks, perhaps such names are more meaningful to the user and will therefore facilitate recall. In this style, recovery depends on the STM, if the error is not reported soon enough, it may be lost from the STM and then no further possibility is left.

During continuous interaction errors appear ... continuously ... but the user keeps correcting them, these systems are reversible, since actions, and their relative consequences, may be undone.

We now recapitulate what has been illustrated so far trying to provide cues for guidelines, for testing and understanding of interfaces for interactive systems.

The three basic activities that we feel are the core of the user's activity may be summarized as: focusing on his goals, understanding which partial results must be displayed/printed along his work and trusting the visual interactive system as defined later.

13.9. Trustable Systems

There are three aspects affecting trustability of a system: one depends on the system and is tied to its usability defined as the ease of learning, of using, of navigating and of obtaining the user's goal efficiently and effectively in the real working environment. The next one, related to the interpretation of the information displayed on the screen, implies that both the human and the working environment must assign, to a given message identical meanings, during the same interaction process.

In every situation met by the user during his work, there will be only one (predictable) result, this condition will ensure that the user will be able to work safely, in our language, trustily.

The next condition, viability, means that no human action may result in a nonmeaningful situation, in a system crash or in a trap (where the user cannot exit without rebooting).

And lastly, orientability which stands for the property that describes the fact that the user will never get lost in the virtual space.

The above picture also shows the evolution of the image, in time, by means of blue arrows at times t1, t2, etc. In this scheme, the image on the screen **materializes** the meaning intended by the sender and must be **interpreted** by the receiver. Two partners play analog roles during interaction: the user (a human) and a computer (the program) which will both materialize the image **i** at successive times and interpret it at each one of these times.

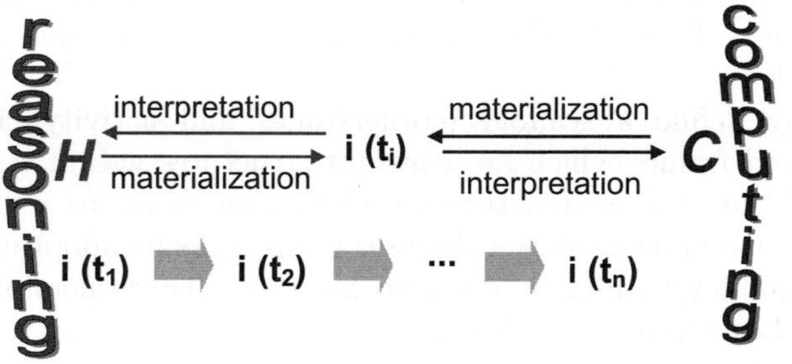

Fig. 13.8. Interaction model.

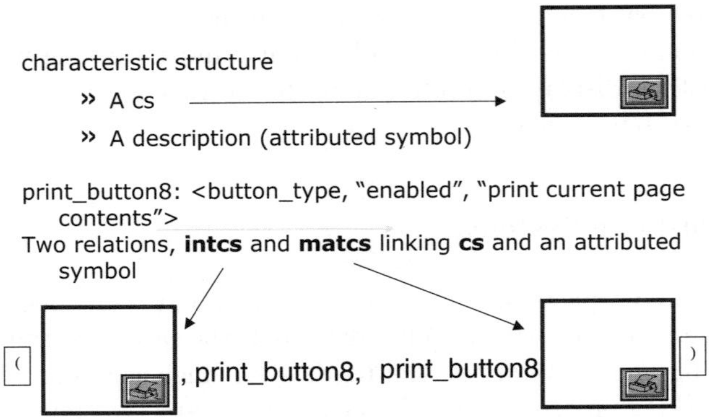

Fig. 13.9. Characteristic patterns.

The notion of characteristic pattern is required to explain the meaning of the basic functions introduced before: interpretation and materialization. In fact, through a graphical and analytical definition (see drawing of printer icon and an attributed symbol grammar description) we may use two expressions which formalize the interpretation of a characteristic pattern (intcs) and its materialization (matcs) respectively.

In order to ensure usability and therefore a unique, non-ambiguous series of visual messages on the screen, rewriting systems on an alphabet of characteristic patterns will be employed where the principal role is played by these characteristic patterns.

Finally, by using translation devices which will transform original specifications in the rewriting systems into control programs, we may build the interactive system which will satisfy the constraints we listed above to guarantee trustiness.

An example of interesting characteristic patterns designed to avoid getting lost in virtual space is the title bar, it contains the standard icons that provide a frame to the screen (like the start-up icon in Windows systems), etc.

We may define a scaffold (cornerstones and activity characteristic patterns) and frames which are constant structures within a set of visual sentences (defined as a structure associating an image to a meaning). In this way we may now facilitate the user in his tasks by adopting a notation which is familiar to him to describe his task, the cornerstones and the required actions to achieve his goals.

The notation coming from a working domain embeds the user's procedural knowledge, the description of his tasks and the context in which he will be operating. The embedding may be explicit or implicit, in this second case the arrangement of objects, their relations and relative positions, contain important information (to the user) about their meaning and their relevance within the task.

An example of interesting characteristic patterns designed to avoid getting lost in virtual space are the title bars, the standard icons that provide a frame to the screen (like the start-up icon in Windows systems), etc.

We may define a scaffold (cornerstones and activity characteristic patterns) and frames which are constant structures within a set of visual sentences (defined as a structure associating an image to a meaning). In this way we may now facilitate the user in his tasks by means of the adoption of a notation which is familiar to him to describe his task, the cornerstones and the required actions to achieve his goals.

The notation coming from a working domain embeds the user's procedural knowledge, the description of his tasks and the context in which he will be operating. The embedding may be explicit or implicit, in this second case the arrangement of objects, their relations and relative positions contain important information (to the user) about their meaning and their relevance within the task.

As for the interpretation, we want to impose that only one single meaning is valid and common to both the user and the program when the screen contents are interpreted, for this reason each characteristic structure, even if present in different visual expressions, implies that both the human interpretation and the program interpretation must be total functions.

From the communication point of view, the assignment of a meaning to a visual message must be unique (the same for human and program) as reflected in the expression where PL stands for pictorial language (the common one between user and program) and H-int($i(t)$) stands for the human interpretation of an image i at time t (and correspondingly for the visual information system — the program — interpretation of the same image at the same time). Unfortunately, this equality can only be validated experimentally.

13.10. Conclusions

Many features influence the design of modern interfaces seen under the light of the peculiarities of humans and of the nature of human–computer interaction, when humans perform their everyday work in their offices. This paper reports material taken from a number of different sources which are listed at the end of this section.

The field is constantly being updated with new studies on usability, on human cognitive abilities, on the use of multimedia and multimodal systems, on learning theory, on new methodologies of design, particularly those user-centred where the user may be seen as a codesigner.

I hope that these pages may shed further light on this exciting field where the requirements of computation must marry those of human psychology and perception.

References

1. P. Bottoni, M. F. Costabile, S. Levialdi and P. Mussio, *Trusty Interaction in Visual Environments*, 6th ERCIM, Workshop on User Interfaces for All, Florence, eds. P. E. Emiliani, C. Stephanidis, pp. 98–109, 2001.
2. P. Bottoni, M. F. Costabile, D. Fogli, S. Levialdi and P. Mussio, *Multi-level Modeling and Design of Visual Interactive Systems*, IEEE Symp. Human-Centric Computing: Languages and Environments, Stresa, 2001, pp. 256–263.
3. P. Bottoni, M. F. Costabile, S. Levialdi and P. Mussio, *From User Notations to Accessible Interfaces through Visual Languages*, Proc. UA-HCI 2001, New Orleans, USA, pp. 252–256.
4. A. Dix, J. Finlay, G. Abowd and R. Beale, *Human–Computer Interaction*, Second Edition, Prentice Hall, 2000.
5. H. R. Hartson and D. Hix, (eds.), *Advances in Human–Computer Interaction*, Ablex Pub. Corp., Norwood, NJ, USA, 1992.
6. D. A. Norman, *The Invisible Computer*, the MIT Press, Cambridge, MA, 1998.
7. J. Raskin, *The Humane Interface*, Addison-Wesley, Reading, MA 2000.
8. B. Shneiderman, *Designing the User Interface*, Third Edition, Addison-Wesley, 1999.
9. J. W. Sullivan and S. W. Tyler, *Intelligent User Interfaces*, Frontier Series, ACM Press, 1991.
10. H. Thimbleby, *User Interface Design*, Frontier Series, ACM Press, Addison-Wesley, 1990.

Exercises

Beginner's Exercises

1. How would you define an "interface"?
2. List the main features that a usable interface should have.
3. Why are formal approaches to the design of an interface hard?
4. What are the differences between short term memory and long term memory?
5. What are the differences between computer memory and human memory?

Intermediate Exercises

6. Explain what is intended by User Model and System Model.
7. Why is model matching so important?
8. Describe the priming phenomenon.
9. Account for the relevance of the Cognitive Dissonance effect in the context of user choices.

Advanced Exercises

10. Provide examples of affordability in objects visible on the screen.
11. Discuss the validity of user classes (naïve, experts, casual).
12. Explain the relevance of the recovery command UNDO.
13. What is a trustable system?

Index